The General Method of Social Work Practice:

A GENERALIST PERSPECTIVE

THIRD EDITION

Maria O'Neil McMahon

East Carolina University

With a Foreword by Carel B. Germain

Allyn and Bacon

Boston   London   Toronto   Sydney   Tokyo   Singapore

Executive Editor: Karen Hanson
Managing Editor, Social Work: Judy Fifer
Vice President, Social Sciences: Susan Badger
Series Editorial Assistant: Jennifer Jacobson
Executive Marketing Manager: Joyce Nilsen
Manufacturing Buyer: Aloka Rathnam
Cover Administrator: Suzanne Harbison
Editorial-Production Service: Electronic Publishing Services Inc.

Copyright © 1996, 1990, 1984 by Allyn & Bacon
A Simon & Schuster Company
Needham Heights, Massachusetts 02194

Library of Congress Cataloging-in-Publication Data

McMahon, Maria O'Neil
   The general method of social work practice / Maria O'Neil McMahon; with a foreword by
Carel B. Germain.—3rd ed.
     p. cm.
   Previous ed. published under title: The general method of social work practice.
   Includes bibliographical references and index.
   ISBN 0-13-063280-5
   1. Social work education. 2. Social work education—Curricula. 3. Social service.
4. Holism. I. McMahon, Maria O'Neil. General method of social work practice. II. Title.
HV11.M374   1995
361.3—dc20   95-9214
                                                                                      CIP

Printed in the United States of America
10 9 8 7 6 5 4 3 2 1   00 99 98 97 96 95

Contents

Foreword to the Third Edition

A serious need in social work is a practice framework for beginning professional practitioners that reflects the distinctions between beginning and advanced practice methods, goals, and skills. Professional values, purpose, and core knowledge are common to both. But despite many helpful attempts to clarify the differences, confusion persists about what the beginning professional social workers "really does" and whether it is "really different" from what the advanced professional social worker "really does."

The General Method of Social Work Practice helps meet that need and reduces that persistent confusion. In developing a framework for the distinctive practice method, goals, and skills for the beginning level workers. Dr. Maria O'Neil McMahon constructs what she calls the "holistic foundation." It comprises selected concepts from general systems theory, ecological ideas, and professional wisdom derived from her experience as a social work educator and practitioner. Incorporating this foundation, students focus their perceptions and conceptions for practice on people and environment as a unitary system. People are regarded as biological and psychological beings engaged in continuous exchanges with their social environments, physical settings, and cultural contexts. This knowledge foundation is broad but is not as developed in depth as it would be at the advanced level.

But the book is not overburdened with theory. It is a how-to book written with the learning needs, concerns, and interests of students in mind. It anticipates their experiences and questions as they begin their methods course and enter the practicum. Not only is it a text for the classroom, but it will also be helpful to field instructors in planning appropriate practice experiences. Curriculum developers in foundation social work education will find some organizing principles to use as thematic strands in curriculum design.

Basic social work processes from engagement through evaluation and termination are described and analyzed for individual, family, group, and community work. Skills and techniques associated with each, identified as appropriate for the beginning practitioner, are described and illustrated. Dr. McMahon seeks to enhance in her student readers the capacities for feeling and thinking, understanding and knowing, and caring and doing. Diagrams to clarify concepts, supplemented by imaginative exercises for skills development, support this learning objective. Diverse practice illustrations show how beginning social workers use the General Method to provide services to people experiencing a variety of human predicaments in a variety of environments. Goals set by client and practitioner and the skills of the Method are clearly delineated, and careful attention is paid throughout to the diversity of race and ethnicity, gender, and sexual orientation.

Thus the reader gains clarity about the difference between the two levels of practice and education for practice. The entry-level practitioner learns and applies a general method of working with people and their environments, with limited but significant goals and circumscribed skills of moderate complexity. The beginning worker is skilled in general service provision, in assessing and managing readily amenable and accessible person-environment needs and problems, and in making informed judgments about when to refer more complex or intractable problems to the advanced practitioner.

As the author's analysis and the practice examples show, beginning social workers are prepared to relieve life problems and environmental needs not requiring complex interventions. They provide reassurance, support, and tangible resources; link people to formal and informal helping systems; furnish needed information; and work collaboratively with others in assuring continuity, coordination, and comprehensiveness in basic social welfare services. They are skilled in outreach activities with defined populations in at-risk situations. And their practice in both urban and rural areas spans a variety of institutional bases, including social agencies, health and mental health agencies, schools, industry, housing projects, police precincts, and so on. *The General Method of Social Work Practice* will facilitate the learning of these many professional tasks and skills by the student. It will also meet the interests of the experienced B.S.W. practitioner in ongoing professional development.

—Carel B. Germain

Preface to the Third Edition

I have come to refine my understanding of "generalist" and "advanced generalist" practice through continued effort to develop the meaning of each concept and to explain more clearly their relationship and interdependence. In this edition, I offer revised and additional diagrams and conceptualizations to promote a greater understanding of the generalist perspective and to assist in the development of identity and expertise in generalist practice.

The value of social work generalists who can work at multiple levels with diverse populations, problems, policies, and environments is becoming increasingly recognized. There has been a gradual movement, particularly in public social services, to give entry-level generalists (B.S.W.s) priority over other baccalaureate graduates in hiring for social work positions. This parallels the growing evidence that social service delivery is improved when services are carried out by such professionals. In addition, an increasing number of B.S.W. practitioners are seeking "advanced" generalist preparation as they are promoted into administrative positions. In writing my book, *Advanced Generalist Practice, With an International Perspective* (Prentice-Hall, 1994), it became very clear to me that advanced generalists must first have a solid foundation in generalist practice. I hope that this third edition of *The General Method*, with its *Instructor's Manual*, will serve as a major source of guidance and clarity for all those seeking quality generalist education and practice.

The General Method of Social Work Practice is used extensively by social work educators throughout the United States and in other countries. I was particularly gratified by the extremely positive reception I received when I presented the content of this book at a social work educators' conference in Stavanger, Norway to educators from five different countries (Norway, Sweden, Denmark, Finland, and

Latvia). I understand also that human service providers find the book very helpful and relevant to such fields as counseling, criminal justice, education, and nursing.

The number of new authors who are offering additional texts on generalist practice is impressive. Their models readily reflect the original problem-solving process presented in the first and sequential editions of this book. Generalist practice is nationally and internationally identified by such core characteristics as a problem focus, problem-solving process, multi-level approach, open selection of theories and interventions, and an ecological-systems perspective. A major contemporary challenge is to articulate what constitutes "advanced" generalist practice and to demonstrate how it truly expands the qualities that are central to generalist practice. In taking on this challenge, both generalist and advanced generalist practice are enriched and refined. The need is here; the process has begun.

I am grateful to so many people who have helped me to find the motivation and information needed for writing this third edition. Thanks to Harris Chaiklin, University of Maryland, Emma Quartaro, Seton Hall University, and Frank Baskind, Virginia Commonwealth University, who reviewed this edition. Particular thanks to all those schools, faculty, and students, here and abroad, for their affirmation and enthusiastic reception of earlier editions. I deeply appreciate the assistance of Sr. Mary Joan Cook of Saint Joseph College for her editing of the manuscript, and for the help and perseverance of my graduate assistants at East Carolina University.

The Foundation for Social Work Practice: A Holistic View

In my judgment, one of the profession's most important tasks in theory development is the formulation of a way or ways of thinking about social work as a whole. It has always seemed strange to me and somewhat unfortunate that while we have had theory about casework, group work and community organization we have had little, until recently, about social work itself. The serious consequences of this deficiency in the theory of social work is that it has led us to practice as specialists more than as generalists and without a generalist base to anchor our specialties.

—Gordon Hearn[1]

Over the last twenty-five years, noted social work educators and practitioners have worked diligently at clarifying the educational needs and role expectations for a beginning social work professional.[2] Controversy and confusion have often resulted from the use of such related terms as *basic, core, general,* and *generic* to describe the foundation of social work practice. In addition to the search for appropriate descriptive words, studies have been conducted to identify the specific knowledge, values, and skills that are essential for beginning practice.[3] Even with these components to constitute the base for practice, the search continues for a conceptual framework that will integrate the various dimensions of social work into a unified whole.

Achieving preciseness in identifying and unifying methods, skills, theory, knowledge, values, attitudes, policies, and programs for social work will remain a challenge, owing to the artful and evolving nature of the profession. This book is an attempt to offer a comprehensive conceptualization of content for understanding and describing professional social work practice at the entry level today. The beginning worker is described as a professional who has been socialized into the role of a social work generalist. More specifically, the theoretical and experiential preparation for practice as outlined in this book presents a picture of an ecological generalist: someone who works with a variety of client systems and services, using various theories within an ecological systems perspective guided by a general problem-solving methodology. After presenting a holistic view of the foundation for social work practice and an overview of the essential elements for generalist practice, the focus of the book will be to explore the general method that is commonly used in the education and practice of beginning social workers.

The Search for Holism

In the profession of social work, among the human services and within the human person, there is a growing expression of a desire for holism. As a concept, *holism* has become increasingly popular in diverse professions since the 1970s. It is currently defined and used from various perspectives. In essence, holism refers to a totality in perspective, with sensitivity to all of the parts or levels that constitute the whole and to their interdependence and relatedness. The terms *health, wholeness,* and *the holy* are often used when describing holism.

The roots of holism may be found in the writings of Jan Smuts,[4] Claude Bernard,[5] Walter Cannon,[6] Kurt Goldstein,[7] Andras Angyal,[8] and others. In 1926, Smuts introduced holism as a philosophical theory in his book *Holism and Evolution*. He based the word *holism* on the Greek word *hole*, meaning complete, entire, and whole. Smuts describes the determining factors in nature as "wholes" that are irreducible to the sum of their parts. Focus is on the functional or organic relations between parts and wholes. Evolution in the universe is seen as the recording of the making of wholes.

Bernard (1927) and Cannon (1939) view the human body as a whole and describe the body's capacity to maintain inner balance or equilibrium. A person's "internal environment" is seen as having regulators to cope with external and internal disturbances.

Kurt Goldstein (1939), a neuropsychiatrist, is the major exponent of organismic theory. In this theory, the organism is described as a united whole, with mind and body undifferentiated. Organs and faculties of the body are not independent; what happens to any part has an effect on the whole. Although Goldstein recognizes that the organism is influenced by the environment, he gives predominance to the human organism.

Andras Angyal (1941), a successor to Goldstein, states that it is impossible to separate the organism from the environment. Separation would contradict the nature of the whole. Using systems analysis, Angyal conceptualizes the "biosphere," which he describes as a holistic entity consisting of two polarities of individual and environment. The two are seen "as aspects of a single reality which can be separated only by abstraction."[9]

Holistic medicine emerged from the works of Bernard and Cannon, Goldstein and Angyal. In the health field, holism is a concept that describes perceptions of the patient, of the environment of the patient, and of the various providers of services. In holistic medicine, emphasis is on health and coping capacities rather than on disease and sickness. Helping is defined in terms of managing resources rather than treating illness. The physician is encouraged to look beyond the disease and to take a broader look at the patient. Primarily, holism is seen as an approach for viewing the whole person. For example, Goldwag writes:

> Here, the aim is to understand the living organism as a total entity and to understand its parts as integrated, interdependent, interrelated systems that can be understood by studying the parts, but without losing sight of their relation to the whole organism.[10]

For some health providers, the concept *holistic* or *wholistic* means to see and treat the patient within the environment that surrounds and influences him or her. Podolsky writes:

> The term "wholistic", a variant of holistic, signifies that people are treated in the context of their entire environment, including their family situations, social milieu, economic class, and educational attainments, as contrasted with treating only a disease or focusing upon a single complaint.[11]

In addition, a holistic conception has been used to describe a health center where a group of people join their expertise and efforts with a concerted team approach for comprehensive services:

> The City of Health staff also recognizes that no one therapist or single therapy is necessarily the catalyst for healing but rather that a multi-therapeutic approach is the most effective program. With this understanding, the staff works in harmony with one another without the interference of personal ego clouding the attitude of wholeness that prevails.[12]

From this initial overview of the beginnings of holistic theory, it is apparent that early holistic conceptualizations were used predominantly in the field of medicine. Concepts evolved to describe perceptions of the patient, the patient's environment, and the service providers. It is of interest to note that the person recognized as the founder of holistic theory, Jan Smuts, soldier and statesman, was a major advocate of the Commonwealth of Nations and builder of the League of Nations and of the United Nations.[13]

Holism and Human Services

Within the field of human services today, the concept *holism* is commonly applied to consumers of services, their needs, and the services offered. The concept *human services* itself is holistic, in that it draws together professionals and paraprofessionals of diverse backgrounds who are working to meet human needs. The relationship of *human services* to *holistic thinking* is particularly obvious in a contemporary definition by Joseph Mehr. He defines the "generic human services concept" as follows:

> Human services is the field of endeavor that helps individuals cope with problems in living that are expressed in social welfare, psychological, behavioral, or legal concepts. Human services is characterized by an integrated, pragmatic approach focusing on problem solution within the client's life space, utilizing change strategies affecting both the internal person and his or her external environment.[14]

Human service workers include those from fields such as mental health, vocational rehabilitation, corrections, welfare, law, child care, social work, housing, education and physical health.

Professionals and paraprofessionals in human services are increasingly using a holistic conceptualization of the persons receiving services. The client/patient/consumer is seen holistically when focus is on the whole person—body, spirit, and mind—and on the interdependence of each of the major dimensions of *person*. In addition, the client is not seen in isolation, but within his or her life-space environments. The family, culture, physical surroundings, and society of the individual are seen as essential parts of a holistic view of clients.

In considering the needs of a human being holistically, focus is on the whole hierarchy of needs, and on the necessary and sequential relationship of each. Maslow, for example, identifies the needs of a person as crossing over the physical dimension of person (bodily needs), the intellectual dimension (cognitive needs), and the spiritual dimension (aesthetic needs).[15] With a holistic view of needs, human service workers are aware of the interdependence of needs.

In applying a holistic approach to human services, the interrelationships of various helping professionals with one another and with the family and culture of their clients are highlighted. The need for team building and case coordination and management is seen as basic for effective service. Although certain people with particular needs may come to the attention of individual providers or agencies, holistically minded helpers do not lose sight of the fact that each person is very much a part of other persons, that each need is strongly related to other needs, and that a single service can meet neither all the needs of any one person nor one need of all persons. Human service providers are becoming increasingly aware of their dependence on one another within a whole network of human services.[16]

Holism in Social Work

The use of holistic theory is found frequently in social work literature. Weick, for example, stresses the "physical" in the person-in-environment paradigm. In addition to a client's internal and external social environments, she sees the need for workers to become more aware of the physical internal and external environments of clients.[17]

The liberal arts perspective, which is a prerequisite for any professional social work program, is a very holistic conceptualization. It calls for one to have the ability to understand and appreciate different cultures and academic disciplines, and to see their interdependence in a way that is characteristic of a broadly educated person.[18]

Holistic concepts have been used also to describe various aspects of the profession and to describe the whole of social work itself. Certain methodologies and theories have been seen as holistic. For example, in considering different methods of practice, Baer and Federico found that, within a generalist approach, emphasis is on a "holistic assessment and intervention at the level of both people and systems."[19] They see general practice as providing a "holistic perspective" of practice situations.

> The generalist or unitary conceptualization with its emphasis on systems and their interactions, appears to be the approach that best helps the student to understand situations from a holistic perspective.[20]

Brieland, Costin, and Atherton concur with Baer and Federico in viewing a generalist method as holistic when they write the following:

> The small voluntary agency finds that it cannot afford a variety of specialists, and the large public agency has learned that to be effective it cannot separate individual and family improvement from societal change. For those who seek the world in holistic terms, the generalist has come to represent a promising solution.[21]

With the maturation of the social work profession, it is fitting that social work educators and practitioners are using more complex conceptualizations. The recognition of diversity in unity and the identification of multiple-factor causality have been present in social work practice since its foundation; openness and adaptiveness to theory from other disciplines have also prevailed within the profession. At this time, social work leaders are calling for a more comprehensive conception of practice as they continue to engage in exchanging concepts with other disciplines and pursue their search for wholeness.

Generalist Practice in Social Work

Professional social workers may be entry-level workers or advanced practitioners. Social work practice at the entry level is called *generalist practice*. Within the profession, there has been confusion over the use of the concepts *general* and *generic*. Although by definition both terms may be used to describe "what is characteristic of a whole group,"[22] the concept of *generic* is used mainly to refer to what is at the core or root of all practice, and *general* or *generalist* is used to refer to a type of practice that "is not confined by specialization or careful limitation."[23] Over the last twenty years, practitioners and educators have worked diligently at identifying more specifically the meaning and nature of generalist practice. Today, the commonly accepted characteristics of this entry-level practice model include a theoretical perspective and methodology that will be developed throughout this text. Undergraduate social work programs accredited by the Council on Social Work Education offer a generalist curriculum that prepares students for entry-level social work practice. Generalist practice may be found also in the curriculum of graduate programs, along with various concentrations for advanced practice. In Master's degree programs, a generalist curriculum in the first year of study serves as a stepping stone for advanced study in selected concentrations. "Advanced" generalist practice may be a concentration in M.S.W. programs (to be described further in Chapter 10).

A generalist practitioner is expected to have acquired a generic foundation for professional social work and to have integrated this foundation with essential characteristic elements of generalist practice. The generic foundation consists of basic components that are rooted in the identity of all social workers. Generalists draw from foundation components and apply generalist theory and methodology as they practice holistically in diverse environments.

The Foundation of Social Work Practice

In 1956, social work educators and practitioners developed a "working definition of social work practice." They identified five basic elements to describe the "common base" of social work.[24] These elements are Purpose, Sanction, Values, Knowledge, and Method (Skills). Although any profession may be described according to these five fundamental elements, at the foundation of social work, the elements are described within the basic theoretical perspective of "person in environment" (See Figure 1–1).

Periodically, social workers revisit and revise the five basics and theoretical perspective in the light of contemporary practice as encouraged by Harriet Bartlett who in 1958 wrote, "This working definition is a small beginning—but still a beginning—toward conceptualization of the basic elements in social work practice,"[25] and "the formulation can be viewed as tentative, to be revised and refined continuously as knowledge and understanding of practice grow."[26] Whereas the fundamental purpose and perspective of social work generally remain the same, the sanction of social work has greatly changed due to the increasing passage of laws to regulate the practice of social work. The "base" or "foundation" of social work is further explicated through the identification of more specific knowledge, values, and skills that are commonly found in social work today.

Purpose

The primary *purpose* of social work continues to be the enhancement of social functioning.[27] Social workers enable individuals, groups, families, and communities to function more effectively within their various environments. Social workers

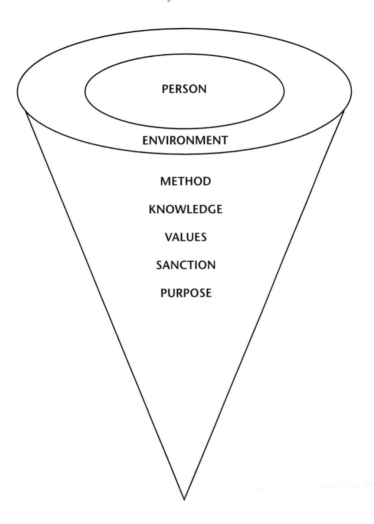

PERSON

ENVIRONMENT

METHOD

KNOWLEDGE

VALUES

SANCTION

PURPOSE

FIGURE 1-1. Foundation of Social Work

strive to eliminate discrimination and to create just social environments. The ways in which social workers implement their purpose take different forms, approaches, roles, and methodologies. Workers engage in direct practice with clients in such roles as counselor, enabler, broker, case manager, and advocate. They may also assume various indirect practice roles, such as supervisors, managers, administrators, teachers, researchers, and consultants. They work to prevent, resolve, or minimize human problems. Their efforts are directed toward the development of the maximum potential of individuals and environments to achieve the highest quality of life.

Sanction

The authority and permissions that *sanction* the practice of social workers in society come from several different sources. These include (1) governmental agency boards with legal regulation responsibility, (2) public or private human service agencies, (3) the organized profession, and (4) the clients served. Since 1992, all fifty states have some form of sanctioning of social work practice through licensing or certification. Thirty states regulate both Baccalaureate and Master level social workers, and twenty states have legal regulation only for social workers with M.S.W. degrees. In twenty-three states, all social workers (B.S.W. and M.S.W.) *must* be licensed or certified to practice. Ten states require licensing or certification for Master level practitioners in clinical or private practice. And, in seventeen states, there is "title protection" only, which means that only social workers using the title(s) identified in the law are required to be licensed or certified (See Table 1–1).[28]

Values

The values of the social work profession are rooted in (1) a belief in the dignity and worth of every human being, and (2) a recognition of the need for a democratic and caring society. Democratic, as used here, refers to a participatory government in which people directly or through elected officials govern themselves, and in which equality of rights is enforced. These two roots of the profession emphasize person and environment and their interrelatedness. The two fundamental values are intertwined and cannot be viewed as distinct or unequal.

Building on a Judeo-Christian value system, social workers recognize that every human being possesses the potential for greatness but also that human beings are fallible, with needs that include protection and support from the environment. A caring society is not only a resourceful system with open doors but also a vulnerable organization in need of direction and control by responsible individuals. Flowing from a belief in the dignity and worth of every person and from the value of a caring society is the commitment of social workers to engage in activities that promote the actualization or potential of both persons and environments. Social workers strive to develop the capabilities of individuals and the resources of societies so that together they may achieve the highest quality of life.

Social work values are more clearly understood when they are explained in terms of actions and interactions. Building on the two fundamental values of person and society, social workers have identified basic practice principles and a code of ethics. Whereas the two essential values reflect the ultimate goals of the profession, the principles and code of ethics serve as criteria for directing professional activities that will lead to achieving the goals of the profession. The two essential values of person and society are found at the roots of all of social work practice. The principles and ethics code flow from the generic values and prescribe appropriate ethical behavior for workers in their work environments.

TABLE 1-1. Social Work Regulation

Jurisdiction (Including D.C., Puerto Rico & Virgin Islands)	Groups Mandated Licensed/Certified or Title Protection	Jurisdiction (Including D.C., Puerto Rico & Virgin Islands)	Groups Mandated Licensed/Certified or Title Protection
Alabama	All Social Workers	Nebraska	All Social Workers
Alaska	All Clinical Social Workers	Nevada	All Social Workers
Arizona	Title Protection	New Hampshire	Title Protection
Arkansas	All Social Workers	New Jersey	All Social Workers
California	All Clinical SW in fee for service	New Mexico	All Social Workers
Colorado	Those who diagnose & treat mentally ill	New York	Title Protection
Connecticut	Title Protection	North Carolina	All Clinical Social Workers
Delaware	Clinical Social Workers	North Dakota	All Social Workers
District of Columbia	All Social Workers	Ohio	All Social Workers
Florida	Clinical Social Workers	Oklahoma	All Social Workers
Georgia	Title Protection	Oregon	Title Protection
Hawaii	Title Protection	Pennsylvania	Title Protection
Idaho	All Social Workers	Puerto Rico	All Social Workers
Illinois	All Social Workers Clinical Social Workers	Rhode Island	Title Protection
Indiana	All Social Workers	South Carolina	All Social Workers
Iowa	Title Protection	South Dakota	All Social Workers
Kansas	All Social Workers	Tennessee	Title Protection

TABLE 1-1. *Continued*

Jurisdiction (Including D.C., Puerto Rico & Virgin Islands)	Groups Mandated Licensed/Certified or Title Protection	Jurisdiction (Including D.C., Puerto Rico & Virgin Islands)	Groups Mandated Licensed/Certified or Title Protection
Kentucky	All Social Workers	Texas	Private practitioner, others title protection
Louisiana	Title Protection	Utah	All Social Workers
Maine	Title Protection	Vermont	Title Protection
Maryland	All Social Workers	Virginia	All Social Workers
Massachusetts	All Social Workers	Virgin Islands	All Social Workers
Michigan	Title Protection	Washington	All Certified SW's who receive fees
Minnesota	All Social Workers	West Virginia	All Social Workers
Mississippi	All Social Workers	Wisconsin	All Social Workers
Missouri	Clinical Social Workers	Wyoming	All Social Workers in Private Practice
Montana	Title Protection		

The basic practice principles, first identified by Felix P. Biestek, S.J., may be conceptualized as individualization, purposeful expression of feelings, controlled emotional involvement, acceptance, nonjudgmental attitude, self-determination, and confidentiality.[29] Although they were initially described as principles for casework, more recent authors have noted the generic nature of these principles for work with systems of any size.[30] Essentially, the principles may be understood as guiding the worker to achieve each of the following:

1. Recognize that every client system is unique and deserving of consideration and respect (individualization).
2. Understand the human need to express one's feelings, and the value in this expression as a means of fostering growth (purposeful expression of feelings).
3. Use one's feelings and emotions appropriately for the service of others (controlled emotional involvement).
4. Demonstrate that human beings have a right to be accepted as they are (acceptance).
5. Avoid passing judgments on people (nonjudgmental attitude).
6. Respect the right of clients to choose for themselves as much as possible (self-determination).
7. Keep information obtained from or about clients confidential (confidentiality).

In concurrence with these principles and with a broader scope for guiding practice, there is the Code of Ethics of the National Association of Social Workers (see Appendix I).[31] In the 1993 revision of the Code, statements are added to emphasize the need for workers to maintain appropriate boundaries in their professional relationships (Sections II.F.4, III.J.12). Particular attention is given to the need for workers not to allow their "personal problems, psychosocial distress, substance abuse, or mental health difficulties" to interfere with their professional performance. Also stressed is the need for workers with personal difficulties that interfere with professional performance to "immediately seek professional help, making adjustments in workload, terminating practice, or taking any other steps necessary to protect clients and others" (Sections I.B.3, I.B.4). Any worker who is aware of a colleague with such personal problems should consult with the person and assist him or her in "taking remedial action" (III.J.13).

Working within agencies, society, and the profession, and with clients and related systems, the social worker draws on the code of ethics and the practice principles of the profession for direction and support. The worker stands at the interface of person and environment with a dynamic value base that is two-sided, relating to both person and environment. This value base is an essential component of the foundation for all social work practice (See Table 1–2).

Knowledge

To carry their commitment into action, social workers need to understand persons and environments and their interdependence. The foundation knowledge base of

TABLE 1-2.   Foundation Values for Social Work

SOCIAL WORK		
PERSON	IN	ENVIRONMENT
Dignity and worth of every person	Practice Principles	Democratic and caring society
	Code of Ethics	

professional social work is selected for an understanding of behaviors, needs, and goals of human systems within the context of their diverse cultures and environments. More specifically, workers need to know about the various systems that constitute their work environment. Components include individuals, groups, families, organizations, institutions, and societies. Social work knowledge includes the study of biology, psychology, sociology, political science, and economics, as well as knowledge of social welfare policies and services. Additional areas include communications, group and family dynamics, and community development.

For intervention to be more than technical activity, the behaviors of the social worker should be directed by careful thought and disciplined knowledge. In addition to gaining knowledge about the profession and social welfare policies and services, social workers study theories relevant to practice. An ability to conceptualize and to theorize is expected of professional workers. Knowledge of particular theories that have been found to help explain the person–problem–situation phenomena of social work practice is included in all social work education programs.

Numerous theories are emerging today that may be considered relevant to social work practice. Many theories interrelate, and some duplicate or contradict others. A worker or student may be challenged and perhaps frustrated in trying to see connections or discrepancies among theories. The large amount of contemporary literature may be unmanageable or somewhat overwhelming. A systematic way of organizing and presenting established and developing theory for social workers is needed. A comprehensive framework for viewing various theories under specific headings would assist workers and educators in organizing theories used in social work.

All theory of relevance to social work may be seen in relation to (1) person, (2) environment, or (3) both in interaction. In Table 1–3, relevant theories are classified according to these three options. The three categories are not mutually exclusive. Theories are grouped according to their predominant focus.

To understand the *person,* a social worker would call on various theories that would collectively provide a comprehensive view of the total person. Theories have been developed in which psychological, physical, social, sexual, intellectual, moral and spiritual dimensions of the human person have been conceptualized

TABLE 1-3. Foundation Knowledge for Social Work

SOCIAL WORK		
PERSON	IN	ENVIRONMENT
Developmental/	Socialization	Organizational theory
life course	Role	Political science
Biological	Behavioral	Legislative process
Psychosexual	Communication	Social policy
Psychosocial	Stress/conflict	Cultural anthropology
Cognitive	Systems	Natural/community
Moral	Group process	resources
Spiritual	Populations at	Public/private services
Self-actualization	risk	Social welfare
Self-awareness		

according to subsystems, stages, and life course developmental milestones.[32] The common and basic human needs for human development and actualization have been described.

Numerous systems that constitute the *environment* for each person have been studied and presented in terms of structure, parts, and processes. Theories regarding cultures, economics, politics, organizations, and systems in general have been identified as essential knowledge for social work professionals.

The middle category of Table 1–3 lists theories that focus on the *interactions* that take place as persons and environmental systems interface. The influence of environment on the person is at the center of such theories as role, socialization, behavior modification, and stress theory.

Although Table 1–3 does not provide an exhaustive list of all theories used in social work, the categorized theories form a framework for theory building. As a person preparing for practice studies each theory individually, it will be easier for him or her to gain a greater sense of the nature of theory if the framework of Table 1–3 is kept in mind. The notions of theory and theory building may be understood as the pursuit of truth, and the conception of individual theories as pieces of the puzzle called "truth" may aptly be viewed as depicted in Table 1–3. When the pieces (theories) are juxtaposed or merged, a greater understanding or clearer view may be acquired.

Method (Skills)

Guided by values and knowledge, a social worker executes a series of activities within the framework of a method with client-related systems to achieve identified goals. These activities constitute the skills of the worker. All social workers are trained initially in a broad variety of basic skills (Table 1–4).

Social workers are known for using interpersonal relationships in a helping process. Sensitivity to feeling has been consistently recognized as an essential

TABLE 1-4.   Foundation Skills for Social Work

SOCIAL WORK		
PERSON	IN	ENVIRONMENT
Relationship skills	Problem-solving skills	Political skills
Listening	Problem identifying	Advocating
Responding	Data collecting	Taking legal action
Feeling/sensing	Assessing/goal setting	Providing evidence
Paraphrasing	Planning/task defining	Bargaining
Clarifying	Selecting and implementing	Organizing
Information giving	intervention	Publicizing
Referring	Evaluating	Demonstrating
	Terminating	

Professional Skills
Recording, research, time-management, teamwork

characteristic of social workers. In addition, problem solving, goal setting, and task defining are commonly identified as central to practice. Through an open, supportive relationship, clients are helped to identify tasks and proceed toward goal accomplishment and problem resolution. In a list of skills for social work practice, obviously, skills for relationship and problem solving would be included (see the "Person" and "In" columns of Table 1–4).

As brought out by Pincus and Minahan, there are times when workers need to interact with systems or organizations that are not client systems. They define a *client system* as "people who sanction or ask for the change agent's [worker's] services, who are the expected beneficiaries of service, and who have a working agreement or contract with the change agent." A client system may be an individual, group, family, or community. In addition to working with client systems, a worker often forms "action systems" to bring about changes in "target systems." *Action systems* are formed when a worker joins with other systems to work with and through them in order to influence a target system and accomplish goals. In identifying causes of problems or sources for meeting needs, workers may find target systems in need of change for goal accomplishment. A *target system* is one that often refuses to accept the change efforts of workers and clients.[33]

The use of relationships or problem-solving skills may be inappropriate and ineffective in work with target systems. This is found to be particularly true in work with large bureaucratic systems. An example of this would be an educational program that rejects minority applicants on the basis of scores on standardized tests known to be biased against certain racial or ethnic groups. Standing at the interface of person and environment, the social worker would need political skills for work with such a target system. In addition to basic supportive and problem-solving skills, therefore, a range of political skills, such as providing evidence, building coalitions, publicizing, bringing legal action, and organizing demonstrations, may be needed (see the Environment column in Table 1–4).

Besides working with client and target systems, social workers are expected to perform certain activities within agencies and as members of a profession. Skill is expected in record keeping, team building, and managing time. Research skills, particularly for practice evaluation, are expected as well.

The list of skills for fundamental social work practice is lengthy and complex. A framework is needed to provide a comprehensive conceptualization of the different types of skills described. Such a framework would suggest to the worker that a whole array of skills is available for individualized selection, depending on the given situation.

Again, the "person in environment" perspective may be seen as a framework in which to diagram the various foundation skills of social workers in practice today. According to Table 1–4, the practitioner would be able to operate with flexibility, using a variety of possible skills. Those skills identified in the diagram indicate the behaviors frequently used by generalist social workers as they apply to the general problem-solving methodology described later in this text. Numerous additional skills are demonstrated in social work practice. The advanced social worker, in comparison with the beginning generalist worker, would have specialized expertise for work with particular methods, problems, or populations. It would be expected that the graduate worker would have competence in the foundation skills as well as in more advanced skills for intensive work.

For example, an M.S.W. clinical worker's skills may range from environmental mobilization to psychotherapy. The clinical worker would have the skills of Table 1–4 and skills for offering interpretations and enhancing insight. The advanced worker with a concentration in policy and planning would have the foundation skills, augmented by skills in complex program and policy planning and development.

A Holistic Conceptualization of the Foundation of Social Work Practice

Table 1–5 offers a comprehensive paradigm of the foundation of social work. The basic "person(s) in environment" perspective which has prevailed throughout social work practice provides a framework for describing the five "common base" components, including a listing of particular values, knowledge, and skills.

The traditional "person in environment" perspective provides a means for the integration of the foundation of social work practice into a systematic and holistic conceptualization. As demonstrated in Table 1–5, the foundation values, theory, and skills for generalist practice may be perceived collectively under the triplex of "person", "in," and "environment." The social worker is positioned in the center, "where the action is." Change efforts may pull from, or be directed toward, either the person or the environment, depending on the need. The social worker actualizes the basic dimensions of the profession through dynamic interactions with his or her work environment.

TABLE 1-5. A Holistic Conceptualization of the Foundation for Social Work Practice

SOCIAL WORK		
PERSON	IN	ENVIRONMENT

PURPOSE
To enhance the social functioning of individuals, families, groups, and communities in their environments.

SANCTION
Clients, Private/Public Agencies, The Profession, Government (Laws)

VALUES

Dignity and worth of every person	Practice principles Code of Ethics	Democratic, caring society

KNOWLEDGE

Developmental/life cycle	Socialization	Organizational theory
Biological	Role	Political Science
Psychosexual	Behavioral theory	Legislative process
Psychosocial	Communication	Social policy
Cognitive	Stress/conflict	Cultural anthropology
Moral	Systems	Natural/Community
Spiritual	Group process	resources
Self-actualization	Populations at risk	Public/private Self-
Self-awareness		services
		Social Welfare

SKILLS

Relationship skills	Problem-solving skills	Political skills
Listening	Problem identifying	Advocating
Responding	Data collecting	Taking legal action
Feeling/sensing	Assessing/goal	Providing evidence
Paraphrasing	setting	Bargaining
Clarifying	Planning/task	Organizing
Information giving	defining	Publicizing
Referring	Selecting and	Demonstrating
	implementing	
	Evaluating	
	Terminating	

Professional Skills
Recording, Research
Time-management
Teamwork

The holistic conceptualization may be viewed as an exciting and needed framework for those involved with beginning practice and education. Graduates of accredited B.S.W. programs, for example, are beginning generalist practitioners. Frequently, administrators and supervisors in social agencies do not understand or appreciate the competence of baccalaureate-level practitioners from accredited professional programs. The role expectations for baccalaureate practitioners are not sufficiently clear for appropriate case assignments and task distribution. The framework of Table 1–5 helps one to understand the parameters of beginning level foundation knowledge, values, and skills; it serves as a guide for administrators, supervisors, and practitioners.

The holistic conceptualization provides a foundation and shows the basic parts or dimensions of social work in relation to one another. The worker is in the center at the point where all of the parts are held in balance for use or redistribution. The General Method of practice, which is set forth in this book, contains various elements depicted in this holistic conception of foundation. The Method pulls from the framework the knowledge, values, and skills as needed in the process of helping (explained further in Chapter 2). It organizes the content needed for the foundation of generalist practice into a comprehensive whole.

Conclusion

In conclusion, the need for greater understanding and development at the beginning practice level has led to the study and identification of a holistic conceptualization to describe the foundation of generalist social work practice. The "person in environment" perspective provides frameworks for comprehending the various components of the foundation.

The generalist builds on the identified foundation and engages in problem solving with a variety of client systems as an entry-level practitioner. The foundation presented in this chapter is a "common base" also for advanced social workers as they acquire increased competence in the use of knowledge, values and skills. Further study is needed to develop and depict the knowledge and skills for each area of concentration in advanced practice. Educators and practitioners at the graduate level and postgraduate levels are working toward greater clarification of what constitutes appropriate preparation for advanced practice. It is hoped that the foundation as presented in this chapter will be helpful as a starting point or model for formulating the principles, theory, and methods for each concentration.

As social work generalists interact with a variety of systems, they use a general problem-solving methodology and other key characteristic elements that activate the foundation knowledge, values, and skills identified in this chapter. An overview of the key elements that characterize generalist practice, with emphasis on the General Method, will be presented in the next chapter. In the remainder of the book, different phases of the General Method will be addressed.

NOTES

1. Gordon Hearn, "General Systems Theory and Social Work," in Francis J. Turner, ed., *Social Work Treatment: Interlocking Theoretical Approaches,* 2nd ed. (New York: The Free Press, 1979), p. 350. Copyright 1979 by The Free Press. Reprinted by permission.

2. Betty L. Baer and Ronald C. Federico, *Educating the Baccalaureate Social Worker,* 2 vols. (Cambridge, MA: Ballinger, 1979); Morton L. Arkava and E. Clifford Brennan, eds., *Competency-Based Education for Social Work: Evaluation and Curriculum Issues* (New York: Council on Social Work Education, 1976); and others.

3. See Baer and Federico, ibid.; Harold L. McPheeters and Robert R. Ryan. *A Core of Competence for Baccalaureate Social Welfare and Curriculum Implications* (Atlanta: Southern Regional Education Board, 1971); Frank M. Lowenberg and Ralph Dolgoff, *Teaching of Practice Skills in Undergraduate Programs in Social Welfare and Other Helping Services* (New York: Council on Social Work Education, 1971).

4. Jan C. Smuts, *Holism and Evolution* (New York: Macmillan, 1926).

5. Claude Bernard, *An Introduction to the Study of Experimental Medicine* (New York: Macmillan, 1927).

6. Walter B. Cannon, *The Wisdom of the Body* (New York: W.W. Norton, 1939).

7. Kurt Goldstein, *The Organism,* New York: The American Book Company, 1939).

8. Andras Angyal, *Foundations for a Science of Personality* (New York: Commonwealth Fund, 1941).

9. Ibid., p. 100.

10. Elliott, M. Goldwag, ed., *Inner Balance: The Power of Holistic Healing* (Englewood Cliffs, NJ: Prentice-Hall, 1979), p. 18.

11. M. Lawrence Podolsky, M.D., "Wholistic Medicine: What Is It, Who Practices It, Who Needs It?" *Modern Medicine* (July 15, 1977): 76.

12. Goldwag, *Inner Balance,* p. 325.

13. *The Encyclopedia Americana,* International Edition (1981) s.v. "Smuts, Jan Christian."

14. Joseph Mehr, *Human Services,* 5th ed. (Boston: Allyn and Bacon, 1992), pp. 16–17.

15. Abraham Maslow, *Motivation and Personality,* 2nd ed. (New York: Harper & Row, 1970); and *The Farther Reaches of Human Nature* (New York: Viking, 1971).

16. Seymour B. Sarason and others, *Human Services and Resource Networks* (San Francisco: Jossey-Bass, 1977).

17. Ann Weick, "Reframing the Person-in-Environment Perspective," *Social Work* 26, no. 2 (March 1981): 142.

18. Council on Social Work Education, "Curriculum Policy Statement for Baccalaureate Degree Programs in Social Work Education," Approved by Board of Directors July 19, 1992 (Alexandria, VA.: Council on Social Work Education, 1992), p. 5, B5.10.

19. Baer and Federico, *Educating the Baccalaureate,* p. 156.

20. Reprinted with permission from *Educating the Baccalaureate Social Worker, Volume II: A Curriculum Development Resource Guide,* Copyright 1979, Ballinger Publishing Company, p. 155.

21. Donald Brieland, Lela B. Costin, and Charles R. Atherton, *Contemporary Social Work: An Introduction to Social Work and Social Welfare* (New York: McGraw-Hill, 1980), p. 146.

22. *Webster's Third International Dictionary of the English Language,* s.v. "generic," "general."

23. Ibid.

24. Commission on Social Work Practice, NASW, "Working Definition of Social Work Practice," quoted in Harriet M. Bartlett, "Toward Clarification and Improvement of Social Work Practice," *Social Work* 3, no. 2 (April 1958), pp. 5–8. See also Harriet M. Bartlett, *The Common Base of Social Work Practice* (New York: National Association of Social Workers, 1970).

25. Harriet Bartlett, "Toward Clarification," p. 8.

26. Ibid, p. 5.

27. Werner W. Boehm, *Objectives of the Social Work Curriculum of the Future,* Curriculum Study, I (New York: Council on Social Work Education 1959), p. 54.

28. National Association of Social Workers, Inc. *State Comparison of Laws Regulating Social Work,* Revised June 1993 (Washington, DC: NASW, 1993).

29. Felix J. Biestek, S.J., *The Casework Relationship* (Chicago: Loyola University Press, 1957).

30. B. J. Picard, *An Introduction to Social Work: A Primer,* 2nd ed. (Homewood, Ill.: Dorsey, 1979).

31. Copyright 1979. National Association of Social Workers, Inc. Reprinted with permission from *Code of Ethics of National Association of Social Workers,* as adopted by the 1979 NASW Delegate Assembly and revised by the 1990 and 1993 NASW Delegate Assemblies, effective July 1, 1994.

32. Specific references for each theory listed in Table 1–3 would be too numerous to identify here.

33. Allen Pincus and Anne Minahan, *Social Work Practice: Model and Method* (Itasca, IL: Peacock, 1973), p. 63.

CHAPTER 2

The Generalist Perspective and the General Method

New configurations of method, a generalist kind of practice, are now emerging that should more accurately translate systemic social work functions into helping procedures.

—Max Siporin[1]

This text focuses on beginning generalist practice as found in baccalaureate social work (B.S.W.) programs or in first-year master's social work (M.S.W.) programs. A copy of the *Curriculum Policy Statement for Baccalaureate Degree Programs,* approved by the Board of Directors of the Council on Social Work Education in 1992, is found in Appendix II. The *Curriculum Policy Statement* for both baccalaureate and master's degree programs draws a distinction between the baccalaureate and master's levels of social work education by stating as follows: "The baccalaureate level prepares students for generalist social work practice, and the master's level prepares students for advanced social work practice in an area of concentration" (*CPS* B5.2, M5.2).[2] In addition to generalist practice at the baccalaureate level, all Master's degree programs in social work offer a "professional foundation which prepares students to apply a generalist perspective to social work practice with systems of all sizes" (CPS, M6.11). In baccalaureate programs, the generalist perspective prepares students for practice as generalists. In graduate programs, the generalist perspective is taught as a base or foundation for advanced practice in selected concentrations. In addition, as stated earlier, "advanced generalist practice" may be a concentration at the graduate level. This text presents the generalist perspective of social work practice as found in the baccalaureate social work programs and in the foundation of master's degree social work programs. Particular attention is given to the methodology used in beginning generalist practice. More specifically, this chapter addresses such preliminary questions as the following: What is the "B.S.W."? What is "generalist practice"? What is the "generalist perspective"? How does the "beginning generalist" compare to the "advanced practitioner"?

The Curriculum of an Accredited B.S.W. Program

What is a "B.S.W."? The B.S.W. is a baccalaureate social worker who practices social work at the entry level of the profession. Any person with a B.A., B.S., or B.S.W. degree, who has completed a baccalaureate social work program in a school accredited by the National Council on Social Work Education, may be called a "B.S.W." Among the many different work settings where B.S.W.'s are employed are public welfare agencies, hospitals, schools, children's and youth services, vocational rehabilitation programs, community action agencies, human resource departments, nursing homes, neighborhood centers, criminal justice programs, and daycare settings for children, adults, and seniors. In 1993, there were 300 baccalaureate social work programs accredited by the Council on Social Work Education and 32 baccalaureate programs in candidacy status.[3]

In order to meet the standards for accreditation by the Council on Social Work Education, "The baccalaureate curriculum must include a liberal arts perspective and the professional foundation" (*CPS* B6.1). Students with a liberal arts perspective are described as being "capable of thinking critically about society, about people and their problems, and about expressions of culture such as art, literature, science, history, and philosophy. Students must have knowledge about social, psychological, and biological determinants of human behavior and of diverse cultures, social conditions, and social problems" (*CPS* B5.9).

An undergraduate social work program must offer students a foundation in social work knowledge, values, and skills with a supervised field experience in generalist practice. Building on a liberal arts base, foundation content must be provided in the areas of human diversity, social and economic justice, social welfare policy and services, human behavior and social environment, research, and social work practice (*CPS* B6.1–16). In addressing the social work practice area, baccalaureate programs offer a sequence of courses that is usually called "method" (*CPS* B6.1–16). According to the Council, the B.S.W. beginning professional is expected to graduate with the identity of a "generalist."

In 1978, Betty Baer and Ron Federico published their intensive study of curriculum for social workers at the baccalaureate level. Although they did not spell out a method for generalist practice, they developed a list of ten generic competencies to be expected of B.S.W. graduates. They are as follows:

1. Identify and assess situations where the relationship between people and social institutions needs to be initiated, enhanced, restored, protected, or terminated.

2. Develop and implement a plan for improving the well-being of people based on problem assessment and exploration of obtainable goals and available options.
3. Enhance the problem-solving, coping, and developmental capacities of people.
4. Link people with systems that provide them with resources, services, and opportunities.
5. Intervene effectively on behalf of populations most vulnerable and discriminated against.
6. Promote the effective and humane operation of the systems that provide people with services, resources, and opportunities.
7. Actively participate with others in creating new, modified, or improved service, resource, and opportunity systems that are more equitable, just, and responsive to consumers of services, and work with others to eliminate those systems that are unjust.
8. Evaluate the extent to which the objectives of the intervention plan were achieved.
9. Continually evaluate one's own professional growth and development through assessment of practice behavior and skills.
10. Contribute to the improvement of service delivery by adding to the knowledge base of the profession as appropriate and by supporting and upholding the standards and ethics of the profession.[4]

As mentioned, Baer and Federico, after considering different methods of practice at the baccalaureate level, concluded that the most appropriate approach is that of generalist practice. They described "the generalist approach" as follows:

All efforts in the generalist, unitary approach to practice are based on the premise that all of a person's needs involve a variety of systems and that the social worker functions at the interface of people and social systems or societal institutions. Social systems theory is the basis for all efforts to explicate the generalist approach to practice.[5]

Baer and Federico realized the limitations in teaching this approach, because it lacked "guides for actions." They hoped that their identification of basic competencies and of the need for a generalist approach in baccalaureate-level practice would assist others in the development of B.S.W. practice methodology as well as competencies. Apparently, much more work was needed by CSWE and B.S.W. educators in the curriculum area of method.

In addition to clarifying what constitutes the general method that guides the actions of the generalist, other central elements that characterize generalist practice will be identified and articulated in this chapter. These elements and the general method may be combined with the social work foundation presented in Chapter 1 to offer a holistic "generalist perspective" of social work practice.

The Generalist Perspective

In generalist practice, the social work foundation, which consists of knowledge, values, skills, purpose, sanction, and the "person in environment" perspective, is developed and expanded through an overlay and integration of identifiable key elements (See Figure 2–1). The essential overriding elements that characterize the practice of generalists are the following:

1. An ecological systems perspective
2. A problem focus
3. A multi-level approach
4. An open selection of theories and interventions
5. A problem-solving process

These elements are not mutually exclusive. They interrelate and overlap as the generalist provides services at various levels.

The five elements highlight the meaning of generalist practice and contribute to the development of an integrated picture that may be called a *generalist perspective*. By definition, a *perspective* means "a view," or "the relationship of aspects of a subject to each other and to a whole."[6] There has been an ongoing debate regarding the most appropriate way to describe social work that reflects these five elements. Should it be called "generalist practice" or "a generalist perspective of social work practice"?

All practice in social work is founded on a common base such as is described in Chapter 1. The "practice" of workers has been more specifically described according to the theory, focus, and methodology used by practitioners over and above this foundation, including such features as "Task-Centered Practice," "Client-Centered Practice," "Casework Practice," and "Macro Practice." In this context, "generalist practice" would be used primarily to refer to the theory, focus, and methodology identified in the five essential elements, with the assumption of the foundation as rudimentary to all practice. The "generalist perspective" would refer more directly to the "whole" (liberal arts, social work foundation, and generalist essential elements) and to the "relationship of aspects of a subject to each other," such as depicted in Figure 2–1. In this figure, it is apparent that the generalist perspective encompasses several subperspectives or "aspects of the subject." These include "a liberal arts perspective," the original "person in environment" perspective, and an "ecological-systems perspective." Whereas the "generalist perspective" refers to a view of *what* a worker *brings* to a problem(s)-person(s)-situation(s), "generalist practice" refers to *what* a worker *does* in a problem(s)-person(s)-situation(s).

A baccalaureate social work education program addresses all aspects of the generalist perspective and "prepares students for direct services with client systems of various sizes and types" (*CPS* B5.2). Although some generalists may serve in such indirect practice roles as supervisors, managers, or teachers, generalist practice is primarily a direct practice model. Entry-level generalists are prepared to work directly with a variety of persons, populations, problems, and environments.

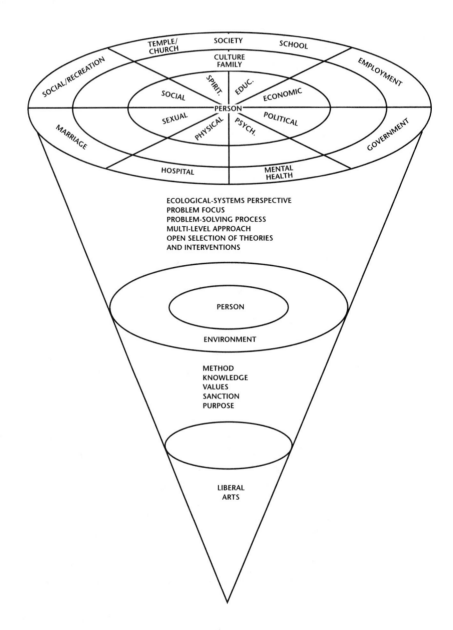

FIGURE 2-1. The Generalist Perspective

An Ecological-Systems Perspective

The theoretical perspective pervasive throughout generalist practice combines general systems, social systems, and ecological theories. Early writers on generalist practice, such as Brieland, Costin, and Atherton, state, "The generalist should understand systems models and use them in problem-solving."[7] Melvin Webber writes, "One of the unifying generalizations is the ecological systems model that views human and social systems as open, self-organizing, self-regulating, and adaptive complexes of interaction and interdependent subsystems."[8] Max Siporin states further, "The integrative trend in the development of practice theory is well exemplified in the ongoing elaboration of the 'problem-person situation' model, or what is now called an 'ecological-systems approach'."[9] And more recently, Karen Kirst-Ashman and Grafton Hull write, "Terms and concepts from both systems theory and the ecological perspective offer useful frameworks for generalist practice."[10] Recognizing the interrelationship of systems with ecology, they write, "The important thing is that both emphasize interactions with the environment."[11]

To understand ecological systems theory as a central element in generalist practice, one must begin by understanding the meaning of "ecology" and "systems." According to Carel Germain,

> Ecology is the science concerned with the adaptive fit of organisms and their environments and with the means by which they achieve a dynamic equilibrium and mutuality.[12]

According to Ludwig Von Bertalanffy,

> A system is a dynamic order of parts and processes standing in mutual interaction.[13]

In an ecological systems perspective, "systems" and "ecology" are integrated by viewing the person(s) as "a system(s)," the environment(s) of the person as "a system(s)," and the fit and interactions between person and environment "ecologically." As depicted in Figure 2–2, the person is seen as a system with various "parts" that are physical, psychological, political, economic (occupational), educational, spiritual, social, and sexual. The environment is viewed as a system consisting of two major "parts" that are "nurturing" (family, friends, community) and "sustaining" (institutions, organizations, programs in society at large).[14] This ecological systems perspective enhances one's view of person in environment by emphasizing the interactions and transactions that take place among the various "parts" and at the boundary at which the person (organism) and environment(s) interface.

A precursor for the application of ecological-systems theory to social work practice may be found in William Gordon's writings on boundary work in social work. Just as ecology concerns itself with the adaptive fit of organisms and their environments, we find that Gordon's seven basic ideas on boundary work consti-

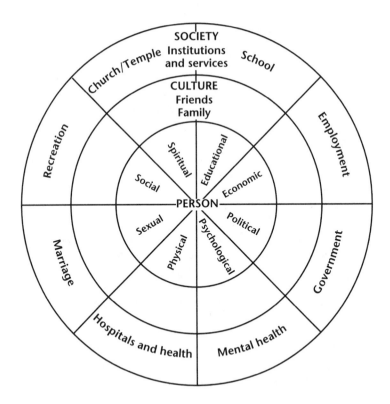

FIGURE 2-2. An Ecological-Systems Perspective of Person in Environment

tute extensive consideration of what occurs at the boundary between a system and its environment. Gordon's seven points were summarized by Hearn as follows:

1. Social work has a simultaneous dual focus. It focuses at once upon the person and his situation, upon the system and its environment.
2. It occurs at the interface between the human system and its environment.
3. The phenomenon which occurs at the interface is a transaction between system and environment.
4. Transaction is a matching effort, whose focus is the coping behavior of the organism on the system side, and the qualities of the impinging environment on the environment side.
5. An encounter between the organism and the environment leaves both changed.
6. The best transactions are those which promote the growth and development of the organism while at the same time being ameliorative to the environment, that is, making it a better place for all systems depending upon the environment for their sustenance.

7. Unattended systems proceed relentlessly toward disorder, evenness, high probability, disorganization, randomness, and continuity, or what is technically called a positive increase in entropy. . . . Thus, for growth and development to occur, there has to be a continuous redistribution of entropy between organism and environment.[15]

The similarities between the ideas of Gordon and those of Germain and Gitterman, as they define ecology, may readily be seen.

Ecology is a science concerned with the relations between living organisms—in this case, human beings and all the elements of their environments. It is concerned with how organisms and environments achieve a goodness-of-fit or adaptive balance and equally important, how and why they sometimes fail to do so.[16]

Rooted in general systems theory, Gordon's work provides the branch for ecological-systems theory to bear fruit in social work.

In ecological-systems theory, the interactions and interdependence between the organism (subsystem) and the environment (macrosystem) are seen as crucial for the survival of both. Any change in one may have a positive or negative effect on the other.[17] The complexity and diversity among people and the various systems that constitute their environments as they exchange and interact continuously for survival is highlighted in this theory.

Ecological-systems theory helps to clarify and to reinforce for social workers the perspective of person in environment. It is not enough to look at people and/or environments. The theory emphasizes the necessary lifeline between the two; it is at the boundary where person and environment meet that most stress or problems occur.

A Problem Focus

The word *problem* has been used to describe the purpose, definition, focus, and process of the profession of social work. For example, in the "Working Definition of Social Work Practice," the first purpose of the profession is stated as follows:

To assist individuals and groups to identify and resolve or minimize problems arising out of disequilibrium between themselves and their environment.[18]

Siporin refers to "social problems" in his definition of practice:

Social work is defined as a social institutional method of helping people to prevent and resolve their social problems, to restore and enhance their social functioning.[19]

According to Pincus and Minahan, the focus of practice is on "the linkages and interactions between people and resource systems and the problems to be faced in the functioning of both individuals and systems."[20] And Charles Levy writes on the assertion that "social work is a problem-solving process."[21]

The meaning and use of the concept *problem* in social work have been debated and criticized. Some critics see the term as too limiting because it refers to pathological or negative situations and appears to overlook the prevention, maintenance, or enhancement functions of social work. The concept is criticized also because it is seen as too general a term for distinguishing the essence of social work from other professions that describe their work as "problem solving."[22]

One may ask this question: What is the meaning of *problem* when used in social work? Does it mean "social problem," "dysfunctional behavior," "pathology," or "undesirable conditions"? More specifically, what is the meaning of *problem* in the General Method of social work? After briefly considering how the concept has been defined by different authors, a definition will be given for "*problem*" as used in the General Method.

The word *problem* goes back to the Greek work *Proballein,* meaning "to throw forward."[23] The word, as found in Webster's, has two central definitions: (1) "a question raised or to be raised for inquiry, consideration, discussion or solution," and (2) "something that is a source of considerable difficulty, perplexity or worry."[24]

In social work research, the word *problem* corresponds to the first of these two definitions. It is the question put forth "that can be studied with hope of adding to relevant knowledge."[25] In describing "an ideal problem," Polansky writes:

> Ideally, it would be cast in theoretical terms (i.e., conceptualized) so that its results might contribute not only to one agency or community but to theory for the field at large, and even beyond social work. At the same time, because this is research for a profession, the hope is to have results that are of immediate, or almost immediate relevance to helping clients.[26]

Perlman seems to lean more toward the second definition in her clarification of the meaning of *problem* within her "problem-solving process":

> "The problem" in the problem-solving model is usually taken to be some difficulty in person-to-person or person-to-task relationships. It is usually focused on as a problem in today's social functioning.[27]

She points out that the problem identified by a client system is not necessarily "the problem" (meaning the basic causative agent in the person's difficulty, the problem of major importance). "It is simply a problem in the helpseeker's current life situation which disturbs or hurts him in some way, and of which he would like to be rid."[28] She also notes that for the majority of people seeking help from social workers, the problem is based on forces outside of themselves and "within their social role transactions."[29]

Merton categorizes social problems as either "deviant behavior" or "social disorganization." He identifies the dual possibility that social problems may originate or result either in the individual or in the society.[30] Siporin builds on Merton's perspectives and describes "problem" as "a reaction pattern to the human-unit environment interaction; it consists of dysfunctional behavior on the part of an individual or social system."[31]

Germain and Gitterman conceptualize "problems" in terms of "disjunction" and "stress" between the person and environment:

> In the Life Model, therefore, human problems and needs are conceptualized as outcomes of transactions between the parts of that whole. Thus they are defined as problems in living which have created stress and taxed coping abilities. Within the interface where person and environment touch, the problem or need reflects a disjunction between coping needs and environmental nutriments.[32]

According to Pincus and Minahan and to Laura Epstein, there must be an evaluator or definer for "a problem" to exist as such. Epstein, for example, writes as follows:

> Problems are not fixed, explicitly bounded things with firm substance. They ordinarily cannot be clearly recognized in a uniform manner by following particular rules of observation. Conditions become defined as problems by a complex and fluid process. Problem definers are those who give voice to an issue.[33]

And Pincus and Minahan state:

> It is useful in this context to define a problem as a social situation or social condition which has been evaluated by someone as undesirable. In this view, no social situation is in itself inherently a problem. When a situation is referred to as a problem, it must be realized that an implied evaluation of it has already been made.[34]

The concept *problem* has been used to describe the central focus of the three traditional methods of casework,[35] group work,[36] and community organization.[37] In generalist practice also, "the problem" is the initial focus and pervasive threat throughout a problem-solving procedure.

Problem in generalist practice is a very broad and inclusive concept referring to an issue, need, question, or difficulty. *Focus* means that which is the center of attention or interest. A *problem focus,* as an essential element of generalist practice, refers to the issue, need, question, or difficulty brought to the attention of the generalist for study and action at any given time.

Traditionally, the focus of attention for study and intervention by social workers was determined according to their method of practice (The traditional methods were casework, group work, and community organization). The "focus" of practitioners was predetermined through their educational preparation and practice experience. Today, in generalist practice, the "problem" presented to generalists becomes the focus of attention and directs the theory and interventions they use in a general problem-solving methodology. Depending on the problem and related goals, the worker selects the most appropriate theories and interventions needed for problem assessment and resolution. The problem is the pivot or the focal point of the spiraling six-stage problem solving process to be explained further throughout this text (see Figure 2–3).

A Multi-Level Approach

Generalists are prepared to work with systems of different sizes (*CPS,* M6.11 and B5.2). Their focus, theory, and methodology do not constrict their practice or expertise to working only, or mainly, with individuals, groups, or communities. Their client systems may be individuals, families, groups, communities, or organizations. Any one of these systems may be seen as a "target" or "action" system. As a "target," the system is viewed by the generalist as needing to change in order to meet the goals of the worker (change agent) and the client system. As a member of an "action system," a particular system is mobilized to work with the change agent and perhaps other systems to bring about change in a target system and to accomplish goals.[38] The generalist often works with multiple and various systems as client, target, or action system.

Another way to cluster or categorize systems of different sizes is according to "level" of practice. The *micro* practice level means "one-on-one" or individual level. *Mezzo* refers to group, and *macro* is "large-scale" practice, such as community, organization, institution, or society.[39] In generalist practice, workers practice at whatever level is needed depending on the problem in focus as assessed from an ecological-systems perspective. The generalist may be working with a particular level at a given time or with more than one level concurrently or sequentially. The *multi-level approach* connotes a readiness for level diversity based on the problem in focus and the generalist's knowledge and skills for problem solving.

An Open Selection of Theories and Interventions

The meaning of *an open selection of theories and interventions* refers to the fact that generalists do not specialize in one theoretical approach. Their use of theories to

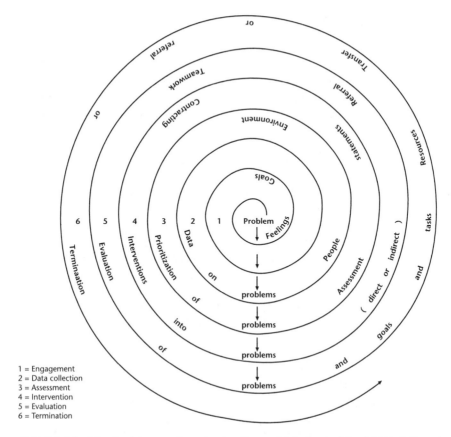

1 = Engagement
2 = Data collection
3 = Assessment
4 = Intervention
5 = Evaluation
6 = Termination

FIGURE 2-3. The Problem as Seen in the General Method of Social Work Practice

understand (assessment) and to direct their actions (intervention) varies according to the problem in focus. Their only constriction may be due to their limited ability and experience in using more advanced theories and specialized models of interventions. In situations where the problem calls for a more specialized approach, generalists make referrals.

The scope of attention or intervention by the generalist may extend from a person, to a family, to a group, to a community, to an organization, to society at large. In focusing on a problem, a whole range of possible causes and solutions must be considered. Although a generalist does not have great theoretical depth or specialized competence, the worker is challenged to think with conceptual complexity and to have the ability to identify the particular system and point of interface in need of attention. The generalist is open to select the most appropriate theory, intervention, or resource for an accurate assessment and planned intervention in the particular person–problem–situation.

CASE EXAMPLE

John, 18 years old, has had a difficult time maintaining passing grades in high school, owing to limited cognitive abilities and physical stamina. Because of these limitations, he is unable to help with or eventually to take over his father's business. This is a role expected of the oldest son according to the culture of the family. John is feeling rejected by his father and relatives. He walked into an outpatient clinic for help.

The worker for this case would need to know cognitive theory and understand the client's culture and physical limitations. Role theory would be useful in assessing the problems (role skills, role expectations, role enactment) within the client–environment situation. Figure 2–4 shows how the worker uses Figure 2–2 and Table 1–3 in the application of theory. The lines of the circle in Figure 2–4 are the places where theories under the "in" category of Table 1–3 would fall. Role theory is indicated as RT at the interfaces between person and family and between family and employment/society. In the sections within the circles would fall the theories categorized under "person" or "environment" in Table 1–3; cognitive theory (CT) is in the "education" section; physiological theory (PT) is in the "physical" section; and theory about culture is in the second circle, "family."

Generalist practitioners, using the foundation theories as presented in Table 1–3, would selectively and collectively apply theory to practice. They would understand the meaning of theory and would grasp the concepts, statements, sources, and application of each of the theories. In addition, with the help of the ecological framework, the generalist would be able to view the relationships and complementarity among the basic theories for collective application and more effective practice. The theories as presented in Table 1–3 would support the generalist in using the general social work method that will be presented in the remainder of this book.

A Problem-Solving Process

Several contemporary writings used in social work education and practice describe the "how to" of practice in terms of a basic sequential process. The skills and stages of the processes may be stated in different words, but similarities and overlap among writers are apparent.

Helen Harris Perlman writes that her casework problem-solving process is actually applicable to any problem-solving efforts "in the normal course of living."[40] She identifies several "operations" that are essential to the process. They are seen as not necessarily occurring in order but as possibly taking place simultaneously or even out of sequence. Basically, the components of the process are problem identification; feelings identification (client's); examination of causes and effects of the problem; search for means of solution and alternatives; and choices or decision making and action on decisions or alterations of plans and action. In

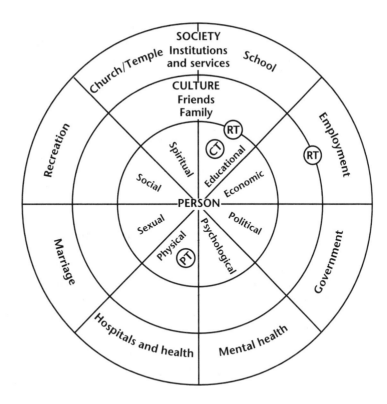

FIGURE 2-4. Use of Theory in Case Example

the casework process, Perlman sees the factors of "relationship" and "involvement with significant others" as necessarily present within the process.[41]

In an early analysis of the change process, Kurt Lewin identifies the three phases of "unfreezing," "moving," and "freezing."[42] Lippitt, Watson, and Westley expand the process to the following seven general phases:

1. The development of a need for change
2. The establishment of a change relationship
3. The clarification or diagnosis of the client system's problem
4. The examination of alternative routes and goals; establishing goals and intentions
5. The transformation of intentions into actual change efforts
6. The generalization and stabilization of change
7. Achieving a terminal relationship.[43]

The authors state that the process does not necessarily progress in the orderly sequence listed. Often, more than one phase occurs at the same time. Process is seen as "a kind of cyclic motion starting over and over again as one set of problems is solved and a new set encountered."[44] Lippitt, Watson, and Westley were among the first to identify their process as applicable to work with individuals, groups, organizations, and communities.

Pincus and Minahan describe three "guide posts for the process" in their "Model and Method."[45] They stress that the activities of a worker are cyclical in nature and that at any point there may be overlap in the steps of the process. The major "successive points" in their process are described as "contact," "contract," and "termination." In the contact stage, the worker begins to engage in communications with various systems. In contracting, the worker forms agreements with clients ("primary" contracts) or with other related systems ("secondary" contracts). After contracting, the worker begins to move toward termination.[46]

Compton and Galaway identify three basic phases similar to those of Pincus and Minahan, but they develop the phases with additional activities incorporated into the process. The "contact phase" of Compton and Galaway includes "problem identification, initial goal setting and data collection." The "contract phase" refers to "joint assessments, goal setting and planning." There is also an entire section in their work on the "implementation of the plan" and on "evaluation." Their "ending phase" includes "referral, transfer and termination."[47]

Max Siporin distinguishes between "the basic helping approach" and "special and eclectic approaches" in practice theory. He presents four "characteristic helping processes" in practice. They are (1) "educational socializing and structure building process," (2) "relational process," (3) "rehabilitative therapeutic process," and (4) "the problem solving and crisis resolving process." The stages of the problem-solving process are "assessment, planning, interactive action, evaluation monitoring and corrective action."[48] In addition, Siporin develops a "general helping process," also called an "action process," which has the "helping procedures" of "engagement, assessment, planning, intervention, monitoring, and termination."[49]

Gerard Egan presents a three-stage helping model. The three principal stages of his helping process are (1) "responding to the client/client self-exploration," (2) "integrative understanding/dynamic self-understanding," and (3) "facilitating action/action." He calls his model "developmental," with "progressive interdependent stages."[50]

Shulman introduces "A Model of the Helping Process" based on the work phases called "preliminary," "beginning," "work," and "ending." In the preliminary phase, workers are concerned with empathy, communication, responding, and reporting. Central to the beginning phase is the art of developing a working relationship. It includes early contracting and clarification of boundaries. The work phase, according to Shulman, involves a series of skills, including elaboration, containment, and working with silences. The ending phase occurs when the separation process is carried out and skills for transition are utilized.[51]

Within task-centered practice, there is an identifiable "sequence of discrete steps" that may be seen collectively as constituting a process. Although the steps are to be applied systematically, Reid recommends that there be sufficient flexibility to allow for adaptation to the individual circumstances of each case.[52] The sequential steps, called "the task implementation sequence," are stated by Dean Hepworth as follows:

1. Enhancing the commitment of the client to carry out a specific task
2. Planning the specific details of carrying out the task
3. Analyzing obstacles that may be encountered
4. Modeling and rehearsing the behaviors embodied in carrying out the task
5. Summarizing the plan for the implementation of the task and conveying encouragement along with the expectation that the client will carry out the task.[53]

A comparison of the different processes reveals that the authors are in basic agreement in recognizing a general process for practice, and that the process consists of progressive stages that lead to goal accomplishment. Several writers stress the need for flexibility in applying the process, with the expectation of overlap and occasional inconsistency in the sequencing of phases. In addition to describing foundation values and knowledge, it is apparent that leaders in the profession of social work have worked diligently at finding ways to describe the basic actions or "systematic mode of procedure" used by social workers. Building on these earlier works, this book will describe a problem-solving process, called *The General Method*, that has characteristics similar to those of the processes identified. As with the cyclical nature of theory building,[54] it is hoped that the General Method that is emerging from these earlier writings will offer greater understanding and utility for practice.

Method Defined

In the "Working Definition of Social Work Practice," method is defined as "an orderly systematic mode of procedure.[55] Schwartz describes method as "a systematic process of ordering one's activity in the performance of a function."[56] According to Siporin, method refers to "the 'how' of helping, to purposeful, planned, instrumental activity through which tasks are accomplished and goals are achieved."[57] And, in *Webster's*, method is defined as "a procedure or process for attaining an object" or "a particular approach to problems of truth or knowledge."[58] Basically, *method* means an orderly process of action. The concept connotes thought and purpose in addition to activity.

Morales and Sheafor state: "The social worker's skill is expressed within the framework of one or more social work methods."[59] In addition to skill, a social work method should reflect the knowledge and values of the profession. Method puts the knowledge, values, and skills of a worker into action. As pointed out by Siporin,

The societal task functions of social work are realized through the "how" of methodic action, in an application of knowledge, attitudes, and skill.[60]

The first methods identified in social work practice focused on the way a social worker proceeded in working with an individual, running a group, or organizing a community. The traditional methods of social casework, social group work, and community organization were seen as separate and distinct methodologies. Each method had its own integral set of theories and skills.

Although some workers and agencies continue to use predominantly one of the traditional methods, there has been a growing recognition of the need for workers to be able to work with systems of different sizes. In some graduate schools, students identify at least two methods for concentration. In many schools, traditional methods have been combined into micro (casework and group work) and macro (community, organization, social planning) practice. It has become apparent, as brought out by Carol Meyer, that "the traditional separation of casework, group work, and community organization is no longer tenable."[61]

At the undergraduate level, there is a strong movement toward identifying a procedure that is common to all methods. Schwartz suggests that from experiences with different size systems "the common methodological components of the helping process in social work" can be extracted.[62] Although Gordon discouraged "the dubious task of trying to extract from each (traditional method) what was common to all,"[63] he recognizes "such broad stages as assessment, planning, taking action and evaluating, [as] characteristics of any rationally based problem solving approach."[64] At the base level of practice, Siporin identifies a "common base of method." He does not find "a generic method" in practice, but he uses an emergence of various "modes of social work intervention."[65] In Morales and Sheafor, there is reference to a "generic practice method," but its meaning is not developed.[66]

Many contemporary writers in social work have begun to describe an "orderly systematic mode of procedure" (NASW definition of *method*), but refer to it as something other than a method. There is obvious hesitancy in using the word *method*. The term seems to be reserved for the three methodologic foundations of the profession. Although social workers appreciate the contributions of the original methods that served as pillars for practice, it is time for them to accept and to encourage the emergence of new, relevant methods for contemporary practice at both the B.S.W. and M.S.W. levels.

The General Method

Using the definition of *general* to mean what belongs to the "common nature" of a group and "not confined by specialization or careful limitation"[67] (as stated in Chapter 1), and the definition of *method* to mean "an orderly systematic mode of procedure,"[68] it is possible to identify a General Method of social work practice. This method may be seen as common to all methods and not bound by careful limitation. It is a basic method consisting of a purposeful procedure ordered according to six major stages.

The sequential stages of the General Method are engagement, data collection, assessment, intervention, evaluation, and termination. In the succeeding chapters, each stage will be described in greater detail. The stages of the method are not mutually exclusive. They serve as systematic guidelines for organizing the thoughts and actions of workers as they interact with diverse systems. In reality, the stages frequently occur simultaneously or out of order. Within each stage of the process, there may be combinations of such basic components as communication, data collection, contracting, evaluation, and termination. The General Method is a dynamic process composed of clusters of skills according to stages.

The method may be utilized when working with individuals, groups, families, or communities. It is not restricted to any particular system. It is inclusive of work with target and action systems as well as with client systems.[69] The General Method is built on the holistic base of knowledge, values, and skills presented in Chapter 1. Its main purpose is to serve as a guide for the actions of entry-level social workers.

The General Method is more than the selection and sequencing of skills found in the foundation of social work practice. It is more than an action chain made up of six stages. The General Method is a problem-solving process carried out within the context of the generalist perspective. This means that throughout the process and during each stage of it, the worker focuses on identifiable problems, brings an ecological-systems theoretical framework, selects openly from a range of theories and interventions, and readily practices at different or multiple levels.

The generalist, as described in this book, uses the General Method, intended to serve as a guide for beginning social work practitioners at the entry level. In the following sections of this chapter, a comparison will be made of the beginning generalist with the advanced practitioner and of their methodologies. In a later chapter, consideration will be given to the placement of the General Method within the broad sphere of methodologies that exist in human services today.

The Beginning Generalist Versus the Advanced Practitioner

Brieland, Costin, and Atherton distinguish between the practice of the baccalaureate level generalist (B.S.W.) and the master's level generalist (M.S.W.). The master's level generalist can demonstrate traditional or specialized methods as well as the General Method. While in graduate school, these workers study both general and specialized methodologies. An example cited is the University of Chicago model of an M.S.W. generalist. Workers from this program begin their helping procedure with a problem-solving approach similar to the General Method of B.S.W. workers. When the time comes for assessment and intervention, however, the graduate workers may utilize specialized methods such as casework or group work if they are needed.

In this process all social work methods, traditional and innovative, are utilized singly or in combination to meet reality needs and to alleviate stresses in ways that enhance or strengthen the inherent capacities of client systems.[70]

Anne Minahan and Allen Pincus suggest that "all social workers are generalists." They define a generalist as "a person with a broad view who can look at an entire social situation, analyze the interactions between people in all the resource systems connected to that situation, intervene in those interactions, determine which specialists are needed from a variety of disciplines, and coordinate and mobilize the knowledge and skill of many disciplines." Building on a generalist identity, they see students in advanced education (M.S.W. programs) developing a specialization or becoming "a more expert generalist." The advanced generalist acquires "increased competence in assessment, knowledge, and skills related to interactions between resource systems."[71]

As stated, a social work generalist is a human service provider with broad-based skills, foundation knowledge of persons and environments, and a commitment to social work values. The generalist demonstrates basic competence for working with individuals, groups, families, communities, and other related systems within an ecological-systems perspective. A social work generalist is described also as an entry-level person who uses an open selection of theories and interventions and a problem-solving process called in this book the General Method of social work practice.

The advanced practitioner is a person who has the foundation knowledge, values, and skills of the generalist and advanced knowledge and skill for working with a particular population, problem, or area of practice, who may use a traditional or a specialized method or methods. This social worker has an M.S.W. degree in which, or beyond which, there was at least one full year of advanced study and field work in the identified area of concentration. In an M.S.W. curriculum and in M.S.W. practice, competence is expected beyond the knowledge, values, skills, and method identified in this book.

CASE EXAMPLE A

Mrs. A, a single parent, came to the town social service department on the advice of a friend. She stated that she and her son had been doing fine until recently when she started having problems with him and with her landlord. Her son, J, was 16 years old and failed to follow Mrs. A's rules and directions. They frequently argued, resulting in J's walking out of the home. In addition, their apartment was in poor condition, with leaking pipes and cockroaches. Mrs. A said she had complained several times to the landlord, but she appears to be ignored by him.

INTERVENTION PLAN A (BEGINNING GENERALIST)

Worker (B.S.W.) helped Mrs. A clarify her presenting problems and goals. Data collecting included interviews with J and the landlord. An intervention plan was developed and implemented in which (1) Mrs. A received ongoing support from the worker, which included information and discussion regarding the needs of adolescents. As a result, Mrs. A was able to establish more realistic expectations for her son. (2) J was referred to an adolescent activity group, where he had opportunities for peer support and male identification (male B.S.W. group leader). (3) Worker met with landlord and cited the housing code regulation that indicated that if he continued to ignore Mrs. A's complaints, he would be in violation of the code. Mrs. A was informed of the rights of tenants and the resources for housing-code enforcement. When the landlord did not make any improvements, Mrs. A contacted the Housing Code Enforcement Bureau, which notified the landlord that it would take court action if he did not follow up on the defects reported by Mrs. A.

CASE EXAMPLE B

Mrs. B, a single parent, came to the family service agency because she was referred by the social worker from the school attended by her daughter, Marie, age 14. Mrs. B said her daughter was defiant and not doing well in school. She was also having trouble with her landlord in her apartment because of inadequate heating. Mrs. B had tried contacting the Housing Authority, but the landlord told them that the problem was Mrs. B's failure to pay her heating bill. Mrs. B said she knew that many tenants in the apartment building were having similar problems with the landlord.

INTERVENTION PLAN B (ADVANCED PRACTITIONER)

In gathering information, the worker learned that Mrs. B's feelings of inadequacy and discouragement were longstanding and not just related to her daughter and the landlord. In addition, the worker learned that Marie had difficulty getting along with her teachers and peers as well as with her mother. Mrs. B had received reports from Marie's school that she was always trying to be the focus of attention in her classes. Mrs. B's neighbors had told her that they would be glad to meet as a group to take action against the landlord.

Based on these findings, an intervention plan was developed in which (1) Mrs. B was referred for intensive casework to a clinical social worker who helped Mrs. B gain insight regarding her feelings of inferiority and depression. (2) Marie was referred to a small therapy group that was led by male and female co-workers, both with M.S.W. degrees and concentrations in adolescence and psychotherapeutic group work. (3) The housing problem was brought to the attention of a community organizer of the local neighborhood center, a person who had extensive experience in the area of housing.

In Intervention Plan A, beginning generalists used foundation values, knowledge, and skills in a general method to work with individuals, groups, and community resources. The skills utilized included basic relationship, problem-solving, and political skills. The advanced practitioners of Intervention Plan B would be expected to have more extensive knowledge, skills, and experience. The skills of these workers would include providing insight and dealing with transferences, as well as complex community organizing and case advocacy. Depending on the worker's concentrations, greater knowledge of relevant theory, housing, legislation, group dynamics, depression, and mental illness would be expected. Workers would be using specialized methodologies. Such knowledge, skill, and methods would be in addition to what is identified in the generalist perspective of social work practice.

Methodologies

Focusing more specifically on methods, it has been stated that the beginning generalist is guided by foundation knowledge, values, and skills while he or she uses the General Method in working with a variety of systems. Within an ecological theoretical perspective, the generalist acts according to a basic helping procedure. Realizing human characteristics and, therefore, the uniqueness of each situation, the beginning practitioner is able to move back and forth across lines or stages of the Method, depending on the current reality. The General Method provides the worker with a basic guide for operation.

In contrast, the more advanced methods—traditional or otherwise—may include much that is found in the General Method but may also reflect the usage of advanced knowledge, skills, and procedures for work with particular systems, problems, or populations. Although practitioners and educators at the graduate level of practice have identified knowledge and skills for traditional social work methods, further development is needed in clarifying the content of methods for advanced practice. The worker with a concentration in the area of children, for example, may have a specialized method for working with children through the use of play. The family specialist may have a distinctive method for family therapy.

How does one decide whether the general or an advanced method of practice is needed in a particular situation? To answer this question, one must consider several factors. Primarily, it is necessary to collect data on the severity of the problem or need being addressed and on the strength and coping capacities of the persons in need. As depicted in Figure 2–5, when the severity of the problem or need is *great* and when the client has *little* ability and motivation for dealing with the problem, there is a strong indication that an advanced worker is needed (see point 1 in Figure 2–5). To bring about the greatest possible improvement in the client's situation, it is desirable that the M.S.W. practitioner has advanced expertise as well as general expertise. When the problem or need is of little severity and the client system has obvious strengths and coping capacities, the beginning generalist will be able to intervene with high expectancy for goal accomplishment (see point 2 in Figure 2–5).

For example, if Mrs. W has a history of being depressed, with periodic outbursts against her children, and if she is very defensive when approached about her problems, the worker would need to be highly skilled to work with her effectively. If Mrs. W had a history of excellent caretaking of her children, but recently found herself losing control and therefore came to an agency seeking help, there is a strong possibility that a worker could use the General Method to help Mrs. W with her current stressful situation.

As shown in Figure 2–5, some client–problem situations may be serviced by either an advanced or beginning general practitioner. Either the General Method or an advanced method could be used successfully.

Where there is similarity in the assessed severity of the problem with the assessed strengths of the client, a balance may result. In these cases, there is greater question as to whether the advanced or beginning generalist methods should be used for effective goal accomplishment. For example, although Mr. B may have lost his job on the same day his daughter had a serious car accident and he received a doctor's report that he needed major surgery, Mr. B and his family may be strong enough to be able to find ways of coping with their difficulties with the help of a generalist. The advanced practitioner may not be needed, even though there are major (life-and-death) issues, because of the great strengths of the client system (see point 3 in Figure 2–5).

In cases where the problem or need falls in the middle of the scale of severity and the client system's strengths are assessed as between the great and little indicators, the selection of method may be arbitrary. For example, the community concerned with an increase in neighborhood crime may have some strengths for mobilizing itself to work on the emerging problem with the help of either a beginning generalist or an advanced practitioner. The general problem-solving method or the specialized community-organization method could be effective (see point 4 in Figure 2–5).

Figure 2–5 may be a helpful tool for case assignment or planning. To use the tool, however, it is important to understand the meaning of the indicators of problem/need severity and of the client system's strengths. A problem or need is assessed at "little" severity when it has recently emerged (time consideration)

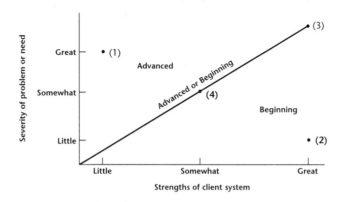

FIGURE 2-5. Beginning and Advanced Methodology

with limited scope (how many, how deeply involved) and when it has little life-or-death magnitude. When the client system is assessed as having "little" strength, it means that the persons involved have very limited coping capacities, motivation, and resources. As the assessment moves higher on either scale, it means that there is evidence of a greater degree of client strengths or problem severity. Owing to the human and artful nature of social work practice, it is difficult to identify scientific tools for measurement and prediction. Figure 2–5 is a basic tool for comparing the use of the General Method of beginning workers with the use of more specialized methodologies of advanced workers. It is scientifically limited because it relies heavily on personal judgment and inconclusive data. It does, however, provide a framework for beginning conceptualization of distinction in the use of the General Method.

Conclusion

In this chapter, we presented an overview of the characteristic elements of the generalist perspective, with focus on the General Method for entry-level practitioners. We explored the meaning, types, and placement of methods in social work. After a brief description of the General Method, we made some preliminary comparisons between the use of the General Method and the use of advanced methods in social work. The beginning generalist and the advanced practitioner were contrasted in definition and in practice.

In summary, the foundation of social work practice consists of the elements of (1) purpose, (2) sanction, (3) values, (4) knowledge, and (5) method (skills). The major elements of generalist practice are (1) an ecological-systems perspective, (2) a problem-focus, (3) a multi-level approach, (4) an open selection of theories and interventions, and (5) a problem-solving process. The generalist foundation and the elements of generalist practice are depicted in Figure 2–1. Generalists call upon this holistic perspective as they use the General Method of social work practice.

As beginning social work generalists or advanced workers use their practice methodologies when working with a variety of systems, they need to be sensitive to human diversity. In the next chapter, a range of variables that constitute major human diversities found in social work practice will be presented from a holistic perspective. Chapters 4 through 9 will describe more specific examples to demonstrate sensitivity to human diversity in the General Method.

NOTES

1. Max Siporin, *Introduction to Social Work Practice* (New York: Macmillan, 1975), p. 43. Copyright 1975 by Macmillan Publishing Company.

2. Council of Social Work Education, *Curriculum Policy Statement for the Baccalaureate Degree Programs in Social Work Education*, approved by the Board of Directors July 19, 1992 and revised October 1993. (New York: Council on Social

Work Education), B5.2, p. 3, and Council of Social Work Education, *Curriculum Policy Statement for the Master's Degree Programs in Social Work Education,* approved by the Board of Directors July 19, 1992. (New York: Council on Social Work Education), M5.2, p. 3.

3. Council on Social Work Education, "Directory of Colleges and Universities with Accredited Social Work Degree Programs" (Alexandria, VA: Counsel on Social Work Education, July 1993).

4. Reprinted with permission from *Educating the Baccalaureate Social Worker,* Volume I: *Report of the Undergraduate Social Work Curriculum Development Project,* Copyright 1977, Ballinger Publishing Company, pp. 86–89.

5. Ibid, Vol. II., p. 155.

6. *The American Heritage Dictionary: Second College Edition* (Boston: Houghton-Mifflin, 1985), p. 926.

7. Donald Brieland, Lola B. Costin and Charles R. Atherton, *Contemporary Social Work: An Introduction to Social Work and Social Welfare,* 2nd ed. (New York: McGraw-Hill, 1981), p. 144.

8. Melvin Webber, "Systems Planning for Social Policy," in Ralph Kramer and Harry Specht, eds., *Readings in Community Organization Practice* (Englewood Cliffs, NJ: Prentice-Hall, 1969), pp. 417–424.

9. Max Siporin, *Introduction to Social Work Practice,* p. 43.

10. Karen Kirst Ashman and Grafton Hull, *Understanding Generalist Practice* (Chicago: Nelson-Hall Publishers, 1993), p. 12.

11. Ibid., p. 14.

12. Carel B. Germain, "An Ecological Perspective in Casework Practice," *Social Casework* 54 (June 1973): 326.

13. Ludwig Von Bertalanffy, *General Systems Theory* (New York: Braziller, 1968), p. 208.

14. Dolores Norton, *The Dual Perspective: Inclusion of Ethnic Minority Content in Social Work Curriculum* (New York: Council on Social Work Education, 1978), p. 5.

15. Gordon Hearn, "General Systems Theory and Social Work," in Francis J. Turner, ed., *Social Work Treatment: Interlocking Theoretical Approaches,* 2nd ed. (New York: The Free Press, 1979), p. 350, 351, Copyright 1979 by The Free Press. Reprinted by permission.

16. Carel Germain and Alex Gitterman, "The Life Model of Social Work Practice," in Francis J. Turner, ed., *Social Work Treatment: Interlocking Theoretical Approaches,* 2nd ed, (New York: The Free Press, 1979) p. 362. Copyright 1979 by The Free Press.

17. Ibid., p. 302.

18. Commission on Social Work Practice, NASW, "Working Definition on Social Work Practice," in Harriet M. Bartlett, "Toward Clarification and Improvement of Social Work Practice," *Social Work* 3, no. 2 (April 1958): 6.

19. Max Siporin, *Introduction to Social Work Practice,* p. 3.

20. Allen Pincus and Anne Minahan, *Social Work Practice: Model and Method* (Itasca, IL: Peacock, 1973), p. 9.

21. Charles S. Levy, "The Problem in the Social Work Problem-Solving Process," *Journal of Jewish Communal Service* 43 (Summer 1967): 311.

22. Ibid., p. 306.

23. *Webster's Third New International Dictionary of the English Language*, s.v. "problem."

24. Ibid.

25. Norman A. Polansky, ed., *Social Work Research: Methods for the Helping Professions*, rev. ed. (Chicago: University of Chicago Press, 1975), p. 30.

26. Ibid.

27. Helen Harris Perlman, "The Problem-Solving Model in Social Casework," in Robert W. Roberts and Robert H. Nees, eds., *Theories of Social Casework* (Chicago: University of Chicago Press, 1970), p. 147.

28. Ibid, p. 146.

29. Ibid, p. 148.

30. Robert K. Merton and Robert A. Nisbet, eds., *Contemporary Social Problems*, 3rd ed. (New York: Harcourt, Brace & World, 1971), p. viii.

31. Siporin, *Introduction*, p. 22.

32. Carel Germain and Alex Gitterman, "The Life Model," p. 371.

33. Laura Epstein, *Helping People: The Task-Centered Approach* (St. Louis: The C. V. Mosby Company, 1980), p. 55.

34. Pincus and Minahan, *Social Work Practice*, p. 104.

35. Helen Harris Perlman, *Social Casework: A Problem-Solving Process* (Chicago: University of Chicago Press, 1957), pp. 4–5.

36. Gisela Konopka, "The Methods of Social Group Work," in Walter A. Friedlander, ed., *Concepts and Methods of Social Work* (Englewood Cliffs, NJ: Prentice-Hall, 1955), pp. 117–18.

37. Murray Ross, *Case Histories in Community Organization* (New York: Harper and Brothers, 1958), p. 13.

38. Pincus and Minahan, *Social Work Practice*, p. 63.

39. Charles Zastrow, *The Practice of Social Work*, 4th ed. (Belmont, California: Wadsworth Publishing Company, 1992), p. 225.

40. Perlman, "The Problem-Solving Model in Social Casework," p. 137.

41. Ibid.

42. Kurt Lewin, "Frontiers in Group Dynamics", *Human Relations* 2, no. 1 (1947): 5–41.

43. Ronald Lippitt, Jeanne Watson, and Bruce Westley, *The Dynamics of Planned Change* (New York: Harcourt, Brace & World, 1958), pp. 131–42.

44. Ibid., p. 130.

45. Pincus and Minahan, *Social Work Practice*, p. 92.

46. Ibid., pp. 92, 93.

47. Beulah Roberts Compton and Burt Galaway, *Social Work Processes*, rev. ed. (Homewood, IL: Dorsey, 1979), pp. 276–450.

48. Siporin, *Introduction*, pp. 47–52.

49. Ibid., pp. 159–61.

50. From *You and Me,* by Gerard Egan, Copyright 1977 by Wadsworth Publishing Company, Inc. Reprinted by permission of the publisher, Brooks/Cole Publishing Company, Monterey, California, pp. 29–53.

51. Lawrence Shulman, *The Skills of Helping Individuals and Groups* (Itasca, IL: Peacock, 1979), pp. 14–106.

52. William J. Reid, "A Test of a Task-Centered Approach," *Social Work* 22, no. 1 (January 1975): 3–9.

53. Dean H. Hepworth, "Early Removal of Resistance in Task-Centered Casework," *Social Work* 24, no. 4 (July 1979): 318.

54. Gordon Hearn, *Theory Building in Social Work* (Toronto: University of Toronto Press, 1958).

55. Commission on Social Work Practice, NASW, "Working Definition," p. 7.

56. William Schwartz, "The Social Worker in the Group," in Beulah Roberts Compton and Burt Galaway, *Social Work Processes,* rev. ed. (Homewood, IL: Dorsey, 1979), p. 17.

57. Siporin, *Introduction,* p. 43.

58. *Webster's Third New International Dictionary of the English Language,* s.v. "method."

59. Armado Morales and Bradford W. Sheafor, *Social Work: A Profession of Many Faces* (Boston: Allyn & Bacon, 1977), p. 115.

60. Siporin, *Introduction,* p. 43.

61. Carol H. Meyer, "The Changing Concept of Individualized Services," *Social Casework* 47 (May 1966): 284.

62. Schwartz, "The Social Worker," p. 16.

63. William E. Gordon, "A Critique of the Working Definition," *Social Work* 7, no. 4 (October 1962): 5.

64. William E. Gordon, "A Natural Basis for Social Work Specializations," in National Association of Social Workers, *Specialization in the Social Work Profession* (special report of the NASW/CSWE Joint Task Force, December 1980), p. 4.

65. Siporin, *Introduction,* p. 46.

66. Morales and Shaefor, *Social Work,* p. 115.

67. *Webster's Third New International Dictionary of the English Language,* s.v. "general."

68. Ibid., s.v. "method."

69. Pincus and Minahan, *Social Work Practice,* p. 63.

70. Ibid., pp. 146, 147.

71. Anne Minahan and Allen Pincus, "A Conceptual Framework for Social Work Practice," *Social Work* 22, no. 5 (September 1977): 352.

CHAPTER 3

Human Diversity: Populations-at-Risk

A human being is a part of the whole, called by us "universe," a part limited in time and space. He experiences himself, his thoughts and feelings, as something separate from the rest—a kind of optical delusion of his consciousness. This delusion is a kind of prison for us, restricting us to our personal decisions and to affection for a few persons nearest to us. Our task must be to free ourselves from this prison by widening our circle of compassion to embrace all living creatures and the whole of nature in its beauty.

—Albert Einstein[1]

A profession has an identifiable value base. At the roots of the social work profession is the belief in the dignity and worth of every human being. Social workers value human beings of any age, limitation, or diversity. The profession of social work has a commitment to the enhancement of human life.

To be human is to have choice. People need to choose their own lifestyles and behaviors. Social workers respect the need of individuals to choose for themselves. They do not judge the morality of others' behaviors or try to interrupt them, as long as the behaviors of one are not depriving another person of life, choice, or expression. When this is the case, social workers act in support of the oppressed to help them to obtain their freedom and growth.

In social work, each person is seen as unique, with a right to be treated as an individual. Although values and behaviors commonly characterize a particular group, a worker exercises care to avoid stereotyping a member of any group. To *stereotype* means to attribute uniformly a set of characteristics to a group of people and to deny their individual differences. An understanding of the values and behaviors of diverse cultures, however, is valuable to a worker who is trying to communicate and interact in a meaningful way with different systems. Along with the values of life, choice, and individuality, a knowledge of human diversity is needed to guide a worker's actions.

In this chapter, emphasis will be given to a worker's need for sensitivity to human diversity in generalist practice. The General Method presented throughout this text is generic for working with diverse peoples or systems. Individuals and groups, nevertheless, do have distinctive characteristics that a worker should consider as the General Method is applied. Among the diversities found within social work practice are ethnic and class diversity, heterosexual–homosexual diversity, male–female diversity, age and physical/mental development diversity, and rural–urban diversity.

The clients of social workers are frequently identified as members of populations-at-risk. Special groups in American society experience differential treatment due to their human diversity. Populations distinguished by age, gender, sexual preference, religion, ethnicity, or developmental delay or disability are at risk of experiencing discrimination, economic deprivation, oppression or abuse. More recent vulnerable populations in America include people with AIDS and the homeless. Keeping in mind the values of the profession, a worker demonstrates respect for human life through an informed acceptance of human diversity and a resulting sensitive application of method in the service of diverse individuals and populations.

To promote awareness and skill for working with variations among human beings, this chapter explores the major diversities found in social work practice. There will not be a thorough presentation for any one group. Throughout the following chapters, primary attention will be given to the use of the six-stage General Method when working with human diversity in social work practice.

Cultural Diversity

In preparing to communicate with an individual, group, family, or community, a social worker takes time to study the culture of the system to be contacted. *Culture* means the set of values, beliefs, behaviors, language, and thought processes that is learned and exhibited by a group. An *ethnic group* is a subculture within a society, with distinctiveness due to race, national origin, or religion. Some ethnic groups have been identified as *minority* groups. This term is not based on culture or number. *Minority* refers to the extent of a group's power or of its access to the resources and opportunities available in a society. Minority-group members have less control over the circumstances of their lives than do majority members. Minority members experience economic, social, and political inequality, whereas the majority group dominates the society. In the United States, four major ethnic minority cultures have been identified. They are African-American, American Indian, Asian-Pacific American, and Hispanic.[2] Although for some people an ethnic identity provides access and privilege, for members of minority groups, the social meaning of their ethnicity (race) results in discrimination and prejudice.

Cultural sensitivity can be fostered through a knowledge of different fundamental value orientations of ethnic groups. In addition to knowing about the history of a group, it is important for the social worker to have some understanding of how the group basically perceives and values such life dimensions as time, relationships, activity, human nature, and nature itself. Cultures often interlock as individuals from varied backgrounds come together. An Anglo worker, for example, with a future time perspective may become very annoyed with a Mexican-American, present-oriented client who does not save her money to last throughout the month. The client, on the other hand, may become irritated by the worker, who is seen as taking too much time to collect data before providing a direct service.

Certain common tension polarities confront all minority groups. Doman Lum identifies these basic problem areas as (1) oppression versus liberation, (2) powerlessness versus empowerment, (3) exploitation versus parity, (4) acculturation versus culture maintenance, and (5) stereotyping versus unique person.[3] To work with minorities, social workers need to understand these existing polarities and to provide the support necessary for minorities to speak and act for themselves as they organize to overcome such tension areas. Workers demonstrate an understanding of minorities and an appreciation of cultural diversity by working for cultural maintenance and parity rather than expecting acculturation or conformity to exploitation.

If a worker is to be culturally sensitive, it is not enough to know about general characteristics of ethnic groups. To comprehend the specific culture of a person or a group, there has to be further refinement. Careful research of the four major minority groups in America has shown great variation within each group due to intragroup diversity. Valentine, for example, found 14 distinguishable subcultures within the African-American minority group.[4] Clustered in the American Indian category are 98 subcultures.[5] The Asian-Pacific group has 23 subcultures,[6] and at least 5 subcultures are contained within the Hispanic minority group.[7] Each of these subcultures has distinctive customs, attitudes, and lifestyles. Although some similar or common biological characteristics may exist among the members of a minority group—such as the Samoan, Guamanian, Chinese, Japanese, and Vietnamese of the Asian-Pacific American minority—a worker needs to realize that each subgroup has a history and culture of its own. Each subculture frequently has its own language or dialect. There can thus be variation in verbal statements and expressions as well as in the meaning of glances, gestures, and body positionings.

Self-Assessment of Cultural Sensitivity

In the General Method of social work practice, a sensitivity to cultural diversity may be demonstrated within each stage of the process. A worker's sensitivity to the culture of a system is reflected in the way in which that worker (1) engages the system in identifying problems and needs, (2) collects data, (3) makes an assessment and contract, (4) intervenes, (5) evaluates, and (6) terminates. Timing, communications, and actions show the extent to which a worker realizes the value orientations of a culture. The attitude and approach of the worker can also indicate an awareness of the pressures and problems that persist in the lives of people from ethnic minority cultures.

For effective cross-cultural practice (i.e., worker and system from different cultures), a social worker needs to be consciously aware of his or her own culture, as well as that of the system receiving service. Growing in cultural self-awareness can enable a worker to recognize and to appreciate diversity among cultures. It also may help a worker to begin to see any prejudicial or ethnocentric attitudes he or she might have. *Ethnocentrism* is basically the belief that one's own ethnic group has the only appropriate and acceptable practices, values, and customary behaviors.

In Exercise 3–1, questions are proposed for reflection and discussion by workers and students in social work. The purpose of the exercise is to enhance cultural sensitivity and self-awareness. Through identifying, sharing, and comparing the facts, feelings, and experiences addressed in the exercise, one may gain an empathic understanding of diverse groups.

Exercise 3–1   Cultural-Sensitivity Exercise

1. What is your cultural background?
2. Do you identify with a particular ethnic group?
3. Select an ethnic group you come the closest to identifying with, and describe the group's customary behaviors regarding each of the following:

    a. Role of father, mother, children, extended family members
    b. Dating patterns
    c. Eating patterns
    d. Education
    e. Death and dying

4. How do you feel about your ethnic identity? What are the strengths and weaknesses you perceive in your ethnic group?
5. What ethnic groups lived in your home environment when you were growing up? How did your family relate to families of other ethnic groups (consider attitudes, experiences, power relationships; i.e., was one dependent on, or subordinate to, another)?
6. What are your earliest memories of meeting people of minority groups (i.e., African-American, American Indian, Asian-Pacific American, Hispanic)? How did your family relate to people of minority groups? (Consider attitudes, power relationships, experiences.)
7. Are your feelings about your own ethnic group related to any power relationship you experienced with other ethnic groups?
8. Are your feelings about *other* ethnic groups related to any power relationships you experienced with other ethnic groups?
9. With someone from a different ethnic background, compare your ethnic groups according to the factors given in item 3.

10. How do your feelings for your ethnic group compare with this person's feelings for his or her ethnic group?

In the following chapters, a sensitivity to cultural diversity in each of the six stages of the General Method will be more specifically demonstrated. The integration of content on culture and other human diversities within each of the chapters is deliberate, intended to highlight the importance of maintaining this sensitivity throughout any use of the Method.

What is being emphasized at this point is that culture represents a crucial aspect of a person's identity and has a vital impact on that person's social functioning and interactions with human services. Social class, family, and individual differences are also major influences on the whole person. Adding to a sensitivity to cultural diversity, social workers need to be aware of social class, sexual variation (homosexuality–heterosexuality), gender (male–female), age and stage of development, geographic location (rural, urban, or suburban), and other related variables.

Social Class

As stated, in addition to understanding a system's culture, a worker should be aware of the social class of a system. *Social class* is identified through such variables as income, occupation, education, residence, group identification, and, possibly, religious affiliation. When class and ethnicity are seen together, the worker arrives at a clearer picture of a system.

Gordon defines the point where class and ethnicity intersect as "ethclass." He refers to the "ethnic reality" as the dispositions and behaviors that flow from ethclass.[8] Through understanding a system's ethnic reality, a worker may begin to sense more clearly the problems, needs, issues, conflicts, and expectations a system faces. As ethnicity and class interlock, a system may experience pressures that arise from the incongruence between the two.

For example, although a family may have moved into a higher social class (blue-collar to white-collar occupation, private schools, wealthier neighborhood), family members may not be given full participation in the politics and activities of their new environment because of their ethnicity. In terms of consumption, the class level of the family is high, but in terms of power and participation, the same family is a stratified ethnic minority in its environment. This is frequently the case for members of "new ethnics," as described by Blackwell:

> Social class is only one of the two major systems of stratification in the United States. A second and equally powerful system is ethnic stratification. This system by and large expresses where a particular group falls on a social distance scale, that is, how closely it approximates conventional norms and standards of social acceptability of the white Anglo-Saxon society in the United States. In every social distance scale ethnic groups,

particularly the so-called new ethnics—blacks, Chicanos, Puerto Ricans, and Orientals to a lesser degree—are relegated to the bottom position.[9]

People of the new ethnics are often identified as "bicultural" because they live in the two worlds of (1) their ethnic culture and (2) wider society. Moreover, a class system (i.e., upper, middle, lower) is also generally found within each cultural group.[10] The ethnic reality for a minority person, therefore, actually includes the interface of his or her biculture with that of his or her social class according to society at large and according to his or her culture's class system.

Sexual Variations

To work with gay or lesbian clients, social workers need to convey an attitude of acceptance of the human person and a basic understanding of sexual variations among human beings. Building on knowledge and values, a worker applies the General Method with skill and sensitivity in response to the problems or needs identified by gay or lesbian persons.

A homosexual person has been defined as "one who is motivated in adult life by a definite preferential erotic attraction to members of the same sex and who usually (but not necessarily) engages in overt sexual relations with them.[11] McNaught describes two primary types of homosexuals: (1) "transitional"—an individual who is basically heterosexual but engages in homosexual behavior when no one of the opposite sex is available (as in prisons or military service), and (2) "constitutional"—an individual whose sexual orientation toward the same sex is set around the ages of three to five years.[12] Kinsey and his associates formulated a classification system that is a seven-point continuum indicating the extent of overt and covert homosexual experience (see Table 3–1).[13]

The scale ranges from exclusive heterosexuality (0) to exclusive homosexuality (6). On the basis of this scale, the term *homosexual* has been used to refer to those individuals who are at levels 5 and 6, and *bisexual* or *ambisexual* for those who are

TABLE 3-1. Sexual Orientation Scale

0	1	2	3	4	5	6
Exclusively hetero-sexual	Predomi-nantly hetero-sexual	Predomi-nantly hetero-sexual, but more than inci-dentally homo-sexual	Equally hetero-sexual and homo-sexual	Predomi-nantly homo-sexual, but more than inci-dentally hetero-sexual	Predomi-nantly homo-sexual	Exclusively homo-sexual

at levels 2, 3, or 4.[14] Today, an extensive list of "homosexualities" has been identi-fied that extends from a brief encounter in a public bath to an exclusive lifelong relationship between two people of the same sex.

Basically, *homosexuality* is a general term used to describe men or women. As many homosexual men prefer to be referred to as *gay* rather than homosexual, many women prefer the term *lesbian*. To be gay or lesbian involves psychological and sociological experiences as well as sexual attractions or behaviors. The indi-vidual can be better understood if seen in relation to his or her environment and in relation to those who live within that environment. A term frequently used to describe the negative reactions of heterosexual people toward gay men and les-bians is *homophobia*. As defined by Dulaney and Kelly, "Homophobia refers to an emotional reaction of deep-rooted fear and accompanying hatred of homosexual life-styles and individuals."[15] A prevalence of homophobia has been found to exist in this country among helping professionals, particularly social workers.[16] Histor-ically, homosexuality was described in the helping professions as a disturbance or an illness. Today, it is referred to as a sexual orientation or variation.

Numerous studies have been conducted in an attempt to identify physical or environmental factors that are causally related to homosexuality. To date, the eti-ology of homosexuality has not been clearly determined. Although it has been concluded that gender identity, which leads to erotic arousal patterns, is funda-mentally a prepuberty, neurocognitive function, the principles or determinants whereby one's identity is established have not been elucidated.[17]

Studies have been written about the "cure" of homosexuality. The samples for these studies were limited to individuals who sought help because they wanted to become heterosexual. After extensive "treatment," their therapists reported "some increase in heterosexual competence" (rather than a "cure") for only approxi-mately one-fifth of those who sought help.[18] Through additional research, it has been found that the majority of gay men and lesbians do not wish to become het-erosexual.[19] They often seek and receive help from professionals, however, to restore or maintain their self-esteem or to be able to cope with the rejections they experience from family, workplace, and society at large. As brought out by Blair, "Those homosexuals who can withstand the destructive forces of an anti-homo-sexual society emerge usually strong and self-sufficient."[20]

Problems and Needs Related to Sexual Variations

The problems or needs brought to the attention of social workers by gay or lesbian clients are not necessarily related to sexual variations in lifestyle. There are, how-ever, a number of tensions, needs, and problems an individual may experience as a result of being gay or lesbian. A knowledgeable and sensitive worker may assist the individual in these problematic areas.

For example, as a person (at any age) begins to recognize an attraction to members of the same sex or to explore the possibility that he or she may be homo-sexual, he or she may experience strong feelings of fear, confusion, or guilt. For many, there is no one to turn to for an open, honest discussion about their questions and concerns. Some, particularly adolescents, find the internal conflict so overwhelming that they turn to drugs or suicide.[21] Social workers can be very helpful as individuals struggle over questions about their sexual identity or decisions to choose or not to choose a gay or lesbian lifestyle, or to "come out" and make their sexual orientation known publicly. Help may be needed in planning when and how they will share their decisions with significant persons in their lives. If a worker is not able to listen to or to support a person who chooses a homosexual lifestyle, it would be better to make a referral to someone who can, rather than to continue to work with the individual. As brought out by McNaught, "coming out" can be extremely traumatic for a person unless there has been careful planning, with supports available. He writes, "Don't jump into the pool unless there is a support system of some sort waiting for you."[22] What is at stake may include the loss of a job, marriage, or self-esteem. Particularly for lesbians, "coming out" may even result in the loss of their children. Repeatedly, in divorce and custody cases, mothers who were known to be lesbians have been pressured to choose between their lovers and their children. There are organizations now available, such as Custody Action for Lesbian Mothers (CALM), to help women in, or under the threat of, such litigation.[23]

Gay or lesbian persons may seek help from social workers because of problems with interpersonal relationships. The relationship patterns of homosexual life styles have been described as "committed," "independent," or "ambisexual."[24] *Committed* refers to long-term and same-sex relationships. *Independent relationships* are limited to close friendships and brief homosexual affairs. The *ambisexual* lifestyle is one in which individuals have relationships with both sexes for long or brief time periods. Individuals or couples may seek help to decide about maintaining or terminating a relationship or lifestyle. If two gay or lesbian persons decide to make a lifelong commitment to each other, they may ask a social worker to help them find a way to legalize their relationship. The couple may not know about relationship contracts or joint wills. Problems and needs may develop after one of the two dies. The remaining partner may need someone to help him or her to grieve over the loss of the other. Biological family members may have legal access to the remaining assets of the deceased. Even if there has been a joint will, the family may contest it.

As lesbian or gay individuals get older, a number of problems may emerge. These have been classified as institutional, legal, emotional, and medical.[25] Institutional problems may include housing or nursing-home practices that do not permit two nonrelated members to dwell together. If one partner is in a home or hospital, the other may not be allowed to visit or to make medical decisions for the institutionalized person because there is no legal or blood relationship. Legal problems may include restrictive laws regarding property or wills, as cited, or the absence of laws to prevent discriminatory practices by judges, police, or insurance companies. The emotional problems of elderly lesbians and gays may include feelings of rejection by the gay or lesbian community or feelings of abandonment or loss after the death of a partner. In addition, elderly gays who were concerned about concealing their sexual orientation have been found to feel more guilty and fearful of aging and death.[26] The medical problems of homosexuals at any age may include sexually transmitted diseases (pharyngeal or anal gonorrhea, for example; or recently, AIDS, acquired immune deficiency syndrome). Special procedures are needed to diagnose and treat such conditions.

In addition to the help offered directly by a social worker, lesbian or gay persons may need support and services from a variety of professionals and other systems. As they interact with people in diverse settings, they need to be understood and accepted as unique individuals. Social workers can assist by being aware of available, appropriate resources for gay and lesbian clients. The resources needed may include knowledgeable and accepting physicians, lawyers, clergy, and insurance companies. Gay men and lesbians are also enabled to deal with their tensions and problems through active participation in self-help groups, supportive networks, and related political action movements. Social workers may also help gay men or lesbians to locate these resources in their communities and may encourage them to become involved with these services. Sometimes social workers provide services for members of families of gay or lesbian individuals. For example, groups led by social workers for wives of gay and bisexual men may help these women to deal with such feelings and issues as anger, betrayal, homophobia, sexuality, care of children, and support.[27]

Self-Assessment of Homophobia

There is a growing recognition of the need for human service workers to overcome their stereotypical views and attitudes toward gay or lesbian people.[28] The following questions constitute a brief exercise for self-reflection and discussion regarding homophobia. A fear of or antagonism toward homosexuality may be detected as one answers the questions or engages in dialogues about their content.

Exercise 3–2

1. If you learned that a person were gay or lesbian, would it influence your decision about sitting next to him or her?
2. Have you worked with gay or lesbian clients?
3. Do you think gay or lesbian individuals could benefit from being placed in a mixed group (heterosexuals and homosexuals)?
4. Would you protest if an antihomosexual joke were told?
5. Do you think gay or lesbian individuals have had disturbed relationships with one or both parents?

6. Do you have social contacts with gay or lesbian persons?
7. Would you ever discourage gay or lesbian clients from disclosing their sexual orientation to their family, friends, or co-workers? Why?
8. Do you think of homosexuality as a sickness or a natural variant in human sexuality?
9. What would be your response if you learned that your sibling or child was gay or lesbian?
10. Do gay or lesbian persons have a right to be ministers, schoolteachers, social workers, or legislators?

Sensitivity to Gender: Working with Women

In addition to diversity in culture, social class, and sexual orientation, a social worker is sensitive to diversity in gender when applying the General Method. More specifically, a worker is expected to communicate with women and with men in a manner that reflects an understanding of and a responsiveness to their distinctive problems and experiences.

The predominant patriarchal ideology found in American society and in other cultures fosters institutional sexism through which women experience inequality and victimization. *Sexism* means the subjugation of one sex to another. When the term is used today, it basically refers to women being subordinate to men and to the existing attitudes, policies, and practices that demonstrate this discrimination. The unequal treatment of women and the acceptance of male dominance in society are due to differences in gender roles rather than to physiological differences between the sexes. The definitions of masculinity and femininity identified by society dictate the expected behavioral patterns for men and women. These behavioral patterns prescribed by society are called *gender roles*.[29] If social workers are to be helpful to women, it is important that they understand the nature and scope of the female gender role as it has evolved within a sexist society.

The socialization, sex-typed life experiences, and role expectations of women differ from those of men. The traditional gender role imposed on woman as a dependent, long-suffering, conforming, emotionally nurturing, and sweet female has not been a satisfying and health-promoting role for many. Women have often felt constricted and ineffective in this role. They have experienced tensions and conflict that are due to a lack of privilege and power. Some women have internalized society's image of themselves and have accepted a self-concept in which they are helpless, inadequate, and submissive. These women often need help to reject their negative self-attributes and to become resocialized as competent and whole persons.

Problems, such as rape, incest, battering, and harassment, have been concealed and even condoned in society. Women have been found to avoid experiencing success in order to prevent the negative consequences they expected as a result of their accomplishments.[30] In addition, the majority of the poor in America are women.[31] There is evidence that employment and promotion opportunities for women are not comparable to those for men. Women earn $6 for every $10 earned by men.[32] Also, women do not have equal opportunity in the decision-making structures of the job market.[33]

In addition to these problems, some women suffer personally from drinking, drugs, and depression. Although various psychological, physical, economic, and social factors may have an impact on their lives, women with these problems have often expressed strong sentiments of failure as women or helpless feelings of being trapped in a situation where there is no way out.[34] Generally, a relationship can be found between the personal and social problems of women and the negative societal beliefs and practices against women that exist in their culture and environments.

In the past, service providers worked to help women to adjust to their "feminine" role. Today, however, there is an increasing recognition of the need for workers to help women become consciously aware of how they have been socialized and to find ways for them to grow in self-actualization. Social workers need to realize that difficulties which in the past may have been identified as individual, personal problems of women are actually a social problem, with a social cause and possibly a political solution. As a woman discusses her problems with a social worker, she may be surprised and supported in learning that other women have similar experiences and that, collectively, they are victims of sexism in society. Through joining together, women have begun to develop a sense of empowerment and to expose the destructive forces they experience. Organized movements, such as the Suffrage Movement, the Women's Trade Union, the National Consumer's League, and the National Organization for Women have greatly contributed to improving the status of women in American society. Social workers can help women to develop skill in assertiveness, self-confidence, self-reliance, expression of anger, confrontation, organization, and leadership. A sense of independence can be enhanced if the worker assumes more the role of a facilitator than an expert. In the General Method, a collaborative approach is used in which a worker and a client system engage in a shared problem-solving process. This method aptly lends itself to working with women in a sensitive, responsive manner.

Working with Men: A Call for Androgyny

According to Larry Alsbrook, "The man in our society has been seduced into the oppressor role as surely as woman has inherited the oppressed role."[35] Whether or not men are responsible for the development and maintenance of sexism in society can be debated endlessly. It is more important for women and for men to become involved in searching out the positives and the potential for both as they go through the process of redefining gender roles. These issues are currently affecting the basic foundation and institutions of American society. Men may struggle with accepting changes in the feminine gender role because such acceptance necessitates their letting go of power and privilege. Nevertheless, there are possible advantages for men if the results of women's liberation include a change in the demands and expectations for men in a sexist society.

In essence, men may be seen also as victims of sexism. Having to assume the strong, dominant, breadwinning, protector role has had negative and sometimes fatal effects on men. They have been expected to perform with total success at work and at home. Primarily, a man's occupation has been seen as his status determinant as well as his basic identity. As a result, men have frequently developed into workaholics for whom failure in business is perceived as failure in personhood.[36]

The drive to succeed has even influenced men's suicidal actions. The instruments used by men to commit suicide are more certain to complete the task successfully than those used by women. Over 70 percent of all completed suicides are committed by men.[37]

Being a "strong" male has restricted men from expressing or even having emotions. Supportive relationships have been generally limited to a man's wife, with very few sustained peer friendships. Even emotional displays with children have been considered out of character for a man. The stress and tensions felt by men and left unexpressed have resulted in stress-related illnesses and an earlier death rate for men than for women. Such problems, directly related to the masculine gender role, can now begin to be identified and, possibly, resolved if men join in the movement to overcome existing sexism in society. As pointed out by Herb Goldberg:

> The social revolutions of recent years can lessen the male's time-honored burdens, help him reclaim denied emotion, expand his sensual responsiveness, bring new dimensions of honesty and depth to his heterosexual relationships, as well as alert him to the self-destructive compulsions within him.[38]

Rather than respond openly and hopefully to women's liberation, some men are feeling extremely threatened by the changes they witness in their wives, daughters, friends, and associates. They experience shock, hurt, and fear as women change, compete, and achieve in the workplace, the political field, and the family. Instead of fighting the movement, men often react by withdrawal, particularly from encounters with women.[39] Although it may be difficult for a man to seek help with his feelings, a sensitive social worker can help him to understand and to express what he is experiencing. With support, men may begin to see some value in letting go of social norms and moving into a more equal, adult level of sharing with women.

Contemporary social changes have resulted in a variety of significant problems for men. These may include problems in such areas as custody battles, male single-parenting, or fathering after divorce when children remain with their mothers or when parents have joint custody. Social workers are able to help men with these problems through such efforts as establishing support groups for single fathers.[40]

Although sexism has a direct effect on men and women in American society, the problems of racism and poverty overshadow and compound the situation for minority men and women. Nonwhite males have a shorter life expectancy than all females and all other males.[41] Black males, in particular, have the highest risk-status. They constitute the largest group among the prison population. Black males have the highest rate of being victimized by crime and robbery, of experiencing job injuries, of being in low-status service jobs, and of being unmarried. Black prisoners have stated their desire to be able to care for and to protect their women and children as others do.[42] The lack of opportunities in society has frequently led them to try to improve their economic status by participating in illegal activities. Social workers can demonstrate sensitivity to the high risk-status of black men through such efforts as promoting community groups to serve as support networks for black males and through advocating social policies that are responsive to their employment and economic needs. Unless efforts to overcome racism and poverty are sustained and achieved, success in gender egalitarianism will be of little significance for poor, minority men and women.

It is possible that the changes taking place in gender roles may result in new, ongoing problems for men and women in general. Women may go to such an extreme in their efforts to prove their equality with men that they may become engrossed in competition and political power struggles. They, too, may develop stress-related illnesses and a lower life expectancy pattern as they suppress feelings and stress achievement. With men changing their masculine role, one development may be a shift to their demonstrating strength through interpersonal and intellectual skills.[43] This may prove to be equally stressful for men as they strive for success and mastery in these skill areas.

Instead of evolving into new problems, the movement for change in gender roles can be a reciprocal process that produces growth and gains for both sexes. Social workers may contribute to making this a reality by helping men and women to clarify who they are, why they are the way they are, and where they are in the process of becoming. The changes and conflicts men and women experience may be better understood through an awareness of the theory of androgyny.[44] According to this theory, every person has actually or potentially both masculine and feminine characteristics. Each individual is both male and female to some degree. To be a whole person, one needs to recognize and to express both dimensions of personhood. Although someone may initially appear to be "totally masculine" or "totally feminine," he or she will naturally move in time to a stage where there is a felt need to develop and to actualize the other side of his or her personhood. To be fully human, therefore, every person is called to be a psychologically androgynous person.

> The psychologically androgynous person is one who freely engages in both "masculine" and "feminine" behaviors, is both instrumental (task oriented) and expressive (socioemotional) and is both assertive and yielding, when the occasion calls for such behavior.[45]

As men and women strive for wholeness, a beneficial goal to work for is the separation of role and status from gender. Emphasis needs to be placed on individuality, with an acceptance of flexible roles as appropriate to each situation. Social workers can help a man or a woman to develop a definition of self and role that is individualized and sensitive to the person's needs and growth. As Frederick Duhl notes, "There is no one way to be a woman or a man in our society except to develop as an individual."[46] The General Method of social work practice is based on the practice principle of *individuality*. In applying the Method, a worker keeps in mind the unique needs and circumstances of each individual. Ways in which a generalist shows a responsiveness and sensitivity to gender diversity will be explored throughout the presentation of the six stages of the General Method in the following chapters.

Self-Assessment of Gender Sensitivity

As with other types of human diversity, social workers need to be aware of their own personal attitudes and possible stereotypical ideas regarding gender roles. A simple exercise that may assist a student or worker to grow in self-awareness in this area is found in Exercise 3–3. Each individual should ask him- or herself, privately at first, the questions found in the exercise. An open discussion with one or a group of peers may follow.

Exercise 3–3   Gender-Sensitivity Questions

1. What would be your immediate reaction when hearing about a 40-year-old woman marrying a 20-year-old man?
2. How do you feel about having a woman in charge of

   a. Your bank (president)
   b. Your place of employment
   c. The military
   d. Your church
   e. The executive branch of the government (president of the United States)

3. Who did the cooking, cleaning, and shopping in your house when you were growing up?
4. Who does the cooking, cleaning, and shopping in your present home?
5. Who do you think should be responsible for household tasks?
6. What do you think of a man who walks out of a door before a woman who is also trying to leave?
7. Do you ever use the expressions

   a. Woman driver
   b. Henpecked husband

  c. Female gossip
  d. Man-sized job
  e. Catty women
  f. The girls

Other Diversity Variables: The Person

A social worker who is sensitive to human diversity has an awareness of several diversity variables. In addition to culture, class, sexual orientation, and gender, there are related diversity variables that may be conceptualized in terms of *person* and *environment.* To be sensitive to the person, for example, one should consider the age of the person and the developmental stage or stages the individual is going through at the time. When the system of contact is more than one person, the worker needs to be aware of the age and stage of that system-family, group, or community.

A sensitivity to age and stage can help a worker to find the most appropriate way to communicate with the system and to understand the problems and challenges the system may be facing. There are identifiable communication mediums that are found to be more effective than others when working with particular age groups. For example, small children (approximately up to age 3) have been helped through directly involving the child's parents or significant others in providing the service. The worker directs the parent figure, who works directly with the child. Children from approximately age 4 through 11 often find it difficult, if not impossible, to carry on a verbal conversation with an adult. They are used to having adults teach, direct, or parent them. Social workers are usually more effective with children at this age if they communicate through the use of play (see Chapter 7). Adolescents (ages 12–17) are often uncomfortable also with lengthy conversations with adults. An advanced type of play, such as sports, chess, or other game activities, may help to reduce their apprehensions. Using peer groups is also an effective way to reach adolescents. Hearing from peers rather than adults is generally more acceptable for adolescents. The adult, on the other hand, functions in a verbal world. Here too, however, the worker needs to be sure that the language and vocabulary used are appropriate for the particular adults receiving service. Those who may be considered "elderly" (over 65) often feel more secure when the social worker comes to them in their own homes; yet here too, depending on need and attitude toward workers who are usually younger, those who are older may be helped through meeting with elderly colleagues with whom they share common concerns and experiences.

Human systems are in process. They naturally go through various stages in their evolution. The human system is a complex whole with diverse functions that may progress independently of each other. The knowledge base of a social worker includes theories about the developmental processes that take place physically, socially, sexually, cognitively, spiritually, and morally in a person. Although an individual may be at one age chronologically, he or she may not be at a matching stage developmentally in one or all functioning dimensions. For example, a 12-year-old youngster may be operating at a 3-year-old level cognitively. Or, a person who is 30 years old may be functioning socially at a younger, dependent level.

Using knowledge of human development, the worker considers, from the multi-dimensional perspective of *person* (i.e., physical, social, sexual, cognitive, moral, and spiritual), the stage at which a person is functioning. In Table 3–2, conceptualizations for considering stages of development according to complementary theories are outlined and juxtaposed. When a lag is observed in any dimension of development, the worker may have a beginning idea of the needs, problems, and tasks confronting the person at that time. A worker should keep in mind the fact that each person's development is unique and that a number of interrelated and interacting factors contribute to, and direct, one's development. These factors include endowment (to be explained later), culture, and gender.

Before moving into a consideration of additional diversity variables of *person*, the point should be made here that human systems containing more than one person (e.g., group, family, or community) also go through a developmental process. In general, there are the following six basic stages to the process: (1) testing/tuning in, (2) role clarifying, (3) working, (4) reformulating, (5) accomplishing, and (6) terminating. In the beginning stage, members usually observe and conform. As there is movement for role clarification, power struggles may become apparent. With the acceptance of positioning, purpose, rules, and guidelines, the system moves into a work stage. As tasks and goals begin to be accomplished, members of the system grow in confidence, and they may venture out into new behaviors and goals. Reformulating roles and responsibilities may cause tensions and conflicts among members. If communication is open and members are able to change, a more mature, equal, or democratic type of functioning may be reached, with a high level of system accomplishment. Eventually, individual members of the system may break away, or the system may terminate as a whole. Members often join with other outside individuals or systems to form new functioning units. Just as a worker recognizes diversity in stage development of persons, it is necessary to be able to identify the different growth levels of groups, families, and communities. This knowledge and sensitivity helps a worker in problem assessment, progress evaluation, and ongoing facilitation of growth and development within the systems.

Endowment and *personality* are additional diversity variables of *person*. The endowment of a person is a major contributor to his or her development of personality. Endowment refers to the natural gifts, talents, and abilities that a person has at birth. Genetic traits and characteristics, along with the innate mental, physical, and cognitive abilities of a person, are included. Personality development takes place in human beings as they use endowment and interact with others in their environment. Basically, personality is influenced by (1) the endowment of a person, (2) the inherent qualities and opportunities found within a person's environment, and (3) the transactions that take place between person and environment. The personality of a human being consists of the combination and integration of characteristics and experiences that give a person his or her

TABLE 3-2. A Multidimensional Perspective of Human Development

AGE	PHYSICAL	PSYCHOSEXUAL	PSYCHOSOCIAL	COGNITIVE	MORAL	SPIRITUAL
0–3	Marked growth; teething (6–8 months); crawling (9–12 months); self-feeding; walking (1–); bowel and bladder control (2–)	Oral stage (0–1) Anal stage (1–3)	Trust versus mistrust (0–1) Autonomy versus shame and doubt (1–3)	Sensorimotor stage (0–18 months) Object permanence (18 months)	Preconventional level Stage I: Punishment and obedience	Sensing oneness, being cared for
3–6	First permanent teeth; stronger voice; receptive; alert brain; manual and motor power	Phallic (Oedipal stage)	Initiative versus guilt	Preconceptual stage (2–4)	Stage II: Naive instrumental hedonism—conformity for reward	Beginning sense of separateness, self-will
6–12	Increased muscular ability and coordination; girls' growth rate exceeds boys'	Latency stage	Industry versus inferiority	Intuitive stage (4–7) Concrete-operational stage (7–11)	Conventional level Stage III: "Good boy/good girl" conformity to avoid disapproval Stage IV: Authority, maintaining law and order	Experiencing God's attributes through parents and environment; beginning to hear and use religious words Social responses: formal religious education ritual; loyalty to faith of parents; anthropomorphic religious concepts

TABLE 3-2. *Continued*

AGE	PHYSICAL	PSYCHOSEXUAL	PSYCHOSOCIAL	COGNITIVE	MORAL	SPIRITUAL
13–18	Girls— development of breasts, pubic hair, complexion changes, onset of menstruation Boys— development of pubic hair, sperm, voice changes, complexion changes	Adolescence (genital stage)	Identity versus identity diffusion	Formal-operational stage (11–15)	Post conventional level Stage V: Morality of contract; standards of society; individual rights	Religious questioning; religious awakening; varying sense of faith; rebelliousness
18–35	Leveling off of growth	Maturity—to love and to work	Intimacy versus isolation		Stage VI: Morality of individual principles of conscience; universal ethical principles	Crisis/conversion experience Affiliation with (or withdrawal from) organized religious sect
35–65	Change in weight distribution, metabolism and sensory abilities slow down; menopause—women		Generativity versus stagnation or self-absorption			Search for and deepening of personal religious experience, active church participation

TABLE 3-2. *Continued*

AGE	PHYSICAL	PSYCHOSEXUAL	PSYCHOSOCIAL	COGNITIVE	MORAL	SPIRITUAL
65–	Marked decrease in motor coordination; taste buds decline; organs begin to dysfunction		Ego integrity versus despair			Deepening of personal religion; finding religion to give meaning and support for death

*The primary theorists who have conceptualized the processes and stages identified above are: physical—Theodore Litz; psychosexual—Sigmund Freud; psychosocial—Erik Erikson; cognitive—Jean Piaget; moral—Lawrence Kohlberg; spiritual—Gordon Allport and Maria Joan O'Neil. Specific references for each would be too numerous to print here.

unique personhood. Social workers realize that a person's behavior and problems may relate to individual endowment and personality as well as to culture, class, gender, sexual orientation, age, and developmental stages.

Other diversity variables that may be found in *person* and *environment* are religion and values. *Religion* may refer to organized institutions or to an individual's or group's system of beliefs or practices. Although little is found in social work literature regarding the possible impact of religion on practice, there is increasing interest in the topic. Lowenberg, for example, identifies an "urgent need for empirical research to strengthen the social work knowledge base" in the area of religion and social work practice. He writes,

> Practitioners, both those who believe as well as those who do not, must learn to understand religion and its impact on human behavior. Such understanding is a prerequisite for effective practice.[47]

A value system is the collection of beliefs and preferences that are esteemed by a system. People, individually or collectively, have different value systems. As stated earlier, the values of a human being are primarily determined by the culture of the person's nurturing system. In addition, the beliefs, attitudes, and values of a person are also influenced by the value systems that prevail in the larger societal environment.

Self-Assessment of Value Orientation

Social workers and social welfare systems, as well as clients and other work-related systems, may have contrasting values. On this point, Alan Keith Lucas identified three major types of value systems found in American society. They are (1) capitalist-puritan (CP), (2) humanist-positivist-utopian (HPU), and (3) Judeo-Christian (JC).[48] Basic assumptions for each of these three value systems are given in Exercise 3–4. Capitalistic-puritan value assumptions are described in items 1, 2, 7, 8, and 13 of the exercise. Humanist-positivist-utopian assumptions are given in numbers, 3, 4, 9, 10, and 14. And assumptions of the Judeo-Christian system are indicated in items 5, 6, 11, 12, and 15. The instrument (Exercise 3–4) may be used by students, workers, or teachers for self-assessment of underlying value orientations. After the degree of agreement has been entered for all assumptions, the number entered (0–5) for each item is placed below the questionnaire, in one of three lines labeled CP, HPU, and JC. Each line should have five scores, one for each of the items relating to that line's value system (e.g., items 1, 2, 7, 8, 13 for the CP line). The scores in each line are then added, and the line totals are compared. Usually, a person is not totally identified with any one value perspective. The exercise does highlight predominance. It helps workers and students to grow both in awareness of their own values and in sensitivity to the diversity in value systems that often conflict in human welfare services. It is interesting to note that in tracing the history of social work, the profession is rooted predominantly in the Judeo-Christian value system.

Exercise 3-4. Value System Index

ASSUMPTIONS	Totally Disagree 0	1	2	3	4	Totally Agree 5
1. Human beings are responsible for their own success or failure.						
2. Human nature is basically evil, but it can be overcome by an act of will.						
3. The primary purpose of society is to fulfill human needs, both material and emotional.						
4. If human needs were fulfilled, then we would attain goodness, maturity, adjustment, and productivity, and most of society's problems would be solved.						
5. Human beings are fallible but at the same time are capable of acts of great courage or unselfishness.						
6. People are capable of choice, in the "active and willing" sense, but may need help in making their choices.						
7. The primary purpose of life is the acquisition of material prosperity, which people achieve through hard work.						
8. The primary purpose of society is the maintenance of law and order, which make this acquisition possible.						
9. What hampers people from attaining fulfillment is external circumstance, not in general under their control.						
10. These circumstances are subject to manipulation by those possessed of sufficient technical and scientific knowledge, using the scientific method.						
11. Love is always the ultimate victor over force.						
12. The greatest good lies in terms of people's relationships with their fellows and with their creator.						
13. Unsuccessful or deviant individuals are not deserving of help, although efforts should be made up to a point to rehabilitate them or to spur them to greater efforts on their own behalf.						
14. Humanity and society are ultimately perfectible.						
15. Human beings are created beings; one of their major problems is that they act as if they were not and try to be autonomous.						
CP 1, 2, 7, 8, 13						
HPU 3, 4, 9, 10, 14						
JC 5, 6, 11, 12, 15						

The Environment: Rural, Urban, and Suburban

In addition to variables of *person,* a social worker needs to be sensitive to diversity in the *environments* of systems receiving service. Geographic environments differ. A knowledge of distinguishing characteristics of environments helps workers to understand better the people of particular localities and the interactions that take place between different people and different environments.

From a holistic perspective, a social worker explores diversity variables individually and in relation to one another. When studying a person or an environment, a worker is mindful of the ongoing interrelationship between the two. As brought out in ecological theory, an environment is affected by the organisms (persons) contained within it. Conversely, organisms are affected by their environments. More specifically, an environment's growth is directly influenced by the endowment, personalities, values, and functioning of its residents. Interdependently, the growth and development of people are directly influenced by the nature, resources, values, and functioning of their environments. An understanding of rural, urban, and suburban localities can help a worker to be aware of diverse ways in which environments and people may affect each other. If an individual, group, family, or community live in a rural environment, their needs, experiences, values, resources, and development may be very different from those of people who live in urban or suburban areas.

Historically, the term *rural* has been used to refer to "the country" or to mean "countrylike." Rural localities are often defined in terms of low population density (2,500–50,000 inhabitants) and relative isolation. *Urban* is a term that pertains to "the city" or things that are "citylike." It is generally used to describe a highly populated area (over 50,000). Other factors that have been used to distinguish rural from urban areas include income sources and occupations (agriculture versus industry), lifestyle (simple versus complex), and structure and number of available human resources (highly structured and numerous versus informal and sparse).[49] In 1993, 75.2 percent of the American population lived in urban areas, as compared with 24.8 percent who lived in rural areas.[50]

The outlying regions of cities that often bridge urban and rural areas are called suburbs. Legally and demographically, a *suburb* is defined as an incorporated municipality within a Standard Metropolitan Statistical Area (SMSA) other than a central city.[51] Although apparent changes are taking place in suburbia today, the definition traditionally has included a stereotypical conception of "familism, child-centeredness, single-family dwelling units, sharp segregation of workplace from residence, organizational consciousness . . . overlaid by a distinct touch of affluence."[52]

Within each of the three geographic environments, diversity may exist among populations and practices today. There are, however, general characteristics that make urban, suburban, and rural localities distinguishable from one another. Urban locations, for example, generally offer various organized human services that are highly structured, with clearly stated policies and procedures. Rural areas may be devoid of formal, professional services, but there are usually informal, natural helping networks that provide assistance. Whereas the power structure of an urban area may be described as "pluralistic," with several complex, interacting systems, the power structure of a rural area may be seen as "elitist," with decision makers who may not even hold formal positions of authority (see Figure 3–1).[53] There is a boundary "blurring"[54] of political and sociocultural life in homogeneous rural communities. The laws and procedures of an urban legal control system are more explicitly articulated and executed than those of a rural area; in the latter, informal means of regulation are frequently preferred for resolving local problems.[55]

The central and distinguishing problems of rural areas include generational poverty, rigid conservative mores and thinking, and an increasing loss of youth from the area. In addition, 60 percent of the nation's substandard housing is located in rural communities.[56] A core problem for those who live in the city has been described in terms of depersonalization or loss of individuality. As Carol Meyer writes,

> The fact of urban life that characterizes it and no other living condition is the inevitable claim of the crowded, organized, institutionalized city against the freedom and fulfillment of the individual.[57]

In recent years, urban development has led to the renovation of many old buildings in cities. These structures have been changed into upper- or upper-middle-class condominiums or apartments. As a result, the poor and lower-middle-class city residents are often unable to find local housing. The absence of low income housing in urban and suburban areas and the resistance by suburban residents to building such housing, along with the presence of restrictive zoning laws, have contributed to the contemporary housing crisis, particularly for the urban poor. Even when low-income people are relocated in a surrounding area, they often have problems locating transportation to and from their place of employment and needed human services.

Elitism

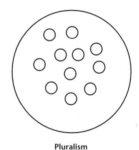

Pluralism

FIGURE 3-1. Power Structures

People from urban and suburban areas discuss their problems and seek out professional help more readily than those from rural localities.[58] When informal networks are not able to provide the assistance needed, and social workers are not accepted by certain individuals in rural communities, a worker may try to work collaboratively with local leaders or neighbors in order to connect the person in need with a needed resource.

For example, if a family is suffering because of such problems as mental illness or alcoholism, and it refuses to discuss its problems with a professional social worker, then the local clergy, doctor, or friend may be willing to speak with the family in behalf of the worker. In rural settings, people are very aware of their neighbors' problems, and are generally more willing to get involved and provide assistance.

In urban or suburban areas, a somewhat similar but more formal approach is used when indigenous leaders or "paraprofessionals" are hired to serve as "outreach workers" to link services with people in need. As brought out, the generalist in the metropolis is usually better able to locate specialized services to help with problems such as those described in the above example (i.e., mental illness or alcoholism). In a rural area, however, the worker may be the only professional resource available. It may be possible to work directly with the family, or it may be necessary to develop a program or write a grant to bring the needed service into the area. During the 1980s, severe economic losses in rural areas, particularly in farm communities, led to a decrease in informal social interactions and an increase in family breakdown.[59] Major withdrawals of federal financial supports, soaring interest rates, declining prices, and rising surpluses have led to an increasing number of farm foreclosures and bankruptcies. Rural land values have declined up to 50 percent and more.[60]

The economic crisis of farmers has been little understood; it has resulted in a high incidence of depression, family violence, and suicide. As stated by one farmer, "The loss of the land is not just the loss of one's job, it's the loss of one's life."[61] This feeling exists especially when the land has belonged to a family for several generations. The farmer who experiences property foreclosure by a bank usually sees this as a personal loss and a family disgrace.

Existing services in rural areas, such as Agricultural Extension or Farm Bureaus, are often unable to cope effectively with the financial, social, and emotional crises facing poverty-stricken rural communities. Human service professionals, social service programs, and schools of social work have made some efforts to join with such services in reaching out to farmers in crisis. They have helped farmers organize groups to advocate fairer policies and prices, and they have helped them to locate other sources of income.[62] Although migrant workers or farm laborers and farm owners have frequently been adversaries in the past, the threat of losing the land has provided an opportunity to bring the two groups together to work for the common goal of keeping the farm operating.

Whereas specialists are utilized in urban localities, generalists have been recognized as the most appropriate practitioners for rural communities.[63] In applying the General Method when working in a rural area, a worker would find it helpful to have knowledge of rural economics (agriculture, mining, industry), regional planning and development, labor organizations and employment patterns, and relationships between public administration and services and local rural governments and services.[64] In addition, a worker in a rural area needs to be sensitive to local etiquette, folkways, values, the probably strong suspicion of outsiders, and the presence of natural helping networks. The programs introduced by a worker should be geographically appropriate. As Lowell Jenkins and Alicia Cook point out:

> Agents of formal services often try to impose a program designed for an urban setting on rural people, ignoring rural values and attitudes. The professional worker frequently fails to respect the local residents who serve as natural helpers. Conversely, those in the natural helping network tend to reject the detached, professional behavior of the formal helper, preferring to "take care of their own."[65]

A worker in an urban or suburban area should have some understanding of the political struggles that take place in their localities over "the metropolitan turf."[66] As the subsystems in an urban or suburban area (whether they are organizations, cultural groups, churches, or geographic communities) compete for space and power in order to live out their values and aspirations, they frequently become involved with the complex political system. Political power, coalitions, public policy, and legal regulation are among the tools used in urban and suburban areas to secure and maintain land and resources.

Cities have been economically drained as people and businesses move out into suburbia. The boundary lines between the suburbs and the central city have been tightened as suburbs have been incorporated with strict zoning and land-use restrictions. Efforts made by suburban communities to dictate the number and types of people allowed to enter their borders are called "growth controls."[67] A decrease in suburban growth may not only reflect a depressed national economy or energy shortage, but may also result from existing discrimination and resistance to growth in suburbia, which are expressed through an increase in the number of growth controls.

Social workers need to be aware of attempts that have been made to consolidate or to coordinate city and suburban governments. In some instances, consolidation has resulted in a loss of space and resources for particular groups.[68] Through an understanding of urban politics, workers are better able to assist and to support local groups and individuals in organizing to advocate for preservation or fair distribution of finite resources within the locality.

Knowledge, skills, and experience beyond those of a beginning generalist may be needed both by the social worker who becomes involved with complex urban or suburban politics and by the generalist who works in a rural area with extensive problems, no formal service-delivery system, and limited natural helping networks. This rural worker would very likely be expected to assume roles in administration, teaching, program development, and policy formation, in addition to direct practice. The urban worker would need to have expertise in the use of the various political tools cited earlier. Unless a worker is prepared with a realistic understanding of the specific work environment and job expectations, he or she could easily "burn out," owing to a disproportionate match between demand and resources. This could be true particularly for the rural worker, because of the absence of local professional support systems. The social worker with a sensitivity to diversity in environments comes to a geographic area with more realistic expectations and preparation. Workers who are realistically prepared are then better able to help client systems, as well as to help themselves cope with, develop within, and bring about change in the environment.

Populations-at-Risk

As stated earlier, groups of people suffering from physical, mental, economic, or social impediments may be subject to rejection, abuse, discrimination, and deprivation in society. Populations-at-risk, such as the elderly, the poor, minorities, and the developmentally disabled, are frequently deprived of adequate and appropriate services. They are often overrepresented in society's criminal justice and mental health systems. These "special populations" are characterized "by de facto second class status in American Society."[69]

Applying traditional professional social work approaches to working with at-risk individuals, groups, or communities is seldom effective. Such vulnerable populations often require long-term assistance from multiple services. Workers need to bring skill and sensitivity for practice in such areas as case management and community-based services. Much of what is needed to prepare for practice with populations-at-risk may be found in a curriculum for generalist practice. Working with vulnerable client systems, as pointed out by Jack Rothman, "requires that the practitioner have baseline competency to operate proficiently on both sides of the psychosocial fence. The ecological systems perspective, . . . offers a comprehensive and balanced conceptualization for carrying out that role."[70]

Felix Rivera and John Erlich suggest that social workers need to "reconsider our definition of community as it relates to minority communities." They do not see minority communities as "gemeinschaft" or "gesellschaft" communities. Instead, they use the concept "neogemeinschaft," meaning "communities becoming and evolving within a hostile environment" where "life experiences take place within a causal, deterministic reality based on racism and economic exploitation."[71] When working in "communities of color," as brought out by Rivera and Erlich, "these communities need to be made to feel as 'subjects' rather than 'objects,'" and, "they must be encouraged to develop a sense of empowerment that leads to productive actions."[72] Again, the generalist curriculum aims at preparing social workers for practice with populations located in "neogemeinschaft" communities. Emphasized in the General Method presented in this text, for example, is the need for self-determination and client system/worker collaboration throughout the empowering problem-solving process.

Additional and more recent populations-at-risk frequently brought to the attention of social workers are the homeless and people with AIDS. Included in both populations are alarming numbers of children who risk serious impairment of their development.

The Homeless

People without the necessary resources to obtain or maintain housing become "homeless." The U.S. Department of Housing and Urban Development describe the homeless as (1) those who encounter economic problems such as unemployment, (2) the chronically disabled, and (3) those in personal crisis.[73] Homeless people are often in poor mental or physical health and lack adequate education and job skills to become self-sufficient. Frequently, they have been victims or offenders in cases of domestic violence or abuse.[74] Families, particularly women with children, are the fastest growing group of homeless. It is estimated that one hundred thousand of the two million homeless in America today are children.[75]

In their study of homeless women, Alice Johnson and Larry Kreuger identified differences between women with children and women without children in shelters. The women without children were described as generally older white women, with a longer history of homelessness, and often with drinking or psychiatric problems. Women with children were usually younger minority women, with a lack of economic and child caring support systems. For effective intervention, the study suggests:

> homeless women without children need more intensive psychosocial services, including psychiatric counseling and alcohol treatment. On the other hand, situationally homeless minority women with children need more extensive housing, public entitlements, parenting skills training, job training, and day care services.[76]

Studies have pointed to a distinction also between rural homeless populations and urban populations.[77] Those in rural areas are found to be younger and more highly educated. They are more likely to be single women or mothers with children. The cause of rural homelessness is more frequently economic factors rather than mental illness or drug abuse. The number of homeless people in rural areas has accelerated as poverty and unemployment has increased in distressed communities. The actual number of homeless in rural areas is difficult to determine because of the scarcity of shelters and social services in these areas. The rural homeless rely heavily on the informal networks of family and friends for assistance. With the number of homeless in rural areas increasing, a significant strain is being placed on traditional support systems. Social workers need to recognize and respond to this growing and complex problem. As pointed out by Richard First and associates,

> An understanding of the relationships between homelessness, poverty, unemployment, and depressed rural economies is missing in the current

view of homelessness and must be addressed more actively by social workers. Ultimately, success in preventing homelessness in rural areas will depend on eliminating poverty and increasing the amount of affordable housing stock.[78]

The problem of homelessness began to be recognized as a major problem in the 1980s as opportunities in the job market decreased and the safety net of basic human services was cut. The Omnibus Budget Reconciliation Act of 1981 resulted in the capping, reducing, or cutting of social programs that helped low-income families, particularly in the areas of housing, health, job training, and child nutrition.[79] The Steward B. McKinney Homelessness Assistance Act of 1987 has guided federal policy and attempts to address the growing problem of homelessness in America. Such efforts, however, have been ineffective primarily because approximately 95 percent of the allocated funding has been used for short-term emergency needs with little effort to address the problem on a more permanent basis.[80]

In May 1993, President Clinton issued an executive order to the federal member agencies acting through the Interagency Council on the Homeless to "develop a single coordinated Federal Plan for breaking the cycle of existing homelessness and for preventing future homelessness."[81] The plan developed by the council recognizes the need for a continuum of multiple services over an extended period of time. The plan holds that "the ultimate answer to homelessness is also the answer to poverty."[82] The continuum of care consists of three main focus areas: (1) Emergency Shelter with outreach, intake and assessment services; (2) Transitional Housing with a variety of supportive services, and (3) Permanent and Supportive Housing.[83] The long-range, future agenda of the plan is described as follows:

> This agenda will encompass long-term community and economic development, education, training and job opportunities, the reinstatement of support services as part of the "welfare" apparatus, and attention to such neighborhood facilities as health clinics and day care centers. But budgetary constraints require a transition to this larger agenda that fully addresses poverty and its accompanying ills.[84]

Shelters for the homeless are clearly an insufficient remedy to resolve the problem of homelessness today. They serve as Band-Aids for a serious illness in society. With the beginning awareness of the multiple problems of the homeless, it is becoming increasingly apparent that generalist practitioners are greatly needed to provide holistic understanding and appropriate multiple services for this growing population-at-risk.

AIDS and HIV

In 1989, it was estimated that there were over 100,000 people with AIDS (Acquired Immune Deficiency Syndrome) in the United States.[85] In 1993, the Centers for Disease Control reported 289,320 cases of AIDS.[86] The disease is transmitted through sexual contact, birth by an infected mother, contaminated blood transfusions, or through the use of contaminated needles, as by intravenous drug users. The acquiring of AIDS is a three-stage process. When first infected, the human system develops antibodies identified as HIV (Human Immune Deficiency Virus). The individual may test "HIV positive" with no apparent symptoms. As the individual moves into the second stage of the illness, he or she develops such symptoms as weight loss, persistent fever, night sweats, and shortness of breath (ARC—AIDS Related Complex). The person in the third stage becomes infected with different diseases, such as pneumonia, Kaposi's sarcoma, gastrointestinal disorders, and enlarged lymph nodes.[87] The Centers for Disease Control defines a person in the third stage as an "AIDS patient." At this time, persons with AIDS are eligible for Medicare and disability insurance.[88]

Individuals with AIDS and their families frequently experience major emotional, social, and economic distress. Social workers may play a central role in providing them with supportive services and a relationship characterized by sensitivity, acceptance, and hope. As suggested by Michael Shernoff:

> Social workers must learn how to empower clients with hope amid their illness. The hope may not be only for a cure, but to stay healthy long enough for the next generation of medical breakthroughs to occur. More time allows social workers to encourage people with AIDS to hope for and work toward improved relationships with estranged family members or friends.[89]

The question of confidentiality is a particularly sensitive ethical issue facing social workers when working with AIDS clients. Even though keeping the illness secret may serve to protect a client from discrimination, keeping secrecy may also prevent the changes necessary to overcome such discrimination and may prevent the protection of others from transmission. On this issue, Marcia Abramson writes:

> On a practical level, secrets can impede understanding, foster isolation, prevent access to services, increase stigma, and interfere with a sense of community, keeping society separated into "us" and "them."[90]

Whenever social workers are in situations where confidentiality may be questioned because of possible threat to the life of others, efforts are made to help clients with self-disclosure. Referring to cases in which clients who are HIV positive refuse to inform their sexual partners, Frederic Reamer writes:

> In many instances, skillful use of clinical intervention to address clients' resistance and anxiety will lead clients to decide to disclose the information themselves.[91]

There may be individuals who will continue to avoid self-disclosure. Social workers may be required by legal regulation or statutes to disclose information about clients with AIDS or HIV to public health officials. Workers may experience a strong ethical dilemma because they feel bound to honor their clients' rights to confidentiality and to preserve their working relationships with them. This ethical issue is a major area of concern for human service professionals. As emphasized by Abramson and Walters, "every profession will need to design a coherent professional ethic governing work with people with AIDS in the years ahead."[92]

AIDS patients frequently experience progressive dementia and become apathetic and withdrawn. Several problem areas may emerge in which social workers could offer valuable assistance. Possible intervention strategies include:

- Problem solving with everyday concerns and difficulties
- Estate planning
- Decreasing the level of hypochondriacal preoccupation
- Guidance in designing adequate structure and limits for activities of daily living
- Assisting with family conflict[93]

Another growing related area in need of attention is service provision for children with AIDS. In January 1987, 410 pediatric (under 13 years of age) cases of AIDS were reported to the Centers for Disease Control in Atlanta. By March 1993, there were 4,480 reported pediatric AIDS cases.[94] The child welfare system in America finds it difficult to locate homes for these children. Social workers have become involved in developing and maintaining foster care programs specializing in serving children with AIDS.[95]

A Holistic Framework for Sensitivity to Human Diversity

As stated, several factors need to be considered if a social worker is to be sensitive to human diversity in practice. The variables of diversity introduced in this chapter are culture, class, sexual variation, gender, age, developmental stages, endowment, personality, value systems, health, and environment. These variables may be organized within a "person-in-environment" framework, as outlined in Table 3–3. Using a holistic perspective, a worker identifies the unique combination of factors that constitute the identity of the system receiving service.

TABLE 3-3. Human Diversity

PERSON	IN	ENVIRONMENT
Gender	Culture	Class
Age/developmental ability	Value system	Geographic location
Endowment/health/personality	Sexual orientation	Institutions/services
	Populations-at-risk	

In addition to the factors in the concept of *person,* the *whole* person is not fully understood without also considering his or her functioning *in* his or her *environment.* Besides having an awareness and acceptance of an individual's distinguishing age, gender, developmental abilities, health, endowment, and personality, the worker needs to be sensitive to a client's culture, value system, sexual orientation, and populations-at-risk to which he or she may belong, and must be able to understand his or her social class, geographic location, and available environmental institutions and services.

A profile describing all of these factors about a system can be extremely helpful to a worker who is preparing to contact the system and to actualize the General Method. As information is gathered prior to contact, the framework in Table 3–3 may serve as a guide to alert the worker to possible areas of diversity.

A social worker may also benefit by drawing up a self-profile according to the areas found in Table 3–3. When, in any of the variables listed, there is a difference between the profile of the worker and that of a system receiving service, the worker should honestly appraise his or her sensitivity toward, and ability to work with, the identified diversity. Preparation may need to include research and dialogue with one's supervisor or with someone who shares the diversity of the system to be contacted. The system in need of service may find it difficult to work with a social worker who, in one or several of the areas listed, does not share a commonality. Whenever possible, the system should be given the opportunity to work with someone who is not different. The service system should be able to provide a change in workers when it is believed that differences are preventing goal accomplishment.

Conclusion

A sensitivity to human diversity from a holistic, multi-variant perspective is essential for effective social work practice. Although some central concepts and definitions were presented for each of the diversity variables introduced in this chapter, far more extensive reading is necessary for a worker to develop a sound understanding of any one of the variables identified. What has been given is an overview and a framework for conceptualizing the major diversities found by social workers in practice. A social worker must be sensitive to human diversity and the plight of populations-at-risk throughout the entire process of service delivery.

In the following chapters, attention will be given to the need for sensitivity to human diversity during each stage of the General Method. Examples will demonstrate the use of skills and sensitivity when working with different systems in a variety of fields of practice.

NOTES

1. Cited in Elliot M. Goldwag, ed., *Inner Balance: The Power of Holistic Healing* (Englewood Cliffs, NJ: Prentice-Hall, 1979), p. ii.

2. Jacquelyn Dupont-Walker, Region IX Child Welfare Training Center, University of California at Los Angeles, School of Social Welfare, *Ethnic Minority Cultures—Shades of Difference?* (Ann Arbor, MI: National Child Welfare Center, 1982), p. 2.

3. Doman Lum, "Toward a Framework for Social Work Practice with Minorities," *Social Work* 27, no. 3 (May 1982): 246–48.

4. Charles Valentine, "Deficit, Difference and Bicultural Models of Afro-American Behavior," *Howard Educational Review* 41, no. 2 (May 1971): 137–57.

5. Eddie F. Brown and Timothy F. Shaughnessy, eds., *Education for Social Work Practice with American Indian Families*, American Indian Projects for Community Development, Training and Research. (Arizona: School of Social Work, Arizona State University, 1979), cited in Dupont-Walker, *Ethnic Minority Cultures*, p. 16.

6. Royal F. Morales et al., *Asian and Pacific American* Curriculum on Social Work Education (Los Angeles: Asian American Community Mental Health Training Center, 1976), p. 2.

7. Dupont-Waker, *Ethnic Minority Cultures*, p. 2.

8. Milton M. Gordon, *Assimilation in American Life* (New York: Oxford University Press, 1964), pp. 51–54.

9. James E. Blackwell, *The Black Community: Diversity and Unity* (New York: Harper & Row, 1975), pp. 67–68.

10. Ibid, p. 74.

11. Judd Marmor, ed., *Homosexual Behavior: A Modern Reappraisal* (New York: Basic Books, 1980), p. 5.

12. Brian McNaught, *A Disturbed Peace* (Washington, DC: A Dignity Publication, 1981), p. 4.

13. Adapted from Alfred C. Kinsey, Wardel B. Pomeroy, and Clyde E. Martin, *Sexual Behavior in the Human Male* (Philadelphia: Saunders, 1948).

14. Marmor, *Homosexual Behavior*, p. 8.

15. Diana Dulaney and James Kelly, "Improving Services to Gay and Lesbian Clients," *Social Work* 27, no. 2 (March 1982): 8.

16. Teresa A. DeCrescenzo and Christine McGill, "Homophobia: A Study of the Attitudes of Mental Health Professionals Toward Homosexuality" (M.A. thesis, University of Southern California, School of Social Work, 1978).

17. J. Money, "Factors in the Genesis of Homosexuality," in George Winokur, ed., *Determinants of Human Sexual Behavior* (Springfield, IL: Charles C. Thomas, 1963).

18. E. Hooker and others, *Final Report of the National Institute of Mental Health Task Force on Homosexuality* (1969), reprinted in the *SIECUS* Newsletter (December 1970): 3–14.

19. Clifford, Allen, *The Sexual Perversions and Abnormalities* (London: Oxford University Press, 1949).

20. Ralph Blair, *Etiological and Treatment Literature on Homosexuality* (New York: National Task Force on Student Personnel Services and Homosexuality, 1972), p. 18.

21. McNaught, *A Disturbed Peace*, p. 9.

22. Ibid, p. 18.

23. The Association of Women in Psychology, *Considerations in Therapy with Lesbian Clients* (Philadelphia: Women's Resources, 1979), p. 24.

24. Adapted from Raymond M. Berger, "The Unseen Minority: Older Gays and Lesbians." Copyright 1982, National Association of Social Workers, Inc. Reprinted with permission, from *Social Work* 27, no. 3 (May 1982): 240.

25. Ibid., pp. 237–40.

26. Ibid., p. 237.

27. Sandra Auerback and Charles Moser, "Groups for the Wives of Gay and Bisexual Men," *Social Work* 32, no. 4 (July–August 1987): 321–25.

28. DeCrescenzo and McGill, "Homophobia."

29. Det P. Romero, "Biases in Gender-Role Research," *Social Work* 22, no. 3 (1977): 214.

30. S. V. Levine, L. E. Kamin, and E. L. Levine, "Sexism and Psychiatry: Theory and Review," *American Journal of Orthopsychiatry* 44, no. 3 (April 1974): 327–36.

31. Maryann Mahaffey, "Sexism and Social Work," *Social Work* 21, no. 6 (November 1976): 419.

32. Mimi Abramovitz, Thomas J. Hopkins, Victoria Olds, and Mary Wring, "Integrating Content on Women Into the Social Policy Curriculum: A Continuum Model," *Journal on Social Work Education* 18, no. 1 (Winter 1982): 33.

33. Marita Williams, Liz Ho, and Lucy Fielder, "Career Patterns: More Grist for Women's Liberation," *Social Work* 19, no. 4 (July 1974): 466.

34. Marcia Guttentag and Susan Salasin, "Women and Mental Health," in Libby Cater, Anne Scott, and Wendy Martyna, eds., *Women and Men: Changing Roles, Relationships, and Perceptions* (Palo Alto, California: Aspen Institute for Humanistic Studies, 1976), p. 2: Sharon C. Welsnack, Marc Schuckit, eds., *Alcoholism Problems in Women and Children* (New York: Grune & Stratton, 1976), pp. 37–60.

35. Larry Alsbrook, "Marital Communication and Sexism," *Social Casework* 57, (October 1976): 522.

36. John F. Longreas and Robert H. Bailey, "Men's Issues and Sexism: A Journal Review," *Social Work* 24, no. 1 (January 1979): 27.

37. Herb Goldberg, *The New Male* (New York: New American Library, 1978), p. 47.

38. Ibid., p. 1.

39. Ibid., p. 220.

40. Helen A. Mendes, "Single Fatherhood," *Social Work* 21, no. 4 (July 1976): 312.

41. Lawrence E. Gary and Bogart R. Leashore, "High-Risk Status of Black Men," *Social Work* 27, no. 1 (January 1982): 55–56.

42. Sister Maria Joan O'Neil, Small-group discussions with inmates at Somers Maximum Security Prison, Somers, CT, 1980–83.

43. Joseph H. Pleck, "The Male Sex Role: Definitions, Problems and Sources of Change," *Journal of Social Issues* 32, no. 3 (Summer 1976): 155.

44. Sandra L. Bem, "The Measurement of Psychological Androgyny," *Journal of Consulting and Clinical Psychology* 42 (April 1974): 155–62; and "Sex Role Adaptability: One Consequence of Psychological Androgyny," *Journal of Personality and Social Psychology* 31, no. 4 (April 1975): 634–43.

45. Joyce B. Lazar, "Sex Role Adaptability" (Rockville, MD: Alcohol, Drug Abuse and Mental Health Administration, 1980), p. 3.

46. Frederick Duhl, "Changing Sex Role-Concepts, Values and Tasks," *Social Casework* 57 (February 1976): 89.

47. Frank H. Lowenberg, *Religion and Social Work Practice in Contemporary American Society* (New York: Columbia University Press, 1988), p. 149.

48. Alan Keith-Lucas, *Giving and Taking Help* (Chapel Hill: University of North Carolina Press, 1972), pp. 138–43.

49. Emilia E. Martinez-Brawley, "Identifying and Describing the Content of Rural in Social Work," *Arete* 5, no. 1 (Fall 1980): 23.

50. U. S. Bureau of the Census, *Statistical Abstract of the United States: 1993* (113th edition). Washington, D.C., 1993.

51. Robert L. Lineberry, "Suburbia and Metropolitan Turf," *The Annals of American Academy of Political and Social Science* 422 (November 1975): 3.

52. Ibid., p. 2.

53. Emilia E. Martinez-Brawley, personal interview, October 19, 1982, New York.

54. Marion H. Wijinberg and Louis Colca, "Facing up to the Diversity in Rural Practice: A Curriculum Model," *Journal of Education for Social Work* 17, no. 2 (Spring 1981): 92.

55. H. Wayne Johnson, "Rural Crime, Delinquency, Substance Abuse, and Corrections," in Leon H. Ginsberg, ed., *Social Work in Rural Communities,* Second Edition (Alexandria, VA: Council on Social Work Education, 1993), p. 206.

56. Owen K. Weber, "Preparing Social Workers for Practice in Rural Social Systems," in Wayne Johnson, ed., *Rural Human Services* (Itasca, IL.: Peacock, 1980), p. 206.

57. Carol H. Meyer, *Social Work Practice: A Response to the Urban Crisis* (New York: The Free Press, 1970), p. 80.

58. Arnold J. Auerbach, "The Elderly in Rural Areas: Differences in Urban Areas and Implications for Practice," in Leon H. Ginsberg, ed., *Social Work in Rural Communities* (New York: Council on Social Work Education, 1976), p. 105.

59. Janet M. Fitchen, *Poverty in Rural America: A Case Study* (Boulder, CO: Westview, 1981).

60. Rex R. Campbell, "Crisis on the Farm," *American Demographic* 7, no. 10 (October 1985): 30–34.

61. Maria J. O'Neil and John R. Ball, "The General Method of Social Work in Rural Environments" (Paper presented at the Council on Social Work Education, Annual Program Meeting, Saint Louis, MO, March 9, 1987), p. 2.

62. Emilia E. Martinez-Brawley, "Social Work and the Rural Crisis: Is Education Responding?" (Paper Presented at an Invitational Session, Council on Social Work Education, Annual Program Meeting, Saint Louis, MO, March 9, 1987), p. 2.

63. Leon H. Ginsberg, "Introduction: An Overview of Rural Social Work," in Leon H. Ginsberg, ed., *Social Work in Rural Communities,* Second Edition (Alexandria, VA: Council on Social Work Education, 1993), pp. 6–7.

64. Emilia E. Martinez-Brawley, "Historical Perspectives on Rural Social Work: Implications for Curriculum Development," *Journal of Education for Social Work* 16, no. 3 (Fall 1980): 49–52.

65. Lowell Jenkins and Alicia J. Cook, "The Rural Hospice: Integrating Normal and Informal Helping Systems," *Social Work* 26, no. 5 (September 1961): 415.

66. Lineberry, "Suburbia," p. 4.

67. James W. Hughes, "Dilemmas of Suburbanization and Growth Controls," *The Annals of the American Academy of Political and Social Science* 422 (November 1975): 61.

68. Lineberry, "Suburbia," p. 8.

69. President's Commission on Mental Health, *Mental Health in America 1978,* Vol. III (Washington, DC: U.S. Government Printing Office, 1978): 731.

70. Jack Rothman, *Practice With Highly Vulnerable Clients* (Englewood Cliffs, NJ: Prentice-Hall, 1994), p. 14.

71. Felix G. Rivera and John L. Erlich, *Community Organization in a Diverse Society* (Boston: Allyn and Bacon), p. 83.

72. Ibid., p. 259.

73. U.S. Department of Housing and Urban Development, "A Report to the Secretary on the Homeless and Emergency Shelters," Office of Policy Development and Research, May 1984.

74. Ralph DaCosta Nunez, *Hopes, Dreams and Promises: The Future of Homeless Children in America* (New York: Institute for Children and Poverty, Homes for the Homeless, Inc., 1994), p. 32.

75. Children's Defense Fund, *Children 1990: A Report Card, Briefing Book, and Action Primer* (Washington, DC: The Fund, 1990).

76. Alice K. Johnson and Larry W. Kreuger, "Toward a Better Understanding of Homeless Women," *Social Work* 34, no. 6 (November 1989): 537–540.

77. P. Fisher, *Endangered Spaces, Enduring Places: Change, Identity, and Survival in Rural America* (Boulder, CO: Westview Press, 1991); P. Rossi, *Down and Out in America* (Chicago: University of Chicago Press, 1989); Richard J. First, John C. Rife, and Beverly G. Toomey, "Homelessness in Rural Areas: Causes, Patterns and Trends," in Leon H. Ginsberg, Ed., *Social Work in Rural Communities,* Second Edition (Alexandria, VA: Council on Social Work Education, 1993): 244–259.

78. First, Rife, and Toomey, "Homelessness in Rural Areas," p. 257.

79. Nunez, pp. 17–19.

80. National Law Center on Homelessness and Poverty, *Beyond McKinney: Policies to End Homelessness* (Washington, DC: National Law Center on Homeless and Poverty, November, 1992), p. 1.

81. William J. Clinton, "Executive Order Mandate to the Council," Executive Order 12848 of May 19, 1993, in *Priority: Home! The Federal Plan to Break the Cycle of Homelessness,* HUD 1454-CPD, March 1994.

82. *Priority: Home!*, p. 14.

83. Ibid., p. 73.

84. Ibid., p. 35.

85. W. Heyward and J. Curran, "The Epidemiology of AIDS in the U.S." In Gary Carlson, ed., *The Science of AIDS: Readings from the Scientific American* (New York: W. H. Freeman, 1989), pp. 39–49.

86. Centers for Disease Control, "HIV/AIDS Surveillance Report," 5, no. 1 (May 1993): 6.

87. U.S. Public Health Service, "Facts About AIDS," (Washington, D.C.: U.S. Government Printing Office Group, 1985).

88. Martha N. Ozawa, Wendy F. Auslander, and Vered Slonim-Nevo, "Problems in Financing the Care of AIDS Patients," *Social Work* 38, no. 4 (July 1993): 370.

89. Michael Shernoff, "Why Every Social Worker Should Be Challenged by AIDS," *Social Work* 35, no. 1 (January 1990): 7.

90. Marcia Abramson, "Keeping Secrets: Social Workers and AIDS," *Social Work* 35, no. 2 (March 1990): 172.

91. Frederic G. Reamer, "AIDS and Social Work: The Ethics and Civil Liberties Agenda," *Social Work* 38, no. 4 (July 1993): 415.

92. Abramson, "Keeping Secrets," p. 169. See also, L. Walters, "Ethical Issues in the Prevention and Treatment of HIV Infection and AIDS," *Science,* 239, pp. 597–603.

93. Stephen I. Buchingham and Wilfred G. Van Grop, "Essential Knowledge About AIDS Dementia," *Social Work* 33 (March– April 1988): 112–115.

94. Centers for Disease Control, May 1993, p. 6. Phyllis Gurdin and Gary R. Anderson, "Quality Care for Ill Children: AIDS—Specialized Foster Family Homes," *Child Welfare* 66, no. 4 (July/August 1987): 291–302.

95. Phyllis Gurdin and Gary R. Anderson, "Quality Care for Ill Children: AIDS—Specialized Foster Family Homes," *Child Welfare* 66, no. 4 (July/August 1987): 291–302.

CHAPTER 4

Engagement

Social work is concerned with the interactions between people and their environments which affect their ability to accomplish life tasks, alleviate distress and realize aspirations and values in relation to themselves, the rights of others, the general welfare and social justice.

—CSWE[1]

The first stage of the General Method is called *engagement*. Whether the generalist begins to work with a client, target, or action system, and whether the system is an individual, group, family, community, or institution, the first thing the worker tries to do is to open up the boundary between them (system and worker) for positive interaction. Frequently, there is some resistance by a system to any possible change or intrusion from the outside. From the inception of contact with a system, the generalist needs to use skill and knowledge along with professional values and principles for effective engagement.

In the first stage of the General Method, the worker has three guiding landmarks that help in the initial movement of the procedure. As the generalist begins to interact with a system, the three focal points of problems, feelings, and goals are kept in mind. All three are often in focus at the same time in the conversation and transactions between worker and system. The generalist makes sure that all three points have been addressed before proceeding to the next stage of the method.

In this chapter, each of the three central elements of the engagement stage will be studied. Techniques will be presented for working with diverse systems on their problems, feelings, and goals. Case vignettes will demonstrate the first stage of the General Method with a variety of systems. Considerations will include the use of the social work foundation (Table 1–5, Chapter 1) during the engagement stage of generalist practice.

Getting to the Problem

Before actually discussing the problem with a system in any depth, it is necessary for the worker to prepare for the contact. The social worker tries to learn as much as possible about the culture, needs, and resources of the system. The worker tries not only to understand the system that he or she will interact with, but also to understand his or her own culture, needs, and resources and how the two, worker and system of contact, may form a "fit" for positive interactions. If it appears that there will be stress or difficulty in the match between worker and system, the practitioner seeks help from a supervisor.

At the point of initial contact, after brief introductions, the purpose for coming together needs to be expressed. Within the description of purpose, a problem may be mentioned. The worker keeps this in mind for reference when the time is appropriate.

If the contact is initiated by the worker, he or she states the purpose. If the contact was initiated by a client or some other system, the worker encourages the system to say why the contact was made. For example:

CASE 1: Worker-Initiated

Worker: Good morning, Mrs. B. I am Mary Costello, the school social worker. I would like to talk with you about your son Johnnie and how he's doing at school.

CASE 2: Client-Initiated

Worker: Good morning. I am Mary Costello, the school social worker. I understand you wanted to talk with me.

Client: Yes, I'm Mrs. B, Johnnie's mother. His teacher said that maybe I could talk to you about the problems I've been having with my son lately.

The generalist asks himself or herself: What is the issue, problem, need, or question that appears to be the major concern for this client system? Is there really a problem (or problems) that the system will identify and invest energy in for resolution? The worker begins to clarify the problems he or she and the system are going to work on together.

The General Method is permeated with ecological-systems theory. The generalist knows that when an environment gives an organism the inputs needed for thriving, there are certain outputs that the environment expects from the organism. The environment and the organism have role expectations for each other. Each is expected to behave and produce in a way that is conducive to the well-being of the other. In the General Method, the problem is defined initially in terms of what is taking place at the point of interface and interactions between organism and environment. The problem is seen at the boundary point where a system interlocks with some aspect of its surrounding environment or with some other system in that environment. The expected inputs and outputs for each problem situation are considered.

In time, the plan of intervention developed in the procedure may be directed toward a system or its environment rather than toward the boundary where the two come together. As brought out by Hearn: "In short, social work activity is focused inside, outside, and at the boundary between the system and its environment."[2] The initial problem description, however, focuses on the boundary point where there is a need or desire to direct attention to the functioning of system and environment in relation to each other.

For example, in Case 1, the problem as presented by the worker is between Johnnie and the school. He is not behaving or performing academically at the level expected for him to "fit" into the system and be promoted by the school. The problem as introduced by Mrs. B in Case 2 is between Johnnie and his mother at home. He is not acting in the manner his mother expects and thus is not receiving her approval and affection. Every effort should be made to relate the problem as directly as possible to the system in contact with the worker. The more distant the problem, the more difficult it is to involve the system in a timely change effort. Usually it is not necessary to identify clearly the causes of the problem in the engagement stage. During data collection, stage 2, there is opportunity to obtain information on causes. Sometimes, however, facts relating to causes may need to be presented to promote greater incentive for cooperation. The worker may need to present data in order to determine the validity of the apparent causes of a problem presented by the system.

For example, if Mrs. B identifies the main problem as Johnnie's not getting along with his teacher, she may think there is little she has to work on to improve the situation. If, on the other hand, it is pointed out to Mrs. B that Johnnie's school problems are showing up in classes with different teachers, and if she is helped to see that his problems started around the time her husband was laid off from work and she began working, Mrs. B may begin to get more involved in looking at the problem.

The timing and techniques used in presenting facts to stimulate involvement are dependent on the sensitivity and skills of the worker. Presenting facts too soon or too abruptly may cause the client to become defensive or inhibited. Mrs. B, for example, may find it difficult to talk about her husband or the financial constraints that necessitated her going to work. She may become defensive as she begins to see a correlation between her son's school problems and what is happening with herself and her husband.

In beginning to identify the problem with a system, the skilled generalist is sensitive to delicate, feeling-filled areas. The worker knows that feelings relevant to the problems must be recognized and expressed if there is to be real movement toward problem resolution. As feelings are disclosed, new problems or a clearer understanding of the problem may emerge. As stated, problems are not fixed, but evolving, and feelings are a force that helps to move the problems into clearer focus.

Identifying Feelings

A basic practice principle, as described in Chapter 1, is *purposeful expression of feelings*.[3] The social worker does not encourage indiscriminate ventilation of feelings about any or every issue. The General Method is a purposeful process that calls for the worker to have expertise in the realm of feelings. The generalist strives to become aware of the feelings of the client system as they relate to the problem situation. The worker recognizes when the system is expressing unrelated feelings and uses skill in deciding whether or not these feelings indicate other problem areas in need of attention or whether their expression is an attempt to avoid facing the problem at hand. If the former, the worker and system may need to reconstruct or add to the identified problem; if the latter, the worker may need to discuss the avoidance with the system and redirect the conversation back to the identified problem.

There is also the basic principle called *controlled emotional involvement*.[4] It points to the need for the worker to have self-awareness in terms of his or her own feelings surrounding the problem-client system-environment situation. Prior to and throughout the process of working with others, the generalist realizes the fact that he or she has feelings also. At times, these feelings may be very strong and in need of control while he or she works with particular systems or problems. If this is difficult for the worker, he or she should seek help from a supervisor.

In the General Method, the identification of feelings, as well as problems, is done basically on a rational level. The theoretical foundation of social work practice looks at the whole of human nature and enables the worker to be aware of unconscious as well as conscious factors that influence human behavior. In general practice, however, the feelings encouraged and expressed are mainly conscious and identifiable. The approach of the worker may be described primarily as rational or "cognitive."

> A cognitive approach holds that the principal determinant of emotions, motives and behavior is an individual's thinking, which is a conscious process. The problems the clients bring to social work are considered to be problems of consciousness.[5]

The generalist does not discard the notion of the unconscious in human behavior, but recognizes that his or her competence is for working on the rational, conscious level. The feelings addressed in practice are conscious or able to be brought into consciousness with a little effort.

Carkhuff points out that each feeling has a rational reason that can be identified. He writes:

> The thing the helper must remember is this: Regardless of the apparent nature of the cause of a particular helpee's feelings, each of those feelings will always turn out to have a sufficient and rational reason! One of the

most important goals of all helpee exploration is to identify—to the helper as well as to the helpee—the real reason for each of his or her real feelings.[6]

Even though feelings may be conscious, the worker knows that often they are difficult to share. It may be awkward for a person to engage in a discussion about private feelings with a professional person in the early stages of a working relationship. As stated earlier, in some cultures, words are seldom used to express feelings, particularly with someone outside of the family.[7]

In his book *You and Me,* Gerard Egan lists the following feelings that are commonly "difficult to express": "feelings of being no good," "feelings about not being able to do things," "feelings about not being able to do something about a situation," "not being able to handle affection from others," "feelings of being hurt or rejected," "feelings that come from a need to punish someone else," "feelings coming from a need to be punished," "feelings of guilt," "feelings of shame," "feelings of being dependent on a person," "feelings of being passive," and "feelings of helplessness."[8]

Poor families have been described as unable to express concerns well enough to talk about them with a social agency, and "so inarticulate that they literally did not have the words for their emotion."[9] Hollis disagrees with this judgment and reports that most social workers do not have difficulty getting clients to express their feelings if the workers themselves use appropriate language. She points out that workers should not let "simplicity of language" be understood as "incapacity." Often simple words or expressions are the most valid and meaningful. She writes:

> Exploration may sometimes proceed at a slower pace than the more verbal, better educated client. But once the low-income client's confidence has been established, he is likely to speak freely, particularly of feelings of anger and frustration, sometimes directed against the worker himself.[10]

To be able to help a system discuss relevant feelings, the generalist needs to have a broad vocabulary to describe feelings. As brought out by Hallowitz:

> The worker also helps the client with feelings that impair his ability to deal with the problems at hand—e.g., anxiety, conflict, resistance. He encourages the client to do the problem-solving work to the fullest possible extent. When the limits of this are reached, he contributes his own thinking and suggestions.[11]

The suggestions offered to help a client with describing feelings have to be carefully and appropriately selected. The word list in Table 4–1 may be helpful to workers as they search for ways to describe particular feelings most aptly. Each word may be modified for more accurate indications of degrees of intensity by using such descriptive words as "a little, "somewhat," "rather," or "very."

TABLE 4-1.   Words to Describe Feelings

POSITIVE FEELINGS	NEGATIVE FEELINGS
Relaxed	Uptight, nervous
All together	Spacey, mixed up
Whole	Falling apart
Confident, adequate, potent	Confused, unsure, inept
Graceful	Awkward, clumsy
Well organized	Disorganized
Accepted	Rejected, abandoned
Appreciated	Unappreciated
A part of things	Out of step, left out
Loved	Unloved
Full of life	Burned out, exhausted
Strengthened, firm	Weakened, weak
Witty	Dull
Able to cope	Overwhelmed
Good	Bad
Warm	Cold
Delighted	Unhappy, frustrated
Great	Small
Glad	Sad
Pleased	Displeased, angry, outraged
Loving	Hateful, hostile, furious
Daring	Afraid
In control	Out of control, helpless
Hopeful	Hopeless
Full	Empty
Built up	Put down, crushed
Serene	Disturbed
Energetic	Exhausted
Healthy	Sick
Powerful	Powerless
Free	Trapped

Feelings are not described in one or two words. They may be expressed through phrases, behavioral descriptions, and stated desires.[12] For example, to feel "happy" may be described as "I feel great"; "I feel as free as a bird"; "I feel I could jump for joy"; or "I feel I would like to reach out and hug everyone here." The important point in the engagement stage is not so much *how* the feelings are expressed but *that* they are expressed in whatever manner has the most meaning to the system. Central to the art of social work practice is the awareness of feelings in human systems and of the value in their purposeful expression.

As stated earlier, when feelings are expressed, the worker needs to explore with the system of contact "the rational reason" for the feelings.[13] A technique frequently used as the practitioner clarifies the feelings is to say, "I understand that you are feeling _____ because _____," or "Is it that you feel _____ because _____?" "You seem to be feeling _____ because _____."

It is always necessary to receive feedback from the system after a reason for feelings is suggested. This may be accomplished by adding such statements as "Is that correct?" "What do you think?" "Am I right?" or "Is that it?" In this way, the system is encouraged by the worker to participate in the process of finding reasons for feelings, and to accept, modify, or reject the suggested description of feelings offered by the worker.

As the worker moves with the system from the identification of feelings to the reasons for the feelings, the worker tries to utilize the ecological perspective. An effort is made to incorporate a view of the system in relation to the environment within the definition of the reason for feelings. The more the members of a system see their roles in the reason for the feelings, the more chance there is that they will begin to use their feelings in dealing with the problem. For example, the worker may say in Case 1,

Mrs. B, I can see that you are troubled because you can't understand why your son is not getting along in school lately. Is that right?

or

Mrs. B, you seem to be very upset right now. Is it because you don't want to hear that Johnnie is having school problems at a time when you and the family are having so many other difficulties?

In the second case, the worker might say:

You are feeling very frustrated because you can't seem to get along with your son lately. Is that it, Mrs. B?

or

You are very angry with your son lately because he is not behaving the way you expect of him. Is that correct?

The reason for the feelings may be closely related to the problem as presented, or after further exploration, the worker may find that the reason for the feelings as clarified becomes a means for uncovering issues that need more immediate attention. In the first case, for example, the worker may begin to see that Mrs. B is currently feeling overwhelmed because of extensive family problems, and Johnnie's behavior at school is but an indicator of a very troubled family situation. In the second case, Mrs. B expressed feelings that relate directly to the presenting problem. The feelings she expressed were caused by a problem in parent–child interaction.

As the feelings are refined and the problem reformulated, it may become apparent through the exploration of feelings and their reasons that there is a problem needing to be addressed, but that it is outside the scope of the compe-tence of the generalist or the agency's services. A referral to another service may be necessary. A resource may need to be contacted for a collaborative effort, when several problems have emerged and at least one problem continues within the worker's domain. It is important for the worker to keep in mind that every step in the process of the General Method may change the nature of the problem. As pointed out by Spitzer and Welsh:

> Problem focused practice requires an ongoing and continuing process, since problems are rarely totally resolved. As a result of intrapsychic or environmental events, the impact of the social welfare response system, or the responses to the problem by other segments of society, new elements are introduced and the nature of the problem constantly changes.[14]

When needs or expectations are unmet, system members begin to feel unful-filled. Negative feelings, including anger and rage, may develop. Negative feelings drain energy from a system. When the reason for these feelings is identified and if through some process or intervention the reason may be reversed, there is then new energy available for more effective social functioning. Positive feelings gener-ate vitality and energy for growth-promoting transactions. The reasons for positive feelings are seen as something to be maintained or enhanced. As long as the rea-sons persist, the energy level continues or expands for effective social functioning.

The reasons for feelings may relate closely to the problems and also to the goals. The stating of reasons for negative or positive feelings helps to move the worker and the system into recognizing and discussing goals. Frequently, the ini-tially stated goals either reflect the opposite of identified reasons for negative feel-ings, or they reflect an expansion of stated reasons for positive feelings. A tech-nique used to bridge the elements of feelings with goals is to state the reverse side of reasons for negative feelings or to highlight and develop the reasons for posi-tive feelings. For example, the worker would say:

> You are angry at yourself because you are not able to give your children the attention and direction they need, and you wish you could give them more attention and direction. Is that so?

or

> You are feeling happy because you and your son are getting along better lately, and you would like to see this continue and grow as time goes on. Right?

The introduction of suggestions for preliminary goals should come only after the client has confirmed the stated reasons for feelings. If the suggested goals are unrelated to the feelings of the client, they may be a reflection of the worker's hopes and expectations rather than the client's actual goals.

Feelings in Macrosystems

The engagement stage initiates the General Method as used with systems of any size or type. Even when working with a target or action system, the generalist tries to discern how the problem is perceived, what feelings exist about the situation, and what goals would be acceptable and feasible for involvement by the system.

As defined earlier, target systems need to change for goal accomplishment. They do not necessarily want to or agree to work with the social worker. Action systems cooperate with the worker to achieve goals or influence target systems. And client systems request or agree to work with the worker to receive benefits from the service.

A target, action, or client system may be an individual, family, group, community, organization, social institution, or society. These are the systems of contact in social work practice. As the generalist works with diverse systems, an important consideration is the distinguishing characteristics that are generally recognized among systems. As depicted in Figure 4–1, human systems have a basic set of characteristics that vary according to the type of system. The worker prepares for contact with a system by recalling or trying to find out as much as possible about the system. Working from foundation knowledge, the practitioner makes every effort to become aware of the system's characteristics and the degree of intensity of feelings.

For the range of major systems of contact in social work, there are characteristic polarities with intervening degree scales that may be considered (Figure 4–1). The polarities include facts versus feelings, goal orientation versus process orientation, formality versus informality, explicit nature versus implicit nature, organization versus little organization, structure versus little structure, objectivity versus intimacy, social control versus human concern, and law and work versus circumstance and love.

Individual . . . Family . . . Group . . . Community . . . Organization . . . Institution . . . Society

Feelings _____ Facts
Process orientation _____ Goal orientation
Informality _____ Formality
Implicit nature _____ Explicit nature
Little organization _____ Much organization
Little structure _____ Much structure
Intimacy _____ Objectivity
Human concern _____ Social control
Circumstance _____ Law
Love _____ Work

FIGURE 4-1. Polarities in Systems

In Figure 4–1, feelings and goals are associated with certain types of systems. As indicated in the diagram, there are basically greater expectation and awareness of feelings and process with smaller systems and greater expectation and awareness of facts and goals with larger systems. In beginning to work with a larger system, the generalist sees the need to come prepared to present facts and to work with structure and formality. Generally, feelings are not readily considered or expressed in larger systems.

To work with any system, the worker deals with human beings who naturally have feelings. The worker tries to identify feelings as they relate to the problem and to the worker's efforts. Skill is used to distinguish between those feelings that are the personal feelings of individual representatives and those of the larger system. Whereas the worker may be able to discuss feelings and relationships with individuals, it often takes longer to recognize and discuss them with individuals who represent a large system. There is a possibility that the expression of feelings will not be able to influence or change a situation in a larger system because of policy and structure. Carefully presented facts, however, could be most effective.

In terms of goals, larger systems enter very readily into a dialogue about their goals and expectations. They usually have explicitly stated goals that can be utilized as the worker tries to engage the system in mutual goal setting. The smaller system, however, may take more time and need more help in understanding and expressing its goals.

As implied in Figure 4–1, while working with the three major components of the engagement stage (i.e., problem, feelings, and goals), the worker usually finds a natural tendency to get into feelings and relationships with the smaller systems (i.e., individuals, groups, families, and some communities), and to get into facts and goals with larger systems (i.e., some communities, as well as organizations, institutions, and society). As stated, however, all three components—problems, feelings, and goals—must be considered by the worker for successful movement in the engagement stage.

Goal Recognition

The worker asks the question, What is it that this system really wants? In the first case cited, the worker is hearing that Mrs. B wants Johnnie to remain in school and get promoted, but she also wants some relief from heavy family burdens. In the second case, Mrs. B is clearly focusing on the goal of improving her relationship with her son. Such clarification of goals is imperative for the worker to determine how to proceed with the system. Goals have to be expressed, understood, and agreed on by both system and worker before they can move on to the second stage of the method.

What is a goal? Epstein gives a very direct answer when she writes:

> The idea of a goal is straightforward. It is the end toward which effort is directed. A goal is a point beyond which something does not or cannot go. . . . Therefore a goal is an attainable wish.[15]

Werner interchanges goal with "objective" and relates the terms to "motive." He writes:

> A motive is a goal or objective which we choose on the basis of a personal conception of what is necessary for our welfare, happiness or success.[16]

Epstein points out four main types of goals in social work, "agency, professional, practitioner and client goals." She stresses the need for the client goals to be predominant when working on cases.

> Agency, professional, and personal practitioner goals are never out of sight or out of mind. They provide a general climate of opinion and requirements. However, so long as client goals do not seriously contradict vital segments of the broader goal structure, they should determine the individual case goals.[17]

In the General Method, a goal is conceptualized as including objectives, motives, and attainable desires. It is the end toward which the worker and the system or systems direct their efforts. Goals are explicated in the General Method when there is mutual agreement by worker and system. It is possible that the method may be arrested because no goals can be established by mutual agreement. To proceed without this mutuality would be futile.

Although initial goals may be expressed in broad, general terms, the practitioner and the system work toward formulation of concrete goals. General and specific goals of the General Method are of a social-functioning nature, and they are conceptualized from an ecological-systems perspective. General goals relate to social situations in which the exchange at the point of interface between system and environment is central. As the goals are stated, clarified, and refined, the worker keeps in mind the need to have goals be measurable and attainable. They should be practical, limited in number, and obviously related to the identified problems.

As the General Method proceeds into data collection, assessment, and planning, goals may be reformulated and refined for greater specificity. Goal setting leads to the identification of specific tasks that need to be performed for goal accomplishment. The actions needed to obtain the stated goals will be clarified within an identifiable and realistic time span. When completed, the identified problem should have been addressed, alleviated, or resolved.

Moving from identifying preliminary general goals that are stated ecologically and that are related directly to the presenting problems, the generalist helps the systems to develop more specific measurable and practical goals and tasks. For example, a general goal stated by Mrs. B may be to improve interactions between herself and her son. As the worker gets more involved with Mrs. B and her son later on in the course of the Method, they would be expected to agree on the general goal and to identify their specific goals and tasks in terms of behaviors and conditions. These might include, for example:

1. To give themselves more time together by spending at least half an hour a day listening, talking, and relaxing together (both)
2. To grow in understanding each other by attending biweekly sessions with the social worker until June (both)
3. To develop greater understanding of self and other parents and skills for parenting teenagers by attending the parenting-skills class on Tuesday nights for six weeks (Mrs. B)
4. To grow in understanding self and other teenagers and how to get along with parents by attending the teen meetings until June (Johnnie)
5. To avoid losing temper and striking out at son by talking about upsetting behavior with him at home and during sessions with the worker (Mrs. B)
6. To try to obey mother and avoid getting sarcastic with her by talking about upsetting behavior with her at home and during sessions with the worker (Johnnie)

In item 1, the specific goal is to give themselves more time together, and the measurable task is to spend at least one-half an hour a day listening, talking, and relaxing together.

Goals in the engagement stage of the General Method are beginning goals in a process of goal setting. The main purpose for goal identification in the initial stage is to let the system know that the worker is listening and that he or she hears what the system is saying about wants, needs, or values. The worker skillfully begins to engage the system in thinking about goals, with the hope that this engagement will motivate the system for deeper involvement in a collaborative problem-solving effort. As the Method proceeds, the worker and the system gain a clearer understanding of problems, feelings, and goals.

Working with Different Systems

The following complex case situation is offered to provide a better understanding of the application of the engagement stage of the General Method to different systems. The worker for the family will begin to use the General Method to work with client, target, and action systems. The systems of contact range from an individual to a large business.

CASE SITUATION

Mrs. Armez was sent to the Unity Social Service Department by her pastor. Her husband had to go into the hospital for an operation and, after a few weeks, was told by the doctor he could return to work. When Mr. Armez tried to return, he was told they didn't need him any longer, and he was laid off. While he had been in the hospital, Mr. Armez's place of employment had changed hands, and Mr. Armez thinks the new management does not like Hispanic people. Mr. Armez continues to feel weak and doesn't know if he could work the way he used to. Mrs. Armez said that since Mr. Armez's unemployment benefits ran out and the family went on welfare, he hasn't been acting right. He drinks more, and he fought with her when she began to do some part-time work. The children are not doing well in school lately, and the school social worker is afraid that they are being overly disciplined by Mrs. Armez and her husband.

EXAMPLE 1: Generalist with Mrs. Armez (Client System)

Worker:	Good afternoon, Mrs. Armez. My name is Katherine Brown. I understand Rev. Growth suggested that you get in touch with us.
Client:	Yes, he thought you might be able to help me.
Worker:	I'd be glad to work with you, Mrs. Armez. Where would you like to begin?
Client:	I'm not sure. It's just that nothing seems to be working out right now, and I don't know how to explain it.
Worker:	I can imagine that it isn't easy for you to begin to talk with me. Was it difficult for you to come in today?
Client:	I came right after work. I know my husband would be mad if he knew I stopped off here. I just can't let things go on the way they've been going these last few months.
Worker:	It sounds like you are under a lot of pressure right now. Am I right?
Client:	I'm so upset with all that's happening at home. It's too much for me to take.
Worker:	You're feeling very upset because you just don't know how to handle the many problems at home right now.
Client:	Yes, please understand, I love my children and my husband. It's just that everything is going wrong. He's changed since he lost his job. He can't get work, and he's mad that I'm working. I can't let my children starve. I iron for some people in the morning, and that helps a little. The welfare money isn't enough. He just doesn't care—I don't know how to reach him. He's drinking so much lately.
Worker:	I can see that you love your children and your husband. You're feeling confused because you can't understand your husband any more, and he doesn't seem to understand what you are trying to do. Is that it?
Client:	Yes, but—he's just a man, and in his country, women don't work. He's feeling bad he can't get work. I don't blame him.
Worker:	You are trying very hard to understand him. I can see that.
Client:	Yes, and it's not just him. The kids are sick a lot lately, and the school is saying they are not behaving themselves. I try to get after them, but they're getting so fresh. And that place where we live—it's getting worse. The landlord doesn't care. I try to clean it, but with my husband home all day—I'm tired of fighting with them.

Worker:	Mrs. Armez, I hear you mentioning many problems that you are facing right now—your husband can't find a job and you're worried about his drinking, your children are often sick and having troubles in school lately, you are not pleased with where you are living, and you and your husband and children are not getting along. I can understand that you are feeling overwhelmed because you can't handle all of these problems by yourself.
Client:	(Shakes head and begins to sob.) I can't deal with it. It's just too much. I need some help.
Worker:	I can see that you are feeling very helpless because you can't change the situation, and you want some help with trying to deal with it all. What is it that you are hoping for, Mrs. Armez?
Client:	If only things could be different. I wish Hector could go back to work. He liked where he was, and we were getting along fine. And I wish the kids weren't so sickly and that they would mind in school. I guess I just want things the way they were. Maybe we should move away but how? It's just so bad right now. If only something could be done.
Worker:	I'll be glad to begin to work on it with you, Mrs. Armez. We can't tackle all of these problems at once, but we can take one at a time to see what can be done. But first, would you please talk a little more about the situation with me so that I can understand it better?

In this case vignette, the generalist began with introduction and reviewed the purpose for Mrs. Armez's coming. She gave the client time and encouragement to express her feelings about coming and moved on to clarify problems, feelings, and goals. With the identification of so many problems, the feelings and goals remain at a very broad level until further information can be obtained and until problems are prioritized.

The worker will need to offer Mrs. Armez much support as the procedure moves into data collection. The worker will need to know information to answer such questions as, Why was the husband laid off? How does he perceive the family problems at this time? What are the children's health problems and behavioral problems? How involved is the school or any other agency with the family? When did each problem begin? How motivated are family members to work for change? These questions all fall within an ecological framework for data collection, which will be presented in the next chapter.

The generalist working with the family would use the General Method for working with several interlocking systems. The target and action systems to be contacted could include employment agencies, hospital and health services, the school, the city's Income Maintenance Department, the landlord, housing authorities, programs for alcoholics, shelters for battered wives, protective services, and other agencies or social institutions.

EXAMPLE 2: Generalist talking with the Manager (Bill Jones),
the Personnel Director (Tom Wilson), and, later, the Foreman (Joe
Casey) of the factory where Mr. Armez had been employed (Target
System)

(This interview takes place after the worker had met with Mr. Armez in his home
and received from him permission to talk with his employer.)

Worker:	Good morning. I'm Katherine Brown, a social worker from Unity Social Service Department. I've asked to meet with you to discuss Mr. Armez, one of your past employees. I understand Mr. Armez was not accepted back to work after he recovered from his hospitalization. Is that correct?
Personnel Director:	Yes, Mr. Armez was only with us about a year before he took off, and we had to hire someone else.
Worker:	I see. Mr. Armez wasn't with you very long before he took a sick leave. Let's see. I believe Mr. Armez said he began to work here in October of last year, making it 14 months of employment before he requested a sick leave. Is that correct?
Manager:	I'll tell you, Miss Brown, quite honestly, the company had some concerns about taking him back. We didn't think he was able to work at the level we expect of our employees.
Worker:	I appreciate your honesty, Mr. Jones. You're saying that Mr. Armez wasn't accepted back because the company feared he wouldn't be able to do the work expected. May I ask why you thought that?
Manager:	Well, let's see—do you remember, Tom?
Personnel Director:	Yes, I believe we even had questions about his performance before he took off. Let's check with Joe about that. Joe Casey was the foreman over Mr. Armez. Could we get him up here, Bill?
Manager:	(calls on phone)
Worker:	Thank you for trying to trace this back for me.
Manager:	What's the matter, Miss Brown? Hasn't he found work anywhere else?
Worker:	No, he hasn't. I understand he liked his work here and thought he was doing a good job.
Manager:	Here's Joe. Let's find out how he was doing. Joe, this is a local social worker asking about Hector Armez. Do you remember who he is?
Foreman:	Oh yeah, the Spanish guy. He had to leave for some kind of operation, I think.
Worker:	He had trouble with his arm and needed to be hospitalized for an operation.
Personnel Director:	Joe, his performance on the job wasn't that great, was it? We thought it wouldn't be wise to take him back at the time. Do you remember?

Foreman:	I don't know. He was with us about a year or so and was coming along OK. He was still learning. After he left, we needed someone on the machine. We couldn't wait forever. He had been out a lot, and I had given him a warning.
Worker:	I believe I hear three reasons for not taking Mr. Armez back: (1) He was out a lot, (2) you needed a replacement, and (3) there were questions about his performance level. Is that right?
Foreman:	Well, he was doing OK, but we just couldn't wait that long.
Manager:	And, you know, after being in the hospital and all, maybe he wouldn't be able to man that machine. It's heavy work we do here.
Worker:	There was some risk involved in taking him back?
Manager:	Well, we take risks, but not if we can avoid it. We needed to keep the machines going, and we couldn't count on him.
Worker:	I see. You needed to keep the machines going. May I ask how your personnel policy addresses the need for sick leave?
Personnel Director:	Our employees can take a sick leave when they need it, but we get concerned when it's a new man and he's out a lot.
Manager:	We often get new people, like Armez, who just want to take off a few weeks—or even a summer—and, we can't be bothered with them.
Worker:	It sounds as if you really doubted that Mr. Armez had to leave for medical reasons because he's a member of a certain group of people.
Manager:	Listen, Miss Brown, I don't have anything against Spanish people or any other group of people. We just didn't want to take him back. You heard the foreman say we gave him a warning for his absenteeism, and he continued to take off.
Worker:	I understand that you didn't want to take him back at the time, and I can see that it's not easy to talk about this. I really don't want to cause any difficulty, but I would like to try and see if there is any way that Mr. Armez could come back to work here. I can understand your limitations in keeping someone who misses a lot of work. Could you tell me how many days did he miss while he was working here?
Personnel Director:	I'll have to review his file to find out the exact number of days he wasn't here.
Manager:	Why are you so concerned about him, anyway? Is he asking for welfare? What do you want from us?
Worker:	I am working with the family while Mr. Armez is trying to find employment. Mr. Casey, the foreman, says that Mr. Armez was doing OK on the job, but he was out a lot. I know Mr. Armez had a health problem that needed medical attention. Apparently, Mr. Armez did not have the opportunity to show that he was better after his hospitalization. I hear that your personnel policy does have sick leave written in it, yet Mr. Armez was not given the chance to come back. What

I'm hoping is that there will be some way that we can work together toward giving Mr. Armez the opportunity to return to work here.

Manager: What is he able to do now? Can he take on a heavy job?

Worker: The doctor said he could return to work two weeks after the operation.

Manager: We never saw any doctor's statement. I don't know. We'll have to talk more about it here at our next administrative meeting. I'll meet with you again early next week. No promises.

Worker: All right. I hope we will be able to work together on this.

Manager: We'll see what we can do. I'll need that doctor's statement. Why don't you set up another appointment with my secretary for early next week.

In this vignette, it is obvious that the worker needed to have some basic facts (e.g., date employment began, reason for hospitalization, doctor's statement) to break through efforts at avoidance. She was sensitive to feelings and skillfully recognized them. Confrontation, with mention of legal action, was not needed at this time. Initial identification of problems, feelings, and goals took place. The worker would want to move on to clarify why Mr. Armez was absent, what the company expects of its employees, and what the stated benefits are that Mr. Armez could have expected from the company.

It is possible that a worker will not be able to get beyond the engagement stage with a target system. A worker, either alone or with other systems (client or action), may work toward bringing about change in a target system, even if the system refuses to engage in the process. Strategies may be implemented outside of the target to cause the change necessary for goal accomplishment. The worker may use the General Method to join with other resources and services to form action system.

EXAMPLE 3: Generalist and Doctor at Hospital Clinic (Action System)

(This interview takes place after the worker has received and delivered Release-of-information forms signed by Mr. Armez.)

Worker: Good afternoon, doctor. I'm Kathy Brown from Unity Social Services. Thank you for agreeing to meet with me to discuss Mr. Armez, one of your patients.

Doctor: Yes, Miss Brown, I hope I may be of some help to you.

Worker: Doctor, I am working with Mr. Armez and his family. Mr. Armez has not gone back to work yet. I am wondering about Mr. Armez's condition and his ability to take on a physically taxing job at J.B. Barnes Tractor Factory. I spoke with his employer, and there is hesitancy to take Mr. Armez back. One of the reasons given is their fear he will not be able to do the job because of his operation. Mr. Armez himself says he still feels some weakness in his arm, even though you said he could resume work a few weeks after the operation. I understand that the work Mr. Armez would do calls for heavy lifting and pulling on an

	assembly line that makes tractors. I am wondering if Mr. Armez is able to take on this kind of work, and I would appreciate your professional assistance.
Doctor:	Yes, I'm sorry to hear that Mr. Armez hasn't gone back to work yet. There was a growth on the arm that had to be removed. It was not malignant, and when the wound healed, he was discharged from the clinic. I was not aware that Mr. Armez was continuing to feel weakness in the arm. It could be simply because it hasn't been used for a while and it needs exercise.
Worker:	I see. The employer has requested a written medical statement about Mr. Armez's ability to work.
Doctor:	I am concerned that Mr. Armez continues to feel weakness in his arm. I would be glad to take another look at it, Miss Brown, and let you know what I find.
Worker:	I can see that you are concerned about the situation, doctor, and I am glad you are interested in working with me to help Mr. Armez get back to work.
Doctor:	Yes. If I find that he should be able to do the work, I'll be happy to write up a statement to that effect.
Worker:	I'll suggest to Mr. Armez that he contact you for an appointment and I'll call you after you have seen him. Is that all right with you, doctor?

Here too, the worker tries to engage a system in joint action as they work on the identification of problem, feelings, and goals. The worker senses the concern and willingness of the doctor to get involved in the situation. He doesn't get defensive, but agrees to reconsider his assessment. The worker recognizes this openness and moves quickly to initial goal setting. The doctor agrees to become engaged in the process and will proceed with Miss Brown in collecting data. This stage of the method would not have proceeded so smoothly if the doctor had to bring up policy constraints or rules and regulations of the clinic about taking back discharged patients. In this case example, the doctor as a staff member of the clinic apparently did not find any conflict in being able to cooperate with the worker for goal accomplishment.

As the worker continued to work with the Armez family and their multiple problems, additional client systems might emerge. It is possible she would begin to work with a community or a group that would include members of the Armez family. For example, it could become apparent that poor housing conditions are felt by many people in the apartment complex of the Armez family. A community effort by all of the tenants might be the most effective means to improve the situation.

It could be that the company would not take Mr. Armez back, and that Mr. Armez would tell the worker he knew of six other Hispanic men who were laid off since the company went under new management. The worker could meet with all six as a group, who might collectively agree to involve the Human Rights Commission.

With all of these examples, the generalist begins by engaging the system in the identification and expression of presenting problems, purposeful feelings, and desirable goals. As stated, the General Method is applicable to systems of any size.

Using the Holistic Foundation in Engagement

As the generalist begins to have contact with a system, and throughout the process of the General Method, the foundation knowledge, values, and skills (see Table 1–5, Chapter 1) are called into action. The perspective of the worker is pervasively ecological as he or she observes the matching and interacting of systems and carefully applies theories and skills to practice.

As pointed out in the examples in this chapter, the generalist demonstrates in words and actions an unfolding of the principles of acceptance, individualization, nonjudgmental attitude, purposeful expression of feelings, controlled emotional involvement, self-determination, and confidentiality.[18] In the engagement stage, relationship and problem-solving skills are readily applied. The worker uses skills in listening, responding, guiding, paraphrasing, and clarifying, along with skills for identifying problems, feelings, and goals. It is also possible, as in the target-system example, that some political skills may be needed. In trying to engage a target system in the initial stage of the General Method, the generalist may need to provide evidence, enter into bargaining, or propose legal action.

Knowledge about people, families, organizations, physical conditions, role theory, and stress theory is very helpful to a worker during engagement. In the case vignettes just presented, the worker used knowledge of people, their environments, and the interdependence of both as she formulated descriptions of the problems, feelings, and goals of the situation. Problems were seen as taking place at the interface between a system and other systems in the environment. Feelings and their reasons were related to a need or failure in matching expectations between client systems and environmental systems. Goals were generally described in terms of developing or enhancing the fit and transactions among systems.

The use of foundation knowledge, values, and skills from an ecological perspective continues as a generalist moves into the second stage of the General Method. As data are collected, the worker knows that in the evolving procedure of the Method, a refinement takes place in identifying and expressing problems, feelings, and goals—the three guiding landmarks of the engagement stage. Although each of the six stages of the General Method has its own particular landmarks to guide the worker and system, the elements of foundation and the landmarks of earlier stages remain present and are called upon throughout the procedure.

Human Diversity in Engagement

Culture

As stated earlier, a sensitivity to human diversity may be demonstrated within each stage of the General Method of social work practice. During engagement, for example, as a worker and a client system begin to identify purpose, problems, feelings, and goals, an awareness of the culture of the system can help the worker to create an atmosphere of understanding and responsiveness. Care can be demonstrated even in the selection of place for the initial contact. To foster a sense of security and trust, it may be more appropriate for the worker to meet with members of a particular cultural system outside of the office or agency. For example, outreach in the neighborhood and home visits have proven to be effective, especially within the Hispanic community.[19]

Members of ethnic groups incorporate knowledge of their ethnic history and personal experiences with people of diverse cultures as they relate cross-culturally. (*Cross-culturally* refers to systems of different cultures.) Consumers of services may view service providers and agencies from different perspectives, particularly if there are no apparent members of the consumer's culture in the service-providing system. Guardedness, hostility, fear, and defensiveness are often present when a system begins to have contact with a social worker from a different culture. Defenses vary according to ethnic backgrounds. Chinese culturally derived defenses, for example, include politeness, quietness, and friendliness when the individual is confronted with potential threatening situations.[20]

In approaching a system and beginning to identify the purpose of contact, a worker needs to be sensitive to basic communication patterns, according to the culture of the system. To give and to expect eye-to-eye contact with American Indians or Asians, for example, would be insensitive, because eye contact is generally considered to mean lack of respect in these cultures.[21] Although a worker may feel more comfortable with informality toward clients (i.e., using first names, casual dress, attitude of friendliness), members of certain cultures, such as Asian-American and Afro-American, may need and expect a formal approach from a professional worker, at least initially. Asian-Americans are particularly uncomfortable with functioning in ambiguity. During first contacts, they need to have the purpose and function of a service clearly stated.[22]

In proceeding, the worker keeps in mind the time orientation of a culture. Urban blacks and Japanese may need time to build up a sense of trust and openness; by contrast, Mexican-Americans move quickly into relationships and decision making, relying heavily on inferential abilities. Repetition and calculations are often unwelcomed by Mexican-Americans as they proceed with problem solving.[23]

Diversity is also found among cultures when it comes to identifying and expressing feelings. People from Eastern European ethnic groups, such as Poles, Hungarians, and Czechoslovakians, have strong feelings of shame over having to seek professional help.[24] Members of some ethnic groups are very reluctant to talk about personal feelings and problems with outsiders. This is particularly true of Asians and American Indians. On the other hand, members of Jewish and Italian cultures are often openly expressive of their feelings, needs, and problems.[25]

Problems or needs may be perceived and described from various perspectives, according to culture. For example, Chinese and Mexican-Americans basically see problems collectively rather than individually. The deviant behavior of one is seen as a direct assault on the pride of the community. Also, problems may need to be described in material rather than emotional terms. Pei-Ngor Chen found, for example, that many Chinese clients would only work on emotional problems if they were receiving concrete assistance at the time.[26]

Although a problem may come to the attention of a worker as a personal problem of an individual or group, a culturally sensitive social worker is cognizant of the fact that environments themselves, with their institutional pressures and prejudices, may really be the problem that needs to be addressed. In the engagement stage, a worker fosters a sense of openness when the person or people that make up a system can begin to see that the worker understands both the real problem and how they perceive and experience it.

Goals may be more clearly understood and articulated if a worker is aware of a culture's value orientation. The aspirations and goals of individuals, groups, families, and communities usually reflect the values that have been transmitted through their culture.

The values of *person, family, tribe,* and *community* are commonly upheld by several cultures. There may be, however, discrete meaning for such values in particular groups. For example, although individualism is valued by both Puerto Ricans and the American majority, there is a distinction that should be realized by social workers as they begin to work with Puerto Ricans. Joseph Fitzpatrick offers the following clarification:

> The basic value of Puerto Rican culture, as of Latin cultures in general, is a form of individualism which focuses on the inner importance of the person. In contrast to the individualism of the United States, which values the individual in terms of his ability to compete for higher social and economic status, the culture of Puerto Rico centers attention on those inner qualities which constitute the uniqueness of the person, and his goodness or worth in himself.[27]

An astute understanding of values helps a worker to locate what motivates members of the system and give direction on expressing relevant goals. Members of the Puerto Rican culture, for example, would be motivated to work on goals that appeal to personal responsibility and leadership, rather than those that appeal to platforms or programs.

Sexual Variation

Throughout each stage of the General Method, a social worker should demonstrate sensitivity to sexual variations. During engagement—for example, as purpose and problems are identified—the worker shows respect and acceptance by beginning where the client system is. The worker should focus on only those problems and needs that the client system wishes to address. When a worker knows that an individual is gay or lesbian, there must not be a hidden agenda on the worker's part, in which he or she expects to discuss (or to change) the lifestyle of the individual. If the client system is having difficulties that relate to sexual orientation, a worker may begin to be helpful by making known that he or she is aware of the pressures and problems gay and lesbian persons often have to face in American society. As generally found in helping relationships, a client is usually more comfortable by beginning with external problems (related to societal institutions, policies, and practices). Eventually, problems that are more interpersonal (primary relationships, for example) and then more intrapersonal (dual identities, self-esteem, fears) may be shared.

During engagement, a worker encourages and accepts a client's expression of feelings. For gay or lesbian clients, these feelings may include loneliness, alienation, isolation, hurt, and anger and outrage toward a rejecting, condemning family or society. A worker who becomes defensive or judgmental will be indicating a lack of self-awareness and sensitivity to the needs of the client system. Through supervision, the worker may begin to see that he or she has homophobic tendencies and should discuss the possible need to refer the client to someone else.

As initial goals are stated during engagement, the worker carefully listens and articulates the aspirations and expectations of a client system. If the worker cannot support the goals of a client in any way, this circumstance should be recognized and resolved before proceeding into the second stage of the General Method. As with members of other minority groups, the problems faced by those who are gay or lesbian are frequently caused by discriminatory practices of large institutions. Goals, therefore, are often long-range, social-change goals as well as personal, immediate-need goals. The worker takes time throughout the Method to engage the system in the process of realistically stating, understanding, and refining long- and short-range goals, which may be personal, interpersonal, institutional, or societal in nature.

Gender Sensitivity

With each stage of the General Method, a social worker may also indicate sensitivity to gender diversity. In engaging a system in the first stage of the Method, a worker begins with an awareness of the sex of those in the system as well as of his or her own sex. If there is a gender difference, the sensitive worker is attuned to the way in which he or she is being perceived by the system.

If, for example, the system of contact is a man or a group of men who are strongly identified with the masculine, "macho" role, and if the worker is a woman, it may be difficult initially for the man or men to see the social worker as a unique individual with expertise in problem solving. In engagement, as the worker proceeds with the process of identifying problems, feelings, and goals, he or she may find it equally difficult for men to express or to admit that they have problems and feelings. There may also be hesitancy in articulating goals to be worked on collaboratively with a female.

If the system of contact is a woman or a group of women who are strongly identified with the female, dependent role, it may be difficult for the worker to engage the woman or women in a shared, problem-solving process, particularly if the worker is male. Time and skill will be needed in either case for the worker to create an open, trusting atmosphere of mutual respect and interdependence.

During engagement, a worker would also be mindful of the other diversity variables identified in Chapter 3 under the headings of "person," "in," and "environment." These include the age and stages, endowment and personality, value system, class, and geographic location of the system receiving service.

Engagement in Diverse Field Areas

Each chapter of this text that describes one of the six stages of the General Method (Chapters 4 through 9), contains a section that has case examples from diverse areas of the field of social work. Examples are selected from the areas of child welfare, gerontology, public social welfare, community services, education, corrections, and homeless shelters. The examples demonstrate the apparent applicability of the General Method, with its six stages and major focal points for each stage, in all areas of the field of practice. Although the persons, problems, and needs addressed in each example relate directly to a specific field area, the General Method is used by all of the workers.

In the following section, the application of knowledge and skills during the *engagement stage* of the General Method will be demonstrated by entry-level generalists in six diverse field areas.

I. Field Area: Child Welfare
A. Agency: State Department of Children's Services
B. Client System

> *K is a 15-year-old female of French-American ethnicity. The police referred her to Children's Services two and a half years ago because she was physically abused by her mother. K had also been sexually abused by her stepfather on two occasions. She was committed to the state and placed in a group home, where she lived for over two years. She then requested and was placed in foster care. After two months in a foster home, K ran away. The police picked her up and placed her in an emer-*

gency shelter. She was at the shelter when the case was assigned to a new worker from the State Department of Children's Services.

C. Engagement

Problem: *During engagement, K said she knew she had two problems: (1) She had no place to go to live, and (2) she was missing school. She said she did not want to return to her foster home, but would not say why she ran away. She shared that she had run away with a boyfriend, who left her after a few days. K spoke about hating herself and knowing that no place or school would want her. She described herself as "dumb" and "ugly." During engagement, the worker identified additional problems. These included the personal problems of (1) poor self-esteem, (2) identity confusion, (3) problems concerning her sexuality and how to relate to males, and (4) depression.*

Feelings: *K expressed feelings of nervousness and loneliness. She said she knew she was "jittery" and just couldn't settle down to anything. She also said that she "hated" her mother and stepfather and never wanted to see them again. She wished she could live with her "real father."*

At one point, K began to cry and left the room. When she returned, the worker identified feelings of pain and depression. K admitted that she was "really down" and believed that no one really cared if she lived or died. She said that her "rotten boyfriend" got tired of her, even though she "gave him everything," and she knew her parents couldn't stand her either.

Goals: *K's stated goals were (1) to obtain and maintain a permanent placement* (permanent placement *means a place to live until adulthood), and (2) to get back into school as soon as possible. K said she wanted to leave the shelter but didn't know where to go. She thought she would like to go back to the group home where she had lived before she had been placed in the foster home. The worker hoped that K would eventually see the need for help with her more personal problems, although K was not ready to discuss this need at the time of engagement.*

D. Charted Progress

By the end of the engagement period, the worker recorded the items in Table 4–2 to begin to chart a formal plan of action (explained in detail in this chapter). The date of contact, the problems identified at the time by the worker or the client, and the goals mutually agreed on by both K and the worker were listed as in Table 4–2.

II. Field Area: Gerontology

A. Agency: Seaside Nursing Home

B. Client System

Mrs. J is an 80-year-old Portuguese woman who was admitted to the skilled-nursing facility at Seaside Nursing Home two weeks ago. She

TABLE 4-2. Initial Recording

DATE IDENTIFIED	PROBLEM/NEED	GOAL
1/12	No permanent home	a. To obtain a perma-nent placement
		b. To maintain a per-manent placement
1/12	Out of school	c. To reenter school
1/12	Personal problems a. Poor self-esteem b. Identity confusion c. Sexuality (relation-ships, behavior) d. Depression	

was released from the hospital with a diagnosis of "organic brain syndrome." The summary from the hospital social worker indicated that Mrs. J was a housewife with no formal education. Her family refused to be involved with her and left no name or address for contact. Mrs. J cannot remember where members of her family live. At the nursing home, she remained seclusive and appeared to be afraid to leave her room. An entry-level generalist was assigned to work with Mrs. J to help her adjust to the nursing home.

C. Engagement

Problem: During the first interview, Mrs. J expressed displeasure with her placement in the institution. She said she did not like it at the nursing home and wished she could go somewhere else. She did not respond when asked where she would like to go. Mrs. J could not speak English fluently, and wished there was someone who could speak Portuguese with her. She said she was afraid that if she left her room, her things would be stolen. She would only leave her room if someone came to take her to the dining room for meals.

Feelings: Mrs. J began to express feelings of distrust, anger, and abandonment. She did not feel comfortable in a cross-cultural environment. Whenever the worker began to talk about where Mrs. J came from or where she would like to go, Mrs. J became quiet and looked very sad and hurt. She would shake her head and look out the window. During the second interview, she said she had three children but they all had gone away and left her. She would not talk about her husband.

Goals: Mrs. J said that she wished she were able to go out on her own. She realized that she had first to be able to leave her room before she could go anywhere else. She did not think she liked the people at the nursing home, but was willing to meet twice a week with the worker to talk about how she was getting along. She said she hoped that someone who spoke Portuguese would come to see her.

The goals for Mrs. J that were agreed on by herself and the worker during engagement were the following:

1. To be able to leave her room on her own
2. To have someone who speaks Portuguese visit with her
3. To get to know the staff and resources of the nursing home.

D. Charted Progress

The worker charted progress at the end of the engagement stage, identifying dates, problems, and goals as shown in Table 4–3. At this time, it was also possible to record the initial contract for biweekly meetings of the worker and Mrs. J.

III. Field Area: Public Social Welfare

A. Agency: State Social Services

B. Client System

Mr. and Mrs. P and their two children, ages 2 and 4, arrived at the agency with their suitcase. Mrs. P's father had called the agency a week earlier, saying that his daughter and her two children had come to live with him, but he didn't have any room. He wanted "the state" to find housing for his daughter and grandchildren. He also said that his daughter and her husband were separated, but that her husband was waiting at their old apartment to take their AFDC check (Aid to Families with Dependent Children). Mrs. P's

TABLE 4-3.   Initial Recording

DATE IDENTI-FIED	PROBLEM/ NEED	GOAL	TASK	CONTRACT	DATE ANTICI-PATED
9/25	Poor adjust-ment: seclu-siveness— not leaving room alone	To be able to leave room alone			
9/25	Cultural iso-lation: need to commu-nicate in native lan-guage	To be visit-ed by someone who speaks Portugese			
9/27	Unfamiliar with staff and resources of the nursing home	To get to know the staff and resources of the nurs-ing home	To meet twice a week	Worker and Mrs. J	10/4 and every Tuesday and Thursday thereafter

father wanted the check held for his daughter, who would come in to pick it up. When the P family arrived at the Social Services unit, the case was assigned to an entry-level generalist.

C. Engagement

During the initial interview, because of the urgent nature of the situation, the problem, feelings, and goals of engagement were explored and specific data were collected. Preliminary assessment, planning, and intervention also took place during the first day of contact with the family,

Problem: *In this situation, housing was the obvious immediate problem. Because of repeated tardiness in paying their rent, the P family had been evicted from their apartment. Mrs. P thought that she and her children could find temporary shelter with her father. After two weeks, however, he said they would have to leave. Mr. P expected to take the money from their welfare check and return to Maine, where his mother lived. He said he had planned to send for his family once he got settled. At this time, however, Mr. and Mrs. P said that they decided they would prefer to find another apartment locally.*

Feelings: *Mrs. P was feeling rejected by her father and blamed him for their current problem. Mr. P was angry at the state for not sending their check and food stamps. (After the initial call from Mrs. P's father, the check and food stamps had been held by the post office and were later returned to the central welfare office.) Both felt that no one really wanted them or cared. They appeared to be confused and said that they were feeling helpless and did not know what to do.*

Goals: *When asked what they hoped the worker could do for them, the P's said that they wanted him to find them a place to stay. The worker clarified his own role and said that he could assist them by locating temporary shelter, but that they would have to become active in searching for and in documenting their search for more permanent housing. The immediate goals agreed on by the worker and Mr. and Mrs. P were (1) to find emergency shelter for the family (short-range goal) and (2) to locate an apartment in the local or neighboring geographic area for extended residence by the family (long-range goal).*

D. Charted Progress

As the worker began recording for a formal plan of action, the basic information obtained through engagement was charted as in Table 4–4.

TABLE 4-4.   Initial Recording

DATE IDENTIFIED	PROBLEM/NEED	GOAL
9/28	Housing for P Family	a. To find emergency shelter for the P family
		b. To locate an apartment for long-term residence by the family

IV. Field Area: Community Services
A. Agency: Clayton Neighborhood House
B. Client System

> *Mrs. T lives with her husband and three children in a one-room apartment at 33 L Street. She came to Clayton House to request clothing for her children and to complain about the lack of heating in their room. She informed the worker that there were three other Hispanic families in their building who also were without heat. None of the adults in the four families spoke English. A Spanish-speaking entry-level generalist went out and visited all four families. They met to organize and work together to obtain heating in their homes.*

C. Engagement

> *Mrs. T was encouraged to express her problems, feelings, and goals when she met with the worker. Her initial request for clothing was granted on the same day at the first interview. She was directed to the clothing room at Clayton House and told to take whatever she needed.*
>
> *After the worker and Mrs. T talked together about the heating problem, the client system in this case expanded to include members from the other three families who shared the problem. Before trying to resolve the issue with Mrs. T, the worker wanted to meet with the others who were experiencing the problem and to find out more about the situation. After visiting each family individually in their apartments, the worker met with members of all four families in Mr. and Mrs. T's room. Together, they began to identify problems, feelings, and goals.*
>
> Problem: *The basic problem identified during the engagement period was the lack of heat on the second floor of the L Street apartment building. All of the residents who met with the worker lived on the second floor. They said that they had had very little, if any, heat over the past month. There were some nights when the temperature dropped below freezing, and the only means of keeping warm was to turn on all of the burners and the ovens of their stoves.*
>
> *When the worker inquired about the residents on the first floor, she was told that they do not have a heating problem. They were described as "English speaking," and it was felt that they received better treatment from the landlord.*
>
> Feelings: *The community of residents who met with the worker shared feelings of frustration and victimization. They felt helpless and angry. They did not think that their landlord listened to them or cared about what happened to them. They were afraid that if they put pressure on the landlord, he would evict them and they would not be able to find another place to live.*
>
> Goal: *All present agreed that something had to be done. They asked the worker to help them. A mutually agreed-on goal was to get their apartments heated. They wanted assurance that heating would be provided consistently throughout the winter.*

TABLE 4-5.   Initial Recording

DATE IDENTIFIED	PROBLEM/NEED	GOAL
12/3	Lack of heat on second floor	To obtain consistent, adequate heating for second floor residents of L Street apartment house.

D. Charted Progress

The worker recorded the basic information obtained during engagement as outlined in Table 4–5. She saw a possible problem of discrimination by the landlord, but decided to wait until further data were collected before recording the problem in the record.

V. Field Area: Education
A. Agency: Keeney Elementary School
B. Client System

Jim G is an 8-year-old black child in third grade. His teacher referred him to school social services because he began to miss school or to come late each morning. His behavior was becoming increasingly inappropriate. He often kept his head down on his desk and remained silent when his teacher called on him. He no longer raised his hand in class or showed any interest in learning. His grades were beginning to drop, and his teacher feared he would get so far behind in his work that he might have to be moved to a different classroom. The teacher also noted that Jim was not eating his lunch. These behaviors were not apparent until the second month of the school year. An entry-level generalist was assigned to talk with Jim and to make a home visit.

C. Engagement

Problem: *When Jim entered the worker's office, he sat at the table and kept his head down. The worker asked if he knew why she wanted to see him, and he shook his head negatively. She reviewed his teacher's concerns and assured Jim that the people at school wanted to try to help him so that he would not get behind in his schoolwork. The worker wondered if Jim could talk about what was bothering him lately. Jim didn't answer, but got up and walked over to the bookcase containing toys and games. He asked who the toys were for, and the worker explained that any of the children who came to the office could use them. Jim took out the game Chutes and Ladders and asked if the worker wanted to play it with him. As they were setting up the game, the worker said that she could see that it wasn't easy for Jim to talk about what was troubling him, but she hoped that he would eventually. With his mother's permission, the worker began to see Jim twice a week in her office.*

After the first meeting with Jim, the worker visited his mother at home. Jim lived with his mother and father in a middle-class neighborhood. Mrs. G expressed concern over her son's regressive school behavior and said that she noticed that he was acting somewhat strange at home also lately. He wouldn't go to sleep at night unless his mother stayed in his room and kept a light on. She could not identify anything different or painful that Jim might have experienced since school began. She said that her son had done excellent school work when he was in first and second grade, and she could not understand what was happening to him to bring about the changes he was going through. She offered to work with the school in whatever way possible. She said that she would see that Jim got to school on time each day even if she or her husband had to drive him. Mrs. G agreed to come to school to talk with the worker again in two weeks.

The problems identified during the initial interviews with Jim and his mother were (1) school tardiness and absenteeism, (2) declining academic functioning (interest, participation, grades), and (3) refusal to sleep without his mother and a light in his room.

Feelings: In early sessions with Jim and with his mother, very little feeling was expressed by either of them. Jim avoided talking about anything personal. Mrs. G only expressed concern over her son's school performance.

Goal: Mrs. G and the worker agreed to work together to help Jim to improve his attendance at school and his academic performance. Both agreed to talk with Jim to try to motivate him to want the same goals.

D. Charted Progress

As the worker extended the engagement period with Jim and his mother, she recorded the initially identified problems as found in Table 4–6. She also recorded the goals and tasks that she and Mrs. G developed.

TABLE 4-6.   Initial Recording

DATE IDENTI-FIED	PROBLEM/ NEED	GOAL	TASK	CONTRACT	DATE ANTICI-PATED
11/1	Jim's school tardiness and absenteeism	Jim's regular school attendance (on time each day)	1. See that Jim gets to school on time each day	1. Mrs. G	11/5—each day thereafter
11/1	Jim's declining academic performance	Improved academic functioning (interest, participation, grades)	1. Talk with Jim about school problems	1a. Worker and Jim b. Mrs. G and Jim	11/6 and twice a week thereafter
11/2	Jim's getting to sleep at night				

VI. Field Area: Corrections
A. Agency: Juvenile Court
B. Client System

A group was formed for seven male adolescents, all age 14, who were on probation for burglary, theft of automobiles, or minor larceny (shoplifting). The usual probationary period was six months. If a youth attended and participated regularly in group meetings and met all of the other requirements of probation, the time of probation could be reduced to four months. All of the group participants knew that they were expected to attend weekly group meetings from four to six months, depending on when their probationary period would be over. A new B.S.W. female social worker was assigned to co-lead the group with an M.S.W. male worker who had worked in corrections for six years and who had specialized in social group work while in graduate school.

C. Engagement

Problem: The presenting problem shared by all of the youths was being on probation for illegal actions. Discussion centered on clarifying the problem. Was it being on probation or was it committing illegal acts? At this time, most of the group members saw the problem more in terms of having gotten caught rather than having broken the law. One member said that their basic problem was "law-breaking leading to probation." All agreed that this was a good way to describe it.

As group participants began to talk more about themselves, several other common problems began to surface. The youths were surprised to learn that all of them were in special classes in school because of learning disabilities. They all said that they had "bad tempers" and made some reference to problems at home. Two of the youths mentioned their drug habits.

Feelings: In early group sessions, members expressed strong feelings of mistrust, particularly toward the group leaders. Some members complained about having to come to the group but eventually admitted that they were angry really because they had gotten caught by the police and put on probation. They said that it was "dumb" of them to get caught. Members repeatedly indicated a sense of little self-worth.

Goals: The goal most clearly expressed by all of the participants was to get off probation as soon as possible. They also admitted that they wished they could stay out of trouble, but that it was not easy. They said, too, that they would like to be able to handle their tempers better. They expressed interest also in being able to understand more about "the changes" they were going through.

Although reference had been made to problems they were having with parents, there was not a general agreement that group members wanted to work on getting along better with their parents. They also did not like to talk about the fact that they did not think they were worth very much.

TABLE 4-7.   Initial Recording

DATE IDENTI- FIED	PROBLEM/ NEED	GOAL	TASK	CONTRACT	DATE ANTICI- PATED
10/1	Law-breaking leading to probation	To get off probation in four months	1. To attend weekly group meetings	Seven members, two workers	10/1 and each Monday at 4:00 P.M. for at least four months
10/1	Bad tempers	To learn to control tempers in school, home, neighborhood			
10/1	Need to understand "changes" of teenagers	To learn about "changes" youth go through			
10/1	Parent-son conflicts				
10/1	Low self-worth				

D. Charted Progress

The worker recorded the problems and goals that were identified by the group during the engagement period, as found in Table 4–7. She did not list the problems of learning disabilities and drug habits, because the youths were receiving help with these problems from other services. The preliminary agreement of group attendance and participation in order to get off probation was recorded in the columns called "task," "contract," and "date anticipated."

VII.   Field Area: Homeless Shelter

A. Agency: West End Community Shelter

B. Client System

José Gutierrez, a 37-year-old Hispanic male, came to the emergency shelter on May 7. He had gone to the County Department of Social Services for assistance and they referred him to the shelter. During his intake interview with the shelter social worker, an experienced B.S.W., Mr. G. said that he had been recently evicted from his apartment and that he was HIV positive. He had come to the mainland United States from Puerto Rico twenty years ago. He was divorced with no children.

C. Engagement

Problem: *Mr. G. told the worker that he had completed a drug detox program six years ago and thought he had put his life in order. He was working as a chef in a nursing home when he found out that he was HIV positive. He quit his job because he did not think he would be allowed to work in a kitchen. He did not realize that he could not be fired because he was HIV positive. He could not find another job. After his money ran out, he lost his apartment, and his friends seemed no longer to be interested in him. His immediate needs were identified by Mr. G. and the worker as for shelter, food, and health care.*

Feelings: *Mr. G. was feeling abandoned and depressed. He said that he had no place to turn and did not know what was going to happen to him. He knew he was not feeling well physically and was afraid that he was getting worse.*

Goals: *Mr. G. said that he would like to get medical help for his condition. He also said he needed a place to stay. He understood that the shelter had a 60-day limit and he would need some place to go after that. He wondered whether the shelter would keep him even for sixty days if his sickness got worse. He said he wished he could be working. He wanted to be able to pay for his food and lodging. Goals were identified as (1) to get medical care, (2) to locate housing (short- and long-term), and (3) to locate employment (part- or full-time).*

D. Charted Progress

The identified needs and goals agreed upon by Mr. G. and the worker were recorded (See Table 4–8). The worker knew that Mr. G. eventually would not be able to work and would need some other source of financial support. At the present time, however, Mr. G. was highly motivated and appeared able to engage in some type of employment.

TABLE 4-8.   Initial Recording

DATE	PROBLEM/NEED	GOAL
5/8	HIV positive	Medical care
5/8	Homeless/hungry	Immediate housing/food
		Long-term housing
5/8	Unemployed	Employment—part/full
	(No financial support)	Long range—public assistance/social security

Conclusion

In this chapter, focus was on the engagement stage of the General Method. The three focal points of problem, feeling, and goal were highlighted. Skills for working in these three major areas were pointed out. The use of ecological-systems theory throughout the stage was emphasized. The traditional purpose of social work, to enhance social functioning, was evident as the engagement process was described within an ecological perspective.

Case vignettes offered a demonstration of the use of skills, the ecological perspective, and the three guiding landmarks of the engagement stage. Examples described the work of a generalist as she began to engage a family, a business employer, and a health care service in the General Method. The use of foundation knowledge, values, and skills during engagement was discussed. Additional examples included cases from diverse field areas. Several ways in which a worker demonstrates sensitivity to human diversity during engagement were also described.

The expected timing of the engagement stage was not stated in this chapter because actual timing of any stage in the General Method is not clearly predictable. Sometimes a worker and system may move through engagement or any other stage in one interview. Sometimes it takes months, or as discussed, it may never be completed. The Method and each of its stages have an evolving, dynamic, and relative nature.

In the next chapter, the generalist will be seen in movement to the second stage of the Method, data collection. The overlap and natural flow from the first to the second stage will be shown. In the second stage of the systematic procedure, worker and system of contact take a deeper and sharper look at the issue, need, question, or difficulty brought forth for study and action.

NOTES

1. CSWE Commission on Educational Planning, *CSWE Curriculum Policy Statement* (New York: Council on Social Work Education, March 1981). p. 3.

2. Gordon Hearn, *The General Systems Approach: Contributions Toward an Holistic Conception of Social Work* (New York: Council on Social Work Education, 1969), p. 69.

3. Felix P. Biestek, S. J., *The Casework Relationship* (Chicago: Loyola University Press, 1957), p. 33.

4. Ibid., p. 48.

5. Harold D. Werner, "Cognitive Theory," in Francis J. Turner, ed., *Social Work Treatment: Interlocking Theoretical Approaches,* 2nd ed. (New York: The Free Press, 1979), p. 243.

6. Robert R. Carkhuff and William A. Anthony, *The Skills of Helping: An Introduction to Counseling Skills* (Amherst, MA: Human Resource Development Press, 1979), p. 243.

7. Bok-Lim C. Kim, "Casework with Japanese and Korean Wives of Americans," *Social Casework* 53, no. 5 (May 1972): 273–79.

8. From *You and Me,* by Gerard Egan. Copyright 1977 by Wadsworth Publishing Company, Inc. Reprinted by permission of the publisher, Brooks/Cole Publishing Company, Monterey, California, pp. 80–83.

9. Florence Hollis, "Casework and Social Class," *Social Casework* 46, no. 10 (October 1965): 466.

10. Ibid., p. 469.

11. David Hallowitz, "Problem-Solving Theory," in Francis J. Turner, ed., *Social Work Treatment: Interlocking Theoretical Approaches,* 2nd ed. (New York: The Free Press, 1979), p. 111.

12. Egan, *You and Me,* pp. 87–88.

13. Carkhuff and Anthony, *The Skills of Helping,* p. 79.

14. Kurt Spitzer and Betty Welsh, "A Problem-Focused Model of Practice," in Beulah Compton and Burt Galaway, eds., *Social Work Processes,* rev. ed. (Homewood, IL: Dorsey, 1979), p. 259.

15. Epstein, *Helping People: The Task-Centered Approach* (St. Louis: The C.V. Mosby Company, 1980), p. 125.

16. Werner, "Cognitive Theory," p. 244.

17. Epstein, *Helping People,* p. 133.

18. Biestek, *The Casework Relationship.*

19. Ted R. Watkins and Richard Bonzales, "Outreach to Mexican Americans," *Social Work* 27, No. 3 (May 1982): 246.

20. Doman Lum, "Toward a Framework for Wocila Work Practice with Minorities," *Social Work* 27, no. 3 (May 1982): 246.

21. Wynetta Devore and Elfriede G. Schlesinger, *Ethnic-Sensitive Social Work Practice* (St. Louis, MO: C.V. Mosby, 1981), p. 173.

22. Ibid, p. 194.

23. Jerome B. Kernan and Lawrende L. Schkade, "A Cross-Cultural Analysis of Stimulus Sampling," *Administrative Science Quarterly* 17 (September 1972): 351–58.

24. Joseph Giordano and Grace P. Giordano, *The Ethno-Cultural Factor in Mental Health—A Literature Review and Bibliography* (New York: American Jewish Community, 1977).

25. Mark Zborowski, "Cultural Components in Response to Pain," *Journal of Social Issues* 8, no. 4 (1952): 16–30.

26. Pei-Ngor Chen, "The Chinese Community in Los Angeles," *Social Casework* 51 (December 1970): 591–98.

27. Joseph P. Fitzpatrick, *Puerto Rican Americans* (Englewood Cliffs, NJ: Prentice-Hall, 1971), p. 90.

Data Collection

The social worker should respect the privacy of clients and hold in confidence all information obtained in the course of professional service.

—NASW Code of Ethics[1]

In the second stage of the General Method, information is gathered systematically for understanding and planning. When the information that the worker collects can be verified as fact, it becomes data. Demonstrating the scientific aspect of professional social work, the generalist uses research skills to distinguish fact from impression or assumption. Inasmuch as possible, the worker strives to acquire information that is factual in the data-collection stage of the General Method.

The worker organizes the collected data under the three categorical headings of (1) problem, (2) person, and (3) environment. Using an ecological framework, the generalist directs inquiry to find out about the problems presented, the persons involved in the problems, and the potential or actual resources and restraints in the environment that may affect the person-problem-environment situation.

Gathering Data

After an initial engagement period with a system, the generalist begins to collect specific information according to the three general categories cited. Workers may obtain information in a variety of ways. The most direct means of gathering data is through question and answer in a personal interview. Kerlinger describes the interview as "a psychological and sociological measuring instrument." He points out that a respondent's answers to carefully planned questions may be translated into measures and used as data.[2] Having begun to identify what information is needed for an accurate assessment, the worker also begins to plan how to formulate questions to be used in interviewing for gathering the needed data. Thought is also given to finding other possible ways for obtaining relevant information.

In addition to the direct approach of questioning in interviews with primary sources of information, workers may find answers through listening and observing. Whereas direct questioning may cause fear or defensiveness, skilled listening and observing may disclose the information needed without provoking anxiety or discomfort. A worker may find out if a mother has grown in patience with her child by observing their interaction at home. A group's interest in a particular problem may be identified by noting their reaction when the problem is mentioned in a general discussion. If a worker has any doubt about how he or she is interpreting what is seen or observed, further validation is to be solicited. Sometimes, formal testing is requested for precise information.

Data may be collected through secondary sources such as reading records, documents, and written materials, and also through verbal or written communication with outside systems. All data about clients should be collected only with the client's knowledge and permission. Before any information is obtained, written release-of-information forms must be signed by the client and sent to the sources from which information is being sought. An example of a release-of-information form may be found in Figure 5–1. What type of information is being requested and why the information is needed should be clearly explained to clients before a worker asks for information or a signature on a release form. If data are being obtained through a study of public documents (i.e., state records of births, marriages, deaths, etc.), no permission is needed. Only information that is relevant and necessary for an accurate assessment should be sought by the worker. It is possible that the system of contact will not allow the worker to collect information on some problems, and that the worker will, therefore, have to limit the focus of attention to those problem areas accepted by the client for study and intervention. If a client will not give permission to release information that must be obtained in order to proceed with a case, the worker may have to point out to the client that services will be terminated unless the information is made available.

Fact Versus Assumption

As a worker collects data, skill is needed to distinguish between fact and assumption. Interpretation of what is heard or seen may be influenced by the worker's frame of reference, past experiences, values, needs, and impressions. Through unconscious association, a worker may quickly assume that one word, description, or event is similar to another, and a label may be given that is actually incorrect. When a worker believes data have been found, he or she should ask: How is this documented? Did I really see this—hear this—find this?

FIGURE 5-1. Release-of-Information Consent Form

I _____give permission
(person giving consent)

for _____to release to
(system with information)

_____ the following
(system to receive information)

information:

_____

_____

_____

_____

_____

_____

I understand that _____
(system receiving information)

will use this information for the following purpose:

_____

_____

_____

_____

_____

This consent is to expire on   _____
                                         (date)

Signed _____   _____
                                                  (date)

Witness _____   _____
                                                  (date)

Agency representative _____   _____
                                                  (date)

Facts answer the question: Is this true or false? Assumptions, because they are not based on facts, may be either true or false. With assumptions, missing information is taken for granted. An activity to help refine one's skills for data collection is given in Exercise 5–1.

Exercise 5–1   Information

STORY

A woman was leaving the office when a man appeared at the door and demanded money. The secretary opened a drawer. The contents of the drawer were scooped up, and the man sped away.

If the following statement is true, circle *T*. If it is false, circle *F*. If the statement is an assumption, circle ?

1. A man appeared as a client was leaving the office.	T	F	?
2. The intruder was a man.	T	F	?
3. No one demanded money.	T	F	?
4. The secretary was the woman who opened the drawer.	T	F	?
5. The man took the contents of the drawer.	T	F	?
6. Someone opened a drawer.	T	F	?
7. Money was in the drawer.	T	F	?
8. The man ran away.	T	F	?
9. The man demanded money from the woman.	T	F	?
10. There are three people in this story.	T	F	?

In this exercise, all statements contain assumptions except for number 3, which is false, and number 6, which is true. The assumptions that cannot be substantiated by the words of the story are the following:

1. It is assumed that the woman is a client.
2. It is assumed that the man is an intruder.
3. (False)
4. It is assumed that the secretary is a woman.
5. It is assumed that the contents were taken (not just "scooped up") and that this was done by the man.
6. (True)
7. It is assumed that the contents were money.
8. It is assumed that "sped away" means "ran away."
9. It is assumed that the money was demanded from the woman and not from the secretary.
10. It is assumed that the woman was not the secretary.

These assumptions could be correct, but they could be incorrect also. In this exercise, the question mark should have been circled for 8 out of 10 answers.

A worker tries to tap all possible resources for reliable data before beginning to make an assessment. The validity of each piece of information is considered before an effort is made to categorize and to integrate information. If the worker recognizes that he or she is drawn toward making an assumption, the question "Why am I assuming this?" should be asked. It is possible that the assumption comes from one's "sixth sense," which may be a useful guide to tracking down the facts for a valid assessment.

The Problems

As stated earlier, when data are gathered, they are clustered under the three headings of "problem," "person," and "environment." The "problem" is the need, concern, issue, or difficulty that has been identified for study and action by both the worker and the system of contact. Before deciding what needs to be done, or even which problem should be considered first, the worker and the system need to have a clear understanding of the scope, duration, and severity of each problem.

What is the scope of the problem? How many people are involved in the cause or the effect of the problem? What other systems are feeling this problem? Where can the boundary be drawn between those who have the problem and those who are outside of the problem?

The worker also studies the duration of the problem. When did it begin? How long has it been going on? Has it been continuous or intermittent? The longer a problem exists, very likely, the longer it will take to break the pattern and bring about whatever change is needed. The shorter the duration, the greater the chance of quick and effective intervention.

And finally, the worker asks: How serious is this problem? A guide for understanding the severity of a problem is to consider it in terms of a life-or-death scale. If, for example, the problem is physical, the worker asks: Is the illness terminal? What is the potential for cure? If the problem is more interpersonal or social, the worker considers the possibility of its leading to the breakdown or destruction of the family, the person, the group, the community, or the relationship.

The Persons

Another major category for data collection is the person or persons who are experiencing the problem. A central concern is the coping capacity of the persons who have the problem. To what extent are the persons experiencing this problem capable of maintaining or improving their level of functioning? How have the persons been able to cope with this or similar problems before? Do the persons have physical, psychological, intellectual, economic, and spiritual strengths for dealing with the problem?

In addition to coping capacity, the worker seeks indicators of the extent of motivation the persons have to work on the problem. Do they express a desire to change the situation or to overcome the problem? Do they have hope that things can change? Is any person feeling anxiety, enthusiasm, fear, or pressure that is directly related to the problem, and can this serve as impetus for change? Where do the persons want to begin? Why there? If any person does not seem to have hope that a particular situation can change, why not? What could be a source for motivating this person? What does this person value or want?

The Environment

The third basic category for data collection is that of the environment that surrounds the persons and problems under study. What is there in the environment that could be relating to this person-problem-environment situation? An ecological foundation emphasizes the need and potential for transactions between organisms and their environments. Environmental factors, qualities, or systems may be present that could serve as resources. Currently, the persons may not be utilizing these resources, owing either to a lack of awareness or understanding or to a fear of rejection. To identify formal and informal resources, the worker gathers information from systems in the environment as well as from client systems. The person is asked, What have you tried before? Did you go anywhere or to anyone to receive help with this problem before? Explorations move from a consideration of the person's immediate environment, with informal resources of family, friends, and local community services, to a study of more formal resources, public or private, in the extended societal environment. The worker asks, What resources are available and appropriate to meet this need with these persons at this time?

In addition to gathering data on environmental resources, the worker looks for information about systems or circumstances in the environment that may have a negative influence on the persons or that may be a contributing factor to the problem. These too may be informal sources—family, friends, community—or formal systems, such as schools, hospitals, and organizations. Is the problem caused or compounded by the person's interaction or interdependence with the environment? More specifically, what systems of the environment relate to the person-problem-environment situation, and how do they promote or prevent the growth or functioning of the persons involved?

In summary, the worker asks, What is the scope, duration, and severity of the problem? Do the persons have the capacity and motivation to work on the problem? What resources or influences are there in the environment that could or do have an impact on the problem? After data are gathered in all three categories for each identified problem, the worker proceeds in the General Method to a collective, comprehensive study for preliminary assessments and problem prioritization.

Throughout all of the stages of the General Method, the skilled worker is recognizing and processing data. As with the identified problem and goals of other stages, the information collected is dynamic and changing. Newly acquired data may lead to a reformulation of the problem, goals, assessment, or planned intervention. It is in the second stage of the General Method that particular emphasis is given to procuring and documenting any information that is missing and believed essential for effective assessment and planning.

Maintaining Confidentiality

As stated earlier, throughout the process of collecting data, the worker demonstrates belief in the dignity of persons by respecting a client's right to privacy. The worker understands and upholds the principle of confidentiality when information about a system is requested, released, and utilized. Prior to receiving any information about a client, the worker must be sure of having the informed consent of the client. When requesting information, the worker has the responsibility to clarify why the information is needed, how it will be used, and who will have access to the data collected.

In interacting with client systems, the worker helps the client to understand the implications of sharing information. A client who comes to an agency for help is asking for service from the agency. Occasionally, a client may ask a worker not to tell "anyone," including other agency employees, what is being disclosed. In this case, the worker will need to point out to the client that information is shared with those in the agency whose roles relate directly to service delivery, such as supervisors, secretaries, or other service providers who are working on the case. This type of sharing is not a breach of confidentiality. It is in accordance with the Federal Privacy Act of 1974, which recognizes the need for information exchange among those employees of an agency "who have a need for the record in the performance of their duties."[3]

The client should be assured that information shared with a worker will not go outside of the agency without the client's permission. Exceptions to this (e.g., if the person threatens to harm another person or the worker, or if the record is subpoenaed by the court) should be stated also. Unless a state has privileged-communication statutes for social workers, a worker will be expected to comply if issued a subpoena requesting disclosure of information about a client to the court. A worker who receives a subpoena should consult with an attorney to discuss how information is to be disclosed or retained.

As stated, before requesting or releasing information about a client from or to a third party, a worker needs to have the expressed consent of a client. According to Suanna Wilson, ten conditions must be met if a client is to give his or her informed consent:

1. The consumer must be told that there is a desire or a request to release certain data.
2. The consumer must understand exactly what information is to be disclosed. He cannot intelligently decide if he wants it revealed unless he knows exactly what material is in question.
3. In order for the consumer to know what is to be released, he should actually see the material and/or have it read to him and explained in terms he can understand.
4. The consumer must be told exactly to whom the information is being released—name, position, and affiliation.
5. The client must be told why the information is being requested and exactly how it will be used by the receiving party.
6. There must be a way for the consumer to correct or amend the information to ensure its accuracy and completeness before it is released.
7. The consumer must understand whether or not the receiving party has the right to pass the information on to a third party. The consumer must have the right to specify that this not be done without his knowledge and consent.

8. The consumer should be fully informed of any repercussions that might occur should he (a) grant permission for the disclosure or (b) not give permission.
9. The consumer should be advised that his consent for release of information is time-limited and revocable. He should be advised how he can withdraw his consent and be given periodic opportunities for doing so.
10. The consumer's consent for release of information must be in writing on a "Release-of-Information Consent Form."[4]

Generally, workers are cautious in disseminating confidential information to outside agencies. There are times, however, when workers are somewhat careless in discussing the lives and problems of their clients. Occasionally, workers feel a need to let go of the heavy input received during interviews, and to find outlets during informal situations with family, friends, or colleagues. This is not only a serious failure in confidentiality, but also a failure to use supervision or other appropriate channels for ventilation and support.

As data are received, skill is needed in selecting and documenting information for the record. Clients have the right to verify personally the accuracy of information recorded in the permanent files of the agency. When a worker explains what will be done with the information collected, the client should be told about the kind of record kept by the agency and the policy regarding access to records. Discussion about records and confidentiality does not have to be prolonged enough to cause alarm or suspicion. A worker uses skill in determining when and how to talk about different aspects of confidentiality with a client system.

CASE EXAMPLES

EXAMPLE 1: Agency Boundary

Client: Miss Brown, there's a problem I'm having right now at home that I'd like to talk with you about, but I don't want Mr. Johnson, my husband's worker, to know about it. He would tell my husband, and there would be trouble.

Worker: I'd be happy to talk with you about any problem you may be having, Mrs. Armez, but I'm afraid I can't agree to withholding information from Mr. Johnson. Mr. Johnson and I are working as a team with your family, and we do share information. Is it that you are afraid that Mr. Johnson will discuss the problem with your husband?

Client: Yes, I don't trust Mr. Johnson. He sees my husband every week, and I know they talk about me. He would end up telling my husband what I said.

Worker: You are afraid of what would happen if your husband found out about the problem, is that it?

Client: Yes, I couldn't deal with it if he found out. It would be awful. Do you think Mr. Johnson would tell my husband?

Worker: Mr. Johnson and I talk together to help each other gain a more total understanding of the family situation. We respect what each of you shares with us, and we do not report back on what was said by one to the other.

Client: I don't think I could risk it.

Worker: I can see that you are troubled, Mrs. Armez, and I hope that you will grow in trusting us here at the clinic. I would like to see you get help with whatever is bothering you.

EXAMPLE 2: Release of Information

Worker: Mr. Armez, when I spoke with your employer, he said he needed a doctor's statement indicating that you are ready to go back to work. I understand that you had a doctor's examination last week. Is that right?

Client: Yes, I saw Dr. Gross last Tuesday. He said I could go back to work by Thursday.

Worker: Fine. In order for me to get a statement from the doctor for your employer, I need to have your consent in writing. I will indicate on this release-of-information form that the doctor's statement will be sent to your employer with a copy to be kept in our file. Is this agreeable with you, Mr. Armez?

Client: Yes, sure. That's OK.

Worker: All right. Let's go over what is stated here on this consent form before you sign it.

In the first example, the worker encourages the client to speak about her problems but makes it clear that what she says will be shared with the co-worker for the case. It is better to have the client hold back from sharing at this time than to have co-workers holding back information from each other. The honesty and concern expressed by the worker in this case help to strengthen the client's trust in the workers and in the agency. In the second case, the worker points out what information is needed, from whom, and for what purpose. The content of the consent form is carefully described and reviewed before the form is signed.

Recording Data

Because of the possibility of a client's misunderstanding or misusing information found in his or her record, one might ask why we bother to keep records. A worker needs to record data for several reasons, including:

1. To enhance service delivery through monitoring progress or regression
2. To account for services and to document need
3. To allow for easy transferability if a worker leaves an agency
4. To contribute to research leading to improved services

Each service agency has its own identified methods for keeping records. Three commonly known ways of recording in social work are (1) process recording, (2) summary recording, and (3) problem-oriented recordings.

Process Recording

Most agencies do not use process recording for their permanent records. This type of recording is a lengthy narrative that describes in detail the interactions and communications that took place during a single interview. This recording may be subdivided into four basic parts (1) presenting situation, (2) narrative, (3) worker's impressions, and (4) future plans. An example of a process recording may be found in Table 5–1. After stating the basic information of who, when, where, and why in the section called "presenting situation," the worker narrates what actually took place in the interview. This narrative should include not only what the client said but also what exactly was said by the worker in the sequence as it happened.

The third section of a process recording is for the worker's initial impressions of the person-problem-environment situation and of the worker-system relationship, based on what was said and felt during the interview. This is not a formal assessment of the case but, rather, a current indication of the worker's thoughts about the case and the interview. The worker tries to clarify what he or she thinks now about the persons, problems, and environment and the worker-system interaction that just took place. Impressions may include a consideration of how the worker thinks he or she conducted the interview.

In the fourth section of a process recording, the worker describes future plans for the case. He or she asks the question, What next? This section includes what the worker and the system have agreed on as the next step in the process, and any other actions the worker expects to take concerning the case.

Process recording is primarily a tool for supervision. It is submitted to a supervisor for review prior to a supervisory session. The supervisor reviews the record with the worker and indicates strengths and weaknesses in interviewing skills. The worker is helped to consider possible options or directions for proceeding with the case. Usually, process recordings are kept in a separate folder for the worker and do not become a part of the permanent record.

Summary Recording

Many agencies use a type of summary recording for their permanent records. Here, contacts for a period of time, generally not longer than three months, are summarized. In a summary recording, a worker follows a four-part outline similar to that of process recording. The topical headings used are (1) basic information, (2) content summary, (3) worker's impressions, and (4) future plans. The basic information given in a summary recording states the dates and places of contact, the persons interviewed, and the purpose for coming together. The content section highlights the topics and themes addressed during sessions, along with any major decisions reached during the period of time covered in the

TABLE 5-1. Process Recording

CASE OF MR. D

I. Presenting Situation

Mr. D is a 40-year-old black male who was seen by social services on 10/7 at his own request. He was presently hospitalized for surgery on his ankle, which did not heal properly. The initial injury occurred about a year ago, at which time, according to the patient, he fell off a ladder.

II. Interview

Mr. D was dozing when I entered the room but stirred and said he was willing to talk for a few minutes. I asked him how he was feeling following his surgery ten days ago. He stated that his ankle was better but his hip was sore from being in bed so much. It is still painful if he moves too much.

He then asked me what I had been able to find out about financial help, since he no longer had any health insurance and the money he received for Social Security Disability could not possibly take care of the hospital bills. I said that I had been in contact with our business office, which informed me that the necessary forms had been sent to the Department of Social Services informing them of Mr. D's need for assistance. I explained that DSS would contact him following his release to try to reach an agreement regarding his bills.

At this, Mr. D expressed his impatience over his hospitalization. He said he was anxious to be released from the hospital, feeling that he can sit in bed at home as well as he could here. When I suggested that perhaps he was still in need of special services that could best be delivered in the hospital, he replied that he was not receiving any special services that would keep him from going home. Mr. D stated further that he "doesn't trust" the staff. I asked him why he felt this way. He said the doctors did not tell him the truth when he was seen in the clinic prior to his hospital admission. He said he was left with the impression that they were going to break and reset his ankle. He felt that they knew at the time that more extensive surgery was possible, and that he should have been told about this. He was not informed of their decision to do a bone graft until the day he was admitted to the hospital before his surgery. I suggested that perhaps they had not made a definite decision until they had made a more careful examination of his X-rays following his visit to the outpatient clinic. I agreed that they could have informed him that this type of surgery was a possibility. Mr. D seemed to accept what I said and made no further comments on the subject.

I then asked Mr. D how things were going at home. He said that his mother, who lived in the apartment below, continued to take care of his two boys and that the boys came to see him almost every afternoon. Mr. D seemed a bit reluctant at this point to discuss his home situation in much depth. When asked about his divorce, he said that this did not become final until last April. Neither he nor the boys ever see his ex-wife. He stated that he had to fight to get custody of the boys but felt his wife didn't want them very much, since she makes no attempt to see them. Mr. D mentioned that during his past hospitalization his sister, rather than his ex-wife, had taken care of his daughter. I asked where his daughter was now, and he said that she had fallen through the ice at Carney Park and drowned last winter while he was recuperating at Rocky Neck Veterans' Home. I asked him how he felt about this incident. He said, while looking out the window towards the park, that his feelings did not matter. His concern was for his sons at present, particularly the older boy, age 11, who was with her at the time. When

TABLE 5-1. *Continued*

asked how he felt the boys were doing, he said he thought they had recovered all right, and things were pretty much back to normal. Mr. D seemed particularly uneasy during this part of our conversation, during which time he began fidgeting with his covers and gazing out the window. Since I did not feel that he trusted me enough at this point to explore his feelings any further, I closed this part of the discussion by saying that perhaps in time it would be easier for him to talk about it. He agreed by saying "yes."

I asked Mr. D if he would like me to come back again next week, if I could stop in for a few minutes to see how he was doing. I mentioned that perhaps by then he would be allowed to get up and around a bit. He added that he had hoped he would be home by next week but if he was still here, he wouldn't mind if I came to see him.

III. Worker's Impressions

My impressions of this client, and this interview in particular, were that there was a great deal to be discussed here, but that at the present time, Mr. D was reluctant to discuss many of his feelings with me. He was satisfied insofar as Social Services had met his financial needs. He did not seem to want the help that could be provided in a social work relationship, helping him to work at his feelings in many areas, including his hospitalization, his divorce, and his daughter's death.

IV. Future Plans

While the patient refuses to discuss his feelings and concerns regarding areas such as his daughter's death and his divorce at this time, he may open up after a few more interviews. I plan to see him again next week.

summary. The last two sections give the worker's impressions of what has happened over the period of time covered and the future plans for continued work by worker and system.

Problem-Oriented Recording

Problem-oriented recording (POR) is a clearly identified system of recording that originated with Dr. Lawrence Weed in health-care systems.[5] Several modified versions of this method are presently in use by many human service agencies.[6] Using a problem focus, recording usually begins with a list of all the problems identified to date, with an indication of when the problem was first recognized. For each problem listed, a brief assessment is given according to a "SOAP" format. The *S*ubjective data (according to client's perception of the problem), the *O*bjective data (as documented by testing, observation, and written and oral verification), the *A*ssessment (worker's judgment), and the *P*lan (immediate) for each problem on the list are stated in a concise manner.

For example, a problem listed for Jerry (15 years old, oldest of five children, both parents at home) was "below-average school performance—potential school dropout." The SOAP assessment for this problem was recorded as follows:

S—7/10: Jerry says he finds school boring, and he plans to quit when he is 16. 7/12 and 7/14: His teachers say he doesn't seem to be able to grasp the material, although he tries very hard.

O—Jerry's full-scale IQ is 80 (Performance 90, Verbal 70, WISC-R, 5/21/93). He repeated eighth grade. With current grades, he may have to repeat ninth grade. There is only one ninth grade at Brown Junior High, and it is geared toward students of average or above-average intelligence.

A—Jerry is finding school work difficult, owing to his limited intellectual abilities and his being placed in a class for students with average or above-average intelligence. He has a growing sense of inferiority and will probably drop out if he does not receive help.

P—1. Discuss Jerry's learning needs with Jerry, his parents, the school principal, and Jerry's teachers.
   2. Explore resources for tutoring and supportive services for Jerry.
   3. Explore other schools for Jerry.
   4. Work with all people in item 1 to provide Jerry with the learning opportunities he needs.

Prior to closing a case with POR, a "closing summary" for each problem is stated that includes (1) the status of the problem, (2) the prognosis, and (3) recommendations.

The problem-oriented recording method emphasizes the importance of organization and preciseness in recording. Information is recorded in a manner that is very available for research, documentation, and evaluation. The method offers a framework for immediate recall and immediate information provision. The worker is challenged to clarify problems and to progress in a skillful, accountable way. This recording method is particularly appropriate for general practice in which a problem-solving approach is used throughout the process of service.

Other Record Forms

In addition to the three types of recording cited, information collected on a case may also be recorded on fact sheets and in social histories or referral summaries. In most agency files, a basic fact sheet is found inside the cover of each record (see the example in Figure 5–2). Names of the family members and related resources, dates, addresses, and other factual information are often listed on fact sheets.

In social histories, a brief narrative is given for a variety of general headings. These include family composition, family background, developmental history, education, work, health, religion, economic history, other agencies involved, problem assessment, goals, and future plans. In a referral summary, the worker may add or delete any of these headings, depending on the nature and needs of the setting receiving the referral.

FIGURE 5-2. Identification and Summary Sheet

```
ADMISSION NO. _____ DATE OF ADMISSION _____ ROOM NO._____
PATIENT'S NAME _____ SEX _____ PHONE _____
HOME ADDRESS _____
               street                    town              state        zip
ADMISSION DATE _____ DISCHARGE DATE _____
PRIOR ADMISSION _____ ADMISSION DATE _____ DISCHARGE DATE _____
ADMITTING DIAGNOSIS_____
_____

FINANCIALLY RESPONSIBLE PARTY _____ RELATIONSHIP _____
ADDRESS_____ PHONE _____
POWER OF ATTORNEY        YES _____ NO _____                  home        work
NOTIFY IN CASE OF EMERGENCY _____ RELATIONSHIP _____
ADDRESS _____ PHONE _____
                                                            home        work
DATE OF BIRTH _____ AGE _____ PLACE OF BIRTH _____
U.S. CITIZEN _____ RELIGION _____ CHURCH _____
MARITAL STATUS: S M W D _____ MEDICARE NO. _____
SOCIAL SECURITY NO. _____ BLUE CROSS NO. _____
WELFARE: TITLE XIX NO. _____ OTHERS _____
ATTENDING PHYSICIAN: NAME _____ PHONE _____
ADDRESS _____
PREVIOUS PHYSICIAN: NAME _____ PHONE _____
ADDRESS _____
PHARMACIST: _____ PHONE _____
DENTIST: _____ PHONE _____
PODIATRIST: NAME _____ PHONE _____
FUNERAL DIRECTOR _____ PHONE _____
HOSPITAL PREFERENCE _____ PHONE _____
DISCHARGED DIAGNOSIS _____
_____

DISCHARGE DATE _____ TO _____
```

In any recording for permanent records or referrals, the information presented should be as factual as possible. Workers need to be able to document their statements and to substantiate their conclusions. If a worker is making a statement that is an assumption or an opinion, it should begin with such phrases as "It appears to me at this time that . . . because . . ." or "Based on . . . , my impressions at this time are. . . ." Accurate, effective recording calls for skill and sensitivity. As a worker collects data in the second stage of the General Method, it is essential that he or she have skill in recognizing and recording relevant, accurate data in a systematic and professional manner.

Working with Different Systems

Is there a difference in data collection when it is done with systems of different sizes? Are there variations in the techniques or processes used when a worker is gathering information about a group or community rather than an individual? How is information about a group or community kept confidential when it is frequently disclosed in the presence of several people who are not agency personnel? Is there a different method for recording information when working with a family, group, or community?

The size of a system does not alter the framework for organizing data under the three basic headings of "problem," "person," and "environment." The process and techniques used in collecting data, however, may differ when one is working with a larger system, such as a group or a community. Keeping in mind that the system of contact is made up of distinctive parts, the worker is sensitive to the needs and perceptions of individual members. Focus, however, is directed toward identifying the felt needs of the system as a whole. The worker tries to relate to the system in its entirety and to help its members to grow in an awareness of their common identity and concerns.

Techniques are needed to locate information of a common nature and to sift out uncommon information of a personal nature. To determine the problems, motivation, and capacity of a larger system, and not just of a few outspoken members of the larger system, is a major challenge for a worker. In the data-collection stage of the General Method, the worker tries to become aware of the problems, persons, and environmental resources and influences of the entire system. An effort is made to collaborate with the members of the system in collecting information. They are encouraged to distinguish fact from assumption, to be open to diverse perceptions and feelings, and to focus on common problems and needs.

Even prior to bringing the members of a system together to engage in a working relationship, workers frequently begin the process with a preliminary period of data collection by individual contact. Before convening the entire system, the worker needs to find out what constitutes the boundary of the system and to develop an initial awareness of its members and their felt needs. A worker will often speak with individual members of a family, group, or community to give them the opportunity to share freely and in confidence their perceptions of the system and its problems. This enables the worker to locate motivating issues and potential leaders for the system. Once the system and the worker start to work together for identified goals, they jointly collect data on particular problems, related influences, and resources.

Although the categories for data collection within the ecological framework of problems, persons, and environment are basically the same for all systems, the nature of the content addressed may differ. When working with a larger system such as a community, for example, the resources for and influences on the environment are generally of a formal nature. These may include foundations, federal and local policy makers, and organizations or their representatives. Information collected to be presented to these resources or influences usually has to be clearly factual with documentation. Although skill for recognizing feelings is strongly needed when collecting information with smaller systems, skill in acquiring and presenting facts is paramount in working with larger systems. Workers need to be aware of the general feeling tones of larger systems and their individual members, but change in larger systems is strongly dependent on documented facts. Members of an organization may be very sympathetic toward a cause, but they may not be able to change their larger structure unless there is documented evidence of the need for and value in changing the policies or procedures of the organization. With larger complex systems, the information collected is mainly of a formal, factual nature.

As mentioned, a person may be hesitant to speak out about issues or concerns in a large system. This hesitance may be due to a fear of reprisal later by other members of the system or by outsiders who have been informed of what the person said. Before they can develop confidence in sharing openly, members of a large system need clarification of what will happen when information is disclosed within the system. Although a worker may state how he or she and the agency will handle information obtained, the worker is not able to guarantee that other members of the system will keep in confidence what will be shared. Prior to encouraging the disclosure of information within a system, a worker makes an effort to get the members of the system to mutually agree on a code for themselves regarding how they will treat what is said at their meetings. This code should be restated or reconsidered whenever new members are added or there is some question whether it will continue being enacted.

CASE EXAMPLE

Group
Worker: Before we go on, I would like to talk with all of you about the confidential nature of what goes on in this group. As far as the agency is concerned, anything shared within the group is kept within the agency unless we all give our consent to have certain information shared outside. A summary of each meeting is recorded in the agency record, and any group member may request to review these recordings. The only exception for allowing information to go outside the agency would be if you revealed that you planned to injure someone or if I or our records were subpoenaed to court. Any questions about this?

Mary (group
member): Yeah, but what about everyone else here? How do I know that what I say won't be talked about out on the street by someone here?

Worker: Well, let's talk about that. What do we think about a group member sharing what is said here with someone outside of the group? How do you want to handle what is said during our meetings?

John (group
member): I don't think it's right to go and tell other people. We came here because we wanted help, but I don't want everyone in the world to know my business.

Worker: I hear you saying that you don't think members should talk about what we share here with others. I wonder what the rest of the members think about this.

Others: (Five others speak in support of John's position.)
Worker: Are we saying as a group that we will keep in confidence whatever
               is said within this group? Are there any exceptions to this?

In terms of record keeping, all of the three methods described earlier for recording data collected during an interview (process, summary, problem-oriented) may be used to record contacts with systems of any size. Whether working with an individual, group, family, or community, the worker records fundamental facts about the presenting situation (who, when, where, why), the essential content addressed during the contact (problems, needs, feelings, decisions), and the goals and plans that were established. In recording each contact or contacts over a period of time, a worker may also include his or her impressions of the person-problem-environment situation.

When recording about a large system, a worker needs to distinguish between what is recognized as a problem or need of one or some members of the system and what is seen as a common problem or need of the entire system. For example, when compiling the problem list for problem-oriented recording for a family system, the worker indicates when a problem belongs to one or some members rather than to the whole family.

CASE EXAMPLE

PROBLEM LIST

Active	*Date*
Father's unemployment	10/2
Inadequate housing	10/2
Father's drinking	11/3
Mother–father communication	11/3
Jimmy's sore throat	11/3

In this example, whereas the housing need is common to all, it is apparent that there are individuals within the family who have particular problems that influence the functioning of the entire family: The unemployment and drinking problems are the father's; mother and father have a problem with communication; and Jimmy has the sore throat.

In using summary recording to record an activity group session, a format may be followed such as that illustrated in Figure 5–3. Here again, the worker basically indicates the presenting situation, central content (activity, process, problem), the leader's impressions, and future plans. The recording format provides opportunity for the worker not only to describe the problems and behaviors of the group, but also to identify the problems and behaviors of individuals that influence the functioning of the group.

Making a process record of a community meeting may be extremely lengthy and time-consuming. The framework found in Figure 5–4 provides guidance for

FIGURE 5-3. Weekly Group Record

DATE_____

GROUP _____ LEADER _____

ATTENDANCE: TOTAL MEMBERS PRESENT — MALE _____ FEMALE _____

     VISITORS _____

BRIEF DESCRIPTION OF MEETING: Please record briefly important discussions, decisions, and problems. *Give your own evaluation of the meeting.*

WHAT WAS THE MAIN ACTIVITY OF THE GROUP AT THIS MEETING? Who initiated the main activity, and how did the group as a whole respond to the suggested activities? What program suggestions did you mention or bring up in the meeting?

SITUATIONS REQUIRING INDIVIDUAL ATTENTION: Please record problems, group or individual conflicts, and other incidents that you may want some help with from your supervisor.

LEADER'S INTERPRETATION REGARDING BEHAVIOR OF INDIVIDUALS: If there was any unusual behavior, why do you think the individuals and the group as a whole behaved as they did?

PLANS FOR THE NEXT MEETING:

---

highlighting important aspects of a meeting. Basically, the content addressed includes facts about the presenting situation, content discussed, and future plans and goals. The topics that are covered include how the worker perceived his or her role, before, during, and after the meeting, as well as the worker's impressions. This recording, as with all process recordings, may be used in supervision as a teaching tool. It lends itself to pointing out a worker's skill and sensitivity for working with communities.

FIGURE 5-4. Process Recording for a Community Meeting

I. Presenting Situation
Worker's name
Name of community
Place of meeting
Date of meeting
Who called the meeting?
For what purpose?
Number of people attending
Who were the people at the meeting? (Whom did they represent?)

II. Meeting
What took place? Topics, decisions, actions (including worker's), in sequence.

III. Worker's Impressions
How do the community members see themselves? See you?
Do they see themselves as a community?
What are your impressions of the roles and behaviors of participants?
What do they want to accomplish individually? As a community?
What do they want from you?
Did they and you come away with something as a result of the meeting?
How did you use yourself during the meeting?
How did you feel about the meeting—before, during, and after?

IV. Future Plans
What do they do now?
What do you do now?

Using the Holistic Foundation in Data Collection

In the second stage of the General Method, the social worker uses values, knowledge, and skills from the holistic foundation of practice identified in Table 1–5, Chapter 1. The practice principles of confidentiality, self-determination, and nonjudgmental attitude are strongly apparent in the actions and transactions of the worker during data collection. As pointed out, the client has the right to choose what personal information will be disclosed, as well as to choose how this information will be used. The worker strives to gather factual information for a documented assessment that is free from assumption or personal value judgments.

In proceeding in the helping process with collecting data about persons and environments, the worker uses various theories to comprehend the nature and functioning of client, target, and resource systems. Through observing and inquiring directly or indirectly, he or she obtains information in a manner that reflects the use of theories from the holistic foundation. Seeing the data collected in the light of basic theory, the worker is able to identify such characteristics as coping capacities, developmental levels, communication patterns, and role expectations. Theory also helps the worker to recognize whether certain factors are the cause or the effect of problem situations. For example, in inquiring about the time when 8-year-old Jim started to insist that the light be kept on in his room at night, the worker learned that it was around this same time that Jim started to have learning problems at school, to become increasingly possessive of his mother, and to act fearful toward his father. Knowledge of such theories as psychosexual and psychosocial development, as well as role and stress theory, helped the worker to pursue inquiry for understanding the regressive behavior.

The skills of the holistic foundation that are used in the data-collection stage of the General Method include relationship skills, problem-solving skills, and professional skills. In sifting out facts of importance for understanding and planning, the worker listens, questions, and clarifies. He or she may work with various systems to identify problems and needs or to collaborate in exchanging information for effective teamwork. Recording and research skills are used to test out and to register the findings collected.

Human Diversity in Data Collection

Culture

From an identification of problems, feelings, and goals in the engagement stage, the worker and system move on to gathering information for problem assessment. As a worker begins to collect information about problem, person, and environment, some cultural systems may be hesitant to give information about personal or family problems, particularly to someone from a different ethnic group. The worker, therefore, needs to be explicit in making known what information is needed and how it will be used. Whereas some systems may wish to move quickly through this stage, with reliance on intuition (Mexican-American, for example), others may need to move cautiously, with reliance on fact and reason (Japanese, for example).

To collect data on the actual participants in a problem-person-environment situation, it is important for a worker to understand the roles and structures in the culture of the system. For example, there is a "fourfold structural typology" found among Puerto Rican families. As described by Fitzpatrick, there are (1) extended family systems—a wide range of natural or ritual kin, (2) the nuclear family—father, mother, and children, (3) father, mother, their children, and children of other unions of the husband or wife, and (4) the mother-based family with children of one or more men, but no permanent male figure in the home.[7]

In locating resources or influences in the environment, a worker needs to know who or what resource would be appropriate to contact for certain problems. In the Puerto Rican culture, for example, there may be ready acceptance to have *compadres* and *comadres* (godparents) become foster parents if a child needs to be placed. To mediate in matters such as property disputes, however, it may be more appropriate in this culture to use distant relatives, in order to avoid the risk of losing friendships with closer relatives if they became involved.[8]

Sexual Variation

During data collection in the General Method, as the three focal points of problem, person, and environment are explored, the problems of gay and lesbian clients may be seen more clearly by a worker when the "dual perspective" is applied.[9] In gathering information about person and environment, a worker looks to see if an individual has a "nurturing system" as well as a "sustaining system" in his or her environment. The worker also considers the values and expectations of all three (individual, nurturing system, and sustaining system), realizing that the more they share in common, the greater their congruence, "goodness of fit,"[10] and mutual health and growth. Even if an individual is found to be different or nonacceptable by a sustaining system, he or she can grow and thrive, provided there is a strong, supportive nurturing system. Unfortunately, many gay or lesbian individuals have no nurturing system where they are understood and supported, and they live in a very rejecting, condemning sustaining system. Even if there is a family or cultural community, a gay or lesbian person may not be accepted by them because they reject his or her sexual lifestyle.

In collecting data, a worker inquires about a system's current and potential environment. When working on problems related to sexual variation with gay or lesbian clients, a worker gathers information not only about existing resources in the client system's life space, but also about possible formal and informal resources that could offer support for gay and lesbian persons in their environments.

Gender Sensitivity

In collecting data during the second stage of the General Method, a worker needs to have a sensitivity to gender when information about problem, person, and environment is gathered. Again, a man who believes he should be strong and successful may resist exposure of his personal, family, or social problems. He may withdraw from talking about himself at any length. His environment may be limited in nurturing networks. He may feel comfortable only when talking objectively about his work or society at large with its organizations and institutions.

Women may be in a protective, unknowing position in which they actually or apparently know little about the facts of and influences on their problem-person-environment situation. They may express feelings of helplessness and even fear of succeeding in resolving their problems. They may be struggling over a sense of being disloyal or ungrateful if they criticize or talk about their husbands or family problems. Guilt feelings may emerge if a woman begins to explore and reach out to her extended environment for support and strength.

In collecting data, a worker is also sensitive to the other diversity variables of age and stages, endowment and personality, value systems, class, and geographic location. The worker's skill in inquiry, use of informative resources, and in recognizing facts, custom, and feelings will reflect the extent of sensitivity the worker has to various dimensions of human diversity.

Data Collection in Diverse Field Areas

1. Field Area: Child Welfare
A. Agency: State Department of Children's Services
B. Client System

K, a 15-year-old female in an emergency shelter. (For more background information, see Chapter 4, Engagement in Diverse Field Areas, I. Child Welfare.)

C. Engagement Summary

The feelings expressed during engagement included loneliness, restlessness, hatred of self and others, and depression. The problems and goals identified during this stage are listed in Table 4–2 Chapter 4.

D. Data Collection

Problem: *During data collection, the worker learned that K was well-liked by those who lived in the group home where she was first placed. The group parents described K as quiet and fearful. She seemed to get lost in the group, and therefore, they thought a foster home was a good plan for her at the time. The foster home parents described K as stubborn and pouty. She never seemed to get enough attention and didn't want to do her share of the work. They said they tried to tell K to stay away from the boy she ran away with, but she would not listen to them.*

In school, K had been performing at an average level while she lived in the group home. During her stay in the foster home, she remained in the same school she had attended while in the group home. Her grades started to drop before she ran away. Her teachers said that K daydreamed a lot, but they thought she did have the potential for at least average achievement. As her marks started to drop, the school personnel had a pupil-appraisal team meeting. The Children's Services worker who had the case prior to the current worker attended the meeting. It was agreed at this meeting that K would be referred to the local mental health center for counseling. K refused to go to the center, saying she was not "crazy."

Person: *During data collection, the worker discovered that K was extremely motivated to work on her two stated goals. She said she missed school and even missed her teachers. She wished she could go back to the group home, where they were "nice" to her. K began to say that she knew that she was "messed up," and that she probably needed to go for counseling. She hoped someone could help her so she wouldn't feel "so awful inside." She thought that a boy at the shelter was starting to like her, but she was "afraid of getting too close." The worker at the shelter described K as "shy" and "noninvolved with the activities or residents of the shelter."*

Environment: *The emergency shelter had a residence time limit of four weeks. In exploring possible resources for K, the worker learned*

FIGURE 5-5. Ongoing Recording

DATE IDENTIFIED	PROBLEM/ NEED	GOAL
1/12	No permanent home	a. To obtain a permanent placement b. To maintain a permanent placement
1/12	Out of school	To reenter school
1/12	Personal problems a. Poor self-esteem b. Identity confusion c. Sexuality (relationships, behavior) d. Depression	Personal goals (1/19) a. To feel better about self b. To clarify identity c. To be able to have good friendships with males d. To stop "feeling down"

that K's biological father had moved out of state and left no forwarding address. K's stepfather had been taken to court for child sexual assault, and her mother blamed K for reporting it. K's mother did not want K to be returned home, "ever." There were no relatives interested in caring for K. K's foster parents did not want her to return either. Although there was no opening in K's previous group-home placement, the worker located another group home with an opening in a neighboring city. Services available for residents in this home included ongoing casework by an M.S.W. and weekly peer-group meetings, where discussions focused on such topics as "sex," "parents," and "growing up confused."

E. Charted Progress

During the process of data collection, goals were expanded to include K's expressed desire to get help with her personal feelings and problems. These new, mutually agreed upon goals were added to the two goals identified during engagement and were recorded as shown in Figure 5–5. Since the date when these goals were agreed on was different from the date of problem identification, the later date was recorded in the "goal" column.

Note: *The paperwork required throughout the process of working with K included the following:*

Summary recordings of all contacts with K and related resources

Referral summary for the group home

Case summary for the court in preparation for a petition to seek continuance of commitment

Transfer summary at termination

II. Field Area: Gerontology
A. Agency: Seaside Nursing Home
B. Client System

Mrs. J, an 80-year-old Portuguese woman in a skilled nursing facility. (For additional background information, see Chapter 4, Engagement in Diverse Field Areas, II. Gerontology.)

C. Engagement Summary

The feelings expressed during engagement included distrust, fear, anger, and abandonment. The problems and goals identified during this stage are listed in Table 4–3, Chapter 4.

D. Data Collection

Problem: *The worker attended a patient-care conference on Mrs. J with the staff of the nursing home. She learned at this time that Mrs. J was causing a disruption on her floor. She was fighting with the nurses when they came to give her a bath. She sometimes stood at the door of her room and called the other residents names. On occasion, she would refuse to go to meals or to leave her room. She was often found talking to herself in Portuguese. Also reported were minor incidents of confusion and irrational mood swings.*

Person: *As data were being collected, Mrs. J began to talk more freely with the worker about herself and her background. She said she came to America when she was 20 years old. She married shortly after arriving and had three children by the time she was 25. Her husband left the family when the youngest child was 13 years old. Mrs. J used to clean houses and take in washing to earn money. All of her children had to leave school and get jobs. She said she was "hard" on her children and wished she had been nicer to them. Mrs. J said she wished she could go back to Portugal, where she believes her husband is living. She could not recall the marriage names of her children or the name of her husband's village.*

Mrs. J began to express an interest in knowing more about the other residents. She said she yelled at them because they would not look at her. She was angry at the nurses because they tried to undress her for a bath late in the morning after she was up and dressed. She wished the nurses and the people would like her and agreed that she was willing to try to get along better with them.

Environment: *During data collection, the worker learned from the hospital social worker who made the referral to the nursing home that one of Mrs. J's daughters had admitted her to the hospital. During admission, the daughter stated that her father left the family several years ago and could not be located, and that Mrs. J had been living alone until she no longer could go out by herself. The daughter said that she was moving out of state and would send a forwarding address (which never arrived). She said that her sister and brother also lived out of state.*

The worker also learned that there was no one in the nursing facility who spoke Portuguese. The director of volunteers offered to try to locate someone who spoke the language and who would be willing to visit with Mrs. J. The worker learned from Mrs. J that she used to attend a church where the pastor and several members of the congregation were Portuguese. The worker located the church, and the pastor said he would go to see Mrs. J. Other resources available to Mrs. J in the nursing home included program planning, recreational therapy, choir, and church services. There were also weekly resident meetings that Mrs. J could attend.

E. Charted Progress

During the data-collection stage, the problem list was extended to include Mrs. J's disruptive behavior on her floor. The additional problems were recorded as indicated in Figure 5–6. Mrs. J's organic brain syndrome was not listed as a problem in the social service record because she was receiving treatment for this from the medical staff.

Note: *The recording required throughout the process of working with Mrs. J included the following:*

Intake summary

Weekly summaries of contacts with Mrs. J

Patient-care conference reports

Social service tasks, entered in the problem-oriented recordings of the nursing home

Record of outside contacts made and information obtained as data were collected

On-going contracted plan

Termination summary

FIGURE 5-6. Ongoing Recording

DATE IDENTIFIED	PROBLEM/ NEED	GOAL	TASKS	CONTRACT	DATE ANTICIPATED	DATE ACCOMPLISHED
9/25	Poor adjustment: seclusiveness — not leaving room alone	To be able to leave room alone				
9/25	Cultural isolation: need to communicate in native language	To be visited by someone who speaks Portuguese				
9/27	Unfamiliar with staff and resources of nursing home	To get to know staff and resources of the nursing home	To meet twice a week with worker	Worker and Mrs. J	10/4 and every Tuesday and Thursday thereafter	10/4 10/9 10/11 10/16
10/2	Fighting with nurses over bath	To work out bath schedule with nurses				
10/2	Calling residents names	To stop calling residents names				

III. Field Area: Public Social Welfare

A. Agency: State Social Services

B. Client System

Mr. and Mrs. P and their two children, ages 2 and 4, in need of emergency shelter and more permanent housing. (For more background information, see Chapter 4, Engagement in Diverse Field Areas, III. Public Social Welfare.)

C. Engagement Summary

The feelings expressed during engagement included helplessness, anger, rejection, and confusion. The problems and goals identified during engagement are listed in Table 4–4, Chapter 4.

D. Data Collection

Problem: *Shelter is a basic human need. There is a lack of available housing for low-income families in the local city and surrounding areas. Housing is a crucial need for the P family at this time. The P's have had several moves since their marriage five years ago. They have been evicted from apartments at least three times in the past because they failed to keep up with rent payments. The P's said that they had to use the money they received from AFDC to buy food. The worker also learned that they currently had no money left for food. The family receives AFDC because Mr. P's psychological problems prevent him from maintaining employment (confirmed by Income Maintenance Department's eligibility technician, who has letters from psychiatrists on file). The AFDC check and food stamps for the month are being held at central office until the status and address of the family are clarified.*

Persons: *Although Mr. P said he bought a newspaper to see if there are any available apartments in the area, he and his wife do not appear to be motivated to get involved in apartment hunting. They are anxious to be relocated, but they expect that others (the state or Mrs. P's father) will find a place for them. They are blaming others (the state, Mrs. P's father, landlords, friends) for their problem of being homeless. They express a strong dependency on others to meet their needs. They do not seem to have the ability or the desire to become actively involved in problem-solving or in changing their perspective or behavior. With Mr. P's written permission, the worker contacted his psychiatrist at the mental health center, Saint John's Hospital (where he had been treated), and also got in touch with the Vocational Rehabilitation Department (where he had been tested). Mr. P's mental illness and continued inability to work were verified. The psychiatrist said that Mr. P is faithful in keeping his weekly appointments at the center. The children appear to be in good health. Mrs. P said that it was about time for the children to go for a checkup at the health clinic, but that she had lost their medical card. She said the income-maintenance worker was sending her another one.*

Environment: *Mr. and Mrs. P said that they have no family or friends who are willing to take them in, even for the night. Mrs. P said she knew that her father was trying to find a place where she and the children could live.*

Three possible temporary shelters were located: (1) Salvation Army, (2) City Hotel, and (3) Center City Motor Inn. For more permanent housing, the worker contacted five social service agencies in the surrounding area. None of them were able to provide any information on possible housing. The process of making a Section-8 (rent subsidy) application to the Housing Department was reviewed.

During the initial period of data collection, the worker also explored possible resources for emergency food donations. The following sources were identified: (1) Community Renewal Center, (2) Salvation Army, (3) Saint Michael's Church, (4) Center City Churches Food Bank, and (5) Good News Soup Kitchen.

Throughout the entire process of working with the P family, information continued to be collected as additional needs and possible resources emerged. Data collection extended to information about the following (including referral procedures):

Protective services (possible placement of children)

Social Security

Appeal process when placement extension was refused (fair hearing)

Housing resources

Emergency fuel banks

Moving coverage

Medical transportation service

Appliance repair

Resources for Thanksgiving basket and children's Christmas presents

Community health services

E. Charted Progress

Adding to the recorded problem and goals, the worker listed the immediate need for food and the identified problem of poor money management (Figure 5–7). The family agreed with the goal of securing food, but they were resistant to admitting that help was needed with managing their money (no goal recorded). Although the worker became aware of the additional problems of Mr. P's unemployment and mental incapacity, these problems were not added to the problem list for service from the worker, because they were already being addressed by the Income Maintenance Department and the mental health center.

Note: *Information about Mr. P's unemployment and mental illness was recorded as part of data collection in the record. Additional paperwork during the total time the generalist worked with the P family included the completion of the following:*

FIGURE 5-7. Ongoing Recording

DATE IDENTIFIED	PROBLEM/ NEED	GOAL
9/28	Housing for P family	a. To find emergency shelter for the P family b. To locate an apartment for long-term residence by the family
9/28	Emergency food	a. To obtain emergency food supply b. To find resource to supply food until AFDC check is received
9/28	Poor money management	

Authorization forms for placement of family
Section-8 housing application
Emergency food applications
Documentation that the P's were searching for housing
Letter to authorize medical care
Request for medical transportation
Release-of-information forms
Request for extension of emergency placement
Request for fair hearing
Application for Social Security benefits
Application for energy assistance

IV. Field Area: Community Service
A. Agency: Clayton Neighborhood House
B. Client System
Four Hispanic families without heating in their apartments on the second floor of 33 L Street. (For more background information, see Chapter 4, Engagement in Diverse Field Areas, IV. Community Services.)

C. Engagement Summary
As the worker engaged the families in the problem-solving process, they expressed feelings of frustration and helplessness. There were also feelings of fear and anger expressed toward the landlord. The problem of inadequate heating was identified, and all agreed on the recorded goal, "To obtain consistent and adequate heating for second-floor residences of the L Street apartment house."

D. Data Collection
Problem: *As the worker explored the problem further, she learned that residents were paying a monthly rent of $250 for a one-room apartment. The families were told that heating was included in the rent. Although one person in each of the families was employed, they said that they could not afford any increase in rent or to pay for heating themselves.*

The worker had brought a thermometer with her on the visit. She checked the temperature in each of the apartments, and all of them registered about 50°F.

Since none of the residents at the meeting had lived in the building the previous winter, they did not know if a similar problem had existed last year. They shared how difficult it was for them to find a place to live. No one was requesting help with relocation at this time.

Persons: The worker learned that there were fifteen children (ages 6 months to 16 years) and seven adults (no one over 50) living in the four apartments. Although the residents were motivated to come together to discuss their heating problem, everyone was afraid to have a direct confrontation with the landlord. Mrs. T said that she and her husband had tried to call the landlord, but he was not available and never returned their call. Some members said he is hard to talk with, because he doesn't understand Spanish and they don't speak English. The residents were motivated to work on the heating problem with the worker, but they asked her to contact the landlord in their behalf.

Environment: The worker learned from those attending the meeting that an individual who lived downstairs worked as a janitor in the building. They said that they had complained to him about a lack of heat upstairs, but he told them that they would have to tell the landlord. The worker stopped at the janitor's apartment on the way out, but he was not home. The name and phone number of the landlord were obtained from the residents.

With further inquiry, the worker learned that the landlord lived in a neighboring town, and that he had owned two other buildings in the same area where the L Street apartment was located. The two buildings were recently sold to the city.

When the worker called Mr. X, the landlord, he said that he was not aware of a problem with heating for the second floor. The worker informed him that each of the apartments on the floor was registering a temperature of 50° or below. Mr. X said that he had asked the janitor of the building to help to keep heating costs to a minimum, but he didn't realize this was being done through an uneven distribution of heat in the building. He said he would contact the janitor and have the problem taken care of right away.

The worker inquired if Mr. X knew that his residents had tried to reach him to tell him about the heating problem. Mr. X said he was very busy and often found it hard to find time to return all of his calls. He said also that his secretary finds it difficult to understand what the Spanish-speaking tenants are trying to say over the phone.

E. Charted Progress

The worker entered a summary report of her visit to L Street in the record. She recorded pertinent information collected from speaking with the landlord and the residents. Paperwork completed while working with the community of residents included a planned contract that was developed with the residents (see Chapter 6).

V. Field Area: Education
A. Agency: Keeney Elementary School
B. Client System

Jim G, an 8-year-old African-American third grader with regressive behavior in school and at home. (For more background information, see Chapter 4, Engagement in Diverse Field Areas, V. Education.)

C. Engagement Summary

Although presenting problems and goals were discussed with Jim and his mother (as outlined in Table 4–6, Chapter 4), feelings were not expressed, and there was not a clear understanding of the cause of Jim's problems throughout the first three weeks of contact. The worker proceeded with data collection, realizing that the engagement period needed to be extended.

D. Data Collection

Problem: *The worker reviewed Jim's school record and the nurse's report. Jim was in good health and he had performed at an above average academic level during his first two years of school. His teacher said that in September, when school first started, Jim seemed happy and interested in school. She wondered if he should be placed in a learning-disability classroom because he was getting so far behind in his work. Jim's previous testing and academic performance showed that he did not have a learning disability.*

Persons: *Although Jim seemed to like meeting with the social worker, he did not care if he did not do well in school. He hoped he wouldn't have to repeat a grade. He said his father had told him that school wasn't really that important and that Jim could come to work with him in the car lot when he got older. Whenever Jim or the worker began to talk about home or his parents, Jim became restless and looked a little frightened.*

In one session, after meeting for three weeks, Jim began to play with the black man and woman puppets. He had them begin to dance together and then they started to hit each other. He took the frog puppet and had him yell out, "Hey, stop that!" The worker commented, "It sounds like froggie wants them to stop." Jim continued with the frog shouting, "Stop that fighting, do you hear?" The worker said it looked like froggie was getting upset, and she wondered what froggie was feeling. Jim said, "He's scared. He hates it." The worker said, "I wonder what froggie's afraid of." Jim took the woman doll and put her back on the shelf. He then became quiet and sat down. The worker asked if that was it. "Was froggie afraid that she would go away?" Jim didn't answer. The worker softly said that she knew that sometimes children are afraid that their parents will go away if they fight with each other. Jim looked away. The worker asked if Jim was ever afraid that his mother might go away. Jim whispered, "Sometimes." The worker then asked if Jim ever told his mother what he was afraid of, and Jim shook his head negatively. The worker wondered if Jim would mind if she told his mother what he was afraid of, and as he got up to leave the room he said, "I don't care."

Environment: The worker learned from the school record that Jim's mother was a nurse and that his father managed a car lot. During the second interview with Mrs. G, the worker asked if she could meet with Jim's father, but Mrs. G said that he was always very busy and worked long hours running the car lot. At the third meeting with Mrs. G, the worker shared with her what had happened in play with Jim. Mrs. G's eyes filled with tears. She then told the worker that in October, she learned that her husband had gone out with another woman. She said that she didn't think Jim noticed that she and her husband were quarreling. She recalled that at one point she did tell her husband that she might take off and leave him and the children. She said she wouldn't really do it but just wanted to scare him. She said her husband assures her that he will never see the woman again, but she finds it hard to trust him and to forgive him.

The worker encouraged Mrs. G to talk with Jim about his fear and to assure him that she doesn't plan to leave home. The worker also asked if Mrs. G couldn't talk with her husband about what was happening with Jim. Mrs. G said that she would try to get her husband to take time off to come in to see the worker with her next week.

E. Charted Progress

During the process of data collection and the extended engagement period, the worker added the newly identified problem of Mr. and Mrs. G's strained relationship to the problem list, as shown in Figure 5–8. The plan to have Mrs. G talk with Jim and to have Mr. G come in to meet the worker with Mrs. G was also recorded.

Note: The recording of the worker included an ongoing contracted plan developed by the worker, Mr. and Mrs. G, and Jim (presented throughout Chapters 4–9), which was kept in the social service file. The worker also recorded basic factual information in Jim's school record. In addition, a summary of each contact was included in the social service file, and a closing summary was added at the time of termination.

VI. Field Area: Corrections
A. Agency: Juvenile Court
B. Client System

A group of seven male adolescents (all 14 years old) on probation. (For additional background information, see Chapter 4, Engagement in Diverse Field Areas, VI. Corrections.)

FIGURE 5-8. Ongoing Recording

DATE IDENTIFIED	PROBLEM/ NEED	GOAL	TASKS	CONTRACT	DATE ANTICIPATED	DATE ACCOMPLISHED
11/1	Jim's school-tardiness and absenteeism	Jim's regular school attendance (on time every day)	1. See that Jim gets to school on time every day	1. Mrs. G	11/5–each school day thereafter	11/5–ongoing
11/1	Jim's declining academic performance	Improved academic functioning (interest, participation, grades)	1. Talk with Jim about school problems	1a. Worker and Jim	11/6 and twice a week thereafter	11/6, 11/8, 11/13, 11/15, 11/20, 11/27
				b. Mrs. G and Jim	11/2	11/2
			2. Follow-up	2. Worker and Jim	11/5	11/5, 11/21
			3. Talk with Jim about home tensions and assure him she will not leave	3. Mrs. G and Jim	11/21	
			4. Meet to discuss Jim's problems in relation to parents' problems	4. Worker, Mr.and Mrs. G	11/27	
11/2	Jim's getting to sleep at night					
11/21	Strain in Mr. and Mrs. G's marital relationship					

C. Engagement Summary

During engagement, the primary goal of getting off probation as soon as possible was clearly stated by all members of the group. The youths also wanted help both with controlling their tempers and with understanding better the "changes" they were all going through (as outlined in Table 4–7, Chapter 4). Although they recognized problems they were having in communicating with their parents, they did not want to work on trying to improve their relationships with them. They did not want to talk about their low self-esteem. They expressed anger at having been picked up by the police and put on probation.

D. Data Collection

After an initial period of testing and attempted manipulation of the leaders, group members began to talk more openly about their family backgrounds and life experiences. In addition to collecting data from the youths themselves, the two workers visited the homes of each group member and talked with parents. The workers also talked with the youths' teachers and social workers at the schools they attended. The files of the court for each of the youths were also reviewed carefully.

Problem: The workers learned that each member of the group had committed more than once the offense that led to his being put on probation. All seven of the youths were seen in their schools as "problem students" who had difficulties in learning and in getting along with teachers and classmates. They were described by teachers as "troublemakers" or "attention seekers." Two of the youths were believed to be junior members of the Savage Nomads or the Ghetto Brothers street gangs.

The group members said that they got into trouble usually when they were mad about something or dared to do it by friends. In one case, breaking and entering was required for initiation into a gang.

Persons: Three of the group members were highly motivated to get the most out of the group and to get off probation (MK, ML, and B). Two others laughed a lot and seemed to take the group "as a joke" (J and T). The remaining two were quiet and less easy to understand (A and C). C appeared very upset over being on probation.

The school reported that test scores indicated that two of the boys had borderline intelligence (A and MK). The others had average or above-average intelligence, even though they had problems with learning.

The racial-ethnic backgrounds of the group participants were as follows: one Italian-American; one Irish-American; two white with mixed ethnic backgrounds; two African-American, and one Hispanic.

Environment: All of the youths came from single-parent families. Five lived with their mothers, one lived with his father, and one lived with his grandmother. All came from lower-class or lower-middle-class neighborhoods. The youths had not been active in local recreational centers or programs. Three said they used to attend some church activities for teenagers, but they only went to church when their parents made them go.

The parents and grandmother of the youths expressed interest and concern for their children. Three mothers and T's grandmother said they were afraid that they had no control over their sons (grandson). They all hoped the youths had learned their lesson and would now stay out of trouble. C's father only spoke Spanish. He appeared to be totally overwhelmed, and said he might have to send C back home to Puerto Rico. J's mother had an apparent drinking problem. She said she was thinking seriously of "putting J away" because he was getting too hard to man-

age. She did not say where she thought she might put him. She had heard that J's father was in jail. Three other group members had older brothers who were in jail or correctional centers (A, T, and ML).

E. Charted Progress

Summary recordings were written that briefly described contacts with the group members' parents, teachers, and school social workers. Brief entries were made each week in the records to indicate attendance and participation in the group. Later, detailed studies of each youth were written when he became eligible to be removed from probation.

VII.   Field Area: Homeless Shelter

A. Agency: West End Community Shelter

B. Client System

José Gutierrez, a 37-year-old Hispanic male is homeless and HIV positive. (For additional background information, see Chapter 4, Engagement in Diverse Field areas, VII, Homeless Shelter.)

C. Engagement Summary

Mr. G had worked hard to lead an independent lifestyle. After testing HIV positive, he left his job and lost his apartment. During engagement, he shared with the worker strong feelings of fear and abandonment. The goals they identified focused on locating health care, housing, and employment.

D. Data Collection

Problem: Mr. G believed his illness was caused by his use of unsanitary needles during his drug addiction more than six years ago. He experienced frequent colds and fatigue. He had not been to a doctor in four months because he couldn't afford it and no longer had health insurance.

Person: Mr. G was hesitant to take drugs for his illness because he had previously been a drug addict. He knew he needed to talk with a doctor about this and to find out more about his illness. Mr. G said that he was willing to take any kind of job at this point because he needed money. His work history over the last five years was strong in terms of dependability and performance. Mr. G's work experience and skills were limited to cooking and farming.

Environment: Mr. G was not aware of any relatives in the state. His ex-wife had moved back to Puerto Rico. He said that he regretted that he had fallen away from his church and wished that he could "get back in God's graces."

In the building next to the shelter, there was a free health clinic for people in the neighborhood. The staffing of the clinic was provided through voluntary service from the doctors and interns of the city hospital. A grant provided funding for supplies and equipment. Mr. G would be able to receive medical care and information from the clinic.

With Mr. G's permission, the worker contacted the Social Security Administration and the Department of Social Services. She learned that after Mr. G became "significantly impaired" and became active with AIDS, he would qualify for (1) Social Security and Supplemental Security Income, and (2) general emergency assistance until he received his first SS check.

There was an organization called "Harmony" that offered a variety of services for victims of AIDS or HIV. Services included legal advocacy, a buddy system, a support group, transportation, and limited assistance with paying bills. Also, in the surrounding area, the worker located two residences (Hope Home and Christian House) for persons with AIDS. Currently, all of their nine beds were full (nine beds total).

Following up on Mr. G's interest in returning to his church, the worker was informed of the names and locations of the two Catholic churches in the area. She learned also that there was one church with a weekly service for a large Hispanic population.

Mr. G approved of the worker's contacting his past employer. His employer said that Mr. G was never a problem and that they missed him at the nursing home. He had heard about Mr. G's illness from another employee. He did not have any job openings for Mr. G at the Home. The State Employment office was contacted for a listing of possible job openings, and Mr. G was encouraged to look in the employment section of the shelter's newspaper each day.

E. Charted Progress

During data collection, the worker became aware of Mr. G's desire to return to God and the Catholic church. The need for religious enrichment was added to Mr. G's progress chart. Also added was Mr. G's desire for more information about his illness (See Figure 5–9). Basic information was recorded on the face sheet of his record. In summary recordings, additional information obtained during data collection was included.

FIGURE 5-9. Ongoing Recording

DATE IDENTIFIED	PROBLEM/ NEED	GOAL
5/8	Illness-HIV positive Lack of knowledge	On-going medical care and information
5/8	Homeless/hungry	Immediate housing/food Long-term housing
5/8	Unemployed (No financial support)	Employment — part/full Long range — public assistance/Social Security
5/10	Spiritual void	Return to Church

Conclusion

A frequent mistake of untrained workers is to overlook the need for data collection before intervening with services. Unplanned interventions are often costly, time-consuming, and unsuccessful. Although the process of data collection, which includes recording and documenting facts, may be seen as somewhat arduous and unsatisfying, it is an essential component of professional practice.

In this chapter, central focus was given to identifying and organizing relevant data, distinguishing fact from assumption, understanding the meaning of informed consent, and using appropriate recording formats to document information in writing. These dimensions of data collection are basic to the process, and they prepare the worker to move on to the next stage, assessment. As with all of the stages of helping, circumstances change in human situations, and the art of identifying facts about current realities goes on throughout the dynamic process. A worker must remain open to reformulating or supplementing the information collected, even after it has been organized and used in developing an assessment and planned intervention.

NOTES

1. *Code of Ethics of the National Association of Social Workers,* as adopted by the 1979 NASW Delegate Assembly and revised by the 1990 and 1993 Delegate Assemblies (Washington, D.C.: NASW, 1994), p. 1.

2. Fred N. Kerlinger, *Foundations of Behavioral Research,* 2nd ed. (New York: Holt, Rinehart & Winston, 1973), p. 480.

3. Federal Privacy Act of 1974. Public Law 93-579, December 31, 1974 (effective September 27, 1975), section 552a (b) (1).

4. Suanna J. Wilson, *Confidentiality in Social Work: Issues and Principles* (New York: The Free Press, 1978), p. 57. Copyright 1978 by The Free Press.

5. Lawrence L. Weed, *Medical Records, Medical Education and Patient Care* (Cleveland: Case Western Reserve University Press, 1971).

6. Wilma Martens and Elizabeth Holmstrum, "Problem-Oriented Recording," *Social Casework* 55 (November 1974):554–61.

7. Joseph P. Fitzpatrick, *Puerto Rican Americans* (Englewood Cliffs, N.J.: Prentice-Hall, 1971), p. 83.

8. Sonia Badillo Ghali, "Culture Sensitivity and the Puerto Rican Client," *Social Casework* 58 (October 1977):459–68.

9. Dolores J. Norton, *The Dual Perspective* (New York: Council on Social Work Education, 1978).

10. Carel B. Germain and Alex Gitterman, "The Life Model of Social Work Practice," in Francis J. Turner, ed., *Social Work Treatment: Interlocking Theoretical Approaches,* 2nd ed. (New York: The Free Press, 1979). p. 362. Copyright 1979 by The Free Press.

Assessment

The client's meaningful participation in making decisions and formulating the contract is based on the recognition that people are spontaneously active, seeking, and striving beings.

—Anthony Maluccio and Wilma Marlow[1]

Throughout the helping process, a worker is listening, evaluating, and acting. There is, however, a certain period of time in the process that is specifically designated as the assessment stage. Assessment is a time for appraising the problem-person-environment triplex and for planning interventions. Collaborative judgment and collaborative decision making are central characteristics of this stage of the General Method. Worker and system of contact move into formal planning based on the information collected in earlier stages. After a clear assessment of the nature of the problems as conceived within the context of *persons in environment*, decisions are made concerning where to begin and how to proceed.

The three major components of the assessment stage are (1) an assessment statement, (2) problem prioritization, and (3) the contracted plan. All three dimensions need to be addressed prior to intervening. The worker who moves directly into implementing change, without taking time for assessment and planning, frequently has to undo or add to the actions taken as he or she comes to realize that such interventions were precipitous or inappropriate.

It is possible that in certain situations a worker will have to act before a full assessment has been completed. A client system may have immediate, urgent needs that must be met before the necessary data can be collected for a formal assessment. There may not be time to plan and contract with a system before intervening in a crisis situation. Action may have to be taken immediately in order to stabilize a life-at-risk situation. Once this is accomplished, however, every effort is made by the worker to involve the system in a mutual process of assessment.

Assessment Statement

After much listening and gathering of information, the worker is expected to write an *assessment statement* for each problem identified. In the past, an assessment statement was referred to as a *diagnosis* in social work. In 1917, Mary Richmond modified the concept for greater relevance to the profession by calling it a "social diagnosis."[2] Problems that are frequently brought to the attention of social workers are of a material, interpersonal, institutional, or interdependent nature. Using the term *assessment* rather than *diagnosis* helps to avoid the possible inference that an identified problem is seen as a client's illness.

In the assessment statement, the worker begins by clearly indicating who has the problem, what the problem is, and why the problem exists at this time. By the third stage of the General Method, the worker should have sufficient data to describe the actual scope and cause of each problem. A simple formula to keep in mind for initiating an assessment statement is:

_____ has _____ because _____
   (who)   (what problem)   (why)

The "why," or cause of the problem, may be seen in many layers. Often, an immediate causal factor has touched off the problematic situation. In addition, several sequential factors may have led to the immediate cause. For example, Mr. R may be unemployed because he does not have marketable skills in this state, but he lacks such skills because he came from a country where he was socialized into a work world of a very different nature. Or, a client may be unemployed because he was laid off from his job, and maybe this was the result of fiscal cutbacks by the national administration.

In looking for the cause of a problem, the worker realizes that there is a wide range of possible causes, from personal to interpersonal to structural or societal. The cause cited in an assessment statement should be the one most directly related to the problem. If in the worker's judgment, it is necessary to go back further to preceding causes in order to understand the problem for planning and intervention, these causes should also be cited, with a clear explanation of how they are connected to the problem.

In addition to the opening causal statement, an appraisal of the change potential of the problem should be presented in a full assessment statement. A problem's change potential is dependent on the three variables of problem, person, and environment. All three factors are interdependent, with direct impact on the maintenance or resolution of the problem.

First, the worker and the system of contact consider the nature of the problem itself, asking how serious the problem is and what is its change potential. Is this a problem that can be resolved? Is the problem of such a nature that it is irreversible (e.g., suicide, terminal illness, bankruptcy)? More specifically, how wide or deep is the problem? Are many people involved, and to what extent? How long has it been going on? Although the potential for employment of someone who has been unemployed for years may be assessed as low, the potential for employment of someone with a strong work history who was recently laid off may be considered high.

Secondly, the strengths and weaknesses of the person or persons having the problem need to be assessed. What is his or her or their motivation and capacity to make whatever changes may be necessary? Are they able to cope with it alone or to accept help from others? What is their change potential? In order to document a clinical assessment of the strengths or weaknesses of a person or a relationship, *rapid-assessment instruments* are available for use during interviews. A worker's appraisal of clients in such areas as anxiety level, social interaction, marital adjustment, assertiveness, and alcohol or drug use may be supported by scores obtained on the assessment instruments.[3] Of course, there are limitations in the use of scores from questionnaires. A worker would want to cite additional evidence, such as documentation from other professionals or direct observation, to support the assessment.

The third area to be considered before an integrated assessment of the problem's change potential can be made involves the environment in which the problem is located. What is available in the environment in terms of formal or informal resources to promote the necessary changes? Are there restraining forces in the environment that are stronger than supportive resources? With optimum use of available resources, what is the expected outcome? What is the change potential of the environment for dealing with the problem?

After the three variables of problem, person, and environment are assessed individually, a cumulative assessment of the potential for change may be made for the particular problem within its person-environment context. Basically, the worker's statement may be framed as follows:

The change potential for _____ problem/need of _____
                   (whose)   (what problem)

is assessed as _____ because _____
              (high, somewhat   (reasons: nature of problem,
              high, medium,   person's motivation or capac-
            somewhat low, or   ity, resources and restraints in
                  low)   the environment)

In addition to a causal statement and a change-potential statement, the assessment statement should include a judgment about the seriousness or urgency of the problem. The question to be asked here is, To what extent is this a life-or-death matter for these people (or this person) at this time? Even if the change potential for a problem is judged to be very low, immediate attention has to be given to a life-endangering situation. Action must be taken in whatever way possible to protect the lives of those involved. In critical situations, the worker may have to make an immediate referral or serve as an advocate, even though there is little support from the persons or environment involved with the problem. Further considerations of types of interventions will be presented in the next chapter. The point being highlighted here is that an assessment statement should include a professional judgment on the urgency and seriousness of the problem, with supportive data.

EXAMPLE 1: Mr. L, 37 years old, French-Canadian, unmarried, no family

PROBLEM—UNEMPLOYMENT

ASSESSMENT STATEMENT

Mr. L has the problem of unemployment because he is unskilled and unmotivated to seek employment. The nature of the problem is such that the potential for change is very low. Mr. L has been out of work since he moved to this state three years ago. His capacity for work is limited because he does not have the skills sought by employers in this area. He has low motivation to seek work because he experienced a series of rejections in his early efforts to find employment. He is feeling hopeless and depressed. Resources for training or hiring unskilled laborers are extremely difficult to locate in this state. For these reasons, the overall change potential for Mr. L's problem of unemployment is assessed as very low. This is a very serious problem for Mr. L, because he does not qualify for public assistance in this state, and the savings he brought with him are depleted.

EXAMPLE 2: North Central City Community (approximately 600 families, 6-block area, low-income housing)

PROBLEM—NO PUBLIC TRANSPORTATION

ASSESSMENT STATEMENT

The North Central City Community has a need for public transportation because the local bus company recently cut off its route into the neighborhood. The problem is somewhat serious, because most people in the neighborhood do not have cars, and they now have to walk eight blocks to get a bus. The people of the community are highly motivated for active involvement in resolving the problem, and they have an organized leadership. The bus company has expressed an openness to reconsider its action and to meet with community representatives. In this situation, the change potential is assessed as high, since resources are available inside and outside of the community.

In assessing data according to the triplex of problem, person, and environment, a worker needs to maintain a holistic perspective of the dynamic interrelationships of social, cultural, and psychological factors. Tools and instruments have been developed to help the professional to see the relationship of a client's psychological and social needs with institutional and environmental resources.[4] In juxtaposing one's professional assessment of the problem, person, and environment triplex, a worker may see more clearly how to partialize and prioritize multiple problems in complex situations.

Problem Prioritization

Before entering into the goal setting and contracting of this stage of the method, the worker and the system of contact need to prioritize the problems identified and assessed. The questions asked are: What problem do we work on first? Where do we begin? On what basis should a problem be selected as the primary focus for intervention?

As the worker compiles, categorizes, and reviews data, it often becomes apparent that several problems are in need of attention. In response to the question of where to begin, the worker and the system of contact enter into a process for prioritizing the problems identified. To select the most appropriate starting point, the worker must reconsider the initial assessment of the information that was gathered according to the problem-person-environment triplex for each identified problem.

In studying each problem or triplex, the worker keeps in mind the fact that a client needs to build up a sense of trust in the worker's and agency's ability to be helpful. To foster client involvement in a growing, working relationship with the worker, there has to be an experience of success or satisfaction of need as soon as possible. The worker, therefore, tries to select *first* a problem that has a high change potential for resolution or need satisfaction.

As stated earlier, in writing an assessment statement for a problem, the worker asks: What is the change potential of the problem itself, of the persons involved, and of the related environment? Only after assessing all three dimensions for a problem will the worker be able to arrive at a comprehensive and accurate prognosis that can be used for problem prioritization. For some problems, the persons may have high motivation and capabilities, but the environment may provide little opportunity to actualize the persons' potential. An unemployed person, for example, may have skills and high motivation to find a job, but there may be no job openings in the environment. A person may have a problem or need that does not appear to be serious in nature, such as an absence of a support system. If, however, the person has little motivation, or if there are no available support groups or resources in the environment, the prognosis for change in this problem area is low. After considering the total change potential for problems such as those just cited, the worker would continue to try to find a problem with high potential for change in all three areas before beginning to intervene with the system.

At times, it may be impossible to find a starting problem with high change potential in all three areas. From a list of problems, it may be very difficult to distinguish and select the one that should be given priority. A tool has been developed to assist a worker in conceptualizing and analyzing a number of problems.

It serves as a framework to compare change expectations for different problems and, through juxtaposition, to visualize which problems have the greatest change potential.

According to the tool depicted in Table 6–1, each problem is studied and scaled according to an assessment of the change potential of the problem-person-environment triplex. On the basis of data collected previously, the worker estimates the potential for change, using a scale of 0–10. Scoring criteria are as follows: 0 = no potential, 1 = very low, 2 = low, 3 = somewhat low, 4 = medium—leaning toward low, 5 = medium, 6 = medium—leaning toward high, 7 = somewhat high, 8 = high, 9 = very high, and 10 = maximum potential for change. For example, in looking at the problem identified as "child's illness" in Table 6–1, the worker first asks about the nature and duration of the illness. If information has been gathered that indicates the child has just developed a strep throat, and the worker knows that there is a high incidence of cure for this illness, the change potential for "problem" may be scored as high (8). If there are accessible health care resources and the parents and child will take or administer the prescribed medication, the change potential in "person" and "environment" is also high (scored 8 and 9). Because the total change-potential score for the problem of "child's illness" is very high (25), this problem may be seen as the highest priority on the list of problems for initial intervention.

The change potential scores for the problem identified as "father's drinking" are not as hopeful. On the basis of data observed and obtained, the worker has assessed all three categories with extremely low scores. In looking at the nature and duration of the problem itself, the worker knows that the problem has gone on for years and that alcoholism is a serious physical and socially pathological illness (scored 2). In terms of the father's motivation and capacity to change at this

TABLE 6-1. Problem Prioritization

PROBLEM LIST	CHANGE-POTENTIAL SCORES (0–10)			TOTAL CHANGE POTEN-TIAL	PROBLEM PRIORITIZA-TION	SEVERITY
	PROBLEM	PERSON(S)	ENVIRON-MENT			
Child's illness	8	8	9	25	1	
Father's drinking	2	1	4	7	8	*
Father's unemployment	5	8	5	18	3	
Mother's depression	6	4	6	16	5	
Wife abuse	3	2	4	9	7	*
Housing conditions	6	5	3	14	6	
School truancy	8	7	8	23	2	
Husband-wife communication	6	5	6	17	4	

*Life-at-risk situation.

time, the worker assesses the "person" category also as very low (1), because the father denies he has a drinking problem and refuses to go for help. The worker studied the formal and informal resources of the father's environment and averaged out a score of 4. Although formal resources are available in the environment to help the father with his drinking problem (AA and local hospital and clinic), his wife and family deny that the father has a drinking problem, saying that he and most of his buddies are just heavy drinkers. Apparently, the total change potential for the "father's drinking" is very low (7). The worker recognizes that it is a very serious problem, but one that will not be resolved in the near future.

In selecting the problem with the highest change potential for beginning intervention, the worker is aware of the fact that there are problems of greater severity in need of ongoing attention. It is expected that these problems will probably take a long time before any marked change will occur. Because of the serious nature of these problems, the worker continues to direct efforts toward overcoming them while at the same time working on those problems or needs for which progress and success may be expected.

For example, in Table 6–1, there are two problems with low change-potential scores (father's drinking; wife abuse). These problems are asterisked in the "severity" column because they are assessed as life-at-risk situations. The worker will continue ongoing efforts to study and intervene in these areas while working with the family on problems that have high potential for change.

Contracting

After a problem has been selected for action, the worker and the system of contact begin to plan what needs to be done, by whom, and when. It is possible that they will choose to work on more than one problem at a time. It is important that they clearly understand, however, which problems are being addressed and which ones are not, and the reasons for the selection.

As pointed out earlier, in the problem-solving approach of the General Method, every effort is made to conceptualize and to verbalize the identified problems and corresponding goals. During the third stage of the Method, worker and system also conceptualize and verbalize the specific tasks that need to be performed in order to accomplish the goals. Not only are the tasks identified, but they are also placed in sequence. Dialogue between worker and system includes a consideration of which tasks need to precede others. The discussion about each task extends to a consideration of possible consequences that may result from its enactment.

Careful planning is needed in determining who should be expected to perform what task. A basic guiding principle is "Inasmuch as possible, a person should do for him- or herself." A worker would agree to carry out a task for a client only when it is apparent that the person or system is unable to perform the needed task and that no other resources are available to call on.

Social workers do not foster dependency. Nevertheless, they do recognize that there are certain actions that some individuals are unable to perform, owing to internal or external circumstances. When such actions are necessary for goal accomplishment, a worker using the General Method would try first to mobilize other resources of the system, such as family, friends, church, or community support systems. If no internal or informal resources are available, the worker may initiate or execute a needed task. As quickly as possible, however, the worker would try to enable the person to perform such tasks for him- or herself.

Example 1

A client may have been trying to contact his landlord for days to register a complaint. Although the landlord has been avoiding contact with the client, he may be more readily available when an agency worker contacts him. The worker would try to arrange for the landlord to meet with the client to discuss the complaint. If necessary, the worker may have to go with the client. If neither of these two options is feasible, the worker may have to go in behalf of the client.

Example 2

A woman recuperating from an operation may be unable to drive her son to the clinic. The worker would try to see if another family member or neighbor could bring him. There may be a volunteer service within or outside of the clinic that could be tapped to provide the needed transportation. Only after options such as these were explored would the worker offer to go out and pick up the child.

During the contracting period, when worker and system of contact clarify who will do what, it is important for both to identify also the date when each task is expected to be carried out. Little progress can be made and time may be wasted unless timing is discussed and there is a sense of expectation for task and goal accomplishment.

As each task is considered and contracted through mutual agreement on task assignments, an anticipated date is stated for the performance of each task, even though the date may have to be altered due to unexpected circumstances. The projection of dates for task execution serves as a guide for general planning and review. If a task is not completed on the expected date, worker and system can grow in understanding the dynamics of problem, person, and environment by asking why it was not accomplished as anticipated. More realistic comprehension and planning could result from this inquiry.

A tool for use in generalist practice has been developed that integrates the essential components of a contracted plan (see Table 6–2). As a worker proceeds in the process of problem solving with a system of contact, this tool may be used to state in writing what is agreed on as (1) the problems or needs to be addressed,

(2) the goals to be accomplished, (3) the tasks to be performed, (4) the persons to execute each task, (5) the dates anticipated to enact each task, and (6) the actual dates of task accomplishment. Once the tool is filled out by worker and system, they may refer to it each time they need to assess progress or impediments to progress. Skill is needed for precise identification of the problems and needs and the goals and tasks. The goals and tasks should focus on behaviors that can be measured or observed.

As each problem or need is selected for action, the name of the problem is entered on the instrument, along with the date when the worker and the system of contact agree that it is a problem for intervention. The list of problems and needs should be prioritized according to the criteria and process stated earlier. The goals for each problem may be stated as long-range goals, short-range goals, or both. The tasks to accomplish the goals for each problem need to be stated in sequence. The person or system indicated as contracting to perform each task should be identified in accordance with the principle of "doing for self as much as possible." The dates anticipated are written down after realistic consideration of what is feasible. As each task is accomplished, the final column should be filled in with the accurate date of completion.

The instrument, as shown in Table 6–2, can be placed in the front of any record for immediate identification of plan and progress. It becomes obvious, on first glance at the "date accomplished" column, whether there are tasks that were contracted but not completed. Rather than having to review all of the recordings of various contacts contained within a record to find out what has been happening with a case, the worker (or supervisor), by reviewing the instrument, can receive a synthesis of the essence of the work being done to date.

The instrument in Table 6–2 fits well with problem-oriented recording (described in Chapter 5). The contracted plan (Table 6–2) may be seen as a direct follow-up and complement to the steps taken for POR. The problems and dates identified on the problem list of POR are readily available for problem prioritization and listing in the first and second column of the contracted plan. Also the "assessment" and "plan" stated in the "SOAP" for each problem with POR will help in the identification of goals, tasks, contracts, and dates anticipated to be listed on the contracted plan. As each task of the contract is performed, its date of

TABLE 6-2. Contracted Plan

DATE IDENTIFIED	PROBLEM/ NEED	GOAL	TASK	CONTRACT	DATE ANTICI- PATED	DATE ACCOM- PLISHED

accomplishment is indicated on the contracted plan. This information will facilitate the writing of summary statements, as expected for each problem in a POR.

The contracted plan (Table 6–2) is a tool for ongoing use. Problems and needs, goals, tasks, and contracted enactor may change in the course of service. Once begun, there is a need for continued updating and review of the plan. As brought out in a later chapter, this tool may also serve as a major instrument for evaluation through goal analysis.

EXAMPLE

An example of a contracted plan for the problems prioritized in Table 6–1 may be found in Table 6–3. For the first problem, child's illness, it is clear in the "contract" column that the worker planned to take Mrs. C and her child to the clinic. She (worker) did this because Mrs. C had a history of missing clinic appointments. Also, Mrs. C had no way of getting to the clinic except by bus. The worker was unable to locate any available informal resources to provide transportation.

As the worker proceeded in problem solving with the family, she found that some of the problems identified during the first interview had decreased, owing to relief in other problem areas. For example, once Mr. C returned to work, Mrs. C was not so depressed and there was less physical abuse by her husband. Both Mr. and Mrs. C recognized their need to better understand and communicate with each other, and they agreed to go for marital counseling. They were also ready to begin to work on finding better housing. Mr. C was not ready, however, to talk about his heavy drinking. He and his wife denied that this was a problem, especially now that Mr. C was back at work. The worker planned to continue to be involved with the family as they worked on finding better housing, but she was not able to go any further with Mr. C's drinking problem at this time.

Working with Different Systems

As stated earlier, the General Method of social work practice is applicable to working with a variety of systems. A worker may be working with a family, an individual, a group, or a community, but in any case, worker and system go through an assessment stage. A question to be considered is, are there any differences in writing an assessment statement, prioritizing problems or drawing up a contracted plan when working with different-size systems? Various writers in the field of social work have focused on the art of assessment with particular systems, such as group[5] or family.[6] The approach and tools presented in this chapter, however, are used in working with any type of system.

In applying and adopting assessment tools to particular systems, a worker is sensitive to the knowledge that exists about each system. In working with a community, for example, the worker knows that a community consists of a complex body of persons with a common characteristic of place, problem, heritage, values, or commitment. There are often very distinctive subsystems within a community

TABLE 6-3. Contracted Plan—The C Family

DATE IDENTIFIED	PROBLEM/ NEED	GOAL	TASK	CONTRACT	DATE ANTICIPATED	DATE ACCOMPLISHED
2/8	1. Child's illness	1. Child's health—no strep throat	1. Call health clinic for appointment	1. Mrs. C	2/9	2/9
			2. Take child to clinic	2. Mrs. C and worker	2/12	2/15
2/8	2. School truancy	2. School attendance daily	1. Speak with mother	1. Worker	2/9	2/9
			2. Speak with child	2. Mrs. C and worker	2/9	2/12
			3. Speak with teacher	3. Mrs. C and worker	2/12	2/12
			4. Wake child on time	4. Mrs. C	3/1	3/1
			5. Put child on bus	5. Mrs. C	3/1	3/1
2/8	3. Father's unemployment	3. Employment of father (steady)	1. Discuss with Mr. C	1. Worker	2/15	2/18
			2. Contact employment agencies	2. Mr. C	2/16	2/19
			3. Check out training programs	3. Worker	2/16	2/17
			4. Locate job or training (J/T) for Mr. C	4. Mr. C, employment agencies, or worker	2/25	3/15
			5. Apply for J/T	5. Mr. C	3/16	3/16

TABLE 6-3. *Continued*

DATE IDENTIFIED	PROBLEM/NEED	GOAL	TASK	CONTRACT	DATE ANTICIPATED	DATE ACCOMPLISHED
2/8	4. Lack of communication between husband and wife	4. Improved husband-wife communication. Talking out instead of fighting out	1. Speak with Mr. C	1. Worker	3/22	3/22
			2. Speak with Mr. and Mrs. C	2. Worker	3/25	3/25
			3. Refer Mr. and Mrs. C to marital counseling center	3. Worker	3/25	3/25
			4. Contact marital counseling center	4. Mrs. C	3/26	3/29
			5. Attend sessions at marital counseling center	5. Mr. and Mrs. C	4/5	4/5
			6. Support their attendance	6. Worker	4/5	4/5
2/8	5. Overcrowded housing	5. Larger living quarters	1. Discuss with Mr. and Mrs. C	1. Worker	4/7	4/7
			2. Explore housing options and contact possible resources	2. Mr. and Mrs. C and worker	4/8	4/8
			3. Apply for housing	3. Mr. and Mrs. C	5/10	
			4. Move family	4. The C family and movers		

that may contract, contest, and conflict with one another. The worker calls on the knowledge and skills identified in the profession by those who have expertise in community work and supplements their work with the newly developed tools for generalist practice.

In 1955, Murray Ross identified the process of organizing a community according to the following six stages: The community

1. identifies its needs and objectives
2. orders or ranks needs or objectives
3. develops the confidence and will to work at needs and objectives
4. finds resources (internal and/or external) to deal with needs or objectives
5. takes action in respect to them
6. extends and develops co-operative and collaborative attitudes and practices in the community.[7]

The stages for community organization as described by Ross are basically consistent with the stages of the General Method. Each method has a six-stage process. In both processes, worker and community go through phases where problems and objectives are identified, data are collected, and action is taken. Although Ross does not state the specific need for an assessment stage, it is implicit that prior to taking action, problems are prioritized with an appraisal of resources and that actions are planned. Before moving into the action stage (item 5 of Ross), the worker and community now have tools available to help them with prioritizing problems and planning interventions.

For example, in the South End Community, the stated problems and needs were listed as follows:

High prices at local grocery stores

Rat- and roach-infested housing

No local control or input in neighborhood schools

Gang wars among community youths

No traffic light at the corner of Fifth Street and Silver Street

After drawing on assessment statements for each of these problems, the tool for prioritization of problems was completed, as found in Table 6–4.

Apparently, the community was motivated to begin to work on the need for a traffic light and the problem of high prices in local stores. In addition to motivation, the worker assessed the nature and scope of each problem, as well as the extent of related resources. After all factors were considered, it became clear that the problem with the highest change potential was the need for a traffic light. This was a serious (life-at-risk) problem with a good chance of resolution. The problem of gang wars was seen as serious (a youth having been stabbed last month), but community members did not indicate high motivation to work on this. They said gang wars were going on for years because people from certain blocks just didn't

TABLE 6-4.   The South End Community—Problem Prioritization

| PROBLEM LIST | CHANGE-POTENTIAL SCORES (0–10) | | | TOTAL CHANGE POTEN-TIAL | PROBLEM PRIORITIZA-TION | SEVERITY |
	PROBLEM	PERSON(S)	ENVIRON-MENT			
High Prices	3	8	3	14	2	
Infested housing	3	5	3	11	3	
No school control	2	3	2	7	5	
Youth fights	3	4	2	9	4	•
Traffic light	8	7	8	23	1	•

*Life-at-risk situation.

get along. Also, few resources were available for youth in the area. The worker, while not losing sight of this problem, would begin with an issue with high success potential in order to build up a sense of trust and accomplishment within the community.

After prioritizing problems and needs, the worker and community would move to planning specific tasks and responsibilities for goal accomplishment. The tool for contracted planning could aptly be used at this point. An example of how a contract could be developed with this community is found in Table 6–5. In this case, as community members begin to witness success from their efforts, a sense of pride and power develops. They begin to hope for greater accomplishments and to demonstrate motivation to work on complex tasks, such as finding funding sources and writing grant proposals. In time, the community begins to focus on what could be as well as what was, on prevention as well as problem resolution. Residents begin to talk about the need for them to overcome their interpersonal conflicts because they could gain so much more by working together. Some people identify past feelings of helplessness or isolation. According to Table 6–5, once the community finds out that there is funding for building a youth recreational center, they begin to think about other projects for enriching the community. The social worker's role as leader and activator decreases as members feel more confident and assume more leadership themselves.

Although the complexity of community work may be somewhat frightening to entry-level social workers, the general tools for assessment, as demonstrated, enable a worker to partialize and to coordinate the complex dimensions of needs and actions within community practice. As stated earlier, these assessment tools may be applied similarly when working with groups, families, or individuals.

There may be a major shift in the size of the system of contact during the helping process, as tasks become identified and implemented. Client systems may expand or decrease in number. Although a worker may begin contact with an individual, in the course of planning it may become apparent that the worker will need to intervene with the family or a larger system to achieve goals. Fortunately, a worker using the General Method employs knowledge and skills that

TABLE 6-5. South End Community—Contracted Plan

DATE IDENTIFIED	PROBLEM/NEED	GOAL	TASK	CONTRACT	DATE ANTICIPATED	DATE ACCOMPLISHED
3/15	1. Need for traffic light	1. Traffic light at Fifth and Silver Streets	1. Inquire about meeting with traffic commissioner (in three weeks)	1. Mr. G and worker	3/19	3/24
			2. Draw up a petition	2. Petition committee (Mr. and Mrs. K, Mr. F, Ms. Q, Mrs. R) and worker	3/20	3/26
			3. Get 500 signatures	3. Petition committee and six others (Rev. J, Mrs. B, Capt. P, Mr. S, Mr. and Mrs. B)	4/3	4/5
			4. Collect information on accidents at Fifth and Silver Streets	4. Mrs. A	3/20	3/22
			5. Draw up a traffic-flow chart	5. Traffic committee (Mr. and Mrs. M, Mr. McN, Ms. W, Mr. T) and worker	4/3	3/31
			6. Meeting of community	6. Whole community	4/4	4/4
			7. See commissioner with petition and information	7. Petition committee Mr. G, and worker	4/9	

TABLE 6-5. *Continued*

DATE IDENTIFIED	PROBLEM/ NEED	GOAL	TASK	CONTRACT	DATE ANTICIPATED	DATE ACCOMPLISHED
			8. Committee meeting to discuss cancellation by commissioner	8. Community and worker	4/13	4/13
			9. Arrange to meet with mayor	9. Mr. G	4/15	
			10. Meet with mayor	10. Same as for contract 7	4/30	
			11. If task 9 is not possible, meet to plan a demonstration	11. Community and worker	4/20	4/20
			12. Make signs	12. Traffic committee	4/22	4/22
			13. Notify communications media	13. Mr. G and Mrs. P	4/26	4/26
			14. Demonstration at Fifth and Silver Streets	14. Community and worker	4/27	4/27
			15. Get traffic light	15. Town officials	5/3	5/4
			16. Community meeting	16. Community and worker	5/7	5/7
3/15	2. High Prices	2. Lower prices in local grocery stores	1. Compare prices and prepare report	1. Comparative price committee (Mrs. B, Mr. G, Mr. and Mrs. N, Ms. W, Mr. T)	5/12	5/12
			2. Meet with store owners and present data	2. Teams a. Mr. B, Mrs. Q, Mrs. J	5/20	5/27

TABLE 6-5. *Continued*

DATE IDENTIFIED	PROBLEM/ NEED	GOAL	TASK	CONTRACT	DATE ANTICIPATED	DATE ACCOMPLISHED
				b. Mr. and Mrs. K, Mr. F		
			3. Community meeting	3. Community and worker	5/27	5/27
			4. Meet with consumer-protection worker	4. Mr. G, Mr. F, Mrs. J	6/3	6/3
			5. Meet with store owners and consumer-protection worker	5. Comparative price committee, Mr. F, Mrs. J, and worker, store owners, and consumer-protection worker	6/20	6/22
			6. Monitor prices	6. Teams as in contract 2	6/30 and ongoing	
3/15	3. Infested housing	3. Extermination of rats and roaches in community housing	1. Community meeting	1. Community and worker	6/24	6/24
			2. Identify locations and extent of infestation—bring in housing inspector	2. Data collection committee (Mr. and Mrs. M, Mrs. B, Mr. F, Ms. R, Mr. McW.)	7/9	7/8
			3. Draw up petition and get signatures	3. Petition committee	7/17	7/17
			4. See landlords with data and petition	4. Teams a. Mr. F, Mrs. Q, Mr. and Mrs. M	7/30	7/31

TABLE 6-5. *Continued*

DATE IDENTIFIED	PROBLEM/ NEED	GOAL	TASK	CONTRACT	DATE ANTICIPATED	DATE ACCOMPLISHED
				b. Mr. B, Ms. J, Mrs. R		
			5. Speak with Housing Authority and Housing Court	5. Mr. G, Mr. F, Mrs. J	8/6	8/10
			6. Community meeting	6. Community and worker	8/10	8/12
			7. Withhold rents	7. Tenants of infested housing	8/31	8/31
			8. Get publicity	8. Mrs. P and Mrs. Q	8/30	8/29
			9. Hire sanitation specialist	9. Landlords	9/2	9/10
3/15	4. Gang wars	4. End of gang wars	1. Community meeting	1. Community and worker	9/7	9/7
			2. Identify scope and causes—talk with youth and with police	2. Data collection committee (Mr. F, Mrs. Q, Ms. R, Rev. J, Mr. McN)	9/20	9/22
			3. Locate funding to build recreation hall for community youth—talk with local officials	3. Mr. G, Mrs. R, and worker	9/20	9/24
			4. Draw up funding proposal	4. Funding committee (Mr. and Mrs. S, Ms. W, Mr. T)	9/30	10/8

TABLE 6-5. *Continued*

DATE IDENTIFIED	PROBLEM/NEED	GOAL	TASK	CONTRACT	DATE ANTICIPATED	DATE ACCOMPLISHED
			5. Build recreational center (on church grounds)	5. Contractors and community	8/30	11/30
			6. Hire recreation director	6. Recreation center committee (Rev. J, Mrs. R, Mr. and Mrs. M, Ms. Q, Mr. G)	10/30	11/20
			7. Monitor center	7. Recreation center committee	11/1	
6/15	5. No school input or control	5. Direct input into local school	1. Community meeting	1. Community and worker	8/24	8/24
			2. Study structure of school and compare with other schools	2. School committee (Mr. and Mrs. K, Mr. F, Mrs. W)	8/30	9/4
			3. Meet with principal	3. Mr. G, Mr. and Mrs. M	8/26	8/29
			4. Meet with Board of Education	4. Mr. G, Mrs. Q, Rev. J, Mr. W	9/14	9/15
			5. Locate funding sources	5. Mrs. R, Mrs. P, Mr. F	9/11	9/20
			6. Get other community people involved—elderly, singles, etc.	6. Rev. J, Capt. P, Mrs. R, worker		
			7. Draw up proposa for community programs of school	7. Mrs. R, Mr. W	9/30	

are applicable to systems of any size. General practice does not have the limitation of size as found in the traditional methods of casework, group work, or community organization.

Using the Holistic Foundation in Assessment

The skills and approach a worker uses in the assessment stage should reflect the foundation value of *belief in the dignity and worth of every person* (see Table 1–6, Chapter 1). As the worker and system of contact collaborate in assessing and planning, the basic practice principles, particularly individualization, self-determination, and acceptance, are demonstrated.

A system needs to have an individualized assessment. No two people or systems are exactly alike. Each one has a unique combination of problems, needs, resources, and circumstances. Thus, the principle of *individualization* is highlighted in the assessment stage of the General Method.

In prioritizing problems, the worker knows that an essential factor to consider prior to problem selection is the extent of motivation in a system to work on a particular problem or need. Unless there is client *self-determination* in problem prioritization, a worker will undoubtedly meet with resistance and failure. The worker who forges ahead for problem resolution will be unsuccessful without the agreement and support of the client system.

Although it is easy to wish that a system have greater strengths or motivation, the worker must convey an attitude of acceptance toward the system as it is. If several problems are assessed as having low potential for change, the worker may feel a sense of frustration or helplessness. The worker must begin with accepting the system "as a given." Through discussion, support, and assessment, within an atmosphere of acceptance, the worker enables the system to view itself more realistically and to consider possible and desirable goals.

In addition to foundation values and principles, a worker in the assessment stage uses knowledge and skills from the holistic foundation for general social work practice (Table 1–6, Chapter 1). When writing a statement of cause for a problem, the worker may be using such theories as ecology, role, or socialization to explain how a system has been influenced by others. Knowledge of cultures, policies, and formal and informal resources is used in developing priorities for planning and intervention. The worker utilizes various theories to understand persons, problems, and environments and their interactions as an appraisal of their change potential is being made.

The foundation skills that are used during assessment include goal setting, planning, contracting, and recording. As the worker involves the system in contracting, some degree of clarifying, bargaining, and confronting may be needed. The supportive skills of listening, guiding, and feeling and sensing are prevalent throughout the assessment process. With the individualization of each person-problem-environment triplex during assessment, the worker applies foundation skills and theories as deemed appropriate to the situation.

Human Diversity for Assessment

Culture

During the assessment stage, as problems and needs are prioritized and contracts are formulated, a worker and system may find it difficult to determine where to begin, particularly when the work is with minorities. Often, the problems identified are both personal and societal in nature. Although it may be necessary to invest major energy first in providing for immediate material needs, a worker should also plan to deal with the larger social-change issues that need to be addressed. A worker's involvement in the larger issues helps to demonstrate to the client the worker's understanding and acceptance. As interventions are contracted, the worker strives to promote empowerment by strongly encouraging and supporting minority members to speak and act for themselves to meet immediate needs and to bring about institutional change.

In working out a contract with a system, the worker may find different degrees of participation and active involvement by systems, depending on cultural orientations. When a worker is seen as an authority person in a lineal relationship (as with Asian-Americans), members of the system may show passivity and dependence. The speed with which a contract is drawn up may also be influenced by the culture of a system.

The planning and selection of tasks on a contract should reflect a sensitivity to cultural values and beliefs. For example, to suggest institutional care of the elderly as an acceptable plan for many African-Americans, Puerto Ricans, or Asians would be inappropriate. Placing a child with a relative in the tribe would be a much more acceptable plan for an American Indian family than a foster-home placement would be.

Sexual Variation

As pointed out in Chapter 3, the problems listed when working with gay or lesbian clients may also range from personal to broad societal problems. Many personal problems may be assessed as stemming from tensions and rejections the individual has experienced when trying to participate in societal systems. The worker and the system study all of the identified problems, but priority is given to those with high potential for change. The broad, general goals that were stated during engagement are refined during assessment into more specific, attainable, measurable goals for contract formulation. In every possible way, the worker tries to empower the gay or lesbian client system to implement independently the tasks identified in the contract or to implement them with a community of others who face similar pressures or injustices.

Information gathered about potential supportive resources is discussed during assessment, and the plan drawn up by worker and system may include initial contact with outside resources. If no local resources are available, the plan may be developed to organize a support group for gay or lesbian persons in or outside of the worker's agency.

When it becomes apparent that a problem raised by a gay or lesbian client is interpersonal in nature, the worker knows that the most effective and often the only way to help with an interpersonal problem is to involve the other partner in sessions with the worker and the client. The plan and contract, therefore, may need to include a process for bringing into the service a third party who may be hesitant to talk with a professional about his or her gay or lesbian relationship. If it is not possible to include this person, the worker is expected to state clearly to the client the limitations to achieving interpersonal goals.

Gender Sensitivity

During assessment, as the causes of problems are stated, men and women who adhere to narrowly defined gender roles may avoid considering the possibility that their problems may be related to social injustices in a sexist society. In prioritizing problems, they may be closed to the idea of giving priority to a need for change in how they define their gender-role identity. The plan articulated in a contract may reflect a woman's continued dependence, for example, if a worker or others are expected to carry out a major portion of the identified tasks. A man's inability to accept interdependence may be seen in his refusing to allow a worker or other resources to accomplish tasks in behalf of his family or himself.

Using an ecological perspective in planning, a social worker realizes that an individual with a goal to change his or her behavior and image may experience pressure and negative reactions from the environment. In any work on redefining gender roles, whether with men or women, individually or in groups, attention needs to be given to the possible consequences that may result from any change. The reality is that change is usually a painful process for both the individual and the environment. Although a person may become self-sufficient and independent, it is true that no man or woman can be an island, totally independent from others, for very long. Human beings by nature are interdependent. To move into a truly collaborative, balanced interdependence, however, may be impossible for some individuals in their existing environments. Women who have been greatly dependent, for example, may have to go to the other polarity of total independence before they and others can see them as equal, complementary counterparts. The implications of these actions need to be given serious consideration before choices and changes are made. Various support systems and reinforcements need to be located and ensured if change is to be positive and stabilized.

It may be equally difficult for a man who is in a position of power and decision making to move into a more democratic, egalitarian way of functioning within a system, even when he wants to do so. Those who are dependent on him may resist having to assume more responsibility and independence. It may be necessary, therefore, to plan to involve significant others in the helping process.

Thus in writing assessment statements, prioritizing problems, and contracting with different systems, social workers use their knowledge of, and sensitivity to, culture, sexual variation, and gender-role diversity. They also make reference to the additional diversity variables of age and stages, endowment and personality, value systems, class, and geographic location (described in Chapter 3).

Assessment in Diverse Field Areas

I. Field Area: Child Welfare
A. Agency: State Department of Children's Services
B. Client System

K, a 15-year-old female in an emergency shelter. (For more background information see Chapter 4, Engagement in Diverse Field Areas, I. Child Welfare.)

C. Summary of Preceding Stages

The problem and goals identified during engagement and data collection are listed in Table 5–5. During engagement, K expressed feelings of loneliness, hatred, nervousness, and depression. In collecting data, the worker learned that K had experienced some difficulty adjusting in both the group home and the foster home placements that she had before she ran away, particularly in the foster home. Her schoolwork had also deteriorated prior to her running away and being placed in the emergency shelter. After exploring informal and formal resources in the environment, the worker located a group home for young women (ages 14–19) in Jewett City that had an opening. K expressed a strong desire to move into a group home, to return to school, and to get help with her personal problems.

D. Assessment

Assessment statement: *K has no permanent residence because she cannot live at home with her abusive parents (mother and stepfather), and she ran away from her foster home. She has personal needs (problem 3 in Table 5–5) that interfere with her functioning. The etiology of K's personal problems go back to her traumatic home environment, where she was physically and sexually abused. K is out of school because she is living in a temporary shelter awaiting placement. Her school performance had dropped to below average while she was living in the foster home because she became involved with a boyfriend and was having an increasing number of arguments with her foster parents.*

The change potential for K's problem of homelessness is assessed as somewhat high because K is motivated to accept a group-home placement and a resource is available. The change potential for K's need to reenter school is assessed as somewhat high because there is a school near the group home. The change potential for K's problems with adjustment to placement and school is assessed as somewhat high because K is now motivated to accept ongoing help with her personal problems and because there will be opportunity for K to receive help individually and in group while living in the group home.

Problem prioritization: *The problem-prioritization tool was used by the worker, as recorded in Table 6–6.*

The need for a placement is given top priority because it has the highest change potential (24) and also because of the urgency (severity) of the situation (living in temporary shelter). Finding a school placement is not a difficult problem to resolve. It received the second-highest score and became second in priority.

The personal problems have lower change scores because it is expected that these problems will take more time for resolution. K is particularly motivated to try to get over "feeling down." She is ready to talk about how hurt and angry she is. She also wants to feel better about herself and to understand what has happened to her. She hesitates to talk about her sexuality, even though problems related to her sexual identity, behavior, and relationships are assessed as serious (severity). K ran away from home when she became involved with a boyfriend, and she fears new heterosexual friendships. Since the worker has been able to locate environmental resources for all the problems listed, the change potential scores in the "environment" column are high (9's). Even though the problem relating to K's sexuality is prioritized last, the worker sees the seriousness of this problem and will bring it to the attention of the person who will be working with K individually in the group home.

Contracting: *Building on the list of problems and goals identified during engagement and data collection, the worker and K then began to plan the tasks that needed to be performed to achieve the stated goals. They also identified who would be responsible for carrying out each task, and they set the dates when task completion could be anticipated. Their contracted plan is given in Table 6–7.*

II. Field Area: Gerontology
A. Agency: Seaside Nursing Home
B. Client System

Mrs. J, an 80-year-old Portuguese woman in a skilled-nursing facility. (For more background information, see Chapter 4, Engagement in Diverse Field Areas, II. Gerontology.)

TABLE 6-6.   Problem Prioritization

PROBLEM LIST	CHANGE-POTENTIAL SCORES (0–10)			TOTAL CHANGE POTEN-TIAL	PROBLEM PRIORITIZA-TION	SEVERITY
	PROBLEM	PERSON(S)	ENVIRON-MENT			
No permanent home	7					
Out of school	7	8	9	24	1	.
Personal problems		7	9	23	2	
Poor self-esteem	5					
Identity confusion	5	6	9	20	4	
Sexuality	5	6	9	20	4	
Depression	5	5	9	19	5	.
		7	9	21	3	

*Life-at-risk situation.

TABLE 6-7. Contracted Plan

DATE IDENTIFIED	PROBLEM/ NEED	GOAL	TASK	CONTRACT	DATE ANTICIPATED	DATE ACCOMPLISHED
1/12	1. No permanent home	1a. To obtain a permanent placement b. To maintain a permanent placement	1. Make referral	1. Worker	1/19	
			2. Visit group home	2. K and worker	1/22	
			3. Move to group home	3. K, with worker's help	1/24	
			4. Follow-up	4. Worker, K, and group home staff	1/30 and every second week	
1/12	2. Out of school	2. To reenter school	1. To enroll in local school	1. K and group home staff worker	1/28	
			2. Follow-up	2. Worker, school personnel, group home staff	1/30 and other school conferences on K	

TABLE 6-7. *Continued*

DATE IDENTIFIED	PROBLEM/ NEED	GOAL	TASK	CONTRACT	DATE ANTICIPATED	DATE ACCOMPLISHED
1/12	3. Personal problems a. Depression b. Poor self-esteem c. Identity confusion d. Sexuality	3. Personal goals (1/19) a. To stop "feeling down" so much b. To feel better about self c. To clarify identity d. To be able to have good friendships with males	1. To have weekly individual sessions with social worker at the group home 2. To participate in weekly peer-group meetings 3. Follow-up	1. K and group home social worker 2. K 3. Worker, K, and social worker at group home	1/25 and once a week thereafter 1/25 and once a week thereafter 1/30 and every second week	

179

C. Summary of Preceding Stages

The problems and goals identified during engagement and data collection may be found in Table 5–6. During engagement, Mrs. J expressed feelings of distrust, fear, anger, and abandonment. In collecting data, the worker learned that Mrs. J's failure to adjust included disruptive behavior in the unit. She was agitating the nurses and the residents. More information was obtained about Mrs. J's history and her family, who could not be located. Portuguese-speaking resource people in the nursing home (a new volunteer) and in the community (the church pastor) were being located to visit with Mrs. J. The client herself was becoming more open and motivated to adjust to the nursing home.

D. Assessment

Assessment statement: *Mrs. J is seclusive, uncooperative, and agitating because she is culturally isolated in the nursing home and because she has been abandoned by her family. She will not leave her room alone because she is afraid that the little she has left will be stolen. She finds it difficult to go out and meet with others because she can't speak English fluently, and she feels uncomfortable with people of a different culture. Mrs. J fights with the nurses when they come to give her a bath because it distresses her to have to get undressed at 10 o'clock in the morning. Mrs. J has been yelling at the residents and calling them names because she wants to get their attention and to make them communicate with her. She displays anger and confusion at times, as a result of her organic brain syndrome.*

The change potential for Mrs. J to overcome her seclusiveness is assessed as medium high because Mrs. J is somewhat motivated to be able to leave her room on her own and because she is physically able to do so at this time. The potential to overcome her cultural isolation is assessed as medium because she can speak some English, a volunteer has been located who is Portuguese, and the pastor of Mrs. J's former church will also come to see her. The change potential for Mrs. J to get to know the staff and the resources of the nursing home is assessed as high, because Mrs. J has agreed to meet twice a week with the social worker, and she has expressed interest in meeting other staff members and hearing about available resources. Her involvement in activities at the nursing home will depend on how comfortable she feels with the activities and with those who participate in them.

The change potential for overcoming the bath-scheduling problem is assessed as high because the nurses are open to reconsidering the time Mrs. J is scheduled for her bath. Mrs. J and the head nurse are willing to meet to discuss the problem. The change potential for overcoming Mrs. J's yelling at the residents is also assessed as high, because Mrs. J is motivated to work for better communication with others. She says she will stop the name-calling.

Mrs. J's overall functioning and adjustment are dependent also on the rate of deterioration due to organic brain syndrome.

Problem prioritization: *The worker prioritized the identified problems, using the prioritization tool as shown in Table 6–8.*

The problem of seclusiveness has a high change-potential score (9), because in considering the nature of the problem itself, residents who are physically able to leave their rooms may do so. The change potential for "person" is assessed as somewhat high (7). Although Mrs. J has the physical capacity to leave her room and expresses a desire to get out more, she still feels afraid and strange in the nursing home. "Environment" is also assessed at a 7 for this problem. Resources (persons and programs) in the nursing-home environment are available to help Mrs. J leave her room. They do not, however, reflect her culture, except for one possible volunteer. Mrs. J's problem of seclusiveness is asterisked in the "severity" column, because it can be seen as potentially a life-or-death issue. If Mrs. J regresses to the point of refusing to leave her room even for meals, she could become seriously ill and have to be moved into the chronic-care unit.

In assessing the problem of cultural isolation, the change potential is seen as medium, and "problem" is given a 6. People of different cultures do not have to feel or be isolated. Even though Mrs. J does not speak English fluently, she can carry on a conversation in English ("person" score of 8). She could help others in the environment to understand and respond to her cultural needs. Although there are no Portuguese residents or staff members in the nursing home at the time, this may change, because the number of Portuguese moving into the local geographic area is increasing. Mrs. J has also expressed some desire to get to understand others at the nursing home, and the staff of the home, particularly those who are Spanish-speaking, have indicated an interest in helping Mrs. J feel welcome. They talked about serving Portuguese food and playing music from Portugal at the next resident-and-staff party. The "environment" assessment at this time is scored a 7. If a Portuguese volunteer or Mrs. J's pastor becomes actively involved with her, the environment score may be raised.

TABLE 6-8. Problem Prioritization

| PROBLEM LIST | CHANGE-POTENTIAL SCORES (0–10) | | | TOTAL CHANGE POTEN-TIAL | PROBLEM PRIORITIZA-TION | SEVERITY |
	PROBLEM	PERSON(S)	ENVIRON-MENT			
Seclusiveness:						
not leaving room	9	7	7	23	3	.
Cultural isolation	6	8	7	21	5	
Unfamiliarity with						
staff and resources	9	8	9	26	1	
Fighting with nurses						
over bath	7	8	9	24	2	
Calling residents						
names	7	9	6	22	4	

*Life-at-risk situation.

TABLE 6-9. Contracted Plan

DATE IDENTIFIED	PROBLEM/ NEED	GOAL	TASK	CONTRACT	DATE ANTICIPATED	DATE ACCOMPLISHED
9/27	1. Unfamiliarity with staff and resources of nursing home	1. To get to know the staff and resources of the nursing home	1. To meet twice a week with worker	1. Worker and Mrs. J	10/4 and every Tuesday and Thursday thereafter	10/4, 9, 11
			2. To meet with program planner	2. Worker, Mrs. J, and program planner	10/16	
			3. To meet with a person from recreation staff	3. Worker, Mrs. J, and recreation staff person	10/23	
10/2	2. Fighting with nurses over bath	2. To work out bath schedule with nurses	1. To meet with head nurse to discuss bath schedule	1. Mrs. J and head nurse	10/16	
9/25	3. Seclusiveness: not leaving room alone	3a. To leave room alone (at least once a day)	1. To walk down to nursing station alone at least once a day	1. Mrs. J	10/25 and each day thereafter	
		b. To attend a house activity, program, or meeting (at least once week)	1. To go to a house activity, program, or meeting (at least once a week)	1. Worker or staff member and Mrs. J first two times	Starting week of 10/22	
				2. Mrs. J with residents each week thereafter	Starting week of 11/5	

TABLE 6-9. *Continued*

DATE IDENTIFIED	PROBLEM/NEED	GOAL	TASK	CONTRACT	DATE ANTICIPATED	DATE ACCOMPLISHED
10/2	4. Calling residents names	4. To stop calling residents names	1. To stop name calling 2. To say "hello" to residents	1. Mrs. J 2. Mrs. J	10/16 and thereafter 10/16 and thereafter	
9/25	5. Cultural isolation	5. To share culture with others	1. To meet director of volunteers 2. To visit with Portuguese volunteer 3. To visit with pastor of church	1. Mrs. J, worker, and director of volunteers 2. Mrs. J and volunteer 3. Mrs. J and pastor	10/25 ? ?	

The lack of familiarity with the staff and resources of the home was seen as a problem easily remedied (9). Mrs. J is capable of understanding the staff and resources, and she is somewhat motivated to learn about them (8). The program planner, recreational director, head nurse, chaplain, and others on the staff of the nursing home are very willing to talk with Mrs. J and to develop an individualized program for her. The planned program for Mrs. J could include recreational, social, and spiritual activities. "Environment," therefore, is given a high change-potential score (9) for the problem of "unfamiliarity with staff and resources of the nursing home."

The potential for changing the problem of fighting with the nurses over the bath is assessed at 7. Even though the problem is not a life-or-death issue, changing the schedule for Mrs. J's bath time would affect the schedule for many others. It is possible, however, for the schedule to be changed and thus prevent further fighting by Mrs. J over the bath. The change potential for "person" is 8 because Mrs. J is capable of being cooperative and has said she would like to get along better with the nurses. The nurses are open to rescheduling Mrs. J's bath time, and the head nurse has agreed to meet with Mrs. J about it ("environment" score of 9).

In considering the problem of calling other residents names, the worker assessed the change potential for the problem itself as 7. The act of holding back from name-calling is possible for Mrs. J. She realizes that it isn't right and wants to stop this behavior (9). The residents ("environment") are not interested in going near Mrs. J at this time (change potential of 6), but some will probably respond if they are encouraged by the staff to try and reach out to her.

In totaling the change potential scores, the problems become prioritized as follows: (1) unfamiliarity with staff and resources at the home, (2) fighting with nurses over bath, (3) seclusiveness: not leaving room alone, (4) calling residents names, and (5) cultural isolation.

Contracting: *Building on the prioritized problem list, the worker and Mrs. J began to plan and to contract for what needed to be accomplished in order to achieve their mutually agreed on goals. The contracted plan they developed is shown in Table 6–9.*

III. Field Area: Public Social Welfare
A. Agency: State Social Service
B. Client System

Mr. and Mrs. P and their two children, ages 2 and 4, in need of emergency and permanent housing. (For additional background information, see Chapter 4, Engagement in Diverse Field Areas, III. Public Social Welfare.)

C. Summary of Preceding Stages

The problems and goals identified during engagement and data collection are listed in Table 5–7. During engagement, Mr. and Mrs. P expressed feelings of helplessness, anger, confusion, and rejection. As data were collected, the worker learned that the P's had a history of frequent moves, often caused by evictions due to their failure to pay the rent. The P's were receiving AFDC but had difficulty in planning and budgeting their money. Mr. P was unable to maintain employment because of his psychological incapacity. He was receiving weekly outpatient treatment at the local mental health center. At the time of initial assessment, the P's were asking for help only in locating housing and food.

D. Assessment

Assessment statement: *The P family do not have a place to stay because they were evicted from their apartment two weeks ago. They were evicted because they did not pay their rent on time. They do not plan and budget the money they receive from AFDC to last throughout the month. The P's are in need of emergency food because they do not have any money left from last month, and the check and food stamps for this month are being held at central office until the family is relocated.*

The change potential for the P's housing problem is assessed as low because of the P's limited motivation to become actively involved in searching for an apartment. Although there are possible resources for emergency shelter, the authorized payment for temporary placement is only for a maximum of 14 days.

The potential for meeting the need for food is assessed as high because several resources are available. Finding a way to transport a food supply to the P's should not be a problem unless the worker is unable to get an agency car.

Problem prioritization: *During initial assessment, the worker used the problem prioritization tool for conceptualization. It was clear and urgent that the first two areas in need of immediate attention were food and temporary shelter for the family. In prioritizing, the housing problem was divided into the two parts of (1) emergency shelter and (2) long-term residence. The food need was also subdivided. Considering these two housing needs along with the two food-supply needs, the worker drew up the prioritization shown in Table 6–11.*

The problem/need with the highest change potential is obviously finding immediate food for the family. The second-prioritized area is emergency shelter. The worker and the family will then need to plan for receiving a food supply to last until the P's receive AFDC income and food stamps. The fourth problem area, the last prioritized because of its low change potential, is the need for a long-term residence for the family. There is a pressing need to work on this fourth problem, because the temporary shelter can only be for two weeks. The worker knows also that the only way the temporary placement will be supported financially by the agency is if the P's make ongoing efforts to secure more permanent housing. An extension in temporary placement is granted only if there is evidence that every effort is being made by the family to locate a residence. Through problem assessment and prioritization, it became clear to the worker that pressure needed to be exerted on Mr. and Mrs. P to have them become more actively involved in the search for housing.

Contracting: *The worker and the P's developed the contract identified in Table 6–11. Permission was given by Mr. and Mrs. P to have the worker discuss their plan and progress with Mr. P's doctor and the income-maintenance technician. The worker asked Mr. P's doctor and the family's income-maintenance technician to help with motivating the P's to become more involved.*

IV. Field Area: Community Services
A. Agency: Clayton Neighborhood House
B. Client System
Four Hispanic families without heating in their apartments on the second floor of the 33 L Street apartment building. (For more background information, see Chapter 4, Engagement in Diverse Field Areas, IV. Community Services.)
C. Summary of Preceding Stages
The problem and goal identified during engagement and data collection are stated in Table 4–5. During engagement, residents from four apartments met with the worker and expressed feelings of anger, frustration, fear, helplessness, and victimization. In gathering information, the worker learned that residents were paying $250 for a one-room apartment, heat included. The name and address of the landlord was obtained and he was contacted. Because of the urgent nature of the problem, the worker and the residents moved quickly through engagement, data collection, and assessment.

TABLE 6-10.   Problem Prioritization

PROBLEM LIST	CHANGE-POTENTIAL SCORES (0–10)			TOTAL CHANGE POTEN-TIAL	PROBLEM PRIORITIZA-TION	SEVERITY
	PROBLEM	PERSON(S)	ENVIRON-MENT			
1. Housing						
a. Emergency shelter	8	8	8	24	2	•
b. Long-term	2	1	2	5	4	•
2. Food						
a. Emergency food	9	9	8	26	1	•
b. Until check and food stamps	8	8	7	23	3	•

*Life-at-risk situation.

TABLE 6-11. Contracted Plan

DATE IDENTIFIED	PROBLEM/ NEED	GOAL	TASK	CONTRACT	DATE ANTICIPATED	DATE ACCOMPLISHED
9/28	1. Food—emergency food	1. To obtain emergency food supply	1. Discuss resources	1. Worker and P's	9/28	
			2. Contact resource	2. Worker and P's	9/28	
			3. Obtain food	3. The P's	9/28	
9/28	2. Housing—emergency shelter	2. To move into emergency shelter	1. To locate resource	1. Worker	9/28	
			2. Discuss resources	2. Worker and P's	9/28	
			3. Contact resource	3. Worker and P's	9/28	
			4. To move to resource	4. P's with worker's help	9/28	
9/28	3. Food until AFDC check and food stamps arrive	3. To receive a food supply until AFDC check and food stamps arrive	1. Locate resource	1. Worker	9/29	
			2. Discuss	2. Worker and P's	9/29	
			3. Contact resource	3. Worker and P's	9/29	
			4. Receive food	4. P's and resource	9/29 until check and food stamps arrive	
9/28	4. Housing—long-term	4. To move into an apartment for long-term residence	1. Explore resources	1. Mr. and Mrs. P and worker	9/29	
			2. Contact resources	2. Mr. and Mrs. P	9/29	
			3. Move	3. The P's	10/12	
			4. Update	4. Worker, Mr. P's doctor, income-maintenance technician	9/29 and weekly	

D. Assessment

Assessment Statement: *The four families who live on the second floor of the 33 L Street apartment building do not have adequate heating because the heating for the building has not been regulated for adequate, even distribution. There also is a problem with direct communication between residents and the landlord. The residents and the landlord do not speak the same language, and Mr. X does not return calls made to him by tenants. (The worker added the communication problem to the problem list in the record; see Table 6–12.)*

The change potential for the problem of inadequate heating is assessed as somewhat high at this time because Mr. X, the landlord, is now aware of the problem and has stated that he will see that it gets resolved. As long as the problem of poor communication between residents and landlord remains, however, there is a possibility that a heating loss could recur and that the families would continue to have difficulty notifying Mr. X.

The problem of poor communication has a low potential for change at this time, because neither the families nor the landlord appear motivated to work on improving their communication. The families are afraid that if they meet with Mr. X, he may think that they are complaining too much and raise their rent. Mr. X indicated that he is very busy, with no time to contact residents.

Problem prioritization: *Because there was only one problem that the client system was presenting at this time, the worker did not use the problem prioritization tool. The need for heating was primary and urgent.*

Contracting: *The worker and the residents developed the contracted plan shown in Table 6–12 during their first meeting. The communication problem was added after the worker had contacted the landlord.*

V. Field Area: Education
A. Agency: Keeney Elementary School
B. Client System

Jim G, an 8-year-old African-American child, a third-grader with regressive behavior in school and at home. (For additional background information, see Chapter 4, Engagement in Diverse Field Areas, V. Education.)

C. Summary of Preceding Stages

The problems, goals, and tasks identified prior to a formal assessment are indicated in Table 5–8. Through play, Jim began to express his fear that his mother might leave him. Mrs. G shared feelings of anger and hurt regarding her husband and their relationship. She was finding it difficult to forgive him and to trust him. A meeting was arranged for the worker to meet with Mr. and Mrs. G to discuss Jim's problems and how they were being affected by the problem between Mr. and Mrs. G.

TABLE 6-12.   Contracted Plan

DATE IDENTIFIED	PROBLEM/ NEED	GOAL	TASK	CONTRACT	DATE ANTICIPATED	DATE ACCOMPLISHED
12/3	1. Lack of heat on second floor	1. To obtain consistent, adequate heating for second floor residents of L street apartment house	1. Contact janitor	1. Worker	12/3	
			2. Contact landlord	2. Worker	12/4	12/4
			3. Meet for follow-up	3. Residents and worker	12/5	12/5
12/5	2. Communication problem with landlord					

D. Assessment

When the worker met with Mr. and Mrs. G, they moved into the assessment stage of the General Method. Problems and goals were clarified, and a contracted plan was articulated by the worker, Jim, and both of his parents.

Assessment statement: *Jim has a problem being present at school physically, emotionally, and cognitively, owing to his upset feelings and his fears, which are caused by tension and quarreling at home between his parents. Jim has refused to fall asleep at night unless his mother is with him and a light is on in the room because he is afraid that she will leave him, as he overheard her saying to his father. He was overly tired in school because he was trying to keep awake during the night. He did not want to go to school because he feared his mother would leave for good while he was gone. Mr. and Mrs. G have been quarreling because Mrs. G recently learned that her husband had gone out with another woman.*

The change potential for Jim's school and home problems is assessed as high. The problems have had a short duration. Jim is reacting to external circumstances, and Mr. and Mrs. G are eager to improve the situation. Mrs. G is reassuring Jim that she will not leave him, and she and her husband are willing to go for professional help with their relationship.

Problem prioritization: *The worker used the problem prioritization tool as shown in Table 6–13.*

The change potential for the school tardiness and absenteeism problem was assessed as very high (9), because Jim did not have a history of missing school and the problem merely involved physical presence. The "person" change-potential score was assessed as medium (5). Even though Jim has the capacity to go to school, he did not appear to have the necessary motivation. The potential of the "environment" to change for problem resolution was assessed at a 9, very high, because Mr. and Mrs. G were being very cooperative and gave assurance that they would see that Jim came to school on time each day.

The change potential for the problem of declining academic performance was assessed as a 6 (medium—leaning toward high) because the nature of the problem was reactive (related directly to external circumstances) rather than internalized (present regardless of external circumstances), and because the problems had only become observable over the past month. It could become a serious problem if it persisted and Jim had to be removed from his classroom (asterisk in "severity" column).

The change-potential score for "person" as related to the school-performance problem was assessed as 5 (medium), because here too, although Jim has the capacity to do the work, he is not motivated for school achievement at this time. The "environment" score was appraised as a 9 (high), because Jim was beginning to be helped by his parents and

TABLE 6-13.　Problem Prioritization

PROBLEM LIST	CHANGE-POTENTIAL SCORES (0–10)			TOTAL CHANGE POTEN-TIAL	PROBLEM PRIORITIZA-TION	SEVERITY
	PROBLEM	PERSON(S)	ENVIRON-MENT			
School tardiness and absenteeism	9	5	9	23	1	
Declining academic performance	6	5	9	20	2	•
Sleeping problem	5	3	5	13	3	
Strain in marital relationship	6	8	9	23	1	

*Life-at-risk situation.

the school. His parents were committed to try to reduce the causes for Jim's decline in his school work.

The change potential for Jim's problem with falling asleep was given a 5 (medium), because of the somewhat serious nature of the problem, even though it had only recently developed. If Jim continued to get little sleep, he could become physically ill. The "person" potential was assessed as a 3 (somewhat low) because Jim was too upset to sleep and he continued to want a night light even after his mother assured him she would not leave. The "environment" score was a 5 for this problem, because J's parents were unable to make Jim fall asleep and they did not want to give him sleeping pills.

The change potential for the problem of a strained marital relationship was assessed as high (8) because Mr. and Mrs. G said that this was the first time they had had such a problem. Mr. G said that it was the first time he had gone out with someone else and that it would not happen again. The "person" potential was seen as high (8) because both Mr. and Mrs. G were motivated to work on their problem and to seek outside help. The "environment" potential was seen as very high (9) because several resources for marital counseling were available in the area.

Through problem prioritization, it became clear that the first two areas to be addressed were (1) Jim's school attendance and (2) Mr. and Mrs. G's marital relationship. With improvement in these two areas, it was hoped that Jim's school performance and sleeping at night would improve. Efforts for problem resolution would be primarily directed, therefore, according to the following sequence: (1) Jim's school tardiness and absenteeism, (2) the strain in Mr. and Mrs. G's relationship, (3) Jim's declining school performance, and (4) Jim's sleeping problem.

Contracting:　When the worker met with Mr. and Mrs. G, they reviewed the problems, goals, and tasks that were identified earlier, and

TABLE 6-14. Contracted Plan

DATE IDENTIFIED	PROBLEM/NEED	GOAL	TASK	CONTRACT	DATE ANTICIPATED	DATE ACCOMPLISHED
11/1	1. Jim's school tardiness and absenteeism	1. Jim's regular school attendance (on time every day)	1. Get J to school on time each day	1. Mr. and Mrs. G	11/5—each school day thereafter	11/5–ongoing
11/21	2. Strain in Mr. and Mrs. G's marital relationship	2. Improved marital relationship (less quarreling, growing trust)	1. Explore counseling resources 2. Select resource 3. Contact resource for appointment 4. Attend counseling sessions	1. Worker and Mr. and Mrs. G 2. Mr. and Mrs. G 3. Mr. G 4. Mr. and Mrs. G	11/27 11/27 11/28 Beginning week of 12/3	11/27 11/27
11/1	3. Jim's declining school performance	3. Improved school performance (interest, participation, grades)	1. Talk with Jim about school problems in relation to home problem 2. Check on Jim's performance 3. Update Mr. and Mrs. G on Jim's school performance 4. Continue to meet with Jim 5. Home meeting to evaluate progress	1. Mr. and Mrs. G, Jim, and worker 2. Worker with Jim's teacher 3. Worker 4. Worker 5. Worker, Mr. and Mrs. G, and Jim	11/27 11/28 and weekly 12/4 and 12/11 telephone contacts 11/29 12/17	11/27
11/2	4. Jim's problem getting to sleep at night	4. Jim's going to sleep at night without mother in room	1. Continue to assure Jim that Mrs. G is not going to leave him	1. Mrs. G	11/27 and each night thereafter	

they agreed on the contracted plan outlined in Table 6–14. As highlighted in the "contract" column, Mr. and Mrs. G planned to become actively involved in going for help with their marital relationship and in working with Jim and the school on Jim's school problems.

VI. Field Area: Corrections
A. Agency: Juvenile Court
B. Client System

Seven male youths, age 14, on probation, attending weekly group meetings led by co-workers at Juvenile Court. (For further background information, see Chapter 4, Engagement in Diverse Field Areas, VI. Corrections.)

C. Summary of Preceding Stages

The problems and goals identified by the group during engagement and data collection are outlined in Table 4–7. The youths in the group had low self-esteem and frequently referred to themselves as "stupid." All of the youths were in special classes at school for learning-disabled students. The workers also learned that all of the group participants were from single-parent homes and had trouble communicating with their parents. In visiting the homes and schools, the co-leaders learned that all seven youths were seen as "problems" by parents and teachers. The group members agreed to come to weekly group meetings in order to get off probation sooner (possibly a two-month reduction from a six-month probationary period).

D. Assessment

Assessment statement: *The youths in the group are on probation because they committed the following crimes: three members—breaking, entering, and stealing from homes; two members—theft of automobiles; two members—shoplifting. The problem of law-breaking is assessed as very serious for at least five of the youths (J, T, ML, B, and A). There is a history of law-breaking in their families (by fathers or brothers), and little discipline or support is offered in their homes. All of these five express a desire to get off probation and to make sure they "don't get caught again." They do not have a strong motivation to keep within the law. Although C appears to be sincerely sorry that he got into trouble and upset his father, the problem could become serious if he continues with the street gang he has joined. MK's offense was shoplifting for the third time. His mother said she never has enough money to provide for the children, and she thinks M was trying to bring home things for her and his sisters and brother. Although Mrs. K was finding it difficult to discipline M, she said she had started attending a "parenting" class at church that was helping her to work better with him. She was trying to get M to promise that he would not steal any more.*

The youths in the group are having a problem generally with their development and their feelings because they are entering adolescence

TABLE 6-15. Contracted Plan

DATE IDENTIFIED	PROBLEM/ NEED	GOAL	TASK	CONTRACT	DATE ANTICIPATED	DATE ACCOMPLISHED
10/1	1. Law-breaking leading to probation	1. T get off probation in four months	1. To attend and participate in weekly group meetings	1. Seven members, two workers	10/1 and each Monday at 4:00 P.M. for at least four months	10/1–8/15
			2. To participate in group meetings	2. Seven members	10/1 and each Monday at 4:00 P.M. for at least four months	
			3. To obey rules of school, home, community	3. Seven members	10/1	
			4. To receive weekly reports on behavior from home and school	4. Social workers, parents, school social workers	Week of 10/1 and once a week for four months	
			5. To chart progress at meetings	5. Workers and members	10/22 and at each meeting thereafter	
10/1	2. Bad tempers	2. To control tempers in school, home, and neighborhood	1. Discuss the problem dealing with anger	1. Workers and members	10/22	

TABLE 6-15. *Continued*

DATE IDENTIFIED	PROBLEM/ NEED	GOAL	TASK	CONTRACT	DATE ANTICIPATED	DATE ACCOMPLISHED
10/1	3. Need to understand "changes" of teenagers	3. To learn more about "changes" (including becoming indepen-dent, sex and family planning, and job training)	1. Select first topic	1. Workers and members	10/22	
10/1	4. Parent-son conflicts					
10/1	5. Low self-worth					

195

with low self-concepts and limited support systems at home and in school. Low self-esteem is reinforced by placement in special classes at school. All of the members have said that they don't like being told what to do, and that they get angry when someone puts pressure on them. They wish they could be independent, but they are afraid to try to make it on their own. They don't understand "the changes," physical and emotional, that they are going through, and they said there isn't someone they can talk to about them.

The lack of understanding about their "changes" has a high change potential because issues and topics related to the boys' development can be addressed and discussed in group meetings. Efforts can also be made through the group to help them with gaining temper control. The youths' motivation to work on both of these problem areas ("changes" and "temper") also contributes to an affirmative assessment of change potential.

Problem prioritization: In prioritizing problems, the workers considered mainly those problems that the group members said they wanted to work on. Although parent–son conflicts and low self-worth were seen by the workers as two problem areas, the group proceeded with identifying goals and tasks only for the following: (1) law-breaking leading to probation, (2) bad tempers, and (3) lack of understanding of the changes they were experiencing.

All of the youths knew that probation requirements included abiding by the rules of society and school, attending school, and obeying at home. They were also expected to attend weekly group meetings and to actively participate in them. If the youths had not agreed to the group, they would have been required to have weekly contact individually with a probation officer.

In discussing the prioritization of problems and goals with the group, everyone said top priority was to be given to getting off probation in four months (shortest possible time period). They knew that to achieve this goal, they had to meet all of the requirements of probation. In order to get along and abide by the rules at school and at home, the youths knew that they needed to work on controlling their tempers. They listed this as the second most important problem to be addressed. Finally, they agreed that basically they really didn't understand themselves and what was happening to them. They wanted to talk about the changes they had to learn to deal with.

Without having to use the prioritization tool, therefore, the group prioritized and clarified their goals as follows:

1. To get off probation in four months

2. To control their tempers at home and at school

3. To learn more about some of the changes they were facing (including becoming independent, understanding sex and family planning, and getting training and jobs)

There was a lengthy discussion over goal 1. Some wanted to add "and to stay off." What it would take "to stay off" was debated. Some said it meant they couldn't break the law any more. Others said they would just have to be more careful. The workers said that, hopefully, as participants grew in understanding and respecting themselves and others, they wouldn't need to be involved in law-breaking, and this would ensure their not getting caught again.

Contracting: *Using the prioritized problems and goals, a contracted plan was initiated with the group, as shown in Table 6–15. As indicated in the diagram, no goals or tasks were specifically planned at this time for problems 4 and 5, because the group didn't want to work on these problems. Since the group gave first priority to the goal of getting off probation, the planned contract centered on this problem. Later, additional tasks were added to the contract for accomplishment of goals 2 and 3 (described in Chapter 7).*

E. Ongoing Evaluation

During the assessment period, as the plan was made to chart progress weekly in the areas required for probation, evaluation graphs (explained in detail in Chapter 8) were designed to show the following: (1) group attendance, (2) group participation, (3) behavior in school (i.e., compliance with rules and expectations) and (4) behavior at home (i.e., compliance with rules and expectations). (See Figures 6–1, 6–2, 6–3, and 6–4.) Assessments of group attendance and participation were first scored by the co-leaders, and eventually by the youths themselves. The home assessments were made by the parents and given weekly over the phone to the workers. The school evaluation was made weekly by the youths' teachers and given to the school social worker, who had weekly contact with the court workers.

In addition to these weekly assessments, the workers checked each week to see if any of the group members had been reported to or picked up by police. Any incident was recorded in the youth's record and discussed with the youth individually.

As indicated in Figure 6–1, group attendance was charted by a graph point that indicated the number of the meeting (1, 2, 3, etc.) and an attendance score of 0, 1, or 2. A score of 0 meant "no attendance." A score of 1 was used if a youth came late or left early. A score of 2 meant he was on time and stayed for the full meeting. The youths knew that to get a two-month reduction in probation, they needed to maintain a score of 2 every week unless they were excused by a worker.

In Figure 6–2, group participation was assessed on a 0–4 vertical scale in terms of 0 = none, 1 = little, 2 = some, 3 = much, and 4 = full. The points were plotted to indicate (X) the number of the weekly meeting and (Y) the score for participation. An attempt was made to give more specific criteria for participation scores by the leaders. If a youth came and did not seem interested and never said anything at the meet-

FIGURE 6-1.   Group Attendance

FIGURE 6-2.   Group Participation

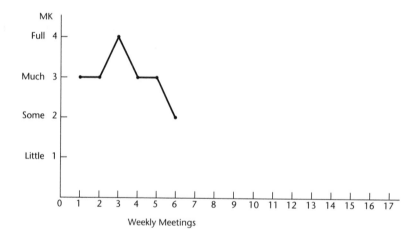

ings, he was given a 0. If he spoke at least once or twice at the meeting, he was given a 1. Speaking up about three or four times and being somewhat interested earned a 2. Sharing or responding five or six times and showing much effort at a meeting to participate was a 3, and being fully involved and fully sharing at a meeting was a 4. Group members were informed that they would need to average 3 points in group participation if they were to have a reduced probationary period.

The graphs for charting home and school reports on behavior had scale points ranging from 0 to 4 (0 = total noncompliance, 1 = poor, 2 = fair, 3 = good, 4 = excellent). The workers requested descriptions of behaviors and incidents if a youth was assessed by his parent or teacher as showing "poor" or "fair" behavior (Figures 6–3 and 6–4).

FIGURE 6-3.   School Behavior (Compliance with Rules and Expectations at School)

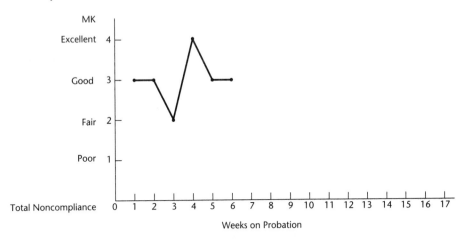

Weeks on Probation

FIGURE 6-4.   Home Behavior (Compliance with Rules and Expectations at Home)

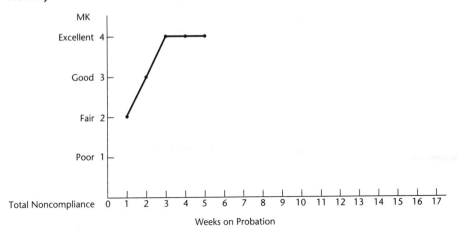

Weeks on Probation

VII. Field Area: Homeless Shelter

A. Agency: West End Community Shelter

B. Client System

Mr. José G, a 37-year-old Hispanic male, is homeless and HIV positive. (For additional information see Chapter 4, Engagement in Diverse Field Areas, VII, Homeless Shelter.)

C. Summary of Preceding Stages

During engagement and data collection, the worker learned Mr. G completed a drug detoxification program over six years ago. Since that time, he had been living a productive, independent life until he learned that he was HIV positive. At the time of intake, Mr. G. was homeless and with-

out any medical care. He had strong feelings of depression and loneliness. In addition to a recognized need for food, shelter, and health care, Mr. G expressed a need for more information about his illness and a desire to return to his Church (See Table 5–10). During data collection, the worker and Mr. G had some success in locating possible resources. These included a local free health clinic, a support system for HIV/AIDS victims, a Catholic church with a large Hispanic Outreach Program, and two residences for individuals with AIDS. They were also exploring possible full- or part-time job opportunities.

D. Assessment

Assessment Statement: Mr. G is not receiving any health care because he has no money or health insurance and because he is afraid of taking medications due to his past history of drug addiction. His physical condition (HIV positive) is expected to become increasingly worse because he has a progressive terminal illness (currently). Mr. G is homeless and without food because he does not have a job and his financial resources have been depleted. He does not have a job because he left his employment as chef in a nursing home when he learned he was HIV positive, and he has limited occupational skills (cooking and farming). Mr. G is recognizing a spiritual void in his life because he has been thinking about the terminal nature of his illness. He dropped away from church ("and God") as he became involved with drugs.

Although the change potential for Mr. G's illness is low because he has a progressive terminal illness, the worker assessed a moderate to high change potential in other problem areas because of Mr. G's strong motivation and the number of available resources. Both the worker and Mr. G recognized that progress in achieving goals was greatly dependent on the extent to which his illness progressed.

Problem prioritization: The problems identified in Table 5–10 were prioritized using the problem prioritization tool as shown in Table 6–16.

The illness received a score of 2 on the problem prioritization scale. Although there currently is no cure for AIDS or HIV, research continues and medications are available to provide some relief from pain and some delay in disease growth. Person (Mr. G) received a 4 due to Mr. G's high motivation, and resources received a 4 because of the availability of the health clinic. The change potential for "lack of knowledge" received a high score (8) because of the increasing amount of information available about the disease, particularly at the free clinic. The shelter could provide immediate shelter and food (total of 27); but, after 60 days, Mr. G would need to go to one of the residences for AIDS patients or find another location (15). Finding a job for Mr. G was seen as possible since he was highly motivated with a good work history, and currently his illness was not too severe to prevent at least part-time employment. It was also possible that if Mr. G's health did become worse he could start to

TABLE 6-16.   Problem Prioritization

	CHANGE-POTENTIAL SCORES (0–10)			TOTAL CHANGE POTEN-TIAL	PROBLEM PRIORITIZA-TION	SEVERITY
PROBLEM LIST	PROBLEM	PERSON(S)	ENVIRON-MENT			
HIV+	2	4	4	10	6	.
Lack of knowledge re: HIV	8	8	8	24	3	
Homeless/Hungry						
a. Emergency	9	9	9	27	1	
b. After 60 days	5	5	5	15	5	
Unemployment	6	6	6	18	4	
Spiritual Void	8	8	9	25	2	

*Life-at-risk situation.

receive public assistance and Social Security (rated a total of 18). Having Mr. G return to church was highly rated since Mr. G was very anxious to go to the church in town where he could be with people of his native culture (25).

Contracting: *After prioritizing the problems, Mr. G and the worker developed a contracted plan of action (See Table 6–17).*

E. Charted Progress

Mr. G's progress in the problem-solving process was summarized in ongoing summary recordings. The problem prioritization tool and the contracted plan developed during assessment were placed in his record for additional information and on-going indication of progress. A copy of the planned contract was given to Mr. G to remind him of the goals, tasks, and dates he and the worker decided upon.

Conclusion

In this chapter, the assessment stage of the General Method was described as consisting of the three major dimensions of (1) assessment statement, (2) problem prioritization, and (3) contracted plan. Tools were presented to assist the general practitioner in this stage of the Method.

Untrained workers have been found to move quickly into intervention after a problem is stated, without taking the time to assess the situation carefully.[8] A point emphasized in this chapter is the need for documented assessments and plans for each case before a worker takes action. Even when working with a crisis, the worker needs to demonstrate skill in planning where, when, and how to intervene. Through practice and supervised experience, the generalist learns to apply the tools in the process of assessment very quickly and accurately.

TABLE 6-17. Contracted Plan

DATE IDENTIFIED	PROBLEM/ NEED	GOAL	TASK	CONTRACT	DATE ANTICIPATED	DATE ACCOMPLISHED
5/7	1. Homeless a. Short term	1. Emergency shelter	1. Enroll in shelter	1. Mr. G & worker	5/8	
5/8	2. Spiritual void	2. Reunited with church	1. Go to service	1. Mr. G	5/10	
5/8	3. Lack of knowledge, re: HIV	3. Gain information	1. Review information at shelter 2. Go to free clinic, ask for help	1. Worker & Mr. G 2. Mr. G	5/9	
5/8	4. No income/job	4. Get income	1. Search for job 2. Apply for job 3. Start job 4. Seek SS/public assistance	1. Mr. G & worker 2. Mr. G 3. Mr. G 4. Mr. G	5/9– 5/15 5/20 Depends on illness	
5/7	5. No housing after 60 days	5. Locate residence	1. Look for apartment or home for AIDS victims 2. Get on waiting list of home for persons with AIDS	1. Worker & Mr. G 2. Mr. G	5/8 5/11	
5/8	6. HIV positive	6. Medical care	1. Make appointment 2. Go to free clinic 3. Continue treatment	1. Worker & Mr. G 2. Mr. G 3. Mr. G	5/8* 5/9 Next appointments	

*Because of the asterisk at problem 6 (life threatening problem), the worker continued to keep this problem in focus even though the problem has the lowest change potential.

The Generalist Method and each of its stages is a dynamic process. As circumstances change, the worker needs to be open to the possibility of having to reassess a situation or to reformulate a contract. There has been evidence that some workers resist finding out new information that would necessitate a reformulation of goals and plans.[9] A major challenge of general practice is to be able to stand on a diversified but solid foundation where one is expected to demonstrate flexibility and adaptation to emerging tensions, growth, and change.

Although the range of tasks and interventions by a generalist appears to be limitless, some parameters and guidelines need to be identified. An entry-level worker does have limitations in knowledge and skills. A skillful assessment may lead to a plan for referral to a specialized service. In the next chapter, an effort will be made to clarify and to categorize the interventions of a general practitioner during the fourth stage of the Generalist Method. In the intervention stage, the worker collaborates with other systems in carrying out the plan that was contracted during assessment.

NOTES

1. Anthony N. Maluccio and Wilma D. Marlow, "The Case for the Contract," in Beulah Roberts Compton and Burt Galaway, *Social Work Processes*, rev. ed. (Homewood, Ill.: Dorsey, 1979), p. 332.

2. Mary E. Richmond, *Social Diagnosis* (New York: Russell Sage Foundation, 1917).

3. John L. Levitt and William J. Reid, "Rapid-assessment Instruments for Practice," *Social Work Research and Abstracts* 17, no. 1 (Spring 1981): 13–19.

4. See, for example, Florence Wexler Vigilante and Mildred D. Mailick, "Needs—Resource Evaluation in the Assessment Process," *Social Work* 33, no. 2 (March–April 1988): 101–104.

5. Rosemary Sarri, "Diagnosis in Group Work," in Robert Vinter, ed., *Readings in Group Work Practice* (Ann Arbor, Mich.: Campus Publishers, 1967), pp. 37–71.

6. Ann Hartman, "Diagnostic Assessment of Family Relationships," *Social Casework* 59 (October 1978): 465–76.

7. Murray G. Ross, *Community Organization: Theory and Principles* (New York: Harper & Brothers, 1955), p. 39.

8. Sister Maria Joan O'Neil, "Study of Direct Service Workers of the Department of Human Resources" (Unpublished report, Hartford, Conn., April 1980).

9. Henry Miller and Toni Tripodi, "Information Accrual and Clinical Judgment," *Social Work* 12, no. 4 (July 1967): 63–69.

CHAPTER 7

Intervention

A professional practice that is defined by its knowledge of theories, its methods, processes, modalities, and techniques, is meaningless to all but its own practitioners if it is not delivered appropriately to those who need its services.

—Carol H. Meyer[1]

The role of the worker during the intervention stage of the General Method evolves according to the tasks identified in the contracted plan described in the preceding chapter. Several roles have been identified as appropriate for an entry-level generalist. These include broker, advocate, reformer, educator, counselor, and mediator.[2] Before assuming any particular role, however, the generalist needs to clarify the nature of the problem to be addressed, the goals to be accomplished, the resources to be utilized, and the plan to be followed. Only after a period of engagement, data collection, and assessment will the worker be ready to assume the role necessary for appropriate intervention at any particular time. A generalist may move from one role to another or may assume multiple roles while using interventions during the process of helping. Often a worker may move from working with one to working with many, from the individual to the large bureaucracy. In general, the various activities of the entry-level generalist may be classified under the four major headings of (1) direct intervention, (2) information and referral, (3) case management and teamwork, and (4) indirect intervention. With each of these four major interventions, particular techniques and skills are used to work with different problems, age groups, or types of systems. In this chapter, the four general types of intervention will be presented as they are found in generalist practice.

As stated earlier, the generalist stands at the interface of persons and environment and carefully tries to collaborate with both systems in a planned intervention process to enhance their fit and interactions with each other. The selection of the type of intervention to be used is based on a skillful assessment.

Direct Intervention

When a worker, in agreement with a system, intervenes directly with the system, that worker is engaging in *direct intervention.* The goals of direct intervention are primarily seen as (1) to give ongoing support to a system as it carries out contracted tasks, and (2) to help a system to bring about change in itself. Either or both of these goals may describe the purpose for direct intervention.

Planned intervention that directly involves a client system and a social work generalist may be brief or extended, depending on the identified need or problem and the capacities of the client and the worker. The extent of direction or leadership offered by the worker in direct intervention is influenced also by the seriousness or crisis level of the situation and by the strengths and coping capacities of the client. The nature of the interaction is usually supportive and growth-promoting.

The generalist uses a broad range of relationship and problem-solving skills in the course of intervening with members of a client system. The relationship itself is central to the entire process. Particularly in the intervention stage, a strong working relationship is necessary. During the course of direct intervention, the worker may use the relationship skills of listening, responding, guiding, paraphrasing, clarifying feeling, sensing, and, possibly, confronting. In addition, the problem-solving skills of problem and need identification, data collection, assessment, problem prioritization, goal-setting, planning, contracting, and evaluating may be repeated as problems are added or changed.

A client may begin with identifying immediate material needs or problems with institutions. As a working relationship develops and the worker is able to help with the presenting problems, clients frequently begin to discuss more interpersonal or personal problems. Information is gathered and assessments are made regarding each of these problems. Worker and client may agree to tasks on the contracted plan that entail direct, ongoing contact between worker and client system. This contact may be seen as a means for the client to achieve greater understanding of self and others or to bring about a change in self. If the goal identified is to bring about a change in someone outside of the client system, the intervention will need to include the outsider directly (becoming a part of the client system) or indirectly (becoming a target system). For example, if Mrs. N wants her husband to overcome his drinking problem, there is little chance of accomplishing this goal just by direct intervention with Mrs. N.

In addition to the foundation skills identified in Table 1–5. Chapter 1, contemporary techniques are being used, primarily by advanced workers, in direct practice with particular systems. Beginning generalists are not expected to use these techniques unless they have studied and practiced them under supervision. For example, eco-maps,[3] sculpting,[4] and genograms[5] are valuable tools to use when working with a family. They provide a technical and vivid means for helping clients to understand diverse perceptions of the family. (These techniques may also be adapted for use in working with individuals, groups, and communities.)

For working with groups, techniques and concepts have been identified to enable a worker to handle disruptive behavior[6] and scapegoating.[7] The use of force-field analysis[8] helps a worker to pinpoint the supportive and the constraining forces that have impact on the life and growth of an organization. The technique of force-field analysis and techniques to handle disruptive behavior and prevent scapegoating may also be adapted for use with individuals and families as well as groups and communities.

For working with adolescents, an effective technique to promote greater self-awareness is the use of the "adolescent grid."[9] By recalling major events within a visible framework, the adolescent can avoid the discomfort often felt in face-to-face interviewing. The grid identifies crisis points chronologically, according to place, family, school, health, activities, and other areas. Adults or children, individuals, groups, or families may also find that this structured instrument is a helpful device for overcoming their fears of interacting with a worker.

The use of play is a valuable technique for working with children. Basically, a child is limited in communicating with words. Play is a natural means for children to express fears, wishes, hurtful experiences, and unmet needs. Repetitious play helps a child to master unpleasant experiences. To expect a child to be able to talk with a strange adult about his or her problems or painful experiences is unrealistic and insensitive. Children usually expect adults to speak to them in order to teach, direct, or correct them. A child may feel great fear and discomfort on being led into a room where there is nothing to indicate that it is a place for children. Social workers can learn how to select appropriate toys and to engage in play that is supportive and helpful to children. This technique is useful during every stage of the General Method when working with children. If it becomes apparent that the child's behavior patterns are inappropriate for the current reality, and that the supportive intervention of the generalist is insufficient to bring about the necessary change, a referral should be made to a child specialist. Through play therapy, a child may be helped to grow in insight and to be free to find appropriate responses to life situations.

As a worker intervenes directly with any person, family, group, or community, it may become clear that giving support or understanding is insufficient to achieve certain goals. If it is necessary for a change to take place in a system, the worker may use some techniques from behavioral modification, as well as problem-solving skills. In addition to helping a client system to develop a rational, systematic way to solve problems, a worker may use specific behavioral techniques for more immediate control of undesirable behaviors, thoughts, or feelings. Although behavior modification in its entirety is a specialized treatment approach, individual techniques such as behavior reinforcement, cognitive restructuring, relaxation exercises, and thought stopping can be selected for use in generalist practice.[10]

As stated, all of the contemporary techniques that have been cited are supplementary to the basic skills found in the foundation of generalist practice (Table 1–5, Chapter 1). Eco-maps, sculpting, genograms, techniques for handling disruptive behavior and scapegoating, force-field analysis, the adolescent grid, communicating through play, behavior reinforcement, cognitive restructuring, relaxation exercises, and thought stopping are tools that enable a client to grow in understanding. Also, they may facilitate change in a client by helping to clarify, objectify, and promote greater control of self or a situation.

There are times when it becomes clear that a client needs to change through gaining insight. If a pattern of behavior emerges that continues to cause problems, the generalist will try to confront the client about it in a cognitive, supportive, and problem-solving type of intervention. Some of the techniques identified above may be utilized. If this is insufficient to bring about the change necessary for goal achievement, the generalist has to be able to realize that a client system may need more intensive help to gain insight and overcome its problematic behavior. For the individual, family, group, or community, this could involve delving into buried feelings or past experiences over a prolonged period of time through an uncovering, sequential process. In time, the client system can be helped to connect current behaviors with feelings that are triggered by certain situations that relate to past experiences. Barriers and dynamics that cause conflict and broken relationships can be exposed. Through this intensive work, the system may be freed to choose more acceptable behaviors in the future.

This intensive direct work is not within the parameters of entry-level generalist practice. Occasionally, a system may come with enough strengths or past experiences to be able to grow in such insight with support from the generalist. Usually, however, the generalist brings the client system with this type of need to the point of realizing that more specialized help is needed, and they enter into the process of referral. Whether the client system is an individual, family, group, or community, there are times when the generalist is unable to help the system bring about the change needed through direct intervention, and a referral is made. A community worker, for example, may find that major factions within a community are preventing goal accomplishment. The power and political struggles may be so intense that the generalist is unable to break through these dynamics. A referral would be made to a community organizer with advanced skills and experience.

Information and Referral

There are times when it becomes apparent that a client system does not have the information needed for problem resolution. Often, clients have received misinformation or they have misconceptions about environmental resources. They may contact a worker to receive assistance which the worker or agency may not be able to provide. In these cases, the worker's intervention is primarily that of information and referral.

The process in which a worker directs a system to another resource for help with an identified problem or need is called *referral*. Often workers are surprised to learn that a resource has not picked up on a case as expected. Several factors can lead to an unsuccessful referral. There is, in fact, an art to knowing where, when, and how to make a referral. Time, planning, and processing are needed for an appropriate match between system in need and available resource. The act of referral may be described as a six-stage process. If any one of the stages is overlooked, the referral may fail. The experience of an unsuccessful referral may build up in the client system feelings of negativism and fear, as well as resistance to reaching out and trying again with another resource.

The referral process consists of the following essential stages to be enacted by worker and system in need.

1. Clarifying and stating the problem or need for which help is sought and of the goals to be accomplished
2. Researching appropriate and available resources and informing client about them
3. Discussing options and selecting resources with the system in need
4. Planning and contracting the means of contact with the selected resource (initial contact, sending information, providing transportation, client-resource meeting)
5. Meeting of system in need with resource
6. Following-up by worker to see if goal is being or has been accomplished

The basic principle of having the client do for him- or herself is paramount throughout the referral process. Only when it is clear that the client does not have the knowledge or ability to carry out a task in the process should the worker intervene and take action.

In stage 1, the generalist helps the client system to clarify what the problem or need is that cannot be taken care of by the generalist. The feelings and goals that relate directly with the identified problem or need are also explored. The feelings both client and worker may have about sending the client to a different resource need to be expressed. Either one might see a referral as a personal failure and feel somewhat guilty. The limitations of the worker and/or the agency should be presented as factually as possible. The client may need to be reassured that the referral is not a rejection by the worker. The worker needs to convey to the client system a sincere desire to see the client system achieve its goals and a strong belief in the ability of a resource to make this possible.

In stage 2 of the process, worker and, if possible, client system work on locating resources to meet the identified needs. Both formal and informal resources are explored. If a need or problem can be resolved through utilizing informal resources (family, friends, community), this may be more desirable to the client. Some clients may prefer not to have these local networks know about their problem, and formal resources (agencies, programs, institutions) will need to be considered.

It is imperative to find resources that are appropriate and available. A resource is appropriate not only because it provides services that address the identified problem or need, but also because it suits the persons and environment of the particular system in need. For example, a person who speaks only Spanish would need to receive help from an agency that understands and works with Hispanic people. Further, if the resource is not accessible to people from the neighborhood or environment of the client system, it is usually not an appropriate resource. If contact with the resource is expected to be brief and transportation can be assured, it is possible to use a resource that is not located near the environment of the client system. Sometimes, workers incorrectly assume that client systems are able to find bus fare or transportation on their own.

Agency resources may not be available for certain clients, owing to the hours when services are provided. Although a resource may be appropriate, it may have a long waiting list because of an insufficient number of staff members available to deliver the services. Moreover, the cost for the service may be outside the price range of some clients and, therefore, the resource is not available to them.

In stage 3 of the referral process, the worker and system share their findings about possible resources, and the client system is the one to choose the resource to be contacted. The worker helps the system to consider alternatives, with probable outcomes or consequences for each option. If there is some question or doubt about a resource, this should be explored. No false hope or reassurance should be given. Even when it appears that an appropriate and available resource has been located and selected, it may prove beneficial to help the client system at this time to identify a second choice in case the first does not work out.

In stage 4 of the referral process, time is given for planning and contracting to decide who will (1) make the initial contact with the resource (usually by phone), (2) give whatever information is necessary for the referral to be accepted, (3) arrange for transportation or provide it, (4) meet with the resource to initiate the services. There is a whole range of possible ways to achieve each of these four tasks. The two extremes on a scale to indicate the range of options would be (1) the client carrying out the task, and (2) the worker carrying it out. In between are different worker–client combinations for which the task may be subdivided. For example, in the first task of initial contact, the worker could (1) dial the number and have the client speak, (2) dial and speak first and then put the client on the phone, (3) have the client dial, but the worker speaks, (4) have a three-way conference call in which worker, client, and resource person all speak together. The initial contact might also involve writing a letter or going to the agency to set up an appointment. These tasks also could be done by the worker, by the client, or by some combination. The same range of options exists for deciding about giving information, arranging transportation, and having the first client–resource meeting. The guiding principle of having the members of the system do for themselves whenever possible should be used as the contract is formulated and tasks are planned.

In stage 5, the new helping process begins as the client system meets directly with the resource. Here, too, the art of referral operates, in the worker's careful assessment of whether or not the client system can or should have the first session alone with the resource. The worker not only considers the motivation and capacity of the client system to have this be a fruitful encounter, but also the motivation and capacity of the resource itself to truly be of help to the system in need. In some individual situations, it may be better to have the worker present in the first contact to offer support, information, or advocacy if needed. As soon as possible, however, the worker should back out and let the system become involved with the resource on its own.

Every referral should have some type of follow-up by the worker. When a person, family, group, or community come to a professional person or agency for help, they share—sometimes painfully—their problems, needs, and aspirations. The professional person and human-service agency show a sense of respect and commitment to people in need by working diligently at getting the necessary help for them. People asking for help are often vulnerable and dependent on the expertise and sensitivity of those sanctioned to give service. Social workers are expected to know what resources are available and how to help people utilize them. It is true that many times circumstances outside of the control of a worker or agency prevent the carrying through of a service. However, the social worker must find out if the person who asked for help did receive it. If the person did not receive help, the worker needs to find out why help was not given and to consider whether anything else could be done.

The worker finds out if help was provided by checking directly with the resource, with the client, or with both. It is important that both resource and client know that the worker will be calling back, and when to expect the follow-up. This should be clarified prior to the worker's last contact with each. In planning, the worker will skillfully discern what a follow-up contact with the client might do to the beginning working relationship of the client and the new resource. The worker will also need to consider what effect it might have on the client system to hear that the worker called the resource to see how things were going. Negative repercussions will be avoided as long as all three parties (worker, client, and resource system) know in advance that the worker will be doing a follow-up and it is clear who will be contacted and when.

When it appears that the goals for the referral are being accomplished, the worker is able to close the case. If there are other problems or needs that are not being addressed by the resource, and the client system continues to ask for the services of the worker, a collaborative arrangement must be worked out between the resource and the worker. Using a holistic perspective, the generalist knows that problems and needs of a system are interdependent, and that when service provision is carried out by more than one resource, collaboration and teamwork among the resources are needed. A third type of intervention frequently found in general practice, therefore, may be identified as teamwork.

Case Management and Teamwork

Because of the nature of the work of the generalist, an entry-level social worker frequently needs to call on other resources for collaboration in providing service. On a contracted plan (Chapter 6), the identification of who will complete the task often includes a worker with one or more other helping persons. The individuals, groups, families, or communities that seek help from a generalist usually have many problems and, therefore, need assistance from several service providers. The generalist has skills to form action systems with these other resource persons in a cooperative effort to achieve their common purpose of providing human services.

Case management is a contemporary term that is used to refer to the actions taken by a worker to mobilize and to bring together the various services needed in a case for efficient, effective service delivery. A case manager tries to coordinate, monitor, and evaluate the services provided.[11] If identified as the case manager, the generalist must use skill to work with the various resources for a case to develop an atmosphere of shared leadership and openness. When diverse resources work together in common planning, decision making, and consolidated action, the efforts of this organized group may be called *teamwork*. Unless the service providers who are working with one system move to become a team, the generalist may carry the heavy burden not only of managing the case, but also of being seen as primarily responsible for its outcome. When resources truly become a team, there is a strong sense of sharing and commitment and of a group responsibility for final outcome.

To begin to grow in the art of teamwork, it is important to realize that there is no *one* model of teamwork that should be used at all times. Some teams have a designated leader, and some have a rotating leadership. A leader needs to have an understanding of group process, as well as goal-directed abilities and skill in bringing forth contributions and leadership from other members of the group.

There are six basic principles for effective teamwork. When a team is not achieving its goals, a review of the principles could reveal possible causes for difficulties incurred. The principles are summarized as follows:

1. *Obtain sanction:* Team members must be free to communicate openly in collaborative service planning and provision. The system in need must sanction the team with the understanding that there will be open communication among members.
2. *Know yourself:* All members of the team must clearly know their own professional identities and the distinctive contribution they and their agencies can make to the team.
3. *Respect one another:* Members of the team must respect each discipline, recognizing similarities and differences without being threatened or "turf protective."
4. *Meet regularly:* The team must meet on a regular basis for shared communication, planning, and evaluation.
5. *Define task assignments:* The team must define clearly each person's tasks and role in providing service.
6. *Share responsibility:* The team must assume collective responsibility for service outcome.

A team proceeds through stages that are similar to the six stages of the General Method. Collectively, members of the team clarify the problem and purpose for organizing, share data, agree on goals and a plan for intervention, assign tasks, evaluate, and terminate contact. The struggle for power or status, the emergence of conflict, and the development of group norms and expectations are important dimensions of a growing team, as they are for any human system.

Although teamwork may be emotionally draining and time-consuming, it can help to avoid duplication and excessive demands on limited, declining resources. Working together as a team can prevent fragmentation or overlap in service delivery. Through a team approach, client systems are not left with the burden of trying to integrate services on their own. A sense of unity and community is fostered.[12]

Indirect Intervention

Currently, the concept "indirect practice" is defined in different ways within the profession of social work. On the one hand, it refers to practice in such areas as administration, supervision, management, or class advocacy. From this perspective, the practitioner is not having client contact. On the other hand, the term "indirect practice" is used to refer to work with target systems or outside agencies in order to achieve goals for a worker's client or clients. Because of possible confusion in the use of the concept, a distinction is made in this edition between "indirect practice" and "indirect intervention." The term "indirect practice" means advanced professional activities, such as administration and management. "Indirect intervention" refers to interactions with systems that affect clients during the intervention stage of the General Method. The worker intervenes with these systems in order to bring about changes needed for clients to achieve their identified goals.

Getting a system involved and responsive frequently uses a worker's political skills. The generalist may find a potential resource that is resistant to the requests of a client or the worker. Such skills as providing evidence, publicizing, bargaining, organizing, demonstrating, taking legal action, and influencing policy development may have to be utilized. For example, a hospital worker with refugee patients has been unsuccessful in obtaining services from a refugee program. The worker knows that the program is being funded to offer the services requested. The generalist may need to present to her supervisor and to the administrator of the refugee program evidence that several requests were made without results. If this intervention is unsuccessful and efforts at bargaining are also unproductive, a form of publicizing may need to take place.

Often a worker will need to use a combination of political skills to bring about change in a target system. For example, legislators may have to be contacted for funding to be allocated to expand needed programs. Evidence of need will have to be presented, and bargaining or demonstration may take place. The generalist may have to give testimony or to speak at open hearings. Interested groups may have to be organized for their participation in the change process. As indirect interventions are planned, the worker keeps in mind the need to involve the clients—those that are suffering from the problems—as much as possible in all of the planned activities.

Indirect interventions may be enacted with any size or type of system. A worker and client system may be unable to achieve identified goals because of a refusal or resistance on the part of an individual, family, group, community, organization, or institution. Frequently, a worker serves a client through indirect interventions with target systems that are represented by members of various professions. Although every effort is made to develop a cooperative working relationship with these representatives, the generalist may have to move into an adversary process in behalf of the client system.

As a client advocate in an adversary process, a social worker tries to persuade a system to decide in favor of the client. The role of adversary is often difficult for a social worker with a basic practice principle of self-determination. The competition or drive for victory in an adversary process can become very strong. It may not be easy for a worker to remain calm and emotionally controlled if the opponent is presenting half-truths or attacking what the worker has presented as valid.

To interact effectively with members of different professions or within their work environments, a social worker needs to understand each profession and environmental system. For example, if social workers are to form alliances or adversary systems with lawyers, they need to have a working knowledge of the vocabulary, methods, and motivations of lawyers, of the requirements of law, and of the functioning of the legal system. Unfortunately, research shows that there is often a tense, untrusting relationship between social workers and lawyers.[13] The frustration that exists as these two professions interface may be due to a basic lack of understanding of each other. The use of words and the approach to problem-solving found in each discipline are different. The professionals may use the same words, but not mean the same thing. For example, the use of the words *contract* and *fact* may cause confusion in communication between lawyers and social workers. A contract used in the process of assessment by a social worker is not the same as the legal contract used in a legal process. Social workers collect data on feelings and attitudes as well as such facts as names, dates, and circumstances. They are concerned with "why" something happened in order to arrive at a plan for problem resolution. A lawyer is concerned with evidence and "what" happened to see if legal action can be taken. Although a social worker may know that something is true, it is not useful information in the court unless it can be documented and admitted into evidence. Whereas the law of the lawyer is technical and specific, the theory of the social worker is dynamic and evolving.[14]

Prior to any indirect intervention, the generalist needs to prepare for interaction with a system by studying the system and its representatives. It may be helpful to consult with someone from a similar system or discipline to identify the most effective way to contact, communicate, and intervene with the system.

Indirect interventions are usually the most challenging and difficult type of interventions for beginning generalists. Social work education programs seldom provide students with a working knowledge of other professional disciplines. Beginning generalists are primarily prepared for direct work with client systems.[15] The entry-level worker, therefore, needs strong educational and emotional support through supervision and consultation to persevere and accomplish indirect interventions.

Designs for General Interventions

The four major types of intervention by a generalist may be depicted in designs composed of circle clusters. In Figure 7–1, the worker (W) is seen in interaction with a client system (C) through overlapping circles. This simple design is used to demonstrate *direct intervention*.

A case example for Figure 7–1 is a generalist working with a family (father, mother, and son) as they grow in understanding the changing behaviors of their adolescent son (age 15).

In Figure 7–2, a *referral* is pictured by a worker (W) interacting with a client system (C) as the client begins to interact with a resource (R). If contact with a particular resource system has not yet been actualized, but is the intent of the intervention, the resource system (R) may be depicted by a broken line. If both a worker and a client have direct contact with a resource, the W circle would extend to the right and intersect the R circle also (Figure 7–3).

An example for Figures 7–2 and 7–3 would be a worker whose client is a depressed woman who is talking about suicide. As indicated in the design, the worker is trying to help the client to face the seriousness of her problem and to admit herself to the local mental health center.

In the design found in Figure 7–4, the worker (W) and other resources (A, B) join together in a team effort. Collectively, the worker (W) and other resources (A, B) interact with a client system (C). The overlapping circles reflect the *teamwork* in human service provision. For example, in working with a community that has experienced a number of unexplained fires lately, a generalist may be working with representatives from the fire department and the local police force to help the community members express their concerns and to find ways to combat fires and to report suspected arsonists. In Figure 7–4, all three resources (worker, fire department, and police) are shown as coming together to form a team for ongoing service to the community. In Figure 7–5, the worker remains in the role of case manager because teamwork has not been established with all three resources to work together. The local police and the fire department are called upon by the worker to meet separately with the community on different occasions. The absence of an ongoing team effort is depicted in Figure 7–5 boundaries that do not overlap (A and B), except with the worker (W) who contacts and coordinates the services for the community.

Figure 7–6 is a diagram of *indirect intervention*. In this design, the generalist (W) is interacting with a target system (T) to mobilize it to meet the needs of a client system (C).

A case example of indirect intervention as shown in Figure 7–6 could involve a group of youngsters who need tutoring. The generalist (W) can be seen as putting pressure on the school system (T) to provide the services needed for the group (C).

Additional designs in intervention may be drawn up to reflect combined intervention types. Sometimes, as shown in Figure 7–7, a generalist (W) may be involved with a number of community resources (A, B) in a team effort to influence a target system (T) for client service (C).

FIGURE 7-1. Direct Intervention

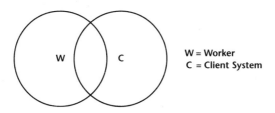

W = Worker
C = Client System

FIGURE 7-2. Referral

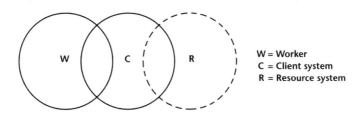

W = Worker
C = Client system
R = Resource system

FIGURE 7-3. Referral—Worker and Client Contact

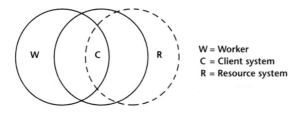

W = Worker
C = Client system
R = Resource system

FIGURE 7-4. Teamwork

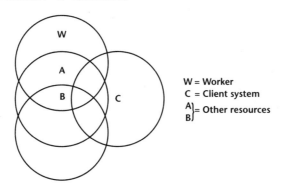

W = Worker
C = Client system
A⎫
B⎭= Other resources

215

FIGURE 7-5. Case Management

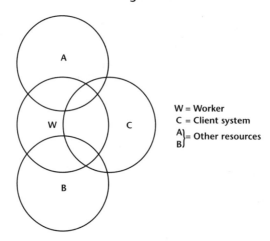

W = Worker
C = Client system
A⎫
B⎭ = Other resources

FIGURE 7-6. Indirect Intervention

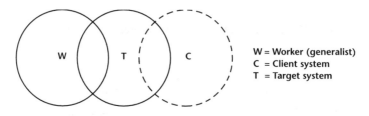

W = Worker (generalist)
C = Client system
T = Target system

FIGURE 7-7. Combined Interventions

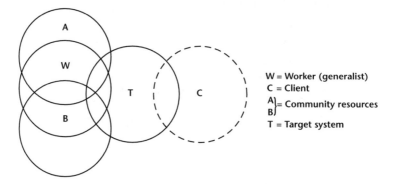

W = Worker (generalist)
C = Client
A⎫
B⎭ = Community resources
T = Target system

216

For example, a generalist (W) working in behalf of an elderly community (C) plagued by vandalism may join with town officials (A) and the local newspaper (B) to advocate better police protection (T) of the elderly community.

In the course of working with a system, a generalist may change the design of intervention as problems or needs emerge or are resolved. At any given time, a worker should be able to identify the design (or designs) currently being used.

Working with Different Systems

As stated in the section on direct interventions, a generalist has skills and techniques for work with systems of any size. In addition to the relationship skills, problem-solving skills, and political skills, as categorized in the foundation framework (Table 1–6 Chapter 1), there is a range of techniques that can be called on as needed with particular systems. Techniques may be appropriately identified as generalist-practice techniques if they can be used with more than one type of system or problem. Specialized techniques are specifically designed for and used in a particular area of specialization, according to problem, population, institution, traditional or specialized method, or theoretical approach. Some techniques that originate in a specialized area may later be extended for use with a variety of systems by the generalist with additional knowledge, skills, and experience under supervision.

For example, although the technique known as "sculpting" has been used primarily in family work, as stated earlier, it could be used with a group or community. Basically, sculpting is a technique in which a person creates a live "sculpture" to portray the way he or she views the members of a system in relation to one another. The worker asks a volunteer to create a space and action configuration: to bodily place all members of the system as he or she sees them—according to distance and body position in relation to one another and to the volunteer. When placed in the position, each person stays as still as a sculpture. The sculptor is encouraged to discuss how and why each person has his or her position, and every member of the configuration is asked to describe what it feels like to be in that position. Each individual in the system is given the opportunity to sculpt out his or her perception of the system. The technique enables all present to grow in understanding the perceptions and feelings of one another. It helps to break down any personal barriers against verbalization and to lessen anxieties. Through this type of play activity, the less powerful or less verbal individuals in the system are freed to express their views and to receive the attention of everyone present.[16]

Often, there is a need within a group or a community, as well as within a family, for greater understanding and sharing among members. Individual members of a group can be encouraged by a worker to sculpt out how they see the interactions and relationships among group members through a sculpted tableau of the group.

In a meeting of a community, a generalist can ask for representatives of the subsystems that constitute the community to portray through space and action positioning how they perceive the relationships among subsystems of the community. Other members of the subsystem may be allowed to help their representative find the best way to depict relationships within the community from the collective eyes of the subsystem. Again, the technique of sculpting can expand the sensitivity of the parts to the perceptions of the whole. Communications within a community can be enriched as fears and feelings of insignificance are exposed.

The sculpting technique may be used also by a group of professionals for team building. If the process of teamwork is not moving along, the technique may be introduced to help members of the team become more aware of how each of them sees the emerging relationships and lines of communication within the team.

Actually, the sculpting technique may be used with different systems during any of the stages of the General Method. In addition to intervention, sculpting may facilitate progress during engagement, data collection, assessment, evaluation, and termination. The technique may be helpful in identifying goals as well as problems and feelings. Not only could the generalist ask the volunteer to sculpt out how he or she perceives the system at present (identifying problems and feelings), but also how he or she would hope to see the system in the future (goals). Through a discussion about each member's views for the future, a consensus may be reached on goals for the system.

Another example of the generic nature of techniques used by a generalist can be found in the behavioral technique of relaxation. The technique of relaxation exercises is done usually on a one-to-one basis. However, just as the individual becomes tense during times of stress, there are obvious periods in the meetings of groups, families, and communities when tensions rise and stress is heightened. As stress builds up within any one of these systems, energy to think and act rationally can become blocked. The generalist can help to reduce the mounting anxiety through a relaxation exercise.

Members of the system are first encouraged to become aware of the reality that tension is building, and they are asked to stop the process and the conversation for a few minutes to relax. One relaxation technique is to have members alternate in tensing and relaxing various muscles and to focus on the different feelings that result. They begin to sense the power within themselves to control the mounting or releasing of tension within their bodies. In addition, members are asked to take deep breaths and to be sensitive to the way deep breathing helps to relax muscles. As the system becomes peaceful and progressively relaxed, some cue words, such as "calm," "still," or "serene," may be said. Later, if tension begins to build again, these words may be used to help the system to recall the relaxed state. With anxiety reduced, the system may be helped to talk about what was triggering the mounting stress. Usually, something has been said that caused members of the system to feel threatened, angered, or afraid.[17]

Force-field analysis is a third example of a technique that may be used by a generalist during intervention with systems of different sizes. This technique, based on Kurt Lewin's "field theory"[18] has been developed primarily as a tool to assist in data collection and assessment of organizations.[19] With a little creative thinking and modification, the technique can readily be used in generalist practice with individuals, groups, families, and communities. Whenever any system is not able to change or to accomplish tasks that were identified in a contracted plan (Chapter 6), there are usually restraining forces operating that are stronger than the driving forces. The generalist may try to offer the system support and understanding of the situation by using a force-field analysis.

Basically, the technique is a procedure that uses a framework to organize information as it relates to the accomplishment of a goal. The forces that influence those individuals responsible for enacting tasks necessary for goal accomplishment are organized and classified as either "driving" or "restraining" forces. The process begins with a clarification of a specific goal. Then, those who are the primary actors or persons needed to achieve the goal are identified. Next, each of the forces impinging on these persons is categorized as either driving or restraining. The forces are then evaluated in terms of their openness to and potential for change. The consistency and stability of each force during a period of change is also questioned. Finally, a judgment is made regarding the strengths of the driving forces as compared with restraining forces in the light of the desirable goal. If there is no imbalance in which the change-producing forces have greater weight, the failure in goal accomplishment can be understood and predicted. The technique could help any individual, group, family, community, or organization to see more clearly why certain tasks are not being performed and goals are not being accomplished. It also provides direction for planned intervention to counteract the restraining forces and to build up those that are change-producing.

The technique of force-field analysis has characteristics similar to those of the tool used for problem prioritization as found in Chapter 6, and also of the procedure used for evaluation through goal analysis to be presented in the next chapter (Chapter 8). In addition to using the technique during direct intervention, the generalist and other resources of a team may find it helpful as they collectively plan strategies for intervention with target systems.

There are several other techniques that a generalist may use in the General Method when working with more than one type of system or problem. The four basic interventions (direct; information and referral; case management and teamwork; and indirect) are selectively applied with a range of techniques as the generalist interacts with different systems.

Using the Holistic Foundation in Intervention

Basic values, theories, and skills used by the generalist during the intervention stage of the General Method are identified in the holistic conceptualization of the foundation for social work practice (Chapter 1). The practice principles that reflect the basic values of social work are very evident in the judgments and actions of the worker as interventions are planned and implemented. Interventions by a social worker are dependent on the willingness of a system to accept and cooperate with the worker. As much as possible, the system of contact is given the opportunity to determine for itself the types of involvement the worker will provide.

Each problem-person-environment situation is individualized as the worker accepts or suggests certain rules or task responsibilities.

Throughout the four major types of interventions, different practice principles are highlighted. For example, *controlled emotional involvement* is a principle that is strongly needed during indirect intervention, especially when the worker is in an adversary process. *Individualization* and *purposeful expression of feelings* are central to direct intervention. *Acceptance* is crucial for effective teamwork. And *confidentiality* and *self-determination* are highlighted during referral.[20]

Knowledge used during intervention varies according to the task at hand. During direct intervention, theories about the type of system (individual, group, family, community, organization) the worker is interacting with are used. With indirect intervention, knowledge of policies, procedures, institutions, and social-change theory is particularly relevant. In referral, the worker uses knowledge about resources. For teamwork to be successful, individual members know about their own profession and other professions, as well as group dynamics and processes.

In addition to the various techniques used by the generalist as described earlier in this chapter, the skills listed in the holistic foundation (Chapter 1) are demonstrated during the intervention stage. Relationship skills and problem-solving skills are pervasive during direct intervention. Political skills are used primarily with indirect interventions. In the referral process and during teamwork, a worker may find it necessary to use all three major types of skills: relationship, problem-solving, and political.

The heart of the General Method may be seen as intervention; the appropriate use of skills and techniques at this time is crucial to the fulfillment of the process. As emphasized, the selection of skills and techniques is guided by a worker's application of basic values and knowledge. The holistic conceptualization of the foundation for practice is a helpful reference for the generalist who must artfully apply foundation knowledge, values, and skills when intervening in each unique situation.

Human Diversity in Intervention

Culture

As brought out in this chapter, the interventions of the generalist may be identified as direct service, indirect service, referral, and teamwork. When a worker is intervening directly with a system of another culture, an interpreter may be needed to overcome language differences. In one sense, direct intervention becomes a type of teamwork when an interpreter is used. Although interpreters repeat what has been said verbatim as they translate, they also need the ability and sensitivity to convey the feelings and attitudes that are being communicated. Interpreters for social workers need to have some understanding of the basic principles and practices of the worker. They need to realize the difference between relating to a friend and to a client, and to be able to convey the personal style of the social worker. Open communication with a strong sense of trust and mutual commitment should exist between the worker and the interpreter. The worker needs to make every effort to communicate directly and respectfully with a client system, even when an interpreter is being used. At no time should any member of the client system be made to feel like an object to supply information or to be talked about. Children should not be used as interpreters for their parents; such action puts them in a position that generally contradicts their role and place in their culture. It may also prevent a parent from dealing with content he or she does not wish to discuss in front of the children.

In working with minorities, the interventions of a worker may be more often indirect than they are in work with people of the majority. In addition to direct provision of services, a worker may serve minorities through various types of indirect involvements with target systems. The nature of such involvements may be primarily educational, with presentations of research findings to document need. A worker may be intervening through applying political pressures on institutions, legislators, or agencies. For example, a worker may become actively involved in promoting legislation to insure an adequate income for all children and families, or in changing policies or structures of traditional agencies that have to be changed if members of minority groups are to receive adequate services. Agencies may need to be encouraged to join up with representatives of minority groups to organize for more sensitive and relevant service provision. As brought out by Leon Chestang, the three essential criteria for programs serving minorities are proximity, relevance, and community participation.[21]

When an agency cannot supply the needed type of intervention, a referral must be made. The worker looks for resources that appear to be sensitive to the culture of the client. This may become apparent by considering (1) the cultural background and languages of those administering and providing the service, (2) the location of the service, (3) the involvement or input by the particular cultural group in the resource, and (4) the extent to which members of the cultural community have received satisfactory services from the resource in the past. Before contacting a formal resource, a worker and system should explore thoroughly the possibility of locating available informal resources. In meeting emotional, social, and personal needs, particularly for minority members, familial and community resources are often far more effective than formal agencies or programs. Also, informal resources usually provide greater stability through ongoing availability. It is in the black community, for example, that members of the African-American culture receive their emotional support and positive identity. As Chestang writes:

> The black person finds emotional solace within the black community. Here are the comforts of family, the protections of supportive institutions such as churches, fraternal organizations and civil rights groups. Here the black person has an opportunity to build self-esteem through the exercise of talents and skills, to develop a sense of personal identity through

enduring relationships with family, friends and significant others, and to struggle in the company of others who face common barriers to the pursuit of a better life.[22]

When a worker intervenes through teamwork with other professionals, it is important to see that team members are sensitive to the culture of the system receiving service. Ideally, there would be at least one member of the team who shares the culture of the consumer. If this is not possible, the team should seek periodic consultation from someone with a cultural background similar to that of the consumer receiving service or at least from someone with knowledge, experience, and demonstrated sensitivity for working with people of the particular culture.

Sexual Variation

The use of groups has been emphasized in the literature as a very effective intervention when working with lesbian and gay persons.[23] Especially for those individuals who do not have a nurturing, accepting family or community network, a group of people who share common values, problems, pressures, concerns, and lifestyle can be very supportive and strengthening. With regard to confidentiality, particular caution may need to be taken by a gay or lesbian group. Some members may not want to have their sexual orientation known outside of the group for various reasons, including the risk of losing job or children. In working with gay or lesbian groups or individuals, a generalist will be promoting self-esteem and self-sufficiency by using the General Method because it is a collaborative, problem-solving approach that encourages assertiveness and empowerment. As presented throughout this text, a guiding principle is to have members of a system do whatever there is to be done for themselves whenever possible.

Gender Sensitivity

The interventions for working with men and women on gender-role problems may include working with groups as well as with individuals. Women may need to be helped, individually or collectively, to speak with self-respect and to find ways to influence their current life situations for greater personal fulfillment. Men may need to be encouraged to form buddyships or to join groups for men and to realize that their emotions are healthy, helpful guides to reality. Workers may join with men and/or women in advocating for changes in policies and practices of sexist institutions. As men and women are enabled to communicate honestly about themselves and their needs and to take action in their own behalf, they begin to experience a sense of freedom and wholeness. As stated, they may need ongoing support from the worker and others as this personal growth is taking place.

In addition to culture, sexual variation, and gender, the interventions of a worker during this stage should also reflect a sensitivity to such other diversity variables as age and stages, endowment and personality, value systems, class, and geographic location.

Intervention in Diverse Field Areas

I. Field Area: Child Welfare

A. Agency: State Department of Children's Services

B. Client System

K, 15 years old, female, moving from emergency shelter into group home. (For more background information, see Chapter 4, Engagement in Diverse Field Areas, I. Child Welfare.)

C. Summary of Preceding Stages

The problems, goals, and contracted tasks identified during engagement, data collection, and assessment are listed in Table 6–7 of Chapter 6. The three major problems were assessed in terms of change-potential scores and prioritized as follows: (1) permanent placement, 24; (2) school placement, 23; (3) personal problems—(a) depression, 21; (b) poor self-esteem, 20; (c) identity confusion, 20; and (d) sexuality, 19.

D. Intervention

The types of interventions by the worker were (1) direct work, (2) referral, and (3) teamwork. In addition to working directly with K and to making a referral to the group home, the child-welfare worker continued as K's state worker (the state maintained custody) and formed an action system (teamwork) with the administrator and other members of the staff of the group home. The worker also participated in school conferences on K, thus forming an alliance with the teacher and social worker of the school. Prior to K's placement in her present group home, the worker had also worked collaboratively with the staff at the shelter. The design that primarily depicts the interventions of the child-welfare worker is found in Figure 7–8.

The direct work with K was primarily to give her support as she carried out the tasks identified in the contracted plan (Table 6–7, Chapter 6) and to discuss her adjustment in the group home and in school. Contacts with personnel from the

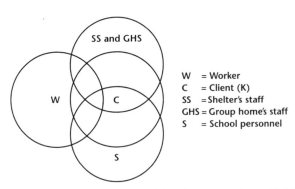

W   = Worker
C   = Client (K)
SS = Shelter's staff
GHS = Group home's staff
S   = School personnel

FIGURE 7-8. Worker's Combined Interventions: Field Area I

group home and school were mainly for the purpose of monitoring K's adjustment and personal growth and to see if any additional services were needed.

A month after K's placement in the group home, K and the worker reviewed the reasons for K's commitment to the state. K understood the need for the worker to petition the court for a continuance of her commitment. This need and its related goals and tasks were added to the planned contract, as recorded in Table 7–1. After K was in the group home for three months, the worker and K evaluated the progress that had been made.

II. Field Area: Gerontology
A. Agency: Seaside Nursing Home
B. Client System

Mrs. J, an 80-year-old Portuguese woman in a skilled-nursing facility. (For additional background information, see Chapter 4, Engagement in Diverse Field Areas, II. Gerontology.)

C. Summary of Preceding Stages

The problems, goals, and tasks identified during engagement, data collection, and assessment are indicated in the contracted plan found in Table 6–9, Chapter 6. During assessment, problems were prioritized as follows: (1) unfamiliarity with staff and resources of the home, (2) fighting with nurses over bath, (3) seclusiveness (not leaving room), (4) calling residents names, and (5) cultural isolation.

D. Intervention

Interventions by the worker in this case were (1) direct work with the client through twice a week sessions, and (2) teamwork with the nursing-home staff (nurses, program planner, recreational staff, volunteer director, and a volunteer) and also with the pastor of the church Mrs. J attended before hospitalization. The designs that demonstrate these primary interventions of the worker are found in Figures 7–9 and 7–10.

Through working with the church pastor, members of his congregation who knew Mrs. J began to visit her and to take her out to special church celebrations (a concert and the Christmas prayer service). Mrs. J was extremely happy to have them visit her and take her out to church activities. She also began to attend Bible services held in the nursing home. At first she went with the worker; later, she

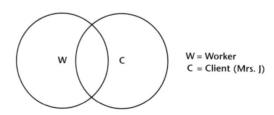

FIGURE 7-9. Direct Intervention:Field Area II

TABLE 7-1. Contracted Plan Continued

DATE IDENTIFIED	PROBLEM/ NEED	GOAL	TASK	CONTRACT	DATE ANTICIPATED	DATE ACCOMPLISHED
2/24	4. Need to remain in custody of state (abusive parents)	4. To obtain continuance of custody	1. Discuss 2. Prepare case summary 3. Petition court for continuance 4. Attend court hearing	1. Worker and K 2. Worker 3. Worker 4. Worker	2/24 2/24 3/1 3/30	

FIGURE 7-10. Teamwork: Field Area II

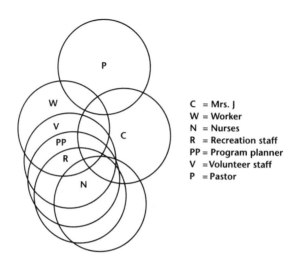

C = Mrs. J
W = Worker
N = Nurses
R = Recreation staff
PP = Program planner
V = Volunteer staff
P = Pastor

FIGURE 7-11. Indirect Intervention: Field Area II

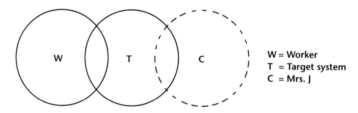

W = Worker
T = Target system
C = Mrs. J

would go with other residents. Mrs. J began to carry on a conversation with other residents at her dining-room table and on her corridor. She became friendly with her roommate, and they would go together to entertainments put on by the recreation department at the home.

Eventually, a Portuguese-speaking volunteer began to visit Mrs. J. This young woman came only three times before she dropped out of the volunteer program. The worker continued to try to locate Mrs. J's family members but was unsuccessful. If family members had been reached, they would probably have been target systems, and the worker's indirect intervention would be depicted as shown in Figure 7–11. If Mrs. J's children had been responsive to the worker's efforts and asked for the worker's help, they would have become an extended part of the client system (Figure 7–9). If they joined with the worker and the home in providing support for their mother, they would be seen as constituent members of the action system and perceived by the worker and the staff as team members in collaborative effort for goal attainment (Figure 7–10).

E. Charted Progress

As the tasks of the contract were executed, the worker recorded their completion by indicating the dates of accomplishment on the contracted plan. Visits by members of her former church were also recorded in the task column (see Table 7–2).

III. Field Area: Public Social Welfare
A. Agency: State Social Service
B. Client System

Mr. and Mrs. P and their two children (2 and 4 years old) in need of housing (emergency and long-term) and food (emergency and supply until AFDC payment). (For additional background information, see Chapter 4, Engagement in Diverse Field Areas, III. Public Social Welfare.)

C. Summary of Preceding Stages:

The problems, goals, and tasks contracted as the worker and the P's moved quickly (crisis situation) through the stages of engagement, data collection, and assessment are indicated in Table 6–11, Chapter 6. The problems and needs of the family were prioritized as follows: (1) food—emergency food, (2) housing—temporary shelter, (3) food supply until AFDC payment, and (4) long-term housing.

D. Intervention

The types of interventions by the worker were (1) referral, (2) direct interventions, and (3) teamwork. The worker placed the family at Center City Motor Inn on the same day that they arrived at the agency. The family rejected the options of Salvation Army (mother and father would be placed in separate facilities) and the City Hotel (disliked the location). Before going to the Motor Inn, the worker took the family to the Good News Soup Kitchen for a meal and picked up a bag of groceries at the Center Churches Food Bank.

While at the motel, Mrs. P asked the worker to try to get a medical card for her to take the children to the health center for a checkup. The worker learned that the medical card was being processed at the central office and that it would take another eight days to arrive. The worker wrote a letter to the health center verifying the status of the P family. The letter was cosigned by the family's income-maintenance technician. Medical transportation was requested and provided for Mr. and Mrs. P and the children to go to the health center.

Mr. and Mrs. P did not actively search for permanent living quarters. They said that they didn't think they liked the locations of the apartments listed in the paper. The worker offered to drive them to look at places, but they only went to two places with him. By the end of ten days, the worker stressed that their time was running out, and the P's requested an extension of time. The application for an extension was denied, and the P's asked for a fair hearing. They were again denied at

TABLE 7-2. Contracted Plan

DATE IDENTIFIED	PROBLEM/ NEED	GOAL	TASK	CONTRACT	DATE ANTICIPATED	DATE ACCOMPLISHED
9/27	1. Unfamiliarity with staff and resources of nursing home	1. To get to know the staff and resources of the nursing home	1. To meet twice a week with worker	1. Worker and Mrs. J	10/4 and every Tuesday and Thursday	10/4, 10/9, 10/11, 10/16, 10/18, 10/23, 10/25, 10/30
			2. To meet with program planner	2. Worker, Mrs. J, and program planner	10/16	11/1, 11/6, 11/8, 11/13, 11/15, 11/20, 11/22, 11/27; 12/6, 12/11, 12/13
			3. To meet with a person from recreation staff	3. Worker, Mrs. J, and recreation-staff person	10/23	10/23
10/2	2. Fighting with nurses over bath	2. To work out bath schedule with nurses	1. To meet with head nurse to discuss bath schedule	1. Mrs. J and head nurse	10/16	10/16
9/25	3. Seclusiveness: not leaving room alone	3a. To leave room alone (at least once a day)	1. To walk down to nursing station alone at least once a day	1. Mrs. J	10/25 and each day thereafter	10/26; 11/6, 11/14, 11/20; 12/3, 12/5, 12/12, 12/15
		b. To attend a house activity (at least once week)	1. To go to a house activity, program, or meeting (at least once a week)	1. Worker or staff member and Mrs. J first two times	Starting week of 10/22	10/24, 12/30

TABLE 7-2. *Continued*

DATE IDENTIFIED	PROBLEM/ NEED	GOAL	TASK	CONTRACT	DATE ANTICIPATED	DATE ACCOMPLISHED
				2. Mrs. J with residents each week thereafter	Starting week of 11/5	11/5, 11/12, 11/21, 11/28; 12/3, 12/7, 12/12, 12/17
10/2	4. Calling residents names	4. To stop calling residents names	1. To stop name calling	1. Mrs. J	10/16 and thereafter	10/16 until 10/20 (argument 10/21) and thereafter
			2. To say "hello" to residents	2. Mrs. J	10/16 and thereafter	
9/25	5. Cultural isolation	5. To share culture with others	1. To meet director of volunteers	1. Mrs. J, worker, and director of volunteers	10/25	10/25
			2. To visit with Portuguese volunteer	2. Mrs. J and volunteer	?	11/13, 11/20, 11/30
			3. To visit with pastor of church	3. Mrs. J and pastor	?	11/14, 11/20, 11/30
			4. To visit with member of church	4. Mrs. J, pastor, and congregation	11/20	11/30
			5. To go off grounds to attend church activity	5. Mrs. J and congregation (Mr. and Mrs. T)	12/4, 12/17	12/4, 12/17

the hearing and told that they would have to leave the motel by the following Monday. When Monday came, the P's informed the worker that they had located an apartment and requested help with moving their furniture from Mrs. P's father's house to the new apartment. After the family got the three required moving estimates, their moving expenses were covered through the Income Maintenance Department.

In their new apartment, the family requested help with obtaining fuel assistance. The worker informed them that they needed to keep their fuel bills and showed them how to apply for assistance. Their AFDC check was detained because of the address change, and the worker hand-delivered the check and food stamps.

The family had a problem with the refrigerator and asked the worker to help them obtain funding to have it repaired. The worker suggested that they try the Salvation Army, which might pay for new parts. The worker learned later that the P's received a new refrigerator and that this was handled through the income-maintenance technician. Mr. P asked if the worker thought he should reapply to Social Security for Supplemental Security Income benefits. The worker inquired about the procedure for reapplication and encouraged Mr. P to begin the process.

Mrs. P asked if the worker knew of any place where the family could go to receive a Thanksgiving basket. Mr. P also wondered if there was any place where he could get Christmas presents for the children. The worker inquired and informed Mr. P that baskets were being given by several local churches and that the Salvation Army had children's gifts.

At one point earlier, when it seemed that the P's were not going to find housing, the worker had explored the process for referring the family to the Protective Services Department. It appeared that placement of the children might be needed until housing for the family was located. Fortunately, this was not necessary.

In the case of the P family, a number of resources were mobilized by the B.S.W. worker. The worker went with the P's to obtain food and shelter. Initial contacts were made by the worker for the P's with the fuel-assistance program, Social Security office, medical transportation services, and Salvation Army (Figure 7–12).

In addition to referral, the worker maintained ongoing direct intervention with the family for three months. (Figure 7–13). Throughout this period, the worker engaged in teamwork with the income-maintenance technician and with Mr. P's psychiatrist. Contact with the income-maintenance technician averaged once a week. The worker spoke with the psychiatrist on five different occasions. These team efforts (Figure 7–14) provided the family with coordinated services and offered the service providers an opportunity for shared service delivery.

E. Charted Progress

As various interventions were identified and enacted, the worker recorded them, along with the dates of task accomplishment, on the contracted

FIGURE 7-12. Referral: Field Area III

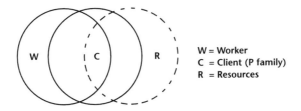

W = Worker
C = Client (P family)
R = Resources

FIGURE 7-13. Direct Intervention: Field Area III

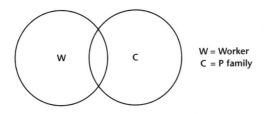

W = Worker
C = P family

FIGURE 7-14. Teamwork: Field Area III

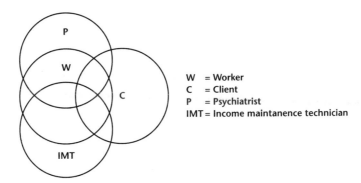

W   = Worker
C   = Client
P   = Psychiatrist
IMT = Income maintanence technician

plan. *After the P's were placed in temporary shelter, the goal of locating a long-term residence took longer to accomplish than anticipated. The efforts to obtain a time extension for temporary placement were also recorded, as were additional problems and needs that surfaced. Goals and contracts for each new problem were developed with the P's and charted on the contracted plan. (See Table 7–3.)*

As indicated in the table, task 3 (move to new apartment) for problem 4 (housing—long-term) was not accomplished until 11/7, even though the anticipated date was "not later than 10/12." The additional

TABLE 7-3. Contracted Plan Continued

DATE IDENTIFIED	PROBLEM/ NEED	GOAL	TASK	CONTRACT	DATE ANTICIPATED	DATE ACCOMPLISHED
9/28	4. Housing—long-term	4. To move into an apartment for long-term residence	1. Explore resources	1. Mr. and Mrs. P and worker	9/29	9/30
			2. Contact resources	2. Mr. and Mrs. P	9/29	9/30, 10/10
			3. Move	3. The P's	10/12	11/7
			4. Update	4. Worker, Mr. P's doctor, income-maintenance technician	9/29 and weekly	9/29; 10/6, 13, 20, 27; 11/3, 10, 17
			5. Request extension for temporary placement	5. Worker	10/11	10/11
			6. Fair hearing	6. Mr. and Mrs. P, worker, and department board	10/31	10/31
			7. Request moving assistance	7. Worker	11/5	11/5
9/28	5. Poor money management					
10/1	6. Medical exam for children	6. To have children examined at health center	1. Find out about medical care	1. Worker	10/2	10/2
10/1			2. See if health center will accept letter of authorization	2. Worker	10/2	10/2

TABLE 7-3. *Continued*

DATE IDENTIFIED	PROBLEM/ NEED	GOAL	TASK	CONTRACT	DATE ANTICIPATED	DATE ACCOMPLISHED
			3. Write letter	3. Worker and income-mainte-nance technician	10/5	10/5
			4. Make appointment	4. Mrs. P	10/5	10/8
			5. Make arrangements for medical trans-port	5. Worker and income-mainte-nance technician	10/8	10/8
			6. Take children to health center	6. Mr. and Mrs. P and medical trans-port service	10/12	10/12
11/14	7. Need for fuel assis-tance	7. To obtain fuel assis-tance	1. Explore resources	1. Worker	11/15	11/15
			2. Discuss	2. Worker and P's	11/16	11/16
			3. Fill out application	3. P's with worker's help	11/20	11/20
			4. Follow up if neces-sary	4. Mr. P	11/26	
11/14	8. Check and food stamps	8. To receive AFDC check and food stamps	1. To find out about delay in deliver	1. Worker	11/14	11/14
			2. To get check at cen-tral office	2. Worker	11/15	11/15
			3. To deliver check to P's	3. Worker	11/16	11/16

TABLE 7-3. *Continued*

DATE IDENTIFIED	PROBLEM/NEED	GOAL	TASK	CONTRACT	DATE ANTICIPATED	DATE ACCOMPLISHED
11/20	9. Malfunctioning refrigerator	9. To fix refrigerator	1. Get estimates on repairs needed	1. Mr. P	11/20	11/20
			2. Explore funding resources	2. Worker	11/20	11/20
			3. Contact Salvation Army	3. Mr. P	11/22	
			4. Have refrigerator repaired	4. Mr. P	11/23	(Problem withdrawn 12/4—new refrigerator)
			5. Send bill to Salvation Army	5. Mr. P	11/26	
11/20	10. Supplemental Security Income	10. To receive Supplemental Security Income	1. Contact Social Security office	1. Worker	11/21	11/21
			2. Discuss	2. Worker and P's	11/22	11/22
			3. Complete application	3. Mr. P	11/22	
			4. Follow-up call	4. Mr. P	11/26	
			5. Go for interview	5. Mr. P	11/27	
11/20	11. Thanksgiving food basket	11. To receive a food basket	1. Explore resources	1. Worker	11/21	11/21
			2. Contact churches	2. Mr. P	11/22	
			3. Go for basket	3. Mr. P	11/24	
11/27	12. Gifts for children	12. To obtain Christmas gifts for children	1. Explore resources	1. Worker	11/28	11/28
			2. Contact resources	2. Mr. P	11/29	
			3. Pick up gifts	3. Mr. P	12/5	

needs of a medical exam for the children (including transportation), fuel assistance, AFDC check delivery, refrigerator repair, Thanksgiving baskets, and Christmas presents for the children were also listed and contracted.

IV. Field Area: Community Services
A. Agency: Clayton Neighborhood House
B. Client System

Four Hispanic families without heating in their apartments on the second floor of 33 L Street. (For more background information, see Chapter 4, Engagement in Diverse Field Areas, IV. Community Services.)

C. Summary of Preceding Stages

The problem, goal, and contracted tasks developed by the worker and the community of residents in earlier stages are outlined in Table 6–12 of Chapter 6. In addition to the need for heating in their apartments, the families recognized that they had a communication problem with their landlord. They were not, however, interested in trying to find ways to improve communication with him at this time.

D. Intervention

The interventions of the worker were both direct and indirect. The worker met with the residents directly to plan and monitor change. She also served as their advocate through indirect work with Mr. X, the landlord. Designs depicting the worker's intervention are found in Figures 7–15 and 7–16.

FIGURE 7-15. Direct Intervention: Field Area IV

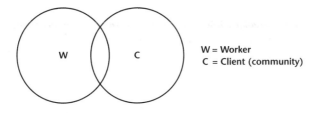

W = Worker
C = Client (community)

FIGURE 7-16. Indirect Intervention: Field Area IV

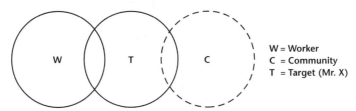

W = Worker
C = Community
T = Target (Mr. X)

When the worker returned to meet with the residents on the day after she contacted the landlord, she found that their apartments were heated. She had brought thermometers with her for each apartment. They registered 68°. The residents expressed gratitude and hoped that the heating would continue throughout the winter. The worker told the group about her conversation with the landlord. They admitted that they didn't really know the man but continued to be afraid to have contact with him. They agreed to monitor the heating in their apartments by checking their thermometers each day. They would meet with the worker in one week to report on their findings.

E. Charted Progress

As the worker and the residents planned additional tasks, the worker recorded the extended plan by adding items to the "task," "contract," and "date anticipated" columns of the contracted plan (Table 7–4).

V. Field Area: Education

A. Agency: Keeney Elementary School

B. Client System

Mr. and Mrs. G and their son Jim, 8 years old, in third grade, with problems at school and at home directly related to his parents' problem with their marital relationship. (For further background information, see Chapter 4, Engagement in Diverse Field Areas, V. Education.)

C. Summary of Preceding Stages

The problems, goals, and contracted tasks identified during preceding stages are outlined in Table 6–14, Chapter 6. The two primary tasks prioritized and contracted for Mr. and Mrs. G were (1) getting Jim to school on time each day and (2) going together for marital counseling. Jim's poor school performance and his sleeping problem were seen as reactions to Mr. and Mrs. G's quarreling and, especially, to Mrs. G's threat that she was going to leave her husband and children. The social worker's primary contracted tasks included meeting with Jim, his teacher, and his parents regarding Jim's school performance and general progress.

D. Intervention

The interventions of the worker may be identified as (1) direct (Jim; Mr. and Mrs. G; Jim and his parents) (see Figure 7–17); (2) referral (marital counseling for Mr. and Mrs. G) (see Figure 7–18); and (3) teamwork (worker and Jim's teacher, working with Mr. and Mrs. G to help Jim) (see Figure 7–19). The worker also attended a student study team conference on Jim with several members of the school faculty (principal, nurse, classroom teacher, learning-disabilities teacher, social service supervisor, worker). Jim's parents had been invited to this conference but they said that they couldn't attend because they were working.

During their meeting with the worker at school, Mr. and Mrs. G invited Jim to join them before the end of the meeting. At this time, Mr.

TABLE 7-4. Contracted Plan Continued

DATE IDENTIFIED	PROBLEM/ NEED	GOAL	TASK	CONTRACT	DATE ANTICIPATED	DATE ACCOMPLISHED
			4. Monitor heat daily in each apartment	4. One person from each family (Mr. T, Mrs. V, Mr. A, and CR)	12/5 to 12/12	
			5. Meet to review findings	5. Worker and residents	12/12	

FIGURE 7-17. Direct Intervention: Field Area V

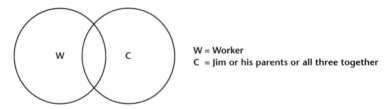

W = Worker
C = Jim or his parents or all three together

FIGURE 7-18. Referral: Field Area V

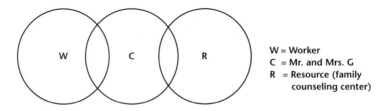

W = Worker
C = Mr. and Mrs. G
R = Resource (family
        counseling center)

FIGURE 7-19. Teamwork: Field Area V

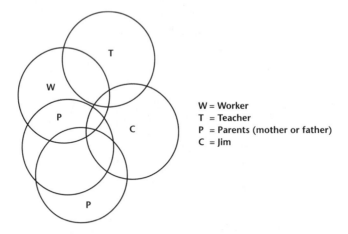

W = Worker
T = Teacher
P = Parents (mother or father)
C = Jim

and Mrs. G informed Jim that they knew that he had been worried about them because he had heard them arguing. They admitted to Jim that they had been having some problems but assured him that they were going to work out their difficulties. They told Jim they were going to get help themselves so they could learn to get along better with each other. They stressed that it was not Jim's problem and that he really didn't have to worry about them. They also assured Jim that neither one of them was thinking of giving up or leaving home. Jim was encouraged to try to do better in school. They said they knew it must have been hard for Jim. Mr. G said he knew it was hard enough for Jim to be "a little man in a big world," and that Jim didn't have to take onto his shoulders the problem of his mother and father. As he hugged his parents, Jim said he would try to work harder in school.

Before leaving this interview, it was agreed by all that the worker would continue to see Jim twice a week and that the follow-up contacts between the worker and Mr. and Mrs. G would be by telephone for 2 weeks. These would be followed by a home visit by the worker, at which time they all would consider termination of planned contacts if progress was apparent.

In talking with Mrs. G on the telephone the following week, the worker learned that Mr. G had made the appointment and that Mr. and Mrs. G had begun counseling sessions at the family counseling center. Mrs. G said that Jim still wanted a light left in his room at night but he didn't need to have his mother with him. He settled for a small night light.

Jim's teacher reported that Jim was beginning to look happier and to show more interest in his schoolwork. The worker continued to meet with Jim in her office twice a week, and Jim was interested in playing age-appropriate games. They drew up ongoing evaluation graphs to chart Jim's progress in school (to be presented in the next chapter).

E. Charted Progress

As tasks contracted in the plan developed by Mr. and Mrs. G, Jim, and the worker (Table 6–14, Chapter 6) were carried out, the worker recorded the date they were completed in the "date accomplished" column of the contracted plan. At the last meeting of the worker with Mr. and Mrs. G in their home, the worker shared the updated plan with them as they reviewed and evaluated progress.

VI. Field Area: Corrections

A. Agency: Juvenile Court

B. Client System

Seven male adolescents, age 14, on probation for burglary, theft of automobiles, or minor larceny (shoplifting), attending weekly group sessions led by co-workers from the Juvenile Court. (For further background information, see Chapter 4, Engagement in Diverse Field Areas, VI. Corrections.)

C. Summary of Preceding Stages

The problems, goals, and contracted tasks identified in earlier stages are outlined in Table 6–15, Chapter 6. The youths prioritized their problems as (1) lawbreaking leading to probation, (2) bad tempers, and (3) lack of understanding of the changes they were experiencing. Group members admitted that they didn't think much of themselves (low self-worth) and that they had problems with their parents (parent–son conflicts), but they didn't appear interested in working directly on these problems. In developing the contracted plan in the group, the need for ongoing evaluation instruments was recognized, and graphs were developed to monitor group attendance, group participation by members, and members' behavior at school and at home.

D. Intervention

The interventions of the B.S.W. worker were mainly varied types of teamwork. The worker and her co-leader met with the seven youths in weekly group meetings, and the workers engaged in ongoing communication with each other as team members. They met at least twice a week to discuss the process, problems, and progress of the group and any developments that were taking place with individual members. The workers went together to visit every home of the group participants. They divided the task of visiting the schools (the B.S.W. went to four schools, the M.S.W. to three) and the tasks of receiving weekly reports from parents and school social workers. The approach used with teachers and parents also highlighted a team effort as they worked together to help the youths accomplish their goals.

The primary teamwork designs to depict the interventions of the B.S.W. worker are found in Figures 7–20 and 7–21.

After charting progress in group attendance, group participation, and school and home behavior, the group began to focus on their problem with their tempers. All saw a relationship between this problem and the problems they were having at home and at school. They agreed to take home an index card each week, and every time they lost their tempers, they would put a check on it. If they forgot during the day to check the card, they would try to remember the incidents and to mark the card each night before going to bed. They would bring the card back each week and report the total number of checks they had for the week to the group. At the meeting, members entered their total number of checks for the week on a weekly chart (Table 7–5). The group members said that they also wanted to check on the other side of the card every time they felt like losing their tempers but didn't. The cards were labeled on each side "temper loss" or "temper control." A matching weekly chart was designed to indicate temper control (Table 7–6). During meetings, the group also discussed ways to let out anger that are acceptable and not seen as a loss of temper. For example, some said they find it helpful when they start to feel angry if they can get out and play ball. Others suggested turning on the radio and singing, going for walks, or finding a friend to talk with. One youth said he learned taking deep breaths and thinking about something that makes him happy help. They joked about what he might be thinking.

After six group meetings, A was picked up by the police and charged with breaking into a store (fifth time). He was found guilty and sent to a correctional institution for six months. J and T often came late to the meetings and continued to say they only came because they had to.

FIGURE 7-20. Worker and Co-worker Teamwork: Field Area VI

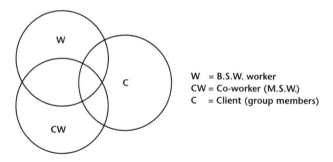

W = B.S.W. worker
CW = Co-worker (M.S.W.)
C = Client (group members)

FIGURE 7-21. Extended Teamwork: Field Area VI

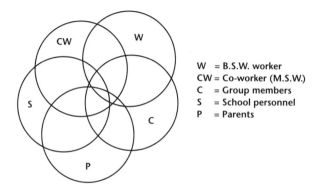

W = B.S.W. worker
CW = Co-worker (M.S.W.)
C = Group members
S = School personnel
P = Parents

As the group began to work on goal 3 (to learn about "changes"), a topic or issue of interest was selected each week by the members, and a plan was developed to study the issue the following week. Topics studied included living in prison, human sexuality and birth control, vocational training and jobs, managing money, and cooking. Films and guest speakers were used to provide information for discussion. The group also went on a trip to visit a vocational-training school.

E. Charted Progress

Each week, as additional tasks were planned by the group, the worker would record them on the contracted plan. For example, the additional tasks that were developed for goal 2 (to control tempers) and for goal 3 (to learn about "changes") were added as outlined in Table 7–7.

VII. Field Area: Homeless Shelter

A. Agency: West End Community Shelter

B. Client System

José G. is a 37-year-old Hispanic male who is homeless and HIV positive. He has no family or close friends. He was referred to the shelter by

TABLE 7-5.   Temper Loss

NAMES	1	2	3	4	5	6	7	8	9	10	11	12	13	14	15	16
WEEKS																
J																
MK																
T																
ML																
B																
A																
C																

TABLE 7-6.   Temper Control

NAMES	1	2	3	4	5	6	7	8	9	10	11	12	13	14	15	16
WEEKS																
J																
MK																
T																
ML																
B																
A																
C																

the Department of Social Services. (For additional information, see Chapter 4, Engagement in Diverse, Field Areas: VII. Homeless Shelter).

C. **Summary of Preceding Stages**

During engagement Mr. G shared his history of past drug addiction and divorce. He worked out a plan with the worker which involved his going to the free health clinic located near the shelter. He also planned to attend a local church service. Data collection continued as the worker and Mr. G began to implement the contracted plan. Mr. G's illness was diagnosed as slowly moving into the second stage of the virus. He was having night sweats and shortness of breath.

TABLE 7-7. Contracted Plan Continued

DATE IDENTIFIED	PROBLEM/ NEED	GOAL	TASK	CONTRACT	DATE ANTICIPATED	DATE ACCOMPLISHED
10/1	2. Bad tempers	2. To control tempers in school, home, and neighborhood	1. Discuss the problem dealing with anger	1. Workers and members	10/22	10/22
			2. Notice when angry	2. Individual members	10/22 and each day	10/22–ongoing
			3. Find acceptable outlet	3. Individual members	10/22 and each day	
			4. Keep track of successes and slipups on card	4. Individual members	10/22 and each day	
			5. Report to group and chart number	5. Individual members	10/29 and each Monday at group	
10/1	3. Need to understand "changes" of teenagers	3. To learn about some of the "changes" (including becoming independent, sex and birth control, and job training)	1. Select first topic—life in prison	1. Group and members	10/22	10/22
			2. Plan program	2. Group members	10/23	
			3. Call Prison Association for speaker	3. Worker	10/23	
			4. Have a talk and discussion	4. Guest and group	10/29	

D. Intervention

Mr. G and the worker carried out the "tasks" of the contracted plan. The worker used direct intervention and referral throughout the process (see Figures 7–22 and 7–23). After the first week, both Mr. G and the worker recognized his need for additional social supports. Mr. G. did not have a car or any money for public transportation. The void in social supports was added to the list of "problems/needs" in the contracted plan (see Table 7–8). Mr. G agreed to contact Harmony, Inc., a service which offered a buddy system and transportation for persons with HIV or AIDS. Mr. G was assigned a buddy who would visit him at the shelter occasionally and take him to the Harmony support group once a week. On the days when Mr. G wanted a ride to church because he didn't feel well enough to walk, he was able to call his buddy for transportation. While attending a church service, Mr. G met a man from his hometown in Puerto Rico. The man told Mr. G that they were looking for additional help at the chicken farm where he worked. He agreed to pick up Mr. G and take him to see the farm supervisor. Mr. G was hired and worked for four weeks before he had to stop because of his illness. He then dropped down to working part-time. On days when he felt able, he would call the supervisor to see if he could work. Mr. G applied for residence at Hope Home.

E. Charted Progress

As planned tasks were operationalized, the worker would indicate on the contract the dates of accomplishment. She shared the process of charting progress with Mr. G to promote his sense of control over what was happening in his life.

FIGURE 7-22. Direct Intervention: Field Area VII

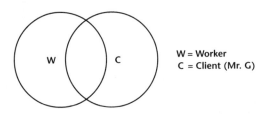

W = Worker
C = Client (Mr. G)

FIGURE 7-23. Direct Intervention: Field Area VII

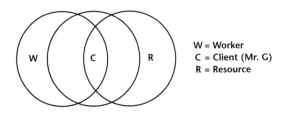

W = Worker
C = Client (Mr. G)
R = Resource

TABLE 7-8. Contracted Plan

DATE IDENTIFIED	PROBLEM/ NEED	GOAL	TASK	CONTRACT	DATE ANTICIPATED	DATE ACCOMPLISHED
5/7	1. Homeless – Short term	1. Emergency shelter	1. Enroll in shelter	1. Mr. G & worker	5/8	5/8
5/8	2. Spiritual void	2. Reunited with church	1. Go to service	1. Mr. G.	5/10	5/10
5/8	3. Lack of knowledge, re: HIV	3. Gain information	1. Review information at shelter	1. Worker & Mr. G	5/9	5/9
			2. Go to free clinic, ask for help	2. Mr. G		
5/8	4. No income/job	4. Get income	1. Search for job	1. Mr. G & worker	5/9	5/17
			2. Apply for job	2. Mr. G	5/15	5/19
			3. Start job	3. Mr. G	5/20	5/21
			4. Seek SS/public assistance	4. Mr. G	Depends on illness	
5/7	5. No housing after 60 days	5. Locate residence	1. Look for apartment or home for persons with AIDS	1. Worker & Mr. G	5/8	
			2. Get on waiting list for home for persons with AIDS	2. Mr. G	5/11	6/24
5/8	6. HIV positive	6. Medical care	1. Make appointment	1. Worker & Mr. G	5/8	5/8*
			2. Go to free clinic	2. Mr. G	5/9	5/9
			3. Continue treatment	3. Mr. G	Next appointments	5/19+

245

TABLE 7-8. *Continued*

DATE IDENTIFIED	PROBLEM/ NEED	GOAL	TASK	CONTRACT	DATE ANTICIPATED	DATE ACCOMPLISHED
5/12	7. Social void	7. Obtain social support	1. Contact Harmony, Inc.	1. Mr. G	5/12	5/12
			2. Meet with staff person	2. Mr. G	5/13	5/13
			3. Meet "buddy"	3. Mr. G	5/20	5/20

Conclusion

In this chapter, the four major types of general interventions were presented. Designs to depict each type of intervention, along with case examples, were given. A number of techniques were identified, and their application to systems of different sizes was demonstrated. The use of these techniques throughout the General Method was also considered.

As the generalist interacts with a system for goal accomplishment, tasks are identified and implemented. The tasks of the worker may be categorized individually or collectively as direct interventions; indirect interventions, information and referral; and case management and teamwork. While working in a helping capacity with one system over a period of time, a worker may use more than one intervention. In addition to direct work, for example, the generalist may need to refer a system to an outside resource and collaborate with the resource in a team effort for integrated service delivery. An individual task may in itself reflect a combination of interventions. For example, a worker may meet with collaborating resources (teamwork), a client system (direct intervention), and a target system (indirect intervention) at the same time.

In each intervention, a worker utilizes knowledge, values, and skills from the foundation for generalist practice. The art of generalist practice is highlighted in the careful selection and application of interventions and techniques at the appropriate time and in a manner that is sensitive to human diversity.

Throughout the General Method, worker and system of contact are charting progress and monitoring change. As each task is carried out during intervention, an appraisal is made of its effectiveness. When all the contracted tasks have been accomplished, a formal period of evaluation takes place. In the next chapter, focus will be on the fifth stage of the General Method, called *evaluation.*

NOTES

1. Carol H. Meyer, "Direct Services in New and Old Contexts," in Alfred J. Kahn, ed., *Shaping the New Social Work* (New York: Columbia University Press, 1973), p. 40.

2. See Frank R. Baskind, *Defining Generalist Social Work Practice* (Lanham, Md.: University Press of America, 1984); Ronda S. Connaway and Martha E. Gentry, *Social Work Practice* (Englewood Cliffs, N.J.: Prentice-Hall, 1988).

3. Ann Hartman, "Diagrammatic Assessment of Family Relationships," *Social Casework* 59, no. 10 (October 1978): 465–76.

4. Frederick J. Duhl, David Kantor, and Bunny S. Duhl, "Learning, Space and Action in Family Therapy: A Primer of Sculpture," in Donald A. Bloch, ed., *Techniques of Family Psychotherapy: A Primer* (New York: Grune & Stratton, 1973), p. 60.

5. Philip J. Guerin and Eileen J. Pendagast, "Evaluation of Family System and Genogram," in Philip T. Guerin, ed., *Family Therapy: Theory and Practice* (New York: Gardner Press, 1976), pp. 450–64.

6. Fritz Redl and David Wineman, *Controls from Within* (New York: The Free Press, 1965), pp. 153–244.

7. James A. Garland and Ralph L. Kolodny, "Characteristics and Resolution of Scapegoating," in Saul Bernstein, ed., *Further Explorations in Group Work* (Boston: Milford House, Inc., 1973), pp. 55–74.

8. George Broger and Stephen Holloway, *Changing Human Service Organizations: Politics and Practice* (New York: The Free Press, 1978), pp. 107–28.

9. James E. Anderson and Ralph A. Brown, "Life History Grid for Adolescents," *Social Work* 25, no. 4 (July 1980): 321–23.

10. William L. Mikulas, *Behavior Modification* (New York: Harper & Row, 1978).

11. Theodore J. Stein, "Child Welfare: New Directions in the Field and Their Implications for Education," *Journal of Education for Social Work* 18, no. 1 (Winter 1982): 107–108.

12. Donald Brieland, Thomas Briggs, and Paul Luenberger, *The Team Model in Social Work Practice* (New York: Syracuse University School of Social Work, 1973); Naomi Brill, *Teamwork: Working Together in Human Services* (Philadelphia: Lippincott, 1976); Rosalee Kane, *Interprofessional Teamwork* (New York: Syracuse University School of Social Work, 1975).

13. Edward E. Mueller and Philip J. Murphy, "Communication Problems: Social Workers and Lawyers," *Social Work* 10, no. 2 (April 1965): 97–103.

14. Patricia Wilson-Coker, "Working Effectively with Attorneys in the Adversary System: Observations and Suggestions for Protective Service Social Workers" (unpublished paper, Saint Joseph College, West Hartford, Conn., 1982).

15. Council on Social Work Education, "Curriculum Policy Statement for Baccalaureate Degree Programs in Social Work Education," approved by Board of Directors July 19, 1992 (Alexandria, Va: Council on Social Work Education, 1992), p. 3, B5.2.

16. Joseph F. Perez, *Family Counseling: Theory and Practice* (New York: Van Nostrand, 1979), pp. 102–104.

17. Mikulas, *Behavior Modification*, pp. 35–36.

18. Kurt Lewin, *Field Theory in Social Science* (New York: Harper & Row, 1951).

19. Broger and Holloway, *Changing Human Service Organizations*, pp. 107–108.

20. Felix P. Biestek, S. J., *The Casework Relationship* (Chicago: Loyola University Press, 1957), p. 17.

21. Leon W. Chestang, "The Delivery of Child Welfare Services to Minority Group Children and Their Families," in *Working with Black Families and Children* (Richmond, Va.: Region III Child Welfare Training Center, 1982), p. 30.

22. Ibid., p. 19.

23. Association for Women in Psychology, *Considerations in Therapy with Lesbian Clients* (Philadelphia: Women's Resources, 1979), p. 33.

CHAPTER 8

Evaluation

Professional accountability demands systematic evaluation. We should not have to rely on infrequent reports of field experiments to learn of intervention effectiveness.

—Edward Mullen and James Dumpson[1]

Evaluation is a time to study and measure the results of the actions taken during intervention. Although a worker and system of contact may frequently stop to consider progress and future plans, a formal evaluative process takes place in the General Method just prior to a worker's termination with a system.

Central to the process of evaluation is an analysis of the level of goal attainment, for which a scale may be used. The contracted plan (Chapter 6) may serve also as a tool to guide the generalist and the system as they go through the process of goal analysis. In this chapter, a model is suggested in which tools and procedures are used by the generalist during the evaluation stage of the General Method. In addition, a tool for ongoing evaluation throughout the Method will be presented.

A balance between art and science, fact and feeling, subjective and objective data is particularly needed during evaluation. The demand for accountability in an age of declining resources strongly supports efforts to develop valid instruments to document the effectiveness of social work intervention. As a worker and system interact during evaluation, the generalist tries to objectify information and procedures and to avoid the biases of client and worker that could lead to an uncritical service appraisal. The worker knows that an evaluation containing documented, unbiased information is less deniable as a reality and that it provides data for research and funding requests. Nevertheless, the worker knows that the primary purpose of evaluation during practice is to enhance the progress of the services being offered to a system. The content addressed and the process used in evaluation, therefore, should remain individualized and sensitive to personal attitudes and feelings in order to have impact on the unique system receiving service.

During the evaluation process, the generalist uses such research skills as data collection, measurement, and analysis. The skills and procedures of the generalist are not, however, strictly based on scientifically sound research methodology. Instead of the hypothesis testing, standardized tests, generalized results, and purely factual data found in scientific research, the generalist uses individualized criteria, personal opinion, and professional judgment. As stated, the worker does try to use measurable goals and systematic procedures in an objective manner, but he or she knows that if the process becomes too technical or impersonal, the system of contact may lose interest and disengage from the process.

Realizing the need to be scientific and at the same time to individualize during evaluation in practice, contemporary researchers in the profession have begun to introduce tools and scientific procedures for individualized case evaluations. For example, "single-system designs,"[2] "practice-outcome inventories,"[3] and "goal-attainment scales"[4] are now being used to evaluate progress and change with a system in practice. A range of scientific, research-oriented techniques, including graphs, scales, and statistical analyses, may be found within these approaches. In this chapter, the model for evaluation that will be presented has some similarity to these contemporary approaches. For example, concepts of a baseline starting point, measured goal accomplishment, and a study of practice outcomes will be contained within the general evaluation process. The model to be suggested is a guiding framework that reflects a balance between research and counseling techniques for evaluation in generalist practice.

Goal Analysis

The fifth stage of the General Method begins with the following question: Has the goal been accomplished? For every task or set of tasks, a goal was stated on the contracted plan. That goal related directly to the problem listed in the column that preceded it. If the goal has been accomplished, the problem should now be resolved or modified, depending on how the goal was originally stated.

To answer the basic question cited, an intensive consideration is made of the change or progress that has taken place since the beginning of the worker-and-system interaction. First, the starting point is recalled; the worker and system of contact ask, What was the problem when we first met? The description that follows of the starting point (which may be referred to as the baseline) should be as precise and factual as possible. For example, if the presenting problem was Mr. and Mrs. S's constant quarreling, the worker will try to be more specific by recalling that Mrs. S said every time she and her husband spoke to each other, they quarreled and that this was at least six times a week. On the contract that was agreed to by both Mr. and Mrs. S, the stated goal read, "To be able to talk and to listen to each other without quarreling." The worker and system would ask, therefore, Has the communication between Mr. and Mrs. S improved? Are they speaking together without quarreling? Can they go a whole week without quarreling?

Answers to such questions may be received from different sources. The primary respondents are the system receiving service and the worker. In addition, information for goal analysis may be requested from other knowledgeable resources, such as family members, teachers, employers, and others. If a worker does not think that the perception of a system of contact joined with the observations of the worker is sufficient, reliable, or accurate, then outsiders may be brought into the evaluation process. As with data collection in the second stage of the General Method, the use of outside resources during evaluation with client systems should be discussed with, and sanctioned, by the clients prior to contacting the resources.

If the answer to the basic question of goal accomplishment is not a clear 100 percent yes, a study is made to determine to what extent the goal has been accomplished. Beginning at the baseline starting point, the question is asked, From where you started when we first had contact, how much closer to or further from the goal have you moved? A scale may be used to help the worker and the system become more specific in answering this question (see Table 8–1). It is a nine-point bipolar scale with an equal number of categories for progression and for regression. The midpoint on the scale (0) indicates the starting point. Descriptive criteria for this point should indicate the problem that led to the stated goal under study. The extreme right of the scale is numbered +4, and the anchoring description for this point is 100 percent goal accomplishment. More specifically, this score indicates that the problem at the starting point has been eliminated or reduced, according to the way it is spelled out in the stated goal. Conversely, the opposite end of the scale is numbered -4, and the descriptive criterion is "goal given up," with no attainment. The intermediate points on either side of the 0 are balanced to reflect movement to a little, some, or a large extent better or worse than the starting point.

The number of scale points to be used depends on the individual goal in each situation. Sometimes the goal may be a single activity that cannot be broken down into a measurable sequence. For example, a goal may be to get food stamps for a family or tutoring for a child. It may be sufficient here to have a simple 3-point scale (-1 = goal given up, 0 = starting point, +1 = goal accomplished). If any movement, even slight, can be detected, it is important to have a scale that can show this. Too few scale points may prevent the recognition of some progress, which could increase hope and motivation. Even the identification of going backwards and a consideration of how the situation may end if regression continues may cause sufficient anxiety to promote greater effort and involvement.

With each individual situation, an attempt is made to use objective descriptors, including numbers or times and events. For example, in the situation presented earlier, the problem at the starting point was Mr. and Mrs. S's repeated

TABLE 8-1. Goal-Accomplishment Scale

-4	-3	-2	-1	0	+1	+2	+3	+4
Goal given up	Large extent worse	Somewhat worse	Little worse than starting point	Starting point	Little better than starting point	Somewhat better	Large extent better	Goal accomplished

quarreling whenever they tried to communicate (at least six times a week). The long-range goal was to have the couple speak and listen to each other without quarreling. During intervention, techniques were used to help them to listen to each other and to try to understand each other's viewpoints. A sensitivity to non-verbal communication was encouraged, and words were suggested to help them express their feelings. After the worker and Mr. and Mrs. S worked together for the period of time indicated in the contracted plan, they began to evaluate goal accomplishment. The scale in Table 8–2 was developed under the guidance of the worker.

In finding regressive descriptors, the worker and the system discern what have been or could be ways in which the situation would grow worse than when the problem was first identified. In the case of Mr. and Mrs. S, they said that at one time they had started to physically fight, and they feared this might happen again. The negative indicators, therefore, reflect the typical pattern of regression for this system. If they had feared an increasing withdrawal from any interaction with each other, then withdrawal would be indicated in the negative descriptors.

What needs to be emphasized is that during the evaluation stage of the General Method, there must be an opportunity to identify possible deterioration as well as growth in a situation. Even with general intervention, the communication between Mr. and Mrs. S, for example, could have become worse than when they first set the goal. The cause of this deterioration would need to be considered as the evaluation progresses. It could be that the intervention was inappropriate because the relationship was too pathological or because Mr. and Mrs. S lacked sufficient motivation or capacity to work on it. The regression in the relationship could be caused by other factors, including those outside of the worker's control, such as influences from individuals or systems unknown to the worker. Before asking why the goal has or has not been attained, however, worker and system need to take time to judge what movement, forward or backward, has taken place on the goal-accomplishment scale. After this appraisal, they proceed to an analysis of why they have arrived at the particular point on the scale. Here again, the contracted plan is a helpful guide to worker and system of contact as they analyze causation.

Contract Review

An evaluation does not stop at this point, even when the first question in the process is answered with a 100 percent yes. Although a goal has been attained, it is important to find out why this has happened. The question to be asked is, Has the goal been accomplished through the planned interventions identified by worker and system in the contracted plan? An honest appraisal of causality can build a stronger working relationship, and it can give direction for further inter-actions between worker and system. It is possible that a goal's accomplishment is due to negative circumstances that may have to be addressed with a reformulation of goals. For example, a goal of getting someone off welfare may have been accomplished because the person was imprisoned rather than because of the

TABLE 8-2. Case Example: Mr. and Mrs. S

-4	-3	-2	-1	0	+1	+2	+3	+4
Goal given up; injury and separation	Large extent worse; no communication without fighting	Somewhat worse; quarrels moving into physical fights half the time they talk	Little worse; quarrels moving into physical fights once or twice a week	Start; no communication without quarreling (at least six times a week)	Little better; communicating without quarreling once or twice a week	Somewhat better; communicating without quarreling half the time they talk	Large extent better; communicating without quarreling most of the time (may be one quarrel a week)	Goal accomplished; open communication without quarreling

interventions of the worker. More immediate goals may emerge, such as providing care for the children of the person incarcerated. If it appears that the goal has been accomplished as a result of the tasks identified in the contracted plan, then worker and system may move on to other problems and goals, or they may move into the process of termination (to be developed in the next chapter).

If a goal has not been accomplished by the date anticipated for the completion of tasks in a plan, the question must be asked, "Why not?" Again, the response may point to some unexpected circumstances; for example, a death or sudden tragedy may have caused the failure in goal accomplishment. If such circumstances are not readily identifiable, the worker and system begin a systematic review of the planned contract, starting with the last column on the right, to find out why the goal has not been attained. The question is not only, "Why has the goal not been accomplished?" but also, "Why has movement toward goal accomplishment reached the point identified on the goal-attainment scale?"

The last column on a contracted plan indicates the dates when planned tasks have or have not been accomplished to date. After recognizing which tasks have not been completed, focus should move over to the next column to find out when it was expected that these tasks would be accomplished. Questions to be asked at this point are, "Was there an error in date anticipation?" "Is more time needed?" "Why was our timing off?" If it appears that what is needed is an adjustment in the date anticipated, this can readily take place, and intervention will be continued. For example, a worker may have worked out a contracted plan with a group of citizens in which it was anticipated that they would meet with a member of congress by a certain date. It was found out later that the politician's schedule was fully booked until two weeks after the anticipated date on the plan. If the reason for a failure to accomplish a goal on the date expected is something other than insufficient time for task completion, evaluation continues by moving over to the "contract" column (the third column from the right) of the plan.

In analyzing the "contract" column, a review is made of the people or system responsible for carrying out the identified tasks. Questions include, "Did the persons or system designated to carry out a task in the plan complete that task? If not, why not?" There are several possible reasons for a failure in task execution. Basically, a review of motivation, capacity, opportunity, and understanding of expectations should be made. The failure could be due to work overload, insufficient resources, or environmental pressures greater than anticipated. A change or redistribution in task responsibilities may be all that is needed to move forward toward goal accomplishment. Perhaps a worker or resource will have to withdraw from carrying out tasks in order to have a client system become more directly involved in problem resolution. Perhaps the worker or a new resource will have to become directly involved in collaborating with a client system to accomplish certain tasks. For example, a worker and Mr. M may have planned that Mr. M would go to the Vocational Rehabilitation Office to complete a set of tests. He was then expected to call the worker to let her know how he made out. What actually happened was that Mr. M changed his mind as the date for the testing drew closer, because he was afraid to hear the results of his testing. When he called the worker, he told her he didn't keep the appointment because he didn't feel well. The worker asked

Mr. M to come in to talk with her, and as they evaluated the plan they had made, Mr. M shared the fact that he couldn't face going for the tests and hearing the results by himself. The contract had to be changed so that the worker would go with Mr. M to the Vocational Rehabilitation Office.

Through analysis of the contract column, it may become apparent that, even when everyone carries out the tasks as agreed to in the plan, goals may still not be accomplished. The next area to be considered then would be the "tasks" column, to see if there could be an error in identifying what tasks had to be performed to fulfill the stated goals. When the tasks outlined in the contracted plan are studied, the question to be asked should call for an evaluation not only of the identified task, but also of the sequencing of the tasks as listed in the plan. The worker asks, "Were the tasks appropriately selected, clearly described, and properly sequenced in order to achieve the goal?" Perhaps some steps were omitted in the process. There may have been resources or influences in the environment that needed to be contacted but were overlooked in the planning. The nature of the task itself may have been inappropriate for a particular system. For example, Mrs. L did not follow through with a plan to take her mother to visit a nursing home. Although Mrs. L passively agreed with the worker that a nursing home would be good for her mother, and Mrs. L said that she would take her on a certain date, she never completed the task. Placing an elderly parent in a nursing home might in some cases be a successful plan to achieve the goal of providing needed care for a parent or of getting relief for a family strained by caring for an elderly person. In this situation, however, sending an elderly parent to a nursing home was not an acceptable or possible option for the family, because it was contrary to their basic cultural beliefs and customs.

Occasionally, tasks are identified, sequenced, and implemented and the stated goals are accomplished, but the problem may continue to be present. At this time, the worker and system would have to review carefully the "goal" column to see whether the stated goal actually related to or reflected the opposite of the identified problem or need. The worker asks, "Did the accomplishment of this goal resolve, reduce, or prevent further growth of, the problem? If not, why not?" It could be that the goal indicated the outcome desired by the worker but not by the client system. The needs of the client may continue to be unmet until the worker clearly understands and expresses the goal of the client. For example, Mrs. F may have expressed strong dissatisfaction with her apartment, complaining about rats and cockroaches, and the worker may have thought that Mrs. F was identifying the goal of extermination of rats and cockroaches from the apartment. When the problem of rats and cockroaches decreased after much activity involving the landlord and the Housing Code, Mrs. F was still dissatisfied with her apartment. Her true goal was to be relocated with the worker's help.

If there is not an overall improvement in a situation even after a contracted plan has been fully implemented, another reason could be an inappropriate identification of the problem or need in the first place. In the case just cited, for example, the worker thought that the client was presenting the problem of infested housing when, in fact, she was trying to give reasons for the worker to help her move. She felt isolated and did not get along with her neighbors. She hoped the worker would be able to arrange for her to move to the south end of town, where some of her relatives lived. As the generalist reviewed the case during evaluation, the question would be asked, "What in fact was the problem?" With hindsight, the worker would be able to see that the real problem with Mrs. F was a lack of social adjustment. The goal she really wanted to accomplish was relocation.

It is apparent, therefore, that a worker may use the contracted plan for evaluation in the General Method. There are six areas or columns that can be analyzed to locate possible causes for failure in problem resolution. At any step in the evaluated process, an understanding may take place that highlights the error in planning and pinpoints where reformulation must take place in the contracted plan.

Contract Reformulation

The General Method is a cyclical, ongoing process. It is more common than exceptional to have the helping process in social work move three steps forward and two steps backward all along the way. By the time the worker and system of contact move into evaluation, however, they are often sensitive to the possibility that the next phase in their working together may be termination. If the evaluation leads to an awareness that little or no progress has been made and that the contracted plan has to be reformulated, there may be resistance or expressed frustration on the part of both worker and system. This is particularly true when it becomes apparent that there is regression in a situation after much time and energy has been invested by both worker and system. A worker may need special support from his or her supervisor and a system of contact may need to receive special support from the worker, if they are to find the energy necessary to persevere in the process of plan reformulation. A worker needs to maintain a flexible, realistic attitude throughout the General Method, and this attitude must be conveyed to the systems he or she is working with.

As problems, goals, tasks, contract, or dates are reformulated during the evaluation period, it is imperative that the system of contact play a major role in the revision. Learning to recognize and accept setbacks, to try again without giving up, to change expectations and plans when necessary, and, finally, to see results from planned and persistent action can be extremely valuable to the growth of any human being.

When the evaluation has taken place that leads to a reformulation of some aspect of the contracted plan, the worker records the dates of the evaluation and the planned revisions on the contracted plan. As shown in Table 8–3, in the "date identified" and "problem/need" columns, the worker indicates the dates when the evaluation took place and the problems that were being evaluated. In the "problem/need" column, the worker also states what reformulations are necessary. In the columns where reformulations are to be made, the worker describes the changes or additions and then proceeds to fill in the other columns of the plan to reflect the revisions.

As shown in Table 8–3, the worker had originally set the goal of having Mr. M grow in awareness of his intellectual potential and marketable skills. He was to complete a battery of tests and learn the results at the Vocational Rehabilitation Office. After he completed the tests and learned their results, he was to call the worker. Mr. M failed to keep the appointment because he was afraid to hear the results. When Mr. M called to say he didn't go for the testing, the worker arranged to meet with him. During this meeting, they evaluated how far they had come and identified where the plan was incomplete. The difficulty was in Mr. M's not being able to carry out task 7 on his own. After much discussion, the worker offered to go with Mr. M for the testing. He agreed, and they also planned to meet again for a follow-up session. The evaluation, with reformulations of tasks and contract, is shown in Table 8–3.

Evaluation Questions

In essence, evaluation may be described as a ten-question process. In addition to those questions already identified that relate to the different areas of the contracted plan, the worker raises questions about external and internal circumstances that may have affected goal accomplishment. As stated earlier, the worker first considers the possibility that planning did not anticipate outside factors that may have caused failure or success in goal attainment. After considering outside factors and after reviewing the contracted plan, the worker and system of contact should also ask if any internal factors or dynamics within their relationship have prevented progress. This would include an assessment of the level of trust, openness, and honesty within the relationship. If it is agreed that there has been some resistance or holding back in their interactions, this should be explored. A direct discussion about the worker-system relationship, its progress, and its setbacks can be a powerful source for movement during evaluation.

Basically therefore, the essential questions to be asked during evaluation may be summarized as follows:

1. Has the goal been accomplished? (yes or no)
2. If yes, has the goal been accomplished as a result of circumstances outside of the contracted plan? (external causes)

If the goal has not been accomplished as expected at this time, the following questions are asked:

3. From when the problem was first identified, how much closer to or further from the goal have you moved? (goal-accomplishment scale)
4. Has the goal not been accomplished as expected because of circumstances outside of the contracted plan? (external causes)
5. Was there an error in date anticipation? (timing)
6. Did a person or system designated to complete a task fail to accomplish it? (contract)

TABLE 8-3. Contracted Plan Continued

DATE IDENTIFIED	PROBLEM/ NEED	GOAL	TASK	CONTRACT	DATE ANTICIPATED	DATE ACCOMPLISHED
2/6	1. Lack of self aware-ness of potential—Mr. M	1. To grow in aware-ness of potential (intelligence, skills)	1. Talk with Mr. M 2. Talk with Mrs. M	1. Worker and Mr. M 2. Worker and Mrs. M	2/13 2/15	2/13 2/15
			3. Talk with Mr. and Mrs. M	3. Worker and Mr. and Mrs. M	2/22	2/22
			4. Call Vocational Rehabilitation	4. Worker	2/23	2/23
			5. Discuss Vocational Rehabilitation with Mr. M	5. Worker and Mr. M	2/28	2/28
			6. Call Vocational Rehabilitation for appointment	6. Mr. M	3/1	3/1
			7. Go to Vocational Rehabilitation	7. Mr. M	3/14	
			8. Call worker	8. Mr. M	3/15	3/15
3/17 Evaluation	Evaluation of problem 1 (as cited above)	Goal 1 (as cited above)	1. Recall goal 1; evalu-ate why not accom-plished; reformulate contract	1. Worker and Mr. M	3/17	3/17
3/17 Contract reformu-lation	Change in contract 7 and in task 8 and con-tract 8		7. Go to Vocational Rehabilitation	7. Worker and Mr. M	3/25	
			8. Meet to review con-tract 7	8. Worker and Mr. M	3/27	

7. Were the tasks inappropriately selected, sequenced, or described? (tasks)
8. If the goal has been accomplished, but the problem continues, was the goal inaccurately identified? (goal)
9. If the goal has been accomplished, but the problem continues, was the problem inaccurately identified? (problem)
10. Was there anything in the worker-system relationship that inhibited goal accomplishment? (internal causes)

As these questions are answered, the causes for failure in goal attainment become increasingly evident. The reason a goal has not been accomplished to the extent anticipated may be pinpointed to some area on the contracted plan or to external or internal circumstances. When there has been clarification of what prevented goal accomplishment, the worker and system then begin to ask, "Why did this happen?" and "What can be done to remedy the situation and make goal accomplishment feasible?" A reformulation of the plan takes place.

Not all of the evaluation questions have to be asked if it becomes clear that a goal has not been attained for a reason suggested in earlier questions. Instead of proceeding with further questioning, the worker and system move into an analysis of why the particular drawback existed and a consideration of what modifications or additions need to be made in the contracted plan. With a reformulation of identified problems, goals, tasks, contract, or dates, the worker and system return to the intervention stage for further action. After the newly developed plan has been enacted, another evaluation takes place. If goals have been attained at this time, the worker and system are then ready either to work on other problems and needs or to move into the final stage of the General Method, called *termination.*

Ongoing Evaluation

As stated, the formal stage of evaluation begins with the question, "Has the goal been accomplished?" This question is asked at the time when it was anticipated on the contracted plan that a particular goal would be attained. In addition to this formal evaluation stage, it is possible to integrate a systematic evaluation throughout the entire General Method. Increasingly, efforts and instruments for ongoing evaluation in social work practice are being described in the professional literature.[5] The value of a concentrated ongoing evaluation is that it helps worker and system to be sensitive to movement and to the long-range goals throughout the process.

A tool may be used to assist a worker and system of contact in an ongoing evaluation process. The tool is a two-dimensional graph, which may begin to be constructed during any stage of the Method. The zero point on the graph represents the starting point when a problem is identified and a goal is first established. The vertical line of the graph intersects the zero point midway, and the line has an equal number of plus and minus points above and below the zero point. The vertical line is the goal line, which is used to chart movement toward or away from the goal as the problem gets better or worse. The highest point at the top of this line indicates goal accomplishment; the midpoint (0) identifies where the problem is when the goal is set; and the lowest point represents total failure in goal accomplishment. Each intermediate point should have some measurable descriptive criterion that indicates progression or regression. Whenever possible, all points should be described in behavioral terms than can be objectively measured.

The horizontal line of the graph is a time indicator. It may represent weeks, days, or months, depending on the nature of the problem. (For a crisis, the intervals may represent days or hours.) The line to the left of the midpoint indicates time intervals prior to the starting point, when there was no contact between worker and system. The right side of the line indicates time intervals during the course of service delivery.

Generally, the graph has four points from the midpoint on each line (see Figure 8–1). More intervals may be added as work progresses, if this appears to be appropriate for a particular situation. During the data-collection stage of the General Method, information may be obtained for plotting dots on the left side of the graph. The worker inquires about the severity of the problem prior to worker-system contact. Usually, this inquiry goes back to at least the previous four weeks. If it is a long-standing problem, a review may be made of the last four months or years. If it is a crisis that just recently began, the inquiry might cover the last four days or four hours. As the problem and goal become clear, the lines of the graph are drawn. As information is gathered about the history of the problem, person, and situation, dots are plotted on the left side of the graph. For example, if the intervals represent weeks, the worker would ask what the situation was like one week, two weeks, three weeks, and four weeks before the system began to have contact with the generalist. As the situation for each time interval is described, an effort is made to locate a point on the goal line which matches the description. A dot is plotted where the time interval and goal indicator meet. In Figure 8–1, for example, one week before contact, the problem was assessed at the -2 point; two weeks before, it was at the 0 point (same as first contact with worker); three weeks before, it was at the -1 level; and four weeks before, it was at the -1 level also. When the points are connected, it is apparent that the problem was at its worst one week before the system began to have contact with the worker. In the case of Mr. and Mrs. S, this would mean that, a week before they contacted the worker, their quarrels were moving into physical fights half the time they talked.

If the tool in Figure 8–1 is used as an ongoing evaluation instrument, each time the worker and system of contact meet, they would plot a point on the graph to show what movement has taken place each week. During the assessment stage, the graph is refined with clear descriptors to measure movement toward or away from clarified goals within an expected time frame as indicated on the contracted plan. As points are plotted and connected, the worker and system begin to envision the direction in which they expect to see the connecting line move, according to time intervals and dates anticipated on the contracted plan.

Plotting and charting movement could continue as the worker and system go through the intervention, evaluation, and termination stages of the General

FIGURE 8-1. Ongoing-Evaluation Graph: Mr. and Mrs. S

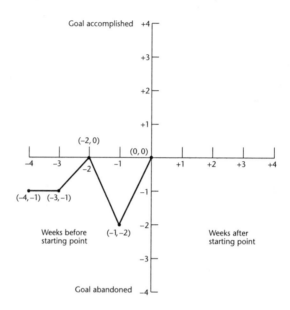

Method. During the formal evaluation stage, a thorough analysis is made of the reasons why movement has been in the directions shown on the graph. The goal-accomplishment scale and the contracted plan may still be used as described earlier to pinpoint the extent of goal accomplishment at the evaluation stage and to locate causal factors that resulted in arriving at the identified point. These tools may be complemented by the ongoing-evaluation graph, which could provide a general perspective of movement throughout the process of service delivery.

Continuing to use the graph during termination helps the worker to detect any regression that may take place as the system begins to realize that contacts with the worker will be terminated. As shown in Figure 8–2, for example, when Mr. and Mrs. S first began to express their problems to the worker, tensions mounted between them. They accused each other of betraying confidences by talking with the worker. The problem increased (point 1, -1). Through further contacts with the worker, Mr. and Mrs. S began to grow in being able to listen to and understand each other. Progress toward the stated goal became evident. They were able to go for three weeks with open communication without quarreling. During the next two weeks of contact, some regression became apparent. The direction of the movement line went slightly downward. This regression was due to the fact that the worker began to talk about termination with Mr. and Mrs. S. They began to talk about the anxiety they were feeling as they thought about having to work on their goals without the help of the worker. A conscious awareness

FIGURE 8-2. Ongoing-Evaluation Graph: Mr. and Mrs. S at Termination

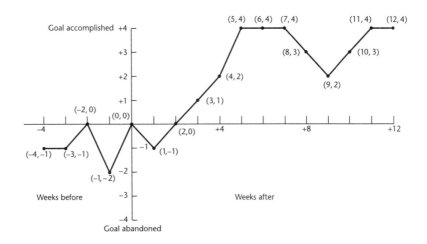

Descriptive criteria for goal line
+4 = Goal accomplished: open communication without quarreling
+3 = Communicating without quarreling most of the time (maybe one quarrel a week)
+2 = Communicating without quarreling half the time we talk
+1 = Communicating without quarreling once or twice a week
 0 = Starting point: no communication without quarreling (at least six times a week)
−1 = Quarreling moving into physical fights once or twice a week
−2 = Quarrels moving into physical fights half the time we talk
−3 = No communication without fighting
−4 = Goal abandoned: injury and separation

of the way they were responding to termination, with strong support from the worker, helped them to experience relief and to find strength to move to goal accomplishment.

The intervals at the right side of the graph on the horizontal line are extended as long as may be needed to indicate length of time receiving service. Although the worker may have gathered data only on the four weeks prior to the starting point (left side of line), the service may continue even beyond a year, and thus the horizontal line on the right would be extended. In Figure 8–2, for example, Mr. and Mrs. S were seen by the worker for twelve weeks. Although there was some regression at the time of termination, they did not go back to where they were during the month before they contacted the worker. The extended graph shows that their goal was attained by the time termination was finalized.

When the ongoing-evaluation graph is used in working with a client system, it is very helpful to ask the client to keep a daily log from the time the goal is first established. If a client is asked to recall what happened over a week or a month (depending on frequency of contacts), it is very likely that there will be some error in what is said. Often, a person's memory of what happened is influenced by how the person is feeling at the time of recall. A daily log can be introduced when the graph is first formulated. The worker asks the system to indicate briefly in the log each day the extent to which the problem and the goal were present. More specifically, the system may be asked to record the number of times or the length of duration of a particular behavior or event. For example, Mr. and Mrs. S would have been asked to jot down at the end of the day in their log how many times they quarreled and also how often they communicated with each other without quarreling during each day. If they bring the log with them each time they meet with the worker, a more accurate plotting of points on the graph can take place. The worker and system need to articulate as exactly as possible the measurable behaviors that are to be recorded and used to indicate movement in goal accomplishment.

One of the main drawbacks in using the ongoing-evaluation graph is the possibility that goals may change during the course of work with a system. With a multiple-problem family, for example, a goal in one area may become abandoned or at least shifted in priority because of a crisis that arises in another area. Progress for the family is then recognized as movement toward a different goal. If more than one goal is being worked on at one time, a number of graphs may be used simultaneously. For example, a child's health problem may be the working goal for a family, when suddenly they receive eviction papers. This new problem has to be addressed immediately. The new goal is to relocate the family within 30 days. A new graph indicating progression and regression in movement toward this goal would have to be developed.

The use of groups and scales as depicted in Figures 8–1 and 8–2 is similar to that used in a single-subject research design. The research methodology includes measurement processes and statistical techniques for testing the significance of results. The short baselines and timeframes of many interventions make the use of these techniques infrequent. The graphic visual presentation of results, however, is extremely beneficial in the course of charting progress.

The ongoing evaluation process used in single-subject design and in the related variation found in Figure 8–1 is applicable to work with a variety of problems, including those of a psychosocial nature. Examples include issues of adolescence, identity, alcoholism, and loss or separation.[6]

Working with Different Systems

No matter what type of system a worker has been working with for goal accomplishment, a time is needed to evaluate how far the system has moved toward or away from the goal. A deliberate, objective study, which includes an analysis of change, identification of impediments to goal accomplishment, and planning or reformulating contracts, may help to break through resistances and to provide direction for future interactions between worker and system of contact.

The tools and processes described in this chapter are general in nature; they may be used in evaluation with individuals, groups, families, or communities. The ten evaluation questions, the goal-accomplishment scale, the contracted plan, and the ongoing-evaluation graph may be adapted for use with any system. Even when working with teams or target systems, the generalist takes time to involve the system in an evaluation, during which the tools and processes suggested may be utilized.

When working with a team, for example, the ten evaluation questions are asked about the goals that the team identified collectively. The contract the team members developed is used to locate causal factors when goals are not accomplished. The timing, contract, tasks, problems, and goals found on the team contract are considered, along with external circumstances not anticipated by the team in planning. Internal circumstances are also considered as possible causal factors. A study would be made not only of the relationships of team members with the client or target system, but also of the relationships among the team members themselves (trust, openness) and how these relationships have affected the process of goal attainment. The goal-accomplishment scale may be used to show how much movement the team believes has taken place for each of the goals it stated. The ongoing-evaluation graph may also be used to monitor direction over a period of time toward or away from the goals.

To cite an example of evaluation in teamwork, a vocational counselor from the State Department of Vocational Rehabilitation, a social worker from the East Side Women's Center, and a child-welfare worker from the Department of Children's Services formed a team to coordinate service delivery for Mrs. Judy E and her 5-year-old daughter, Betty. Mrs. E had been reported three months previously for suspected child abuse. The child welfare worker was monitoring the home situation. She had helped Mrs. E to reach the point where she was asking for skill training to become employed. Mrs. E and the worker developed a plan in which Mrs. E could be referred to the Women's Center and the Department of Vocational Rehabilitation. Mrs. E agreed also to have the workers from the three resources form a team to provide ongoing, coordinated services for herself and her daughter.

Once the team was formed, goals were identified, and tasks were distributed among the members of the team and Mrs. E. The vocational counselor had the task of arranging for Mrs. E to receive skill training. After completing the skill-training program, Mrs. E was to be helped by the vocational counselor to locate employment. The social worker from the East Side Women's Center was at that time leading a support group for unemployed women who needed to develop a sense of self-worth and self-confidence. Mrs. E was to be added to this group. The child-welfare worker was to help Mrs. E to locate day care for Betty. This worker also had the task of case management. She initiated the first meeting of the team and served as the team leader when it began. Rotating leadership was later used.

The main goals, tasks, and contracted responsibilities that were collectively identified by the team are summarized as follows:

1. To help Mrs. E to become employed by her going through a process of testing, training, job locating, being hired—assigned to vocational counselor and Mrs. E.

2. To help Mrs. E to grow in self-worth and self-confidence by her attendance at a weekly women's support group—assigned to social worker at
the Women's Center and Mrs. E.

3. To help Mrs. E to locate appropriate, available day care for Betty through
searching for a resource and completing the application process—
assigned to child-welfare worker, Mrs. E, and Betty.

4. To have Mrs. E participate in the coordinated team effort by encouraging
her to accept the invitation to join and become involved in all team
meetings.

The contracted plan also stated the anticipated dates for completing each of
the identified tasks. As interventions were carried out, the team moved into the
evaluation stage. If a goal and its planned tasks were apparently the direct responsibility of one worker on the team (as in goals 1–3), this member was the one
responsible for developing the ongoing-evaluation graph and/or the goal-accomplishment scale for the particular goal. This team member was asked to lead the
team as members took time to assess the extent to which that goal has been accomplished. Collectively, the team reviewed the ten evaluation questions and the contracted plan. This analysis was conducted with input from the client.

The fourth goal in the team example is one of shared responsibility by all team
members. Each member was expected to encourage Mrs. E to attend and to participate in team meetings. Together, the team designed a goal-accomplishment
scale and an ongoing-evaluation graph for this goal. Because the goal had the distinct dimensions of (1) attendance and (2) participation in team meetings, the team
decided to draw up two graphs and two scales for clarity in assessment of goal 4.
For example, in Tables 8–4 and 8–5 (goal-accomplishment scales) and Figures 8–3
and 8–4 (ongoing-evaluation graphs), the team members—it is hoped including
Mrs. E as a member—discussed and identified what they saw as criteria for identifying movement in goal accomplishment. The dual scales and graphs help to
highlight the multiple options that may exist when the two variables (attendance
and participation) are considered necessary to achieve the one goal (Mrs. E's participating in the coordinated team effort). In Table 8–4, Mrs. E is seen as attending
the team meetings regularly (4 is checked on Table 8–4), but she is not yet participating fully at the meetings (1 is checked on Table 8–5). Both Table 8–4 and Table
8–5 would have to reach a +4 if the goal is to be accomplished totally, according to
the criteria developed by the team.

It should be noted that in the scales of Tables 8–4 and 8–5 and in the "goal"
lines of the graphs of Figures 8–3 and 8–4, there are no minus numbers and line.
This is because there is no degree to which the goal of attendance and participation at team meetings can be less than the starting point (0). The *0* on the scales
means "zero attendance and participation."

The ongoing-evaluation graphs in Figures 8–3 and 8–4 show that there was 0
attendance and participation in team meetings prior to the starting point when
Mrs. E was first invited to attend. The graphs also show the progress that took
place as Mrs. E began to feel more in control of her life, more confidence in herself,
and more comfortable with the other team members.

FIGURE 8-3. Attendance at Team Meetings

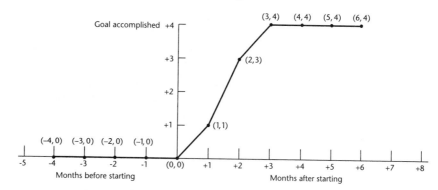

Descriptive criteria for goal line 4a
+4 = Goal accomplished: regular attendance at team meetings
+3 = Attending three out of four meetings a month
+2 = Attending two out of four meetings a month
+1 = Attending one out of four meetings a month
 0 = Starting point: no attendance at team meetings

FIGURE 8-4. Participation in Team Meetings

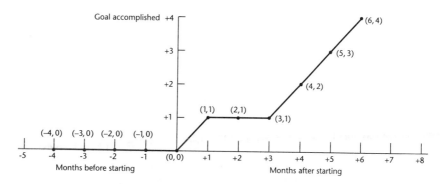

Descriptive criteria for goal line 4b
+4 = Goal accomplished: active participation in flow of meetings
+3 = Speaking up and sharing five or six times during a meeting
+2 = Speaking up three or four times during a meeting
+1 = Speaking up once or twice during a meeting or only when spoken to
 0 = Starting point: no participation in team meetings

In work with a target system rather than a team or a client system, the evaluation process may be somewhat different. Although a generalist may interact with a target system for goal accomplishment, the two may never arrive at a point where they develop a contracted plan together. A worker alone, or with a client or other resource, may initiate contact with a target system to request some assistance or change in service. The worker and other members of the action system

TABLE 8-4.   Attendance at Team Meetings

				X
0	1	2	3	4
Starting point: no attendance	Little attendance: one out of four meetings a month	Some attendance: two out of four meetings a month	Frequent attendance: three out of four meetings a month	Goal accomplished: regular attendance

TABLE 8-5.   Participation in Team Meetings

	X			
0	1	2	3	4
Starting point: no participation in meetings	Little participation: speaking up once or twice during a meeting or only when spoken to	Some participation: speaking up three or four times during a meeting	Frequent participation: speaking up and sharing five or six times	Goal accomplished: active—fully participating in flow of meetings

may state clearly at that time their purpose or goals in making the contact. The target system, however, may not respond favorably. If the worker continues to try to change the target system through repeated contacts and pressures, there may be a time when the worker evaluates with the target system what movement toward or away from the stated goal has taken place since their first contact. Here, a goal-accomplishment scale or an ongoing-evaluation graph may be helpful as the worker tries to make an objective presentation to confront the target system with the reality of the situation.

For example, a generalist may speak to the landlord of an apartment complex in behalf of his tenants, to try to get him to improve the conditions of the apartment. A list is presented indicating repairs, renovations, and improvements needed. To have all 12 items on the list taken care of is the ultimate goal. The generalists and the tenants involve a Housing Code Inspector and the Housing Court in efforts to pressure the landlord to make the improvements. Periodically, the generalist meets with the landlord to continue to bring to his attention the unattended needs of the tenants. As conditions improve or deteriorate, the worker may choose to use an ongoing-evaluation graph or a goal-accomplishment scale to

FIGURE 8–5.   Case Example: Target System—Landlord

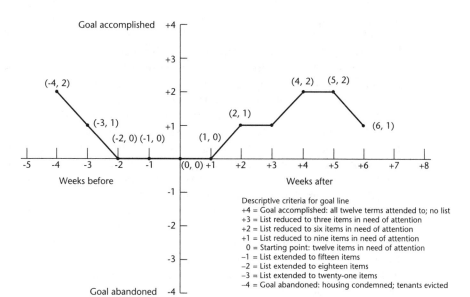

Descriptive criteria for goal line
+4 = Goal accomplished: all twelve terms attended to; no list
+3 = List reduced to three items in need of attention
+2 = List reduced to six items in need of attention
+1 = List reduced to nine items in need of attention
 0 = Starting point: twelve items in need of attention
−1 = List extended to fifteen items
−2 = List extended to eighteen items
−3 = List extended to twenty-one items
−4 = Goal abandoned: housing condemned; tenants evicted

demonstrate what has taken place since the problems and needs were first presented to the landlord (starting point). This evaluative approach may help to create sufficient feelings for progress to be made.

As depicted on the graph in Figure 8–5, the conditions at the apartment complex had deteriorated during the weeks prior to the worker's contact with the landlord. Through various pressures and continued contacts, some improvements were made. After the fifth week of contact, however, there was a tapering off of efforts to improve conditions, and problems increased. The worker used the graph (Figure 8–5) to point out to the landlord what progress had been made, how conditions were starting to get worse, and how far they were from accomplishing the original goal (+4).

Using the Holistic Foundation in Evaluation

The holistic foundation for generalist practice, as diagrammed in Chapter 1 (Table 1–5), identifies the fundamental values, knowledge, and skills used during evaluation. The worker demonstrates care for a system and a commitment to quality service by taking time to analyze movement toward or away from goals. Throughout the evaluation process, the principles of *individualization* and *self-determination* are emphasized. Any assessment of movement or change is strongly dependent on input from the system of contact. Any reformulation of a contract takes place only after a client system, an action system, or, if possible, a target system has spoken with the worker and has given input and consent.

In social work, the worker inquires about changes in feelings and attitudes as well as behaviors. The worker recognizes and encourages *purposeful expression of feelings* during evaluation. If progress has not taken place, the worker conveys a *nonjudgmental attitude* toward the system, as focus is directed to exploring possible causal factors and a reformulation of the plan.

From scientific research, the generalist uses knowledge and skills for measuring, graphing, and scaling during evaluation. In addition to research skills, it may be necessary to use relationship, problem-solving, and political skills. Frequently, the worker guides, clarifies, and confronts as goals are analyzed. Within the evaluation period, such problem-solving skills as problem and need identification, data collection, assessment, and contracting may be reviewed and repeated.

Foundation theories used during evaluation vary according to the problem or goal that is being evaluated. In order to identify indicators of improvement or regression in a problem, the nature and dynamics of the problem must be understood.

Through holistic knowledge, the generalist is enabled to conduct a comprehensive study of causal factors. As the ten evaluation questions are raised and internal and external circumstances are considered, the worker is aided by the foundation theory base, which is integrated within the ecological perspective of *person in environment*. The generalist is sensitive to the complex and multiple factors that interact and influence a system.

Human Diversity in Evaluation

Culture

As the worker and system move into the evaluation stage of the General Method, they begin with the question, "Have the goals been accomplished?" Particularly when working with minorities, the worker must distinguish between long-range goals and short-range goals. The core problems of poverty and racism may be readily identified as basically causing a system to have unmet needs. Long-range goals may be the eradication of these two problems. Although the long-range goals may not be accomplished at the time of evaluation, the efforts made to work toward them should be evaluated. The identified immediate or short-range goals are usually articulated in more precise terms that can be measured for accomplishment. If they have not been fully accomplished, the contract review (described in Chapter 7) may help to highlight the reason why plans are not carried out successfully. Again, the timing projected for goal accomplishment may not have been in line with the time orientation of the culture of the system. The persons or resources expected to carry out the planned tasks, or the tasks themselves, may have been culturally inappropriate. It may be that the goals or the problems were not correctly understood or articulated.

As pointed out, a final question to raise during evaluation is, "Was there anything in the worker–system relationship that inhibited goal accomplishment?" To answer this question, a worker needs to ask him- or herself, "How sensitive and accepting was I toward this person, group, family, or community?" Self-awareness is necessary. If a worker has come to understand and appreciate his or her own ethnicity, it is often easier to recognize and accept the ethnicity of others. As with the systems receiving service, a worker also brings to any new relationship his or her ethnic history and personal experiences with certain cultural groups. Although, admittedly, it may be natural to transfer or stereotype, a working relationship can be very inhibited when those receiving help, or even those providing help, sense that they are not being treated as unique individuals. If goals are not being accomplished, the reason could be related to an absence of cultural sensitivity or of any shared cultural elements, with a resulting stereotyping by both the worker and the system receiving service. When stereotyping is present, studies have shown that participants begin to feel discomfort, and that they retreat into exaggerated behaviors that depict and confirm the ethnic-group stereotype. For example, during an interethnic study between Japanese-Americans and Caucasian Americans, it was found that in time the Japanese-Americans became increasingly quiet and aloof, while the Caucasian Americans became loud and aggressive.[7] An honest evaluation of the worker–system relationship can promote an increase in self-awareness for both worker and system, and it may help to break through some of the discomfort or resistance in the relationship.

Sexual Variation

In the evaluation stage, while making an appraisal of the extent of goal accomplishment and a comprehensive evaluation to locate possible reasons for any lack of accomplishment, a worker who is knowledgeable about sexual variations can better recognize dynamics and factors that may affect or prevent the attainment of goals for lesbian or gay clients. In reviewing the contract, it may become apparent that service providers or other persons who were expected to complete certain tasks may have taken longer than planned or may have changed their minds as the anticipated date arrived. The change on their part could be due to fears, threats, or insincere commitments that surfaced as the plan unfolded. Employers or landlords, for example, who said they would hire or rent to gay or lesbian persons may not have followed through when an opening actually occurred. Clients themselves may have changed their minds and plans as they began to experience pressures from family members, lawyers, judges, or others. An individual who seemed interested in joining a support group, for example, may have failed to show up for meetings because of increased fears of being identified with the group. And finally, here too, it is possible that the worker or the client may be uncomfortable with the working relationship itself and that this discomfort has interfered with goal accomplishment. Perhaps the openness or support needed did not develop, owing to hidden biases or fears. Again, an honest evaluation of the worker-system relationship at this time may result in a breakthrough so that progress can begin.

Gender Sensitivity

When it is time to evaluate goals that relate to gender-role changes, progress in personal and environmental goals should be considered realistically. Both the worker and those receiving service need to realize that only with continued efforts and much time and patience can there be any lasting change in sexist attitudes, practices, and policies. If a goal was to eliminate sexism in a target system and this has not been accomplished, progress may have been made if at least some conscious awareness of the presence of sexism has begun to develop in the target system. On a personal level, to have an individual become aware of his or her self-image and gender expectations may be a major accomplishment, even though the person may not change his or her behavior or life situation.

Here too, a major factor to be reviewed when goals have not been accomplished is the expectations and attitudes of the worker toward those receiving service. A social worker who is finding it difficult to support efforts to overcome sexism or who is comfortable with traditional gender roles may be contributing to the failure in goal attainment. As brought out by Susan Sturdevant,

> If a therapist believes that women are "by nature" flighty, irrational, narcissistic, masochistic, or dependent, etc., he/she will do little to help a client become rational, independent, or stable, since such a change is, according to his/her assumptive world, "impossible" for women.[8]

In addition to a sensitivity to culture, sexual orientation, and gender, during the evaluation stage a worker keeps in mind that goal accomplishment is related to several additional diversity variables, such as age and stages, endowment and personality, value system, social class, and geographic location.

Evaluation in Diverse Field Areas

I. Field Area: Child Welfare
   A. Agency: State Department of Children's Services
   B. Client System
   > *K, 15 years old, female, placed in group home three months ago. (For more background information, see Chapter 4, Engagement in Diverse Field Areas, I. Child Welfare.)*
   C. Summary of Preceding Stages
   > *The problems, goals, and tasks identified and implemented in earlier stages are found in Table 6–6 of Chapter 6 and Table 7–1 of Chapter 7. The worker's interventions included direct work with K, the client; a referral to the group home and a court petitioning for custody continuance; and teamwork with personnel from the shelter, the group home, and the school K is attending.*

D. Evaluation

Goal analysis: *The primary goals of (1) obtaining and maintaining a permanent placement, (2) reentering school, and (3) personal growth were analyzed by K and the worker. They agreed that a placement had been found and was being maintained (goal 1). K was also attending school regularly (goal 2). Her personal problems (3a–3d) were beginning to surface in casework and group sessions at the home, though she was still finding it difficult to believe that she was of any worth and to talk about her sexuality. Goal 4, to obtain continuance of custody, was achieved on 3/30.*

Scales were developed to assess extent to which the first two goals were accomplished. The two dimensions of goal 1 (obtaining placement, maintaining placement) were separated for greater clarity in evaluation (Tables 8–6 and 8–7). The goal of school reentry was expanded at this time to include optimal school performance. Two scales were also used then to evaluate goal 2 (Tables 8–8 and 8–9). The goal regarding personal growth (goal 3) had four subheadings (a–d). Because the child-welfare worker was not working directly on this goal with K, the four parts were reviewed in discussion and evaluated in general, on the basis of input from K, from the worker who was seeing K individually, and from the group-home worker who attended the peer-group meetings.

Goal 1a was evaluated by K and the worker as accomplished (+2). K was placed in a group home where she could stay until adulthood.

According to K and the group-home staff, K was adjusting well to the placement. They thought, however, that she could try to participate more fully in group activities. She was completing her chores and getting along satisfactorily with the other residents. Because K had only been in the home for three months and said she was not completely comfortable there yet, the worker and K evaluated the extent of accomplishment for goal 1b as +2 on the scale.

K was accepted into the local school. Goal for 2a, therefore, was accomplished, as indicated with a +2 on the scale in Table 8–8.

K and the worker considered ways in which they could objectively assess her progress in school. They agreed that they would look at her

TABLE 8-6.   Goal 1a: To Obtain a Permanent Placement

				X
-2	-1	0	+1	+2
Goal abandoned	No place located	Starting point at shelter	Place located	Goal accomplished; placement obtained

TABLE 8-7. Goal 1b: To Maintain a Permanent Placement

	-4	-3	-2	-1	0	+1	+2	+3	+4
							X		
	Goal abandoned; removal from placement	Marked problems; high conflict level	Increased problems	Beginning problems in adjustment	Starting point; beginning placement at new group home	Beginning to adjust	Satisfactory adjustment, but room for improvement	Marked improvement, high comfort level	Goal accomplished; stabilized adjustment

TABLE 8-8.   Goal 2a: To Reenter School

				X
-2	-1	0	+1	+2
Goal abandoned	No school located	Starting point—out of school	School located	Goal accomplished—returned to school

grades and report card from school and that they would ask for verbal assessments from K's teachers through the school social worker. At the time of this evaluation, K's performance was described by her teachers as "satisfactory." They thought she could do better, especially in her writing and class participation. They expected that K would perform at a higher achievement level as she became more familiar with the school. K said that she liked school and her teachers and thought she was learning a great deal. She knew she could try harder and bring up her grades by the end of the semester. K did not believe that she needed a tutor or any additional help with her schoolwork at this time. The worker and K assessed the extent of accomplishment for goal 2b as +2 on the scale (Table 8–9).

K said she continued to find it hard to talk about herself and her personal problems (goal 3). She enjoyed the group meetings because the other residents were able to say things she couldn't. Deep down inside she knew she was feeling happier but was afraid it was "too good to be true." She said she would try harder to talk with her caseworker about herself and her feelings. K's caseworker at the group home thought that K was beginning to relax more during individual sessions and that more time was needed before K would be able to talk freely about herself, her past, or her future.

Contract review and reformulation: During contract review, the worker and K recognized the need for more time before goals 1, 2, and 3 (especially goal 3) could be accomplished. In reviewing contracted tasks, the worker and K agreed that the worker did not have to continue to follow up with K every two weeks. K knew that she could always call the worker if she needed her. They agreed that the worker would begin to visit K once a month, unless there was some reason for additional contact. The worker recorded the process of evaluation that occurred at this stage, indicating the reformulation of contract as found in Table 8–10.

Ongoing evaluation: At this point, the worker and K developed graphs to assess ongoing progress in (1) maintenance (adjustment) in the group home and (2) school performance. The graphs they designed are found in Figures 8–6 and 8–7. The worker and K planned to use the graphs each month when they met for ongoing evaluation and charting of progress.

TABLE 8-9. Goal 2b: To Achieve Optimal Level of Academic Performance

-4	-3	-2	-1	0	+1	+2 X	+3	+4
Goal abandoned: school dismissal or dropping out	Marked persistent problems	Increasing problems	Beginning to have problems in academic achievement	Starting point; beginning new school	Beginning to achieve academically	Stabilizing academic achievement, but room for improvement	Marked improvement in academic performance	Goal accomplished, optimal level of academic performance

TABLE 8-10. Contracted Plan Continued

DATE IDENTIFIED	PROBLEM/ NEED	GOAL	TASK	CONTRACT	DATE ANTICIPATED	DATE ACCOMPLISHED
4/25 Evaluation	Evaluation of problems 1, 2, 3, 4	Goals 1, 2, 3, 4	1. Recall each goal 2. Assess extent of accomplishment 3. Reformulate contract	Worker and K (with input from school and group-home personnel)	4/25	4/25
Contract reformulation	Change in 1. Date anticipated for task 4, goal 1; task 3, goal 3	Goal 1	Task 4—follow-up	Worker, K, group home staff	5/25 and once a month thereafter	
		Goal 3	Task 3—follow-up	Worker, K, social worker at group home	5/25 and once a month thereafter	
	2. Goal statement for problem 2; contract and date anticipated for task 2, goals 2a and 2b	2a. To reenter school b. To achieve an optimal level of academic performance	Task 2—follow-up	Worker and school social worker	5/25 and once a month thereafter	

FIGURE 8-6. Goal 1b: To Maintain Permanent Placement

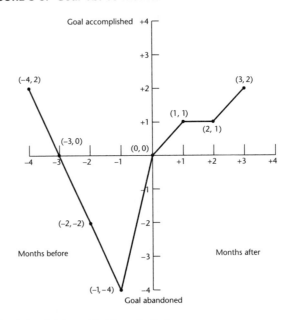

Descriptive criteria for goal line (Y — vertical line)
+4 = Goal accomplished: permanent placement maintained (stabilized)
+3 = Marked improvement: participation in group, high comfort level
+2 = Stabilizing adjustment: satisfactory, but room for improvement
+1 = Beginning to adjust
 0 = Starting point: beginning placement — insecure, withdrawn
–1 = Beginning problems
–2 = Increased problems
–3 = Marked problems in adjustment, high conflict level
–4 = Goal abandoned: removal from placement
Line X – horizontal line = Months in residence
 Plus numbers   = Months in new group home
 0   = Beginning placement in new group home
 Minus numbers   = Months before placement in new group home
 0 to –1   = Placement in shelter
 –1 to –3   = Months in foster home
 –3 and before   = Months in first group home

II. Field Area: Gerontology

A. Agency: Seaside Nursing Home

B. Client System

Mrs. J, an 80-year-old Portuguese woman in a skilled-nursing facility. (For additional information, see Chapter 4, Engagement in Diverse Field Areas, II. Gerontology.)

C. Summary of Preceding Stages

The contracted plan indicating the problems, goals, and tasks identified in earlier stages is found in Table 7–2 of Chapter 7. The worker's interventions were direct work with Mrs. J and teamwork with the staff of the nursing home and the pastor of the church Mrs. J used to attend. The prioritized goals for Mrs. J were the following: (1) to get to know the

FIGURE 8-7. Goal 2b. To Achieve an Optimal Level of Academic Performance

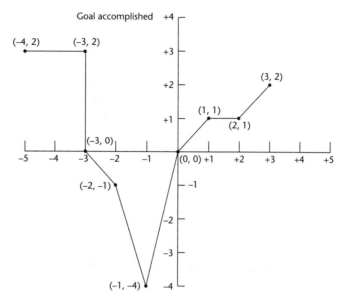

Descriptive criteria for goal line (Y – vertical line)
+4 = Goal accomplished: optimal level of academic performance
+3 = Marked improvement in academic performance (writing and class participation)
+2 = Stabilizing academic achievement, room for improvement
+1 = Beginning to achieve academically
　0 = Starting point: beginning new school – insecure, withdrawn
–1 = Beginning problems in academic achievement
–2 = Increasing problems
–3 = Marked, persistent problems in academic performance
–4 = Goal abandoned: school dismissal or dropout
Line X – horizontal line = Time
　Plus numbers　　= Months attending new school
　0　　　　　　　= Beginning new school
　Minus numbers = Months before attending new school

staff and the resources of the nursing home; (2) to work out a mutually
satisfactory bath schedule with the nurses; (3) to leave room alone (at
least once a day) and to attend a house activity (at least once a week); (4)
to stop name-calling and yelling at residents; and (5) to share her culture with others.

D. Evaluation

Goal analysis:　After three months, the worker and Mrs. J analyzed
the extent of goal accomplishment for the five prioritized goals. Goals 2
and 4 had clearly been accomplished. Mrs. J's bath was scheduled earlier, and she no longer fought with the nurses. She also stopped calling the
residents names and was beginning to feel more comfortable in the home
as she got to know the staff and the resources available (goal 1). She met
with the program planner, the director of volunteers, the head nurse and
other nurses, the chaplain, and staff members from recreational therapy.
Although there were occasional days when she did not leave her room,

she was attending nursing-home activities with her roommate (goal 3) and appeared less fearful of having her possessions stolen. Regarding goal 5, Mrs. J's pastor and two members of the congregation came to see her. They took her to their church for a Christmas prayer service and a concert. A volunteer who spoke Portuguese visited Mrs. J for three weeks in November but then dropped out of the program.

Scales to assess the extent of goal accomplishment for goals 3a and 3b were developed and drawn on a large sheet of paper (Tables 8–11 and 8–12). The scale for goal 3a was expanded into an ongoing-evaluation graph, which the worker reviewed with Mrs. J each succeeding week (Figure 8–8). The nurse at the head station agreed to help Mrs. J and the worker to keep track of the days when Mrs. J was able to leave her room on her own. A small calendar was kept at the head station, and the date was circled when Mrs. J came to the station to say "hello" to the nurse on duty.

TABLE 8-11.   Goal 3a: To Leave Room Alone (at Least Once a Day)

				X		
-3	-2	-1	0	+1	+2	+3
Total refusal to go out of room— goal dropped	Increased refusal to leave room (once a day)	Occasional refusal to leave even when someone offers to take her (about once a week)	Starting point: only leave when someone takes her for meals	Occasional going out of room alone (about once a week)	Increased going out of room alone (once a day)	Going out of room alone freely; maximum goal accomplished

TABLE 8-12.   Goal 3b: To Attend House Activity (at Least Once a Week)

		X	
0	1	2	3
Starting point: attending no house activities (program or meeting)	Attending house activity with worker or staff member (once a week)	Attending house activity with other residents once a week	Attending house activities with residents more than once a week; maximum goal accomplished

The goal does not extend to Mrs. J's going outside the institution on her own. At this time, it is not seen as a possibility. The maximum goal accomplishment considered, therefore, was Mrs. J's being able to freely and frequently go out of her bedroom on her own. The graph in Figure 8–8 demonstrates that Mrs. J was able to live alone up to three weeks before she was hospitalized. She was in the hospital for two weeks prior to her placement in the nursing home. During her first two weeks at the home, she regressed. At the time of evaluation (twelve weeks in residence) she progressed to occasionally leaving her room independently (averaging once a week), which is shown at point +1 on the goal line of Figure 8–8. With the added involvement of the nurses at the station on Mrs. J's floor, the goal reached the point +2 by one week after the evaluation, as shown in point 13,2 of Figure 8–8.

Contract reformulation: *The evaluation conducted by Mrs. J and the worker twelve weeks after she began residency in the nursing home was recorded on the contracted plan (Table 8–13). As indicated, the task for goal 3a was expanded to include Mrs. J's saying "hello" to the nurse at the station on her floor at least once a day after leaving her room on her own. The task of having the nurse chart on the calendar Mrs. J's visit to the station was also added to the contract. In addition, the head nurse and the social worker planned to meet once a week to review Mrs. J's progress, using the charted calendar. The worker would*

FIGURE 8-8. Goal 3a: To Leave Room by Herself

Descriptive criteria for points on goal line (Y — vertical line)
+4 = Goal accomplished: going out of room freely
+2 = Increased going out of room alone (once a day average)
+1 = Occasionally going out of room alone (once a week average)
 0 = Starting point: placement in nursing home; leaving room only when taken to meals
−1 = Occasional refusal to leave room even when someone offers to accompany her (once a week average)
−2 = Increased refusal to leave room even when someone offers to accompany her (once a day average)
−3 = Repeated refusal to leave room even when someone offers to accompany her (more than once a day)
−4 = Goal abandoned: total refusal to leave room
Line X – horizontal line = weeks before and after placement in nursing home

use this information when she met with Mrs. J to chart progress in goal 3a on the evaluation graph each week. As shown in Table 8–13, the contract reformulation and the three-month evaluation were indicated on the contracted plan.

III. Field Area: Public Social Worker
A. Agency: State Social Services
B. Client System

Mr. and Mrs. P and their two children (ages 2 and 4), placed in emergency shelter (Center City Motor Inn) for 44 days, currently living in an apartment. (For additional background information, see Chapter 4, Engagement in Diverse Field Areas, III. Public Social Welfare.)

C. Summary of Preceding Stages

The problems, goals, and tasks identified and enacted in earlier stages are listed in Table 6–10 of Chapter 6 and Table 7–3 of Chapter 7. The interventions of the worker were primarily (1) referral to several resources, (2) direct work with the P family, and (3) teamwork with the income-maintenance technician and Mr. P's psychiatrist.

D. Evaluation

Goal analysis: *After ten weeks of service, the worker and Mr. and Mrs. P evaluated the extent to which the goals of the contracted plan were accomplished. They agreed that goals for problems 1, 2, 3, 4, 6, 7, 8, and 9 were accomplished. These goals are the following:*

1. To obtain an emergency food supply
2. To move into emergency shelter
3. To receive a food supply until AFDC check and food stamps arrive
4. To move into an apartment for long-term residence of family
6. To have children examined at the health center
7. To obtain fuel assistance
8. To receive AFDC check and food stamps
9. To have the refrigerator repaired

Goals 10, 11, and 12 were not accomplished by the time of the evaluation. These goals are:

10. To receive Supplemental Security Income
11. To receive a Thanksgiving food basket
12. To receive Christmas gifts for the children

No goal was ever stated on the contracted plan for problem 5 (poor money management) because Mr. and Mrs. P refused to recognize this problem. They continued to blame others and to deny that their evictions from past apartments were related to their poor management of money.

Contract review: *In reviewing the goals that were accomplished, the worker asked if the attainment of goals was a result of the plan contracted. With the exception of goals 4 and 9, goal attainment directly followed the completion of planned tasks. The contract for goal 4*

TABLE 8-13. Contracted Plan Continued

DATE IDENTIFIED	PROBLEM/ NEED	GOAL	TASK	CONTRACT	DATE ANTICIPATED	DATE ACCOMPLISHED
12/8 Evaluation	Evaluation of problems 1–5	Goals 1–5	1. Review each goal 2. Evaluate extent of accomplishment for each goal 3. Reformulate contract	Mrs. J and worker	12/18 and 12/20	12/18 and 12/20
Contract reformulation	Change in tasks, contract, and dates anticipated for goal 3a	3a. To leave room alone (at least once a day)	(3a)1. To leave room alone and walk down to nurse's station and say "hello" to nurse on duty	1. Mrs. J	12/21 and each day thereafter	
			2. To circle date of visit on calendar	2. Nurse on duty	12/21 and each day thereafter	
			3. To meet to discuss Mrs. J's progress	3. Head nurse and worker	12/27 and each Thursday thereafter	
			4. To evaluate progress toward goal 3a using graph	4. Worker and Mrs. J	12/27 and each Thursday thereafter	

stated that the P's and the worker would collaborate on locating an apartment. For goal 9, the worker and the P's planned that Mr. P would contact the Salvation Army for financial assistance to pay for repairs. Instead, the P's contacted their income-maintenance technician directly, and she arranged for them to receive a new refrigerator.

In analyzing goals that were not accomplished (goals 10, 11, 12), the worker noted that the arrest in the process of goal accomplishment for each of these goals could be pinpointed to tasks contracted to Mr. P that he failed to complete. He did not follow up on his application for Supplemental Security Income, nor did he contact churches for a Thanksgiving food basket or the Salvation Army for Christmas presents for the children.

Even with goal 9 (refrigerator repair), instead of Mr. P's getting estimates on repair costs and contacting the Salvation Army, he and Mrs. P called the income-maintenance technician and requested a new refrigerator. (The worker and the income-maintenance technician real- ized that they should have communicated with each other about this new request before either one enacted a plan—teamwork breakdown.)

The social worker did not use scales to assess extent of goal accom- plishment during the evaluation stage because of the basic nature of the identified goals and the interventions utilized. Although the primary needs for housing and food were being met for the present, the worker realized that there were two continuing problem areas: (1) poor money management and (2) excessive dependency on others to meet their needs. At the time of the evaluation, the P's were not recognizing these prob- lems and did not want to work on either of them. When the worker pointed out that the tasks assigned to Mr. P had not been accomplished, he said he planned to do them when he felt up to it.

Since the P's were not asking for help from the worker with the two cited problems or with any additional problems or needs at the time of the evaluation, and because the worker did not want to continue unnecessary dependency, he began to talk about terminating with the family. Both the P's and the worker agreed that they would begin the process of termination.

E. Charted Progress

The worker recorded the evaluation process on the contracted plan as found in Table 8–14.

In the worker's discussions with the P's, their income-mainte- nance technician, and Mr. P's psychiatrist, the worker shared his con- tinued concern regarding the family's management of money and depen- dence on outside resources to meet their needs. The problem of the family's poor money management had been recorded on the problem list earlier. During evaluation, the family's problem of dependency became more obvious to the worker, and it was added to the problem list when he recorded the evaluation (see Table 8–14). The worker expected that the

TABLE 8-14. Contracted Plan Continued

DATE IDENTIFIED	PROBLEM/ NEED	GOAL	TASK	CONTRACT	DATE ANTICIPATED	DATE ACCOMPLISHED
12/4 Evaluation	Evaluation of problems 1–12	Goals 1–4 and 6–12 (no goal for problem 5)	1. Review goals	1. Mr. and Mrs. P and worker	12/4	12/4
			2. Assess extent of accomplishment	2. Mr. and Mrs. P and worker	12/4	12/4
			3. Analyze progress	3. Mr. and Mrs. P and worker	12/4	12/4
			4. Reformulate contract or begin termination	4. Mr. and Mrs. P and worker	12/4	12/4
Contract reformulation	Add problem 13: family's dependence on outside resources					

285

case of the P family would possibly need to be reopened at a later date, and he thought it would be helpful to have the basic problem of dependency highlighted in the summarized chart.

IV. Field Area: Community Services
A. Agency: Clayton Neighborhood House
B. Client System
Four Hispanic families who needed heat in their apartments on the second floor of 33 L Street. (For more background information, see Chapter 4, Engagement in Diverse Field Areas, IV. Community Services.)
C. Summary of Preceding Stages
The problems, goals, and tasks as identified and contracted in earlier stages are outlined in Table 6–12, Chapter 6, and Table 7–4, Chapter 7. The worker's interventions were direct and indirect, with residents and their landlord. By the third meeting of the worker with the residents, they were ready to move into the evaluation stage of the General Method.
D. Evaluation
Goal analysis: *After the residents monitored the heat in their apartments for a week, they met to share their findings with the worker. Each family reported that the heat was adequate, ranging from 65° to 70° each day. At night the heat went down to 63° to 65°, and this was acceptable to the families. The residents expressed relief and gratitude to the worker. They were hopeful that the heating would continue throughout the winter.*

As the worker and the residents began to recall their identified goal, she presented a scale (as found in Table 8–15) for goal analysis.

The families agreed that at this time their heating during the day is checked as averaging 68° (see the X in Table 8–15). The goal of adequate heating was being accomplished. The continuation of heating throughout the winter remained in question. They wanted to continue monitoring the heat throughout the winter and asked how they could show it on the scale each week. The worker introduced the ongoing-evaluation graph found in Figure 8–9. She explained that the horizontal line represented weeks and that the vertical line indicated temperature. She showed them when and how to plot their findings on the graph. They agreed to meet again the following week to plot their findings.

TABLE 8-15.   Goal 1: To Obtain Consistent, Adequate Heating

							X	
30	35	40	45	50	55	60	65	70
				Starting				

FIGURE 8-9. Temperature Monitoring

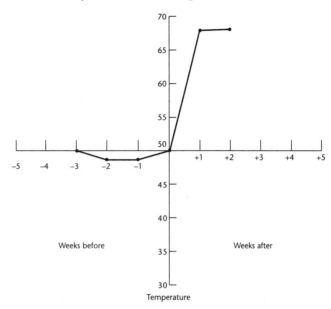

Contract review and reformulation: *In reviewing the contracted plan, the worker reminded the residents that she had never met with the janitor (no entry in "date accomplished" for Task 1, Goal 1, in Table 6–12, Chapter 6). They agreed that there was no need for anyone to say anything to him now that the upstairs was being heated adequately. The residents knew that they continued to have a problem communicating with the landlord, but they didn't want to do anything about it for the present.*

At this time, the worker and the residents agreed to extend their contact for another week. If there was no further problem with the heating and if the residents had nothing else they wanted to work on with the worker, she would terminate with them during the next meeting.

E. Charted Progress

The evaluation and contract reformulation by the worker and the residents was recorded on the contracted plan as indicated in Table 8–16.

V. Field Area: Education

A. Agency: Keeney Elementary School

B. Client System

Mr. and Mrs. G and their 8-year-old son, Jim, in the third grade, who was showing regressive behavior in school and at home in reaction to his

TABLE 8-16. Contracted Plan Continued

DATE IDENTIFIED	PROBLEM/ NEED	GOAL	TASK	CONTRACT	DATE ANTICIPATED	DATE ACCOMPLISHED
12/12 Evaluation	Evaluation of problems 1 (heating) and 2 (communication with landlord)	1. Adequate, consistent heating (no goal set for problem 2)	1. Review goal and problems	Worker and residents	12/2	12/12
			2. Evaluate extent of goal accomplishment			
			3. Reformulate contract			
Contract reformulation	Drop task 1, of goal 1, add tasks 6 and 7 for goal 1		6. Continue to monitor heat daily	6. Mr. T, Mrs. V, Mr. A, and CR	12/12–12/19	
			7. Meet to review findings (and possible termination)	7. Worker and residents	12/19	

parents' strained relationship. (For additional background information, see Chapter 4, Engagement in Diverse Field Areas, V. Education.)

C. Summary of Preceding Stages

The problems, goals, and the tasks that were identified in earlier stages are outlined in the contracted plan found in Table 6–13, Chapter 6. After the joint session with Mr. and Mrs. G, Jim, and the worker at school, Mr. and Mrs. G followed through with going for marital counseling at a local family counseling center, and Jim began to show improvement in his school work.

D. Evaluation

Progress in school performance was evaluated by Jim and the worker as they met twice a week in her office. When the worker called Mrs. G each week, they would evaluate what progress had been made. During the last home visit, the worker, Jim, and his parents reviewed the contracted plan and analyzed the extent of goal accomplishment for all four problem areas.

Goal analysis: *As the worker and Jim met together and focused on his school performance, they looked mainly at the extent to which Jim was (1) paying attention (showing interest in learning), (2) participating in class (raising hand to give answers or ask questions), and (3) bringing his grades up in math and spelling. These were specific areas in need of improvement identified by Jim's teacher. Each week, the worker met briefly with Jim's teacher to receive a report on his progress in the classroom. The teacher showed the worker Jim's weekly test scores in math and spelling. When Jim met with the worker, the teacher's report was reviewed, and scales to evaluate goal accomplishment were used (see Table 8–17).*

By the end of the second week after the meeting with Jim and his parents, Jim's academic performance was assessed as +3 on the interest scale ("much interest") and as +3 on the scale for class participation ("raising hand five or six times a day"); his grades in math jumped from an average of 40 to 90, and his spelling grades went from 50 to 100 (see Table 8–17). There was obvious progress in Jim's investment in school. His school attendance was no longer a problem. He arrived on time each day and was back to walking to school with the neighborhood children. Mrs. G also reported that he was sleeping better at night. When talking with Mrs. G on the phone, the worker learned that Mr. and Mrs. G were not finding the counseling sessions easy, but Mrs. G did think that they were helpful.

Contract review and reformulation: *In the last planned visit with Mr. and Mrs. G and Jim, the worker and the family recognized that all of their goals were being accomplished. More time was needed for Mr. and Mrs. G to work on their relationship, and they planned to continue in counseling for as long as was needed. Jim's problems had apparently subsided and he was back at his earlier functioning level (above average*

TABLE 8-17.   Goal 3: Improved School Performance

INTEREST LEVEL (PAYING ATTENTION)

			X	
0	1	2	3	4
Starting point; no interest	Little interest	Some interest	Much interest	Totally interested

CLASS PARTICIPATION

			X	
0	1	2	3	4
Starting point; not raising hand	Little raising hand (once or twice a day)	Some raising hand (three or four times a day)	Much raising hand (five or six times a day)	Frequent raising hand (seven or more times a day)

MATH GRADES

									X	
0	10	20	30	40	50	60	70	80	90	100
				Starting point						

SPELLING GRADES

										X
0	10	20	30	40	50	60	70	80	90	100
					Starting point					

academically). Mr. and Mrs. G agreed that there was no reason for them to meet with the school worker again unless additional problems developed with Jim.

Jim said he liked to meet with the worker in her office and he didn't want to stop seeing her each week. They agreed that their visits would be reduced to once a week (instead of twice) for two more weeks (once before Christmas and once after he came back from vacation). During these sessions, they said they would talk about ending their work together.

Ongoing evaluation: *Since the worker and Jim would meet to review his progress, ongoing-evaluation graphs were drawn and hung on the worker's wall (see Figures 8–10 and 8–11). The graphs indicated Jim's progress in math and spelling from the time he began school in the fall. Each point on the horizontal line indicated weeks before or after he started working with the social worker.*

The vertical lines indicated grade averages each week, with the center point at the grade Jim was averaging when he first met the worker.

FIGURE 8-10. Spelling

FIGURE 8-11. Math

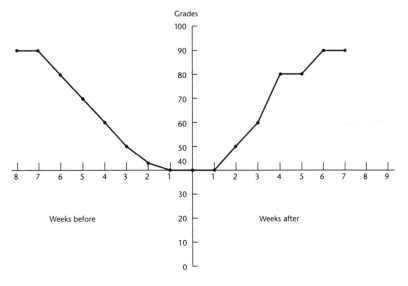

E. Charted Progress

The evaluation of grades and the additional tasks planned at this time were recorded by the worker on the contracted plan as shown in Table 8–18.

VI. Field Area: Corrections

A. Agency: Juvenile Court

B. Client System

A group of six male youths, all age 14, on probation and attending weekly group meetings led by co-workers at Juvenile Court. (For further background information, see Chapter 4, Engagement in Diverse Field Areas, VI. Corrections.)

C. Summary of Preceding Stages

The problems, goals, and tasks contracted in earlier stages are outlined in Table 6–15, Chapter 6, and Table 7–7, Chapter 7. Attendance and participation in group meetings and weekly behavior reports from home and school were charted on graphs from every member of the group at the end of each meeting. Issues of interest or "changes" for the members were selected and discussed each week. After three and a half months (fourteen weeks), the workers began to go through a formal goal analysis with the youths. They also talked about the group process and progress. The ongoing-evaluation graphs and weekly charts that were developed and used earlier (Figures 6–1, 6–2, 6–3, and 6–4 in Chapter 6, and Figures 7–5 and 7–6 in Chapter 7) were helpful in the evaluation process.

D. Evaluation

Goal analysis: *Since the four-month probationary period would be over in two weeks, all of the youths were eager to know if they would be getting off probation and if the group would be ending at that time. In evaluating goal 1 ("to get off probation in four months"), the members were reminded by the workers of the criteria that had been stated earlier for achieving this goal.*

1. *To maintain a score of 2 for group attendance—present each week unless excused*
2. *To maintain an average score of 3 ("much") or higher for group participation*
3. *To maintain an average score of 3 ("good") or higher for behavior at home*
4. *To maintain an average score of 3 ("good") or higher for behavior at school*
5. *To obey the rules of society (no further law-breaking)*

Each of the group members was asked to look over his graphs and to assess the extent to which he met the criteria for accomplishing goal 1. It was obvious that four of the youths (MK, ML, B, C) could be recommended for a reduction in probation from six to four months. One member (A) had already left the group and had been sent to a correctional center. The

TABLE 8-18. Contracted Plan Continued

DATE IDENTIFIED	PROBLEM/NEED	GOAL	TASK	CONTRACT	DATE ANTICIPATED	DATE ACCOMPLISHED
12/4, 12/6, 12/13 Evaluation	Evaluation of problems 1, 2, 3, 4	Goals 1, 2, 3, 4	1. Review and evaluate goal 3 (school performance)	1. Jim and worker	11/27, 11/29 12/4, 12/6	11/27, 11/29 12/4, 12/6
			2. Review and evaluate goals 1, 3, 4 (Jim's school functioning and sleeping)	2. Mr. and Mrs. G, Jim, and worker	12/17	12/17
			3. Review goal 2 (Mr. and Mrs. G's relationship)	3. Worker, Mr. and Mrs. G	12/17	12/17
			4. Reformulate contract or terminate	4. Worker, Mr. and Mrs. G, and Jim	12/17	12/17
Contract reformulation		Change task and date anticipated for task 4, problem 3 (see contracted plan, Table 6-13, Chapter 6)	4. Meet once a week	4. Worker and Jim	12/20 and 1/8	

other two (J and T) had failed to attend and to participate in meetings reg-
ularly. J's home reports averaged "poor" to "fair," and T had "poor" school
reports because he continued to get into fights at school. J and T realized
that they had not accomplished goal 1 and, therefore, would need to con-
tinue to meet with the workers each Monday. They were told that if they
brought their scores up in all areas during the next six weeks, they could
have their probation reduced by a month. They also knew that if they con-
tinued to do poorly, their probation period would be extended.

In evaluating goal 2 ("to control tempers"), each of the youths
reviewed his scores on the weekly chart (Tables 7–5 and 7–6, Chapter 7).
All agreed that they had grown in recognizing when they were begin-
ning to feel angry and it was time to "cool it." They verbalized ways
they had learned to handle their feelings instead of "blowing up." In
looking at the progression of their weekly scores, improvement in temper
control was apparent for all of the youths except T.

In analyzing the third goal (to learn more about "the changes" of
teenagers), the youths reviewed the topics that had been covered during
group meetings. They indicated which issues or speakers they thought
were the most interesting. They described the film on human sexuality
as "kind of stupid," but the talk by the ex-prisoner and the trip to the
vocational training school were "great." They all agreed that they had
grown in understanding some of the changes they were going through.

After the evaluation, it was clear that four of the group members
would probably be leaving the group in two or three weeks. Although the
co-workers would continue to meet with J and T, the plan was made to
begin to discuss in the following meetings "what it is like when you're
off probation and there's no more group."

E. Charted Progress and Contract Reformulation

The worker recorded the group evaluation and contract reformulation as
outlined in Table 8–19. The outline indicates that the anticipated dates for
group meetings would be extended to at least six additional weeks for J
and T. Also indicated in the record is the plan made by the group to begin
to discuss group termination and being off probation at the next meeting.

VII. Field Area: Homeless Shelter

A. Agency: West End Community Shelter

B. Client System

Mr. G, a 37-year-old Hispanic male, is homeless and HIV positive. (For
additional background information, see Chapter 4, Engagement in
Diverse Field Areas, VII, Homeless Shelter.)

C. Summary of Preceding Stages

Mr. G came to the shelter on May 7 feeling afraid and abandoned. Dur-
ing engagement, he informed the worker that he had completed a drug
detoxification program over six years ago and had tried to get his life in
order ever since. Mr. G wanted to go back to work and to get more

TABLE 8-19. Contracted Plan Continued

DATE IDENTIFIED	PROBLEM/ NEED	GOAL	TASK	CONTRACT	DATE ANTICIPATED	DATE ACCOMPLISHED
1/14 Evaluation	Evaluation of problems 1, 2, 3	Goals 1, 2, 3	1. Review goals 2. Evaluate goal accomplishment 3. Reformulate contract or introduce termination	Members and co-workers	1/14	1/14
Contract reformulation	1. Add goal 1a, task 1, contract date anticipated to reflect plan to extend group meetings for J and T for at least 6 more weeks	1a. To get off probation by March 1	1. To attend weekly group meetings	J and T and co-workers	Up to 2/25	
	2. Add beginning termination plan, tasks 1 and 2		1. Introduce termination 2. Discuss being "off probation"	1. Co-workers 2. Co-workers and group members	1/14 1/22	

information about his illness. During assessment and intervention, the worker and he developed and carried out a plan which included Mr. G's going to the free health clinic, getting involved with the Harmony, Inc. program, seeking employment, and returning to church.

D. Evaluation

Goal analysis: Two days after Mr. G applied for residence at Hope Home, the Shelter received a call from the social worker at the Home. The worker said that they were anticipating an opening for Mr. G around the first of the month. They were making arrangements to move a resident to Hospice in Florida where he could be near relatives. Mr. G could come over for a preplacement visit. The worker and Mr. G decided it was time to evaluate what progress had been made in achieving goals and to plan for the future. In using the goal-accomplishment scales, it was apparent that the goals of obtaining emergency shelter, reunion with the church, gaining information regarding HIV/AIDs, obtaining medical care, and getting social support had been accomplished. The goal of locating hous-ing after staying sixty days at the shelter was progressing (+3), but there was some regression in the goal of getting income (1.5) (See Tables 8–20 and 8–21). The reason for the regression was due to Mr. G's having to drop to part-time employment and his not being able to obtain Social Security and Social Services until his condition became worse (See Table 8–20). The worker recalled that during data collection she learned that even when Mr. G's testing indicates that he has AIDS (250 white T-cell count), and he is accepted for Social Security, there will be a 120-day wait before the first check is received. Mr. G could apply for general assistance during the interim period. During evaluation, Mr. G returned to the health clinic and learned that his white T-cell count was at 250. The Doc-tor discussed with Mr. G the medications that would be prescribed.

Ongoing evaluation: While working with Mr. G, the worker used the ongoing evaluation graphs for goals 4 and 5 (See Figures 8–12 and 8–13). These goals were selected because they appeared to be more complex and in need of more time than the other goals identified on the contracted plan.

Contract review and reformulation: The only recognized contract reformulations that were needed at the time of the evaluation were additions to the tasks for goals 4 and 5. Mr. G needed to plan his move to Hope Home, to apply for Social Security and SSI Disability, and to apply for general public assistance. The contracted plan was aug-mented to reflect these anticipated developments for Mr. G (See Table 8–22).

E. Charted Progress

Progress in goal accomplishment was indicated on the contracted plan and the scales and graphs were placed in the record. The social worker entered information obtained from the Hope Home worker and the doc-tor at the clinic in summary recordings.

TABLE 8-20.   Goal 4: Get Steady Income

| | | | | | X | | | |
-4	-3	-2	-1	0	+1	+2	+3	+4
Goal aban- doned								Goal accom- plished

TABLE 8-21.   Goal 5: Locate Residence

| | | | | | | | X | |
-4	-3	-2	-1	0	+1	+2	+3	+4
Goal aban- doned								Goal accom- plished

FIGURE 8-12.   Steady Income

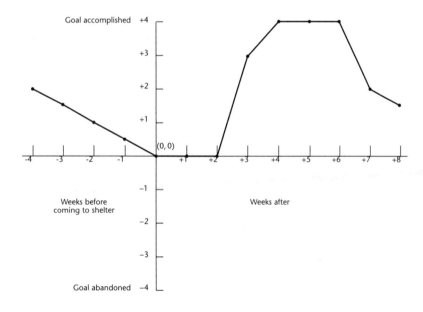

Descriptive criteria (Y Line)
+4 = Goal: Steady income (employment or SS/SSI)
+3 = Almost steady income or more than part-time employment
+2 = Some income or part-time employment
+1 = Little income or brief (one-time) jobs
 0 = Starting Point: No income
−1 = Beginning to go into debt
−2 = Increasing debt
−3 = Major debts
−4 = Goal Abandoned: no work and denied asistance or SS/SSI

TABLE 8-22. Contracted Plan Continued

DATE IDENTIFIED	PROBLEM/ NEED	GOAL	TASK	CONTRACT	DATE ANTICIPATED	DATE ACCOMPLISHED
6/26	Evaluation of problems 1–7	Goals 1–7	1. Recall each goal 2. Assess extent of accomplishment 3. Reformulate contract	1. Mr. G and worker	6/26	6/26
Contract reformu-lation	1. Change task 4, date anticipated, and add tasks 5–8 for problem 4	Goal 4	4. Request Doctor's report 5. Get report 6. Apply for SS and General Assistance 7. Get General Assistance 8. Get SS	4. Mr. G 5. Mr. G 6. Mr. G 7. Mr. G 8. Mr. G	6/26 6/27 6/27 7/5 10/25	
	2. Add tasks 3 and 4 to problem 5	Goal 5	3. Go for preplacement visit 4. Decide about placement	3. Mr. G 4. Mr. G and Home social worker	7/1 7/2	

FIGURE 8-13. Permanent Residence After Shelter

Descriptive Criteria (Y line)
+4 = Goal: Permanent residence
+3 = Going for placement visit for permanent residence
+2 = Applying for place or temporary residence
+1 = Identifying possible places
 0 = Starting Point: Only home is shelter (60 days max.)
−1 = 40 days left/no place located
−2 = 20 days left/no place located
−3 = No days left/no place to go
−4 = Goal Abandoned: homeless

Conclusion

In this chapter, the meaning and process of evaluation in general practice were presented. Evaluation was recognized as a particular stage in and as an ongoing dimension of the General Method. The need and values of evaluation in social work practice were emphasized.

Tools and processes were introduced that may be used during evaluation with any type of system. Various examples were given to demonstrate their applicability. The art and the science of practice are very apparent as a worker objectively and sensitively tries to assess progress and direction in each individualized situation.

As pointed out earlier, evaluation may lead to a reformulation of the contracted plan with additional interventions, or it may serve as a bridge to cross into the final stage of the General Method. Evaluation is a necessary prelude to termination.

NOTES

1. Edward J. Mullen and James R. Dumpson, "Concluding Note," in Edward J. Mullen, James R. Dumpson, and Associates, eds., *Evaluation of Social Intervention* (San Francisco: Jossey-Bass, 1972), p. 244.

2. Martin Bloom and Joel Fischer, *Evaluating Practice: Guidelines for the Accountable Professional* (Englewood Cliffs, N.J.: Prentice Hall, 1982).

3. Man Keung Ho, "Evaluation: A Means of Treatment," *Social Work* 21, no. 1 (January 1976): 24–27.

4. Thomas J. Kiresuk and Robert E. Sherman, "Goal Attainment Scaling: A General Method for Evaluating Comprehensive Community Mental Health Programs," *Community Mental Health Journal* 4, no. 6 (December 1968): 443–53.

5. For examples, see Bloom and Fischer. *Evaluating Practice*; Richard H. Ellis and Nancy C. Z. Wilson, "Evaluating Treatment Effectiveness Using a Goal-Oriented Progress Note," *Evaluation,* Special Monograph No. 1 (1973), pp. 6–11; Tony Tripodi and Irwin Epstein, *Research Techniques for Clinical Social Workers* (New York: Columbia University Press, 1980), pp. 208–29.

6. Ruth Grossman Dean and Helen Reinherz, "Psychodynamics Practice and Single System Design: The Odd Couple," *Journal of Social Work Education* 22, no. 2 (Spring/Summer 1986): 73.

7. Colleen Johnson and Frank Johnson, "Interaction Rules and Ethnicity," *Social Forces* 54 (December 1975): 452–66.

8. Susan Sturdevant, *Therapy with Women* (New York: Springer, 1980), p. 27.

Termination

For everything there is a season, and a time for every purpose under heaven.
—Ecclesiastes 3:1

Human beings need to form attachments. Through an exchange of feelings, thoughts, and actions, trusting relationships develop that may be identified as attachments. There is a natural season for the separation of human systems and for the termination of attachments. Although it is natural for systems to become separated, the process of coming apart may be very painful, even traumatic. As a person anticipates the grief for the loss of a meaningful other, separation anxiety may develop. If the anxiety and feelings around separation are not expressed, there may be a change in behavior and a withdrawal from possible future attachments.

Termination in social work practice is often a time of heightened anxiety for both a worker and a client system, particularly when they have developed a trusting relationship. It is the time to end their ongoing contacts and to plan for the future. Even when working with target or action systems, once goals have been accomplished, a worker needs to take time to end ongoing contacts.

When a social worker begins to disengage with a system, time, skill, and understanding are needed for an effective closure of services. The art of termination involves skillful interactions and procedures with honest sharing in an atmosphere of realistic hope. Although each system is unique with its own individual pace and method of responding to loss, some general patterns of grief reactions are often present during termination and need to be identified.

In this chapter, the knowledge, values, and skills utilized during termination will be presented. The need for a social worker to develop the art of termination cannot be overemphasized. A poorly timed or poorly executed termination may result in marked regression or failure in goal accomplishment. A meaningful, growth-promoting termination experience can stabilize progress and serve as a support and model for a system as it faces new attachments, separations, and losses in the future.

The Meaning of Termination

In this chapter, *termination* means the ending of contact between a worker and a system. As the last stage of the General Method, termination comprises the time taken and the process used when a worker and a system begin to plan the ending of their contacts with each other. Even when there has been only brief contact or little emotional sharing, a time is needed for worker and system to recall goals and evaluate progress, as well as to clarify the reasons and plan for termination, prior to the ending of contact.

Central to an understanding of termination is an awareness of the possible feelings and reactions that may take place as two systems separate. For some systems, the recognition and expression of these feelings may come quite easily at this time. For others, however, strong defenses against these feelings may come into operation. Disguised reactions to particular feelings can make termination a time of confusion and frustration for both client systems and workers.

Children, for example, have been found to experience such feelings as fear, anxiety, sadness, loss, rejection, guilt, helplessness, and cultural shock when they are separated from significant others or familiar surroundings. Instead of being able to express these feelings, some react with such behaviors as hostility, acting out, lack of trust, bed-wetting, poor schoolwork, destructiveness, lying, and running away. Rather than acting out, some children become extremely withdrawn and refuse to form new attachments. In studying this reaction, Ner Littner writes:

> To the degree that he cannot master these feelings and must repress them, the child will need to fend off close relationships, using the various techniques previously mentioned, and suffer the painful consequences of this self-imposed emotional isolation. He will keep bottled up within him an enormous desire for closeness, which he cannot allow himself to really satisfy. It is noteworthy too, that his impaired ability to relate to people may also influence his capacity to be close to his own children, and therefore sometimes directly affects their ability to be close to others.[1]

The clients of social workers have often experienced painful separations and terminations in their lives. They are often guarded and fearful of forming a trusting relationship with a worker. If an attachment is formed, when it comes time to terminate with these clients, strong feelings from past separations may emerge along with feelings over the anticipated loss of the worker. A variety of defenses and reactions may be displayed to ward off past and present hurts and anxieties.

The feelings that are avoided often include a sense of abandonment, fear of being unable to cope alone, helplessness, guilt, failure, and holding oneself responsible for the felt rejection. These feelings may be covered up through one, several, or a sequence of reactive behaviors.

Reactions to Termination

The defenses and reactions of a system during termination may fall within a five-stage termination sequence that is similar to the stages of the grieving process.[2] Although not necessarily in every case, nor in the exact order described below, reactions to termination are often identified as falling within one or all of the following stages:

1. *Denial.* The client may ignore what the worker is saying or avoid any discussion of termination. This may extend to the failing to keep appointments, coming late or leaving early. In a group, individual members or the group as a whole may isolate themselves, refuse to participate in the conversation, or attempt to change the topic of discussion.
2. *Anger.* There may be outbursts of verbal or physical assaults. These may be directed toward the worker, toward other members of the system, or toward a person who is expected to take over the worker's role after termination. Anger may also be turned inward as the client displays a lack of concern or care for self, including possible personal injury. There may be regression to earlier problematic behavior in order to be punished or to punish the worker.
3. *Bargaining.* The client tries to negotiate an extension of time or a modified cutback in contacts. Promises of "being good if" are presented. Gifts or rewards may be offered.
4. *Depression.* The client manifests listlessness, little energy, withdrawal, sadness, helplessness, despair, no motivation to go on. Pain is real and evident. There is regression in accomplishments. Time is needed to mourn. Beginning resignation is apparent.
5. *Acceptance.* With the acceptance of the termination, there is an increase in energy. The client is able to talk about the good and the bad times and to think about the future. There is a "quiet expectation"[3] as the client begins to show interest in forming new attachments. The client returns to the level of functioning prior to the depression and moves away from self-pity or self-centeredness.

During termination, there may not be a clear transition from one stage of the sequence to the next. Frequently, there are signs of regression in the process, and a discussion of fears and feelings will have to be repeated. A worker who is aware of the natural process and reactions found during termination is less likely to take what is happening personally or literally and then react inappropriately.

The Decision to Terminate

After a worker and a system of contact have completed an evaluation of goal accomplishment, they may conclude that the purpose for their coming together has been attained. The scales and graphs suggested in Chapter 8 may have helped to demonstrate the movement and progress that have been made. In addition to these indicators, a worker can assess the appropriateness of moving into termination with a system by (1) reviewing with his or her supervisor the work that has taken place with the system, (2) observing and talking with the system itself, and (3) talking with other knowledgeable sources about the system's readiness to terminate with the worker (with informal consent of system).

If there is some hesitancy to move into termination on the part of the system or the worker, the cause for holding back needs to be identified. A supervisor can help a worker to let go of a system when there may be strong attachment because there has been progress and the worker gets much satisfaction in working with the system, or because progress has been minimal and the worker has feelings of failure.

If the system of contact is holding back from facing termination, this could be caused by the feelings identified earlier or by other problematic areas that the system would like to face with the worker, even though there has been avoidance and fear up to this time. The supervisor might help detect this and might suggest that the worker explore this possibility with the system before moving on to termination.

It may be that a worker wants to terminate with a system even when there is insufficient evidence that goals have been accomplished. Through supervision, the worker may be helped to recognize feelings of anger or helplessness in working with the system, which are causing the desire to terminate prematurely. If a system wants an early termination with a worker, it may be (1) because the worker is beginning to touch on conflict areas that the system does not want to face; or, as brought out earlier, (2) because the system is anticipating the worker's leaving and wants to be in control by initiating the termination; or (3) because the system is taking flight from having to face any of the other feelings already identified (rejection, anger, grief, etc.). Here, too, the worker may need help through supervision to discern the dynamics of the situation.

In observing and talking with a system or other resources about possible termination, the worker assesses the extent of goal accomplishment and also the current functioning level of the system. The questions to be asked are:

1. Have the goals been accomplished according to the contracted plan?
2. Can the system go on functioning at least at the level attained at this time without continued contact with the worker?
3. Although the identified problems may have been resolved and the goals accomplished, if a similar need or problem develops, will the system be able to handle it or, at least, know how to get help?
4. If additional supports will be needed after the worker terminates, are they available?

A worker continues to work with a system beyond the point of achieving contracted goals only for the length of time needed to stabilize goal accomplishment and to go through the process of termination. If the questions above are answered affirmatively, then the system is ready for termination to begin.

Sometimes a system gives the message to a worker indirectly that it is ready to terminate. Perhaps even before a worker begins to discuss the issue, a system may give indicators that it is able to handle problems on its own. Since systems often internalize the coping patterns a worker has demonstrated and, with experience, develop problem-solving skills that are transferable, there may be an apparent decrease in dependency and a desire to handle things independently. When the system is a group or community, attendance may become irregular as members no longer feel the need to meet with the worker or with one another. New sources of support and involvement may have been found by members of the system. Indirectly, the system may be showing a readiness for termination. These behaviors are different when a system reacts to termination by breaking off in anger or as a means to regain control. There is little effect connected with behaviors that indicate a readiness to terminate. Even when a system demonstrates this readiness, some of the feelings and reactions to loss described earlier may become apparent as the worker begins to talk about termination. The thought of not having the worker available for ongoing support may stir up earlier feelings of loss of a significant person. There may be some regression in functioning in order to keep the worker involved and to avoid dealing with fears or feelings of loss. The worker and system may both recognize that it is time to terminate, but opportunity will be needed to identify and express feelings and to plan for termination.

Sometimes a worker has to terminate with a system before goals have been accomplished. This could happen because of the worker's lack of skills to help the particular system or because of an inappropriate emotional involvement. When the decision to terminate is not based on evaluative evidence of the system's readiness, the worker and his or her agency have the responsibility to see that the system continues to receive help from an appropriate resource. Also, time should be given to explain to the system why there has to be a termination and to give the system the opportunity to react to the unexpected closure.

A Life-Cycle Approach to Termination

Throughout the process of terminating with a system, the social worker may use a life-cycle approach. Basically, the worker tries to help the system to step back and review the life cycle of their work together. Initially, as the concept of termination is first introduced and early reactions of the system to the idea may include denial, anger, or bargaining, the worker helps the system to express the feelings underneath these reactions through a review of the *past*. They recall why they first came together and consider how they have moved to the present point in time. Recalling what they have been through together can help to bring out feelings of fear, anger, closeness, or loss. It can help to identify the nature and strength of the current relationship.

As the worker and system move from focusing on the past to the *present*, it can become clearer that goals have been accomplished and that the earlier needs or problems that necessitated help from the worker no longer exist. The instruments used earlier to evaluate progress during the stage of evaluation may be recalled. As the system begins to face the reality that termination is imminent, an attempt may be made to bargain for more time or to locate new problems. The worker may sensitively point out that the system has demonstrated an ability to handle such problems at this time and then begin to talk about the feelings that are making it difficult for the system to terminate. Signs and feelings of depression may begin to appear as the system becomes resigned to the termination. Strong feelings of fear, loss, or grief may emerge. Independently, the system may begin to ask about the *future* and what will happen when he, she, or they will have to manage without the worker. At this point, a plan for termination may begin to be formulated. Much time may be needed before the system has the energy ready to invest in planning for the future. Feelings may need to be expressed repeatedly before a plan is completed. If the system is not ready to move into considering the future, the worker will need to stay with the present, even though this may call for great patience on the part of the worker. In time, a system will move from mourning over the anticipated loss to an acceptance of termination.

When the system begins to accept the termination, more investment in developing and implementing a termination plan can be expected. As the worker discusses the future with the system, frequent reference is made to the needs that were identified in the *past* and to the strengths that are apparent in the *present*, in order to give hope for the *future*.

The life-cycle approach is a dynamic process used throughout the termination stage. Although the three focus points of *past*, *present*, and *future* are not addressed necessarily in an exact sequence, the framework offers some direction and guidance for the worker to help a system move through the process of termination.

Planning the Termination

As soon as possible, an ending date for the final planned contact between worker and system should be set. Ideally, both the worker and the system should mutually agree upon this date and on the extent and times of contacts they will have prior to the termination date. Meetings between worker and client may be gradually tapered off until the closing date, or they may continue on a regular basis until final termination. The termination plan developed by worker and system should be individualized according to the needs and circumstances of the system. The point to be emphasized is that for an effective termination, a plan has to be articulated, understood, and implemented. If it is apparent that a system is ready to terminate with a worker but will need additional supports or services, the process of referral or transfer should be included as an essential dimension of the termination plan.

As brought out in Chapter 7 in the discussion on referral, when resources are being mobilized for a client, every effort should be made to have the client system initiate and follow through on contacting the resource on its own. During termination, unless direct involvement by a worker is absolutely necessary, the worker should try to negotiate a plan in which the system itself establishes linkages with the resources needed. This is particularly the case when resources are informal, such as is the case with family members, church, or neighborhood. Having the system make its own contacts fosters self-confidence and provides the worker with an opportunity to see if the system can develop new relationships independently.

If a worker is terminating with a system that is unable to sustain itself without continued professional help, the worker first tries to transfer the system to another worker in the same helping agency. If the agency already in contact with the system has no workers with the time or skills needed, then the worker locates an appropriate outside resource and makes a referral (see the process for referral in Chapter 7). If a referral (outside resource) or a transfer (inside resource) is needed, a client may have feelings about being referred or transferred that need to be expressed, and there are ways to proceed that can help to insure a smooth transition as a system moves from an old worker to a new service provider.

When a system experiences the loss of a worker, particularly if a trusting relationship has developed, it can be very difficult for the system to begin to bond with a new provider of services. The former worker can help to facilitate the transition process. Generally, only after having expressed some of the reactions to termination, such as denial, anger, bargaining, and depression, can the worker and system begin to rationally consider establishing contact with a new resource. The system in need of continued service may have strong feelings of loyalty to the former worker. There may be a fear of appearing ungrateful or disloyal if the system begins to relate positively to a new resource. The former worker needs to sanction clearly the system's involvement with a new worker. This can be demonstrated in meetings that should be planned for all three parties (former worker, system in need, new worker) prior to the final termination date. At these meetings, the former worker participates in a hopeful and supportive manner. He or she conveys a sense of trust in the abilities of the new worker and of the system in need of continued service to work constructively with each other.

It is necessary for all three parties to know exactly when the former worker is going to terminate with the system and if there is any plan for a follow-up. If there is some expectation of contact after the final termination date, it needs to be clear whom the former worker will contact, when the contact can be expected, and why it is necessary. If the door is left open for the system to reestablish contact with the former worker, there may be a holding back from investment with the new worker. The system itself may contact the former worker unexpectedly by a phone call or a letter. The former worker can be most helpful by acknowledging the contact when received but then directing the system back to the new worker for continued help.

Even when a new resource has entered the termination process, there should be time on the final date for only the former worker and the system to meet together. During their last contact, there is often a planned expression of the significance of the meeting. If the system is a group or community, there is generally a party or some type of ceremony. Pictures may be taken or exchanged. This time provides the opportunity for the final expression of feelings and hopes.

Stating the termination plan in writing helps to avoid manipulation or misunderstanding. A separate format or instrument does not have to be drawn up. The contracted plan that was introduced and developed during assessment, intervention, and evaluation may continue to be used. As the worker and system arrive at a final date and make plans for the intervening period, entries are made in the contracted plan to indicate the what (tasks), who (contract), and when (dates anticipated) of the plan. If it is agreed that new resources will be needed to support the system after the worker leaves, the plan for initiating contact with these resources is included in the written statement. As the termination plan is carried out, dates of accomplishment for each of the tasks are entered on the contracted plan. An example is given in Table 9–1 of a termination plan for a group of young adolescent girls called "the Angels." This group was one of many offered at a neighborhood center each year. All groups terminated at the end of June and began again in September. The worker knew who was expected to take "the Angels" the following year. The new worker was, therefore, invited to meet with the group as part of the termination plan.

Reactions of Service Providers

As human beings, providers of service become attached to others. Social workers, teachers, child-care workers, nurses, and other professionals suffer from feelings of loss when they are separated from systems that have been meaningfully involved in their lives. If there has not been the opportunity to anticipate the loss, move through the reactions, or express the related feelings prior to final termination, a service provider may demonstrate depression, withdrawal, or burnout after one or several terminations of this nature.

In addition to the need for systems receiving services to have time to express feelings and plans prior to termination, social workers and those in collaborative service provision need time to anticipate and express their possible emptiness when a system no longer needs their assistance. A double energy is often used by a service provider in termination: (1) that of helping a system to move away, and (2) that of moving away him- or herself. A provider may deny, become angry, or become depressed during or after the energy drain. Through supportive supervision, peer meetings, and other available environmental supports, a provider may find a place, persons, and convenient time to work on what is happening inside of him or her.

When a provider is employed in an emotionally charged service, such as child protection or work with the terminally ill, the need for supportive outlets is especially apparent. For example, in a residential setting for disturbed children, the child-care director became the main significant other for a 5-year-old boy. The child progressed remarkably and was moved into a foster home. Following his placement, the director became obviously antagonistic toward the social worker

TABLE 9-1. The Contracted Plan Continued

DATE IDENTIFIED	PROBLEM/ NEED	GOAL	TASK	CONTRACT	DATE ANTICIPATED	DATE ACCOMPLISHED
5/3	21. Funding for trip to beach	21. Raise $50 for trip	1. Explore ways to raise funds; begin to plan	1. Group and worker	5/3	8/3
			2. Finalize plans for bake sale	2. Group and worker	5/10	5/10
			3. Have bake sale	3. Group and center	5/15	5/15
			4. Critique bake sale; set date and plan for beach trip; begin to discuss year-end evaluation	4. Group and worker	5/17	5/17
5/24 Evaluation	Year-end evaluation of problems/needs 1–21, as cited above	1–21 as cited above	1. Recall goals 2. Evaluate extent of goal accomplishment	1. Group and worker	4/24 and 6/1	5/24 and 6/1
6/1	Termination process	Satisfactory termination (progress stabilized)	1. Introduce termination	1. Group and worker	6/1	6/1
			2. Discuss feelings and reactions to ending the group; clarify final termination date	2. Group and worker	6/7	6/7
			3. Identify present strengths, discuss the future; plan termination	3. Group and worker	6/14	6/14

TABLE 9-1. *Continued*

DATE IDENTIFIED	PROBLEM/ NEED	GOAL	TASK	CONTRACT	DATE ANTICIPATED	DATE ACCOMPLISHED
			4. Invite new worker (who will have the group after summer vacation) to the next meeting	4. Mary C (for the group)	6/15	6/15
			5. Meet with new worker	5. Former worker, group, and new worker	6/21	6/21
			6. Beach trip	6. Former worker, group, and new worker	6/26	6/26
			7. Closing session and party	7. Former worker and group	6/28	6/28

and increasingly irritable toward the other children. It wasn't until the worker and the director took time to look painfully at what was happening that the director began to touch her feelings of depression due to the loss of the young boy. If the worker or others at the facility had been more sensitive to the natural feelings of the director, more time could have been given to deal with termination prior to the child's discharge, a step that would have prevented some of the reactions that followed.

A social worker who serves as a case manager for a team that is about to terminate with a system can show sensitivity to the needs of the team members by building in a time to talk about the feelings they might have as they anticipate closing the case. Supervisors and administrators also have a major responsibility to help prevent burnout in their employees. If they understand the significance of termination in the provision of services, they can find various ways to assist their workers. For example, in a hospice facility where service providers were repeatedly experiencing the deaths of their patients, an administrator not only set aside times for peer support meetings, but also designated a room on the top floor as "the Tower," where staff could go whenever they felt the need "to yell, cry, or pray." Unless a service provider can reach a point of acceptance with a termination, he or she will not be able to have the anticipation, hope, and energy necessary to invest in new clients, patients, or work assignments.

Developing Sensitivity and Skills

The ideas about termination that are presented in this chapter are often rejected as an overexaggeration. New workers, in particular, find it difficult to believe that their leaving a system can have an impact on the system or on their own selves. A verbal presentation on the dynamics of termination may be only an intellectual consideration unless some aspect of experiential learning can be included. Three basic exercises may be used to help students or service providers to grow in sensitivity and skill for working with termination.

Exercise 9–1   Using Imagery

In this exercise, all the individuals participating in the experience are asked to close their eyes and to picture a significant person in their lives. They are then asked to imagine that this person is talking with them and saying that he or she is going away and does not plan to return. Participants are then asked to identify their immediate feelings. They are next asked to imagine that they express these feelings to the person, but that the person repeats his or her plan to leave. They then imagine the person getting up and walking out. They are asked to let themselves enter into what they would feel when the person has left, and to try to find words to express these feelings. Finally, the participants are asked, "What would you do next?" and then, "What do you need at this time?"

This exercise helps a person to sense some of the feelings that often emerge as one perceives the loss of a meaningful other. Talking about the experience may also lead to a discussion about what actions a person may take in trying to cope with such a loss and what resources might help the person through the experience.

Exercise 9–2   *Small Group Experience*

In this exercise, participants are divided into small groups to discuss a topic such as "timing needed for termination" or "writing up a termination plan." The facilitator moves around to different groups and eventually asks a member of one group to leave and join another identified group. After a few minutes, the facilitator moves to the next group and again directs a member to leave and join a different group, with no explanation for the move. This procedure is continued until every group has lost one of its original members.

In the discussion that follows, participants are asked to describe any thoughts or feelings they had when one of their members was asked to leave. They usually say that they wondered why the person was removed from the group and that they felt some frustration over the departure. They are then asked how they felt about another person joining the group. Here, too, feelings of anger and frustration were often experienced over having to adjust to the entry of a new person. The leaving or entering may have slowed down or stopped the group process. In addition, participants may share feelings of anger toward the facilitator for interrupting the group. Those that were directed to leave a group may disclose that they felt disoriented, isolated, rejected, or perhaps withdrawn as they entered a new group.

Exercise 9–3   *Role Play*

The third exercise is a role play between a worker and a client system. There is a partial script, which is given only to the actor who plays the role of the client system. The person in the role of the worker is directed to begin the play by saying, "I will be leaving the agency in May." To what the worker says, the person playing the client system is directed to feel free to respond as he or she feels like responding. Eventually, however, the "client system" is expected to make the statements (in whatever order seems appropriate) identified in the script.

TERMINATION SCRIPT

Worker: I will be leaving the agency in May.
Client
System: Will I be seeing someone else?

Worker:	(?)
Client	
System:	I had a fight with that neighbor again.
Worker:	(?)
Client	
System:	What did I bother coming here for anyway? You're not really helping me.
Worker:	(?)
Client	
System:	I'll come to see you where you are going—maybe just for a few months.
Worker:	(?)
Client	
System:	Nobody cares about what happens to me anyway.
Worker:	(?)
Client	
System:	May I take your picture before you leave?
Worker:	(?)
Client	
System:	Thanks for everything.
Worker:	(?)

This exercise may also be done as a "fishbowl" experience. Here, anyone watching the role play who believes he or she may have a more appropriate way to respond to the client may come in back of the person playing the role of the worker and tap him or her on the shoulder. The worker then exchanges places with this person, and the new response is given.

In the discussion that follows the role play, the facilitator asks the participants to consider what both actors were feeling as they made different statements. A basic question asked is, "Was the worker responding to the content literally, or was he or she tuning into the feelings of the client system?" The participants are asked to consider other responses the worker could have made to particular statements by the client system. The most important question is, "What does the client need to hear at this time?"

By using these three exercises, workers can become more aware of the following central ideas:

1. Terminations may cause a variety of feelings and reactions that lead to a need for help from others.
2. Departures may cause disorientations and frustration, leading to an arrest in progress, or to withdrawal or anger toward the person who initiated the separation.
3. There are ways to respond to people who are facing terminations that can help to let them know that you understand what they are going through.
4. Workers themselves may have feelings and reactions that they need help with during terminations.

There are other exercises and activities that can enhance a worker's knowledge and skills in the process of terminating with a particular system. For example, process-recording an individual interview on termination and then reviewing the recording by oneself or with one's supervisor or peers can help a worker to better understand the dynamics that are taking place and to locate where the system and the worker are in the termination process. During this last stage of the General Method, a worker's feelings may be so intense that it is difficult to maintain an objective perspective. Using such exercises as process recording, role play, and imagery can help strengthen the worker's comprehension and self-control.

Working with Different Systems

Feelings and concerns of systems during termination differ according to the unique circumstances and perspective of each system. Feelings of loss may extend beyond the loss of a worker to the loss of a support group and its members (group), the loss of an external control system (institution), or the loss of a secure nurturing environment (agency). In trying to identify the feelings a system is experiencing during the termination process, a worker needs to be aware of these variations and other types of feelings frequently felt by systems of particular size or purpose.

When a worker is terminating with a community, for example, members may be planning to continue to work together on issues by themselves, or they may be breaking up because they were a short-term organization with a task focus. Continuing without the worker may be somewhat fearful for them because they depended on the worker's leadership and support. Dissolving this organization may also cause some fears over losing a structure that gave them a sense of power and protection. These feelings will need to be clarified and expressed.

Diversity in reactions to termination also depends on the extent of investment made by each system in the relationship with the worker. This may present a challenge to a worker when the system is a family, group, or community and the extent of investment differs among the individual members of the same system. Although those with little investment may have minimal feeling about ending contacts, others in the system may have strong feelings, with much difficulty in accepting the termination. In this situation, it may be helpful for the worker to plan to meet with each member individually, as well as with the whole system, to work on termination. It is probable that the meetings with the less invested may be light and brief, whereas the meetings with those more invested may be intense and lengthy. Planning to meet with every member individually avoids singling out certain members and yet allows more time for those who need it. Even when an individual has developed no attachment, the worker and this person need to overview the past (purpose for beginning contact), the present (extent of goal accomplishment), and the future (plans for when all contacts are over).

In addition to a review of past, present, and future with members of a system individually and collectively, the worker may ask all of the members to share together how each one perceives the termination. Many times, members are surprised to hear, perhaps for the first time, that they have meant something to one another. Individuals who are hesitant to admit that they have some feelings about the termination may begin to feel freer to talk about them when they hear others openly express their feelings. Also, the sharing may bring about some final efforts to clarify and heal any misunderstandings the members may have had with each other or with the worker.

Using the Holistic Foundation in Termination

As stated earlier, there is an art to termination that calls on the values, knowledge, and skills of a worker. The social work generalist demonstrates this art as various elements from the holistic foundation for social work practice (Table 1–6, Chapter 1) are selected, integrated, and applied throughout the termination process.

As a worker and a system begin to bring their relationship to an end, all of the value principles of individualization, acceptance, self-determination, nonjudgmental attitude, controlled emotional involvement, purposeful expression of feelings, and confidentiality are utilized. The timing, planning, and processing of termination have to be *individualized* according to each system's unique circumstances. If a system is avoiding or denying the termination, the worker patiently *accepts* the defense. Keeping in mind the principle of *controlled emotional involvement,* the worker honestly shares his or her feelings about terminating and artfully encourages the *purposeful expression of the system's related feelings.* If a system does not choose to identify new problem areas or to be referred for additional support, the worker maintains a *nonjudgmental attitude* and respects the system's right to *self-determination.* When a referral or transfer is made or data are collected from an outside resource, all information about the system is treated as *confidential* and released only with the informed consent of the system.

Theories on human development, group dynamics, organizations, and ecological systems are among the theories that give direction and understanding to a worker in the termination stage. In human development theory, the worker learns about the natural needs all human systems have for attachments throughout the life cycle. The trauma of separation and the impact of an abrupt termination on a human system is also presented. Through theories of group dynamics and organizations, the worker learns about the conflicts, tasks, and processes a group, community, or organization undergoes when a person who was seen as the leader (or someone with power and control) leaves the system.

Using ecological-systems theory, the worker perceives the interdependence that develops between a client system and its service-providing environment. The theory helps workers to understand that it may not be feasible to expect an organism to maintain its functioning level when a major nurturer in its environment is removed. The need for a careful assessment of a system's available internal and external resources after termination with a worker is, therefore, highlighted.

In addition to values and theories from the holistic foundation, a worker uses a range of general skills, particularly problem-solving skills, during the termination process. For example, as a worker begins to introduce the idea of termination to a system, skill is needed for a clear identification of what it means to terminate (need-identification skills). In reviewing the past, data collection and evaluation skills are used. As focus is given to the present, a worker uses assessment skills in appraising the strengths and readiness of a system for termination and in locating appropriate supportive resources in the environment. Planning skills, including the sequencing of tasks and contracting, are used as a worker and system begin to plan for the future. Recording skills are needed for writing the termination plan. A variety of interventive skills, including referral and transfer, may be needed in the implementation of the plan. Listening, responding, and clarifying are among the communication skills that are demonstrated repeatedly throughout the entire termination process.

Essentially, the three primary skills needed during termination may be described as (1) sensing skills (recognizing feelings and reactions), (2) timing skills (knowing when to identify, wait, or stop), and (3) processing skills (moving from past to present to future). The art of termination rests in a worker's demonstrated sensitivity to the time and movement needed for a system to be ready to accept termination. All of the actions of a social worker, throughout the process, reflect an artful integration and application of values, knowledge, and skills.

Human Diversity in Termination

Culture

During the termination period, as stated, basic questions asked include the following: (1) Can the system go on functioning at the level attained at this time without continued contact with the worker? (2) Although the identified problems may have been resolved and the goals accomplished, if a similar need develops will the system be able to handle it or, at least, know how to get help? (3) If additional supports will be needed after the worker terminates, are they available? In working with minority ethnic groups, a central need has been described as empowerment. Rather than doing for a system, the worker tries to prevent dependency and to encourage self-help and autonomy. The reality is, however, that the needs of oppressed groups are often multiple and pervasive. A worker and a system may frequently feel overwhelmed or discouraged because little progress is apparent. The worker or the system, or both, may have a strong inclination to terminate, even when goals have not been accomplished and when regression will obviously take place after the worker leaves. Particular care has to be taken by the worker when planning a termination to insure the stabilization of change efforts and the availability of ongoing supports as needed.

Termination, as brought out in this chapter, is a stage when skills in timing and sensing of feelings are especially needed. Again, knowledge of a culture's orientation toward the expression of feelings and the meaning of time is imperative. If a worker has played a meaningful role in the life of a client, he or she will naturally have some feelings and a sense of loss when the worker terminates. The reactions and defenses used by the system will be culturally derived. A skilled worker will understand and enable the system to find the time and the opportunity to express feelings and to prepare for the termination. Expressions of denial, bargaining, anger, or depression may vary according to cultural orientation toward separation and death. The process of moving from past to present to future may also be influenced by the time orientation of one's cultural background. As indicated earlier, members of Asian-Pacific, American Indian, and Afro-American cultures lean toward emphasizing the past, whereas Mexican-Americans are more concerned with the present and Anglo-Saxon Americans are more future-oriented. Recognizing such differences enables a worker to have more realistic expectations of the pace needed by a system to move to the point of acceptance in the process of termination.

Sexual Variation

After an evaluation, the worker and a gay or lesbian client system may decide to terminate, even though long-range goals for social change have not been achieved. With personal, interpersonal, or short-range goals attained, they may decide to continue to address the need to change target systems on their own or in other ways. The worker may continue to advocate equal opportunities and services for gay and lesbian persons through introducing or supporting related legislation, policies, programs, or practices. Gay or lesbian clients may choose to continue their efforts to achieve social change goals through active involvement in ongoing political action groups or movements. When the decision to terminate is reached by both worker and system, it is important for the gay or lesbian client to feel that he or she is welcome to return to the worker or the agency for additional services after termination, if needed.

If a group for gay or lesbian persons is terminating at an agency, individual members generally need to have other formal or informal networks available. This is particularly true for those who have not "come out" and joined the extended gay/lesbian community. As presented earlier, maintaining a hidden identity can be extremely draining emotionally and psychologically. Planning for the future should include thoughtful consideration and efforts to build in appropriate resources for these individuals.

As with any working relationship, a deep attachment may develop between worker and client system in the course of their working together. For lesbian or gay clients, it may be the first time they have met someone who has been able to listen to their questions and concerns and been able to accept and respect them as unique individuals. For workers, it may be the first time they have had the opportunity to get to know and to work with a gay or lesbian individual or group. Terminating the relationship may evoke feelings for both worker and client system that are difficult to face and to express. Again, time is needed for them to overview the life cycle of their relationship and to honestly discuss their feelings, such as anger, fear, loss, and love. It will be easier for both the worker and the client system to accept termination if a sense of acceptance has existed throughout the time they have been together. If there has not been acceptance, either one may continue to feel a need to try to prove something to or to change something in the other.

Gender Sensitivity

As a worker and a system of contact move into the termination stage of the General Method, a key question to be asked is, "Will the progress that has been made be sustained and developed after the worker leaves?" The tendency to regress to gender roles that existed for years before the worker became involved is very strong after the worker terminates. Again, if change is to remain stabilized, it may be imperative that support networks be located and activated before final termination.

As stated earlier, during termination, individuals are encouraged to express their feelings and fears surrounding the anticipated loss of the social worker and perhaps other members of a group. Here too, men who hold back from expressing feelings may not be able to admit that they will miss the worker or the group. Even though, by this time in the process, male clients may have begun to find it somewhat easier to express feelings, there may be a tendency to regress, as generally found before termination. Women, if they have been in the traditional dependent role, may also find it particularly difficult to accept termination and become independent of the worker and the group. If a bonding of mutual respect and support has developed between the client system and the worker or other group members, this experience may serve as a model for the system in future relationships and interactions.

Thus, each stage of the General Method calls for a sensitive application of values, knowledge, and skills as a worker interacts with systems of diverse cultures, sexual orientation, or gender. As brought out in Chapter 3, a worker is sensitive also to diversity in age and stages, endowment and personality, value system, social class, and geographic location. A knowledge of human diversity and an awareness of one's own human responses to various individuals, cultures, life styles, roles, and environments are essential for an effective application of the General Method.

Termination in Diverse Field Areas

I. Field Area: Child Welfare
  A. Agency: State Department of Children's Services
  B. Client System
> K, 15 years old, female, placed in group home six months ago. (For more background information, see Chapter 4, Engagement in Diverse Field Areas, I. Child Welfare.)

  C. Summary of Preceding Stages
> The problems, goals, and tasks identified and implemented in earlier stages are found in Table 6–7 of Chapter 6 and Table 7–1 of Chapter 7. A

summary of the evaluation of goals and contract reformulation may be found in Table 8–10, Chapter 8. Basically, progress was identified during evaluation for all of the stated goals. The goal related to personal growth was the slowest in achievement, and more time was recognized as needed for progress in this area. The contract was reformulated to extend goal 2 to include optimal academic performance, and to change the frequency of worker contact to once a month rather than once every two weeks.

D. Termination

After K had been in her group home for six months, the worker began to terminate because she was leaving Children's Services. K's first reaction to the termination was total indifference. She said she didn't "need the state any more," and hoped she would not have to get another state worker. She was helped to express anger and fear of being abandoned. She admitted that she liked the worker and would miss her very much. She was assured that the worker would miss her also.

As the worker and K began to review the life cycle of their work together, the ongoing evaluation tools described in Chapter 8 (Figures 8–6 and 8–7) were used. Her academic performance and group home maintenance were assessed as +3. They recalled what the past was like for K and how far she had progressed, particularly in her present group home and in school. K knew that she continued to need help with her personal problems (goal 3).

In considering the future, K said she wished to remain in her present group home and school for at least another few years. Her long-range goals included returning to live with her real mother some day. K knew that this was not possible in the near future.

K's case was transferred back to a worker (recently returned from sick leave) who had originally worked with her. K remembered her original worker and said she was glad she didn't have to start all over with someone new. Two weeks before termination, K and the two state workers had a meeting, at which time goals and progress were reviewed. For their last meeting, K and her worker went for a walk. They took and exchanged pictures of each other. K asked if she could write the worker after she left Children's Services, but this continued contact was discouraged.

E. Charted Progress

The termination plan that was developed and implemented by the worker and K is found in Table 9–2. In recording, this plan was added to the contracted plan that was used during assessment and evaluation.

II. Field Area: Gerontology
A. Agency: Nursing Home
B. Client System

Mrs. J, an 80-year-old Portuguese woman in a skilled-nursing facility. (For additional information, see Chapter 4, Engagement in Diverse Field Areas, II. Gerontology.)

TABLE 9-2. Contracted Plan Continued

DATE IDENTIFIED	PROBLEM/ NEED	GOAL	TASK	CONTRACT	DATE ANTICIPATED	DATE ACCOMPLISHED
7/26	Termination process	Satisfactory termination	1. Introduce termination	1. Worker	7/26	7/26
			2. Discuss feelings and termination	2. Worker and K	7/26 and 8/5	8/5
			3. Life-cycle review	3. Worker and K	8/15	8/15
			4. Meet with transfer worker	4. K, worker, and transfer worker	8/22	8/22
			5. Final session	5. Worker and K	8/30	8/30

C. Summary of Preceding Stages

The problems, goals, and tasks identified and contracted in earlier stages may be found in Table 7–2, Chapter 7. The evaluation process and contract reformulation of the preceding stage are outlined in Table 8–13, Chapter 8. At the time of evaluation, progress was noted for all of the stated goals. The least amount of progress was shown for goal 3a (to have Mrs. J go out of her room on her own at least once a day). Additional efforts to work on goal 3a were developed and contracted during the evaluation stage. These included the creation of an ongoing evaluation graph (Figure 8–8, Chapter 8) and more involvement by nursing staff in helping to chart the frequency of Mrs. J's leaving her room by herself. Mrs. J and the worker agreed to assess progress in goal 3a weekly.

D. Intervention

After working with Mrs. J for seven months, the worker began the process of termination because she was leaving the agency. When the worker informed Mrs. J that she would be working at the nursing home for only four more weeks, Mrs. J repeated, "No, you won't" or "You won't go" and refused to discuss it any further. Mrs. J would turn on her television whenever the worker tried to talk about her leaving. One day, the worker went to see Mrs. J at their regular meeting time and Mrs. J was not in her room. She was later located walking on the floor downstairs by herself. She said she didn't know why she was there.

The worker told Mrs. J that she could see that she was upset and angry with her because she was leaving. Mrs. J said she could not understand why the worker had to go. The worker tried to review the progress Mrs. J had made, but Mrs. J said she didn't want to talk about it. She became very silent and refused to speak at all after the worker said she would not be coming back, even to visit Mrs. J. Mrs. J was told that the worker's supervisor would come to see her occasionally and would be available if Mrs. J needed to talk to a social worker. Mrs. J did not respond and remained withdrawn throughout the remainder of the time the worker was at the home.

Realizing that Mrs. J was finding it difficult to accept the termination, the worker's supervisor agreed to see Mrs. J at least once a week for a while after the worker left. During the second-to-last meeting of the worker and Mrs. J, the supervisor dropped in, but Mrs. J said very little to her.

E. Charted Progress

The termination plan was drawn up by the worker, who kept trying to get Mrs. J involved in the process. The plan was recorded as found in Table 9–3.

As apparent in Table 9–3, tasks 2 and 3 (discuss feelings, review life cycle of working relationship) of the termination plan were not accomplished. No dates are entered in last column ("date accomplished") for tasks 2 and 3. The worker was not able to engage Mrs. J either in a

TABLE 9-3. Contracted Plan Continued

DATE IDENTIFIED	PROBLEM/ NEED	GOAL	TASK	CONTRACT	DATE ANTICIPATED	DATE ACCOMPLISHED
4/29	Termination process	Satisfactory termination	1. Introduce termination	1. Worker	4/29	4/29
			2. Discuss termination and feelings	2. Worker and Mrs. J	5/1 and 5/6	
			3. Life-cycle review	3. Worker and Mrs. J	5/1 and 5/6	
			4. Meet with supervisor	4. Worker, Mrs. J, and supervisor	5/15	5/15
			5. Final session	5. Worker and Mrs. J	5/22	5/22

discussion of feelings about the termination or in a life-cycle review. In the termination summary left in the record, therefore, the worker emphasized the fact that the termination process had not been attained. The worker's supervisor planned to focus on tasks 2 and 3 when she met with Mrs. J after the worker's termination.

III. Field Area: Public Social Welfare
A. Agency: State Social Service
B. Client System

Mr. and Mrs. P and their two children (ages 2 and 4), placed in emergency shelter (Center City Motor Inn) for 44 days, then relocated in an apartment; family receiving AFDC because of Mr. P's mental incapacity. (Additional background information may be found in Chapter 4, Engagement in Diverse Field Areas, III. Public Social Welfare.)

C. Summary of Preceding Stages

The problems, goals, and interventions of earlier stages are outlined in Table 6–11 of Chapter 6 and Table 7–3 of Chapter 7. A summary of the evaluation that was completed is charted in Table 8–14 of Chapter 8. The basic goals for food, housing, medical examination, fuel assistance, AFDC payment, and a functioning refrigerator were accomplished mainly through extensive involvement by resources outside of the family. The goals of obtaining Supplemental Security Income, a Thanksgiving food basket, and Christmas gifts for the children were not accomplished (to date) because of Mr. P's failure to complete contracted tasks. The problems of poor money management and excessive dependence on outside resources were identified by the worker but left unresolved because Mr. and Mrs. P refused to recognize them as problems in need of attention. The evaluation culminated with both the worker and the family agreeing to begin the process of termination.

D. Termination

Although the P's said they had no immediate need for continued social services, they appeared a little angry with the worker when the idea of termination was first introduced. They were able to admit that they were disappointed when the worker did not take care of fixing their refrigerator and also when the worker didn't get them a food basket for Thanksgiving. They knew that they should try to do more for themselves and said it was easier for a worker to deal with other programs and services. The worker reminded them that when they really had to get something done, they were able to work it out (such as locating an apartment). At this point, they admitted that Mrs. P's father was actually the one who found the apartment for them. They asked if the worker couldn't come by at least once every month to see how they were getting along. The worker did not agree to this, because he felt it was better for the family to try to solve their problems as they arose and not to hold them until the worker came each month. Again, the worker cautioned them about their need for careful planning in money management and said that if they ever wanted help in developing their skill in this area, they could bring this to the attention of their income-maintenance technician or they could call the Social Services Department directly.

The worker planned to meet three additional times with the family before their final termination. During these last visits, the family continued to complain about how hard it is to maintain a home and raise children these days. They repeated their desire for Christmas presents for the children, and the worker reviewed the tasks identified in the contracted plan. Mr. P did call the Salvation Army (task 2, problem 12, Table 7–3, Chapter 7) on the day of the worker's last visit.

E. Charted Progress

The termination plan carried out by the worker and the P's is recorded in Table 9–4. In the closing summary for the record, the worker emphasized that although problems 5 (poor money management) and 13 (excessive dependency) were never recognized by the P's, these were assessed as continuing and serious by the worker.

IV. Field Area: Community Services
A. Agency: Clayton Neighborhood House
B. Client System

Four Hispanic families who needed heat in their apartments on the second floor of 33 L Street. (More background information is available in Chapter 4, Engagement in Diverse Field Areas, IV. Community Services.)

C. Summary of Preceding Stages

The problems, goals, and tasks identified and enacted during early stages are described in the contracted plan found in Table 6–12 in Chapter 6, Table 7–4 in Chapter 7, and Table 8–16 in Chapter 8. Although the families initially felt victimized and helpless, they expressed feelings of relief and gratitude during the evaluation stage. There was adequate heating in their apartments, and they were actively monitoring the temperature daily. They knew that they continued to have a problem in communicating with their landlord, but they did not want to try to improve their communications at this time.

D. Termination

When the worker returned to meet with the families and review the heating situation, she learned that consistent heat had been provided throughout the week. This finding was charted on the ongoing-evaluation graph given in Figure 8–9, Chapter 8. The worker had mentioned to the families the previous week that if there didn't seem to be any remaining problems to work on when she came for this meeting, she would talk with them about terminating her contacts with them.

Residents first expressed a wish that the worker would continue to visit with them at least once a week. Comments were made, such as "Don't you like us any more?" One tenant said that he had heard that

TABLE 9-4.   Contracted Plan Continued

DATE IDENTIFIED	PROBLEM/ NEED	GOAL	TASK	CONTRACT	DATE ANTICIPATED	DATE ACCOMPLISHED
12/4	Termination process	Satisfactory termination	1. Introduce termination	1. Worker	12/4	12/4
			2. Discuss termination and feelings	2. Worker and P's	12/11	12/11
			3. Life-cycle review	3. Worker and P's	12/11	12/11
			4. Final session	4. Worker and P's	12/21	12/21

325

the landlord was selling the apartment building and that maybe they all would be put out on the street. The worker assured the residents that if they received notice that they had to leave the building, they could contact Clayton House for assistance with relocation.

In reviewing the life cycle of their working together, the worker recalled their first meeting and the way in which they worked on the heating problem. The families were happy to know that they could drop into Clayton House if they ever wanted help with any problem. They were also informed of the regular community meetings and activities that went on at Clayton for children and adults.

The tenants decided that they wanted to continue their daily monitoring of the heat in their apartments throughout the winter. Mrs. T offered to keep track of their findings by marking temperature points on the graph (Figure 8–9, Chapter 8) once a week. If there was any marked regression, she would contact the worker and call a meeting.

The worker shared how much she had enjoyed working with them, even though their contact had been brief. She was invited to drop in any time she was in the neighborhood.

E. Charted Progress

The termination plan was carried out and recorded as outlined in Table 9–5.

V. Field Area: Education

A. Agency: Keeney Elementary School

B. Client System

Mr. and Mrs. G and their son Jim, 8 years old and in third grade, who was showing regressive behavior in school and at home in reaction to his parents' problems with their relationship and Mrs. G's threat to abandon the family.

C. Summary of Preceding Stages

The contracted plan developed and implemented by Jim, his parents, and the worker is found in Table 6–14, Chapter 6. During evaluation, progress was noted for all four identified goals. The goal to improve Mr. and Mrs. G's marital relationship was recognized as needing more time before its accomplishment. Mr. and Mrs. G were motivated to remain in counseling at the family counseling center.

D. Termination

During the last interview with Mr. and Mrs. G and Jim, termination was introduced and discussed. Although it was agreed that the worker did not need to meet with Mr. and Mrs. G again, the contract with Jim was extended to include two additional sessions at school.

As the worker and the G's recognized the progress that had been made, Mr. and Mrs. G expressed gratitude to the worker for her interest in Jim and in them. They said it was good to know that the worker was at the school to help the children and their families. They admitted that

TABLE 9-5. Contracted Plan Continued

DATE IDENTIFIED	PROBLEM/ NEED	GOAL	TASK	CONTRACT	DATE ANTICIPATED	DATE ACCOMPLISHED
12/19	Termination process	Satisfactory termination	1. Introduce termination	1. Worker	12/12	12/12
			2. Discuss termination and feelings	2. Worker and residents	12/19	12/19
			3. Life-cycle review	3. Worker and residents	12/19	12/19
			4. Final session	4. Worker and residents	12/19	12/19

they probably would not have gone for help for themselves if it hadn't been for the worker. They were reminded by the worker that it was Jim who was feeling their pain and reacting to the situation. It was Jim who led them to look closer at what was happening to them and to their family. Using the life-cycle approach, the worker moved from the past to the present and then to the future. In considering the future, the worker strongly encouraged Mr. and Mrs. G to continue their work at the family counseling center, even if it got rough at times. They were assured also that they could contact the worker at school if she could be of any further assistance.

When the worker began to talk with Jim about termination during their last two meetings, he said he didn't want to stop coming. He liked to play with the toys in the office. He liked talking about his grades and keeping track of his improvement on the graphs.

During these sessions, Jim repeatedly asked if the worker had started to see some other child in his place. He was assured that no one could take his place. Jim said he was happy about home, but he was sad that he couldn't continue to see the worker. He told the worker that he might "surprise" her and drop in to see her on his own sometime. Before leaving, he took the graphs that were hanging on the wall with him. He brought the worker a drawing he had made of himself and his family and hung it on the worker's wall. He said that she could keep it—for a while.

E. Charted Progress

The plan for termination was recorded on the contracted plan as outlined in Table 9–6.

VI. Field Area: Corrections

A. Agency: Juvenile Court

B. Client System

A group of six (originally seven) male youths, all age 14, on probation, attending weekly group meetings led by co-workers at Juvenile Court. (For additional background information, see Chapter 4, Engagement in Diverse Field Areas, VI. Corrections.)

C. Summary of Preceding Stages

The group met weekly and focused on the three prioritized goals of (1) to get off probation in four months, (2) to control tempers at home and at school, and (3) to learn more about "the changes" they were facing as teenagers. After three and a half months, the group evaluated their progress in goal accomplishment. Four of the members were achieving the staged goals as planned. They were being recommended for termination of probation. One youth was sent to a correctional center after he had attended six meetings, because he was found breaking into a store. The remaining two members were not meeting the requirements for a reduction in probation. Group meetings were extended for at least an additional six weeks for these two members. After the evaluation, the group begin to focus on termination.

TABLE 9-6. Contracted Plan Continued

DATE IDENTIFIED	PROBLEM/NEED	GOAL	TASK	CONTRACT	DATE ANTICIPATED	DATE ACCOMPLISHED
12/13	Termination process	Satisfactory termination	1. Introduce termination	1. Worker	12/17	12/17
			2. Discuss termination and feelings	2. Worker, Mr. and Mrs. G, and Jim	12/17	12/17
			3. Terminate with Mr. and Mrs. G	3. Worker	12/17	12/17
			4. Further discussion of termination and feelings	4. Worker and Jim	12/20 and 1/8	12/20 and 1/8
			5. Final session	5. Worker and Jim	1/8	1/8

D. Termination

As the group began to discuss what it would be like to be off probation, MK and B said that they were glad they were getting off probation but that they would miss seeing everyone in the group. They asked the group leaders to let them know if the leaders were going on any trips that they could join too. J and T expressed anger over having to come back for group meetings. They began to blame the co-workers for not recommending that they get reduced time, but other group members reminded J and T that they themselves didn't keep up their scores.

As the group discussed the life cycle of their working together (i.e., past, present, and future), they began to recall what it was like when they first started attending. Most of the youths admitted that they didn't think that they could trust the workers and doubted that they would give them time off. C reminded the group about A, saying he was sorry A didn't make it but he should have listened to the probation officers. C also shared how excited he was because his mother and little sister and brother were coming from Puerto Rico to live with him and his father.

All of the youths said that they thought they were doing better than when they first were put on probation. They didn't know if they would be able to stay out of trouble once they were off probation. J and T said they probably would never get off probation. They knew that if they began to do better they still could have a probation reduction of one month (rather than two). In looking toward the future, J and T were told by the workers that if they continued to fail to meet the requirements, the group would stop at the end of its fifth month, but J and T would be expected to meet individually with a worker each week for as long as they remained on probation.

In talking about the future for those who were leaving in two weeks (MK, B, ML, and C), the leaders encouraged each of them to try to get active with local churches or recreational centers. Specific places were identified for each of the youths. They were encouraged also to ask to see the school social worker if they started to have any problems in school.

At the end of the last meeting with all six members, the group had a pizza party. In the following weeks, J's behavior markedly improved at meetings, at home, and in school. He was recommended to be removed from probation one month early. T continued to come late to meetings. His fighting at school continued, and he was not obeying his grandmother. His probation period was extended beyond five months, and he was required to come to see the male worker once a week.

E. Charted Progress

The termination plan was recorded as outlined in Table 9–7.

TABLE 9-7. Contracted Plan Continued

DATE IDENTIFIED	PROBLEM/ NEED	GOAL	TASK	CONTRACT	DATE ANTICIPATED	DATE ACCOMPLISHED
1/14	Termination process	Satisfactory termination	1. Introduce termination	1. Co-workers	1/14	1/14
			2. Discuss termination and feelings	2. Members and co-workers	1/21, 1/28	1/21, 1/28
			3. Life-cycle review	3. Members and co-workers	1/21, 1/28	1/21, 1/28
			4. Final session for MK, ML, B, and C—pizza party	4. Members and co-workers	1/28	1/28
			5. Continue weekly meetings for a month	5. J, T, and co-workers	2/4, 2/11, 2/18, 2/25	2/4, 2/11, 2/18, 2/25
			6. Evaluation of progress of J and T	6. J, T, and co-workers	2/11	2/25 2/11
			7. Final session for J	7. J, T, and co-workers	2/25	2/25
			8. Continue to meet once a week	8. T and worker (M.S.W.)	3/4 and each week until off probation	

331

VII. Field Area: Homeless Shelter
   A. Agency: West End Community Shelter
   B. Client System

Mr. José G is a resident at the homeless shelter and he has AIDS. (For further background information, see Chapter 4, VII. FIELD AREA: HOMELESS SHELTER).

   C. Summary of Preceding Stages

When Mr. G came to the shelter in May, he was unemployed, homeless, and testing HIV positive. During his stay at the shelter, he found a job and worked full- and part-time on a chicken farm. He has become active with the Harmony Program and with Saint John's Church. He started and continues to be seen at the free clinic located near the shelter. Recently, the doctor informed Mr. G that test results indicate that he has AIDS. Mr. G is not able to continue working. He has applied for public assistance and social security. He applied also for residence at Hope Home and was invited for a preplacement visit.

   D. Termination

The decision was made by Mr. G and the staff at Hope home that Mr. G would move to the Home on July 8. The shelter worker and Mr. G took time to plan his termination from the shelter. Mr. G recalled how hopeless he felt that first night when he came to the shelter and signed in for a bed. He expressed deep appreciation for the help he received from the worker and said he would like to come back if he could to visit everyone sometimes. They recognized that Mr. G has been going through a lot of changes in his life and that the road ahead may not be easy. Mr. G said that the doctor helped him to understand the virus better and what he might expect. He said that he was very glad that he had "made peace with God" and his church. He still was afraid but not as much as when he first learned he was HIV positive. He said that he thought he would like the people at Hope Home. He was looking forward to sharing a room with only one person.

   E. Charted Progress

A termination plan was added to Mr. G's contracted plan as found in Table 9–8.

Conclusion

In reviewing the content of this chapter, it may be perceived that the process of termination includes all of the stages of the General Method. The six-stage nature of the Method (engagement, data collection, assessment, intervention, evaluation, termination) is contained within the last stage. During termination, the worker and system begin with an identification of the meaning of termination (engagement). They proceed to gathering information as they move from past to present (data collection). They move on to assessing and planning for the future (assessment). The plan is then implemented (intervention) and evaluated (evaluation).

TABLE 9-8. Contracted Plan Continued

DATE IDENTIFIED	PROBLEM/ NEED	GOAL	TASK	CONTRACT	DATE ANTICIPATED	DATE ACCOMPLISHED
7/2	Termination process	Satisfactory termination	1. Discuss termination past/present/future	1. Worker and Mr. G	7/3	
			2. Plan move	2. Worker, Mr. G and "buddy"	7/3	
			3. Have last meeting	3. Worker and Mr. G	7/7	
			4. Move to Hope Home	4. Mr. G with help of buddy	7/8	

Finally there is closure (termination). The General Method is a cyclical process. In the termination cycle, the process is repeated and completed.

The opportunity for the identification and expression of feelings has been emphasized as essential to the termination process. In this chapter, approaches and exercises for understanding and working with termination feelings have been suggested. The reactions of a system to ending a relationship were described in terms of the five-stage sequence of denial, anger, bargaining, depression, and acceptance. A life-cycle approach containing the three focal points of past, present, and future was offered as a guiding framework for workers during the termination process. Attention was also given to the possible feelings and reactions of service providers as they go through repeated termination experiences. Examples were included to demonstrate a worker's sensitivity to human diversity in the final stage of the General Method and to show how termination is carried out in diverse areas of practice.

New workers frequently say that the most difficult part of working with a system is getting started. In time, workers generally say the most difficult part is the ending. At the beginning, there may be some fears and emptiness because of little experience or knowledge of a system. Seasoned workers know, however, the awesome reality that the emptiness after termination may be filled with memories of the experience, particularly the final stage, that live on.

NOTES

1. Ner Littner, *Some Traumatic Effects of Separation and Placement* (New York: Child Welfare League of America, 1981), p. 22.

2. Elizabeth Kübler-Ross. *On Death and Dying* (New York: Macmillan, 1969), pp. 34–121.

3. Ibid., p. 112.

Identity and Integration

I say this, knowing that the art of doing cannot be taught in any complete sense. Only the principles by which it may be guided, the dynamic elements that operate in "doing," the general nature and direction of the process of being professionally helpful—only these can be taught and learned for the practitioner's creative use.

—Helen Harris Perlman[1]

The General Method—A Purposeful Procedure

As brought out throughout this text, the General Method of social work practice involves a purposeful procedure. Respecting the right of a human system to self-determination, the generalist follows the lead of the system receiving service and offers an approach that is a planned problem-solving procedure. A sensitivity to human diversity enables the worker to be skillful in timing the process and in selecting interventions, tools, and techniques. With the identification of mutual goals, the worker and the system of contact proceed with interactions that have the purpose of goal accomplishment.

The method presented in this book is not actually new to social work. When enacting the traditional methods of casework, group work, and community organization, social workers have often used a problem-solving approach. As articulated and organized in this text, however, the General Method incorporates an ecological-systems perspective, an open selection of theories and interventions, and a multilevel approach. The method is a problem-solving process consisting of six identifiable stages.

The process is dynamic in nature and does not restrict a worker to following a set sequence according to a fixed pattern. The stages of the Method are presented sequentially for conceptualization, but they are not necessarily irreversible. As pointed out earlier, elements of each stage are often observable in every stage. Frequently, there is a returning to an earlier stage as problems or needs evolve. In addition, the general nature of the Method does not restrict a worker to working with systems of a particular size. It may be used with individuals, groups, families, communities, or organizations. Interventions are selected to match the individualized needs of the system receiving service at a given time. A plan to work with members of a system, for example, may include seeing them individually, as a family, and in groups. The Method blends general and individual conceptualizations. A holistic perspective that recognizes individuality and interrelatedness is, therefore, fundamental to the Method.

For beginning workers, the General Method is a guiding framework. Rather than learning about a variety of skills to be applied eclectically, the worker who learns the Method has an organized body of skills. He or she is enabled to be process-minded and to recognize movement in problem solving. The Method guides the generalist and the system receiving service in their collaborative effort for goal attainment.

Classification of Methods in Human Services

The terms *methods, models, approaches, modes,* and *processes* are frequently used interchangeably to refer to the organized use of techniques and skills by helping professionals. In addition to the General Method of entry-level social workers and the traditional methods of advanced social workers, numerous other "methods" may be used by advanced practitioners from social work or other helping disciplines. Depending on theory and value foundations, different interventions are enacted; these are described in the professional literature. Various methods may be different or essentially similar. Frequently, diverse helpers use the same techniques and skills as well as the same terminology and theories. Some approaches, however, are based on contrasting theories and therefore do not work well together. To avoid confusion and increase comprehension, a means of categorizing various helping methods is needed. A systematic framework for distinguishing methods would not only provide a broad overview of different approaches but would also provide greater clarification of the place of the General Method in relation to other methodologies.

There is a way to cluster methods according to their essential characteristics. Basically, all methods may be seen as falling under three major headings: client-focused, problem-focused, or worker-focused. *Client* may be defined as *client system.* As defined earlier, a *client system* means "people who sanction or ask for the change agent's services, who are the expected beneficiaries of service, and who have a working agreement or contract with the change agent."[2] The word *problem* means the issue, need, question, or difficulty facing the client system and being brought to the attention of the worker. And the *worker* may be any member of the helping professionals within the field of human services (as described in Chapter 1). The central consideration in the classification is the role of the worker in the triplex of client system, problem, and worker.

In the first category of methodologies, the *client-focused* cluster, the worker assumes a limited role, giving support mainly through listening and reassuring the clients of their potential for coping with difficulties. There is minimum structure, leadership, and control on the part of the worker. The worker's direct intervention with the problem itself is minimal, if present. The client is seen as strong and well able to deal with his or her problems with a little help from the worker. The methods of Carl Rogers and Robert Carkhuff would come under this category. Consultation and some community locality development may also fall into this category. Developmental, client-centered, and other basic counseling approaches are the types of interventions appropriately clustered in this grouping. As shown in the "Methods A" representation in Figure 10–1, the worker using these methods may be depicted as working directly with client systems, who in turn are enabled to work out their problems or needs by themselves.

In the second major category of methodologies, the *problem-focused* cluster, the worker and the client system work in a more balanced and collaborative effort. Structure, leadership, and control are shared. The nature of the problems or needs is recognized as calling for the involvement of both the professional worker and the client. Although there is belief in the potential of the client system and the hope of eventual withdrawal of the worker, the method is identified as initially calling for some direct intervention by the worker as well as the client. These methods convey the notion of teamwork, as both client and worker focus on the problem in need of resolution. The methods of intervention described in the works of William Glasser or William Reid and Laura Epstein come under this category. Task-centered, problem-solving, functional, and rational approaches and

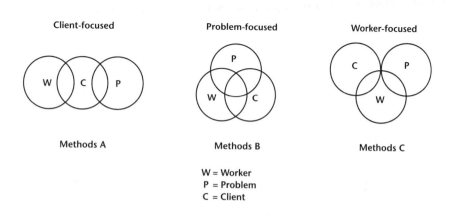

Client-focused   Problem-focused   Worker-focused

Methods A   Methods B   Methods C

W = Worker
P = Problem
C = Client

FIGURE 10-1. Classification of Methods

FIGURE 10-2. The Methodological Process

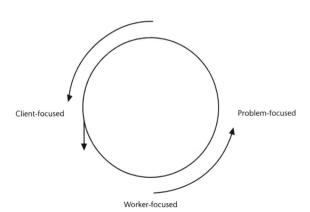

Client-focused   Problem-focused

Worker-focused

some locality development may be identified in this group, as illustrated in "Methods B" of Figure 10–1.

The third and final cluster of methods is described as *worker-focused*. In these interventions, the worker plays a major directive role, assuming clearly the responsibility for bringing about goal accomplishment. Modifying models and aggressive change models calling for specialized interventions by workers are classified here. Behavior modification, class advocacy, Gestalt therapy, psychoanalysis, psychotherapy, and social planning may be among the models of this group. The works of B. F. Skinner and Fritz Perls would contribute to this category of methodologies. As represented in "Methods C" of Figure 10–1, the worker carries the burden of planning, directing, coaching, and structuring for the client.

For further understanding, the categories of methods may be conceptualized as falling at different points on a circle. Usually, in the process of helping, workers move along the line, depending on the progress of the service. Ideally, a worker who begins with a worker-focused method would work toward developing a more problem-focused or collaborative relationship and eventually a more client-focused approach followed by termination, with the client becoming self-actualized (see Figure 10–2). Unfortunately, at times the worker who begins with a less directive approach may see the need for greater worker involvement. If he or she is not qualified for more advanced or specialized interventions, a referral may be necessary.

The General Method in the Classification

In considering the range of methods and the three basic categories, it is easy to find the place of the General Method as a problem-focused methodology. The worker and the client cooperate together at each stage of the General Method. The

FIGURE 10-3. The Scope of Methodology

1 = Beginning generalists   2 = Advanced workers

skills of the generalist may also allow for the use of a client-focused method when the client has the strengths, with support from a professional, to work out his or her own problem. Moreover, the generalist has skill and knowledge to use the General Method when direct problem-intervention by the worker in collaboration with the client system is needed (see Figure 10–3). If the method needed is of the worker-focused type, the generalist has the skill to refer or transfer the client system to an advanced worker. The beginning generalist, however, is not expected to have developed in his or her generalist education the knowledge and skills for worker-focused interventions. The beginning generalist, therefore, is not eclectic when it comes to choosing specialized methods. To practice with these approaches, the entry-level generalist would need further education and supervised experience.

For B.S.W. generalists to have the competence to use client-focused and problem-focused methods, their professional programs would have to include content and field experiences for the development of both types of methods. For advanced workers to have expertise in all three types of methodologies, curriculum content on the three types would have to be addressed in their graduate programs. Presently, skills and techniques used in client-focused and problem-focused methods are found in accredited baccalaureate programs and may also be found in the foundation of graduate social work programs.

The Ecological Generalist—A Basic Identity

The theoretical and experiential preparation for beginning, generalist practice as described in this book prepares the new worker to be an ecological generalist. This person is a human service provider with broad-based skills and foundation knowledge of persons, environments, and the interactions that take place at the interface between person(s) and environment(s). He or she has a commitment to social work values, as well as basic competence for working with individuals, groups, families, communities, and organizations. As described in this text, the ecological generalist is a person grounded in the use of the General Method of social work practice.

According to the Curriculum Policy Statement of the Council on Social Work Education, beginning social workers are prepared primarily for direct practice with a variety of client systems.[3] In addition to direct interventions with client systems, the ecological generalist may use indirect interventions with various systems in the extended environment. As stated earlier, indirect interventions refer to the efforts made by a worker to interact with a system that has the power or potential to respond to problems or needs and to contribute to goal attainment, even though that system itself may be neither experiencing the problem or need nor asking for help from the worker. The indirect interventions of a generalist relate to the needs and goals of particular client systems receiving services (as described in Chapter 7).

The work environment of the generalist includes the five major systems of (1) client, (2) agency of employment, (3) client resources, (4) the profession, and (5) society at large. As depicted in Figure 10–4, ecological generalists (EG) function within an agency structure and as such interface primarily with client systems in direct service. The scope of their work, however, as seen in the diagram, includes moving out to related resources, the social work profession, and organizations or institutions in society at large. To be true to their identity, ecological generalists see and respond to the interdependence that exists among the systems in their work environment. Although most of their formal work time (agency hours) may be used in providing direct services for client systems, generalists take time to be politically and professionally active. Involvement with the extended environment may include advocating for the poor, serving on boards or committees, giving testimony, having personal contact with legislators, and participating in political campaigns or political action groups. Unless ecological generalists maintain an awareness of and some involvement in the development of policy and services in their extended environment, they run the risk of losing their basic identity.

A Forgotten Commitment

As a profession, social work has a history of demonstrated commitment and concern for the poor and the underprivileged. Today, social work generalists and specialists continue to be needed to speak out against social injustices and unmet human needs. As the numbers of people without employment or adequate housing, food, and care increase, social workers are greatly needed to be present once again in the extended environment to stand in solidarity with the underprivileged and to advocate for social change. Unfortunately, some workers have moved away from active societal involvement outside of direct work responsibilities. The "social" dimension of their name and profession has become obscure and perhaps forgotten.

A growing shortage in social work personnel to work with and for the poor, particularly in public welfare, has become increasingly evident in the profession.[4] After studies showed that over 78 percent of social workers in public welfare services had little or no professional preparation for their jobs, CSWE and NASW recognized the B.S.W. level of practice. It was intended that B.S.W. practitioners would fill public welfare positions and enable the profession to continue to serve the needy in public social services.[5] Unfortunately, few current B.S.W. programs

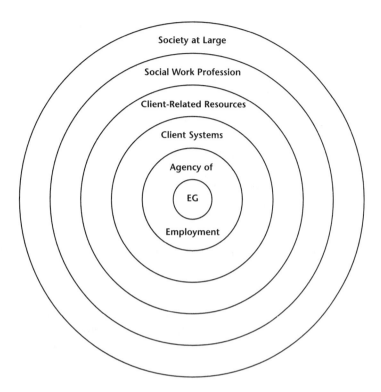

FIGURE 10-4. Work Environment of the Ecological Generalist

and graduates prepare for or enter public welfare services. B.S.W. practitioners move quickly into M.S.W. programs or into private services.[6] There are several reasons why social workers may avoid working in the public welfare system. These may include low pay, large caseloads, limited supervision and number of available professionally trained colleagues, and insufficient or inadequate resources. The results of these circumstances and pressures often include low staff morale and high staff burnout and job turnover. Special support and recognition should be given to those who persevere in the system because of a strong commitment and dedication to serving those without resources and with multiple needs in what is frequently the most degrading and impoverished of service systems (see, for example, talk given to DSS workers in Appendix 3).

Addressing the broad and multiple needs of the poor often calls for political skills and strategies. Although basic political skills have been identified as fundamental to practice at the beginning level (see Figure 1–4, Chapter 1), new workers will need to have models and supervisors in their agencies who promote and demonstrate the use of these skills. If there is little activity by advanced workers in the extended environment, new generalists may lose sight of their commitment and ecological identity.

The call for renewed and intensified involvement by social workers with the disadvantaged in American society today is very clear and urgent. Robert Stewart writes as follows:

> If social work abandons its traditional commitments, there will be no ethnically pluralistic professional group in society concerned with poor and disadvantaged populations. Social work is the last hope for a professional societal bastion for all economically exploited and disadvantaged groups in America.[7]

Bertram Beck extends the need to a global perspective when he writes this statement:

> Adherence to the interest in social issues and social action that characterized our forebears and still characterizes social work leadership is the right direction and the only direction that can ultimately bring about a world order characterized by peace and justice.[8]

As finite resources are becoming depleted and inaccessible, human service consumers and providers are beginning to witness a movement from a concern with quality to a concern with survival. Social welfare programs and policies that took years to be developed are being modified or eliminated in order to save on federal funding. To combat this regressive process, social workers are urged to sharpen and demonstrate political expertise. Ron Federico describes future social workers as follows:

> The professionals of the future must be astute political actors, who can work within the existing social structure to utilize available resources, and still find and use opportunities to affect social policy.[9]

Current changes taking place in social policy and programs call for an updating of curriculum and learning opportunities for social work students. As the implications of new legislation and policy changes are being studied, social work educators, students, and practitioners need to have ongoing communication, with opportunity for observation and validation of what is happening in the field.

Legislation, such as the Omnibus Budget Reconciliation Act of 1981, has had a profound impact on human service delivery. Through the creation of block grants, programs have had to be consolidated, with a reduction in their funding. Although the 1981 act gave states increased flexibility in deciding how to use block-grant funding, it frequently resulted in a growing competition among programs and special-needs groups competing for limited resources.[10]

For legislators, decision makers, and groups with needs, social workers with research and political skills can assist in identifying and documenting priorities. In addition, a worker with an understanding of policy development and with relevant political skills can contribute to the introduction and passage of legislation that reflects human priorities. Because of their theoretical foundation and identity, ecological generalists understand and can help explain the strong correlations that are emerging between program cutbacks and increasing social problems in society. Anne Minahan comments:

> Social work perspectives on the interaction of person and environment and on interdependence can help us demonstrate that the intertwined factors of inflation, unemployment, and reductions in income maintenance, health and support programs have a direct relationship to hunger and pain and poverty and alcohol and drug abuse and despair and violence against people.[11]

Although social workers do engage in some political activities, they are found generally to be ineffective in the political arena. One reason for their limited success has been identified as "insufficient skills for political action," particularly "overt political behavior." For increased effectiveness, the skill development of workers may need to be expanded to include such "overt" activities as lobbying, campaigning, negotiating, boycotting, testifying, and conducting sit-ins.[12]

In the area of interpersonal communication, as brought out by Specht, "the management of interpersonal processes in sociopolitical interaction differs from the management of other professional interaction." When working with policy makers, funders, landlords, or employers, the worker needs to find ways to interact selectively in order to gain the attention and support of the sociopolitical other.[13]

Curriculum content for social work students could include guidelines for giving testimony and other techniques and tactics for legislative advocacy. For example, Cecilia Kleinkauf has developed a "Guide to Giving Legislative Testimony," in which a basic process may be identified as to (1) research the bill, (2) analyze the committee conducting the hearing, (3) prepare the testimony, (4) give the testimony, (5) deal with questions, and (6) conduct a follow-up.[14]

Using this process in researching a bill, the worker begins by finding out about related existing statutes and studies them in relation to the proposed bill. Next, he or she explores the strengths and weaknesses of the bill and of suggested amendments. Information about the bill's history, cost, supporters, and opponents is collected. The worker also needs to know about the procedures, composition, and members of the committee conducting the hearing. Knowledge about committee members includes information about their voting records, philosophy, interests, and constituencies.

Testimony is prepared orally and in writing. The testimony should be brief, and its contents should be accurate. The worker, or the person selected as witness, should address the issue as well as the bill itself. Copies of the testimony should be given to committee members, because legislators are often distracted or called out during the hearing. It is important for the worker or other witness to state clearly who he or she is and what position he or she is taking on the bill. Legislators frequently ask questions of the witness. If answers are not known, the worker should not attempt an answer, but rather should say that the information will be obtained for the legislator. Workers must be sure to follow up with information promised to legislators. After the hearing, workers need to keep track of the progress of the bill. It may be necessary to give additional testimony if the bill is passed on to another committee.

Before introducing or advocating for legislation to develop new social programs, workers should be sure that they are aware of already existing programs that attempt to meet the identified need or problem. Various frameworks are available to analyze existing social welfare programs. For example, Winifred Bell has outlined eight basic criteria for evaluating program effectiveness. They are (1) objectives, (2) legislative authority, (3) source of funding, (4) administrative structure, (5) eligibility requirements, (6) coverage, (7) adequacy, and (8) equity.[15] Workers could use a similar approach to compare proposed new programs with those that have been or are in existence. Legislators are usually very interested in seeing the comparison and in learning how the new program would be more advantageous.

Research by Ronald Dear and Rino Patti has shown that certain political tactics have been particularly effective in influencing the passage of legislation. They identify, as essential, the following seven tactics:

1. The bill should be introduced early in the season or, ideally, before the session has begun.
2. It is advisable to have more than one legislator sponsor a bill.
3. The advocate of social legislation should seek to obtain the sponsorship of the majority party. . . . It is even more beneficial to obtain meaningful bipartisan sponsorship. . . .
4. Whenever possible, the advocate should obtain the support of the governor and of relevant state agencies.
5. The advocate should seek influential legislators as sponsors of proposed legislation, provided that they are willing to exercise their influence in promoting the bill.
6. The advocate should press for open committee hearings on the bill and, when such hearings are held, attempt to arrange for testimony in behalf of the bill by expert witnesses.
7. The advocate should use the amendatory process as a strategy for promoting a favorable outcome for a bill.[16]

The overt skills, list of tactics, and testimony guide are all helpful tools for social workers as they become involved in the legislative arena. An adaptation of the General Method may also serve as a helpful framework for workers as they engage in political activity in the extended environment.

Using the General Method for Social Development

A social worker who perceives needs on the broader societal level may wonder where to start and how to carry through with efforts to bring about social change or development. Time and energy limitations of the worker should be realistically recognized, with activities carefully planned to avoid wasted effort. The method of the ecological generalist is a process that may be adapted for use by workers as they engage in work with diverse structures and systems in society.

For social change or development, the General Method is somewhat modified, because the system of contact usually does not have the identified need, nor does that system see any reason to respond to the need, even though it has the power to do so. Although the Method has been described repeatedly as a collaborative process between a worker and a system, in this type of work the worker often executes the process alone. Sometimes the work involves advocacy for particular clients. In these cases, every effort is made to involve and to empower the clients in each step of the process. At times, however, a worker is advocating for a class of people or for a policy change that affects people in society at large. Although a worker may try to join with others in coalitions or teams to bring about the desired change, it is possible that the process will have to be initiated and perhaps completed by the worker alone. Whether alone or with others, the procedure for work in the extended environment can be guided by the six stages of the General Method.

An outline of the General Method as designed in this text is repeated in Table 10–1. Having first identified both a need in society and the systems primarily responsible for meeting the need, a worker can follow the outline as a guide for action. The questions raised during each stage of the Method may he modified or expanded for greater relevance. For example, the three main components of the first stage are shown as "problems," "feelings," and "goals." In beginning to engage in the process, the worker first studies the problem, need, or issue in the extended environment by asking the following questions:

1. **What is the problem or need as perceived by**
   a. **Me (worker), my agency, my profession?**
   b. **The systems with the power to respond to the problem or need?**
   c. **Others**
      i. The group of people feeling the problem or need?
      ii. People in society at large?

The worker then proceeds to an inquiry about feelings and goals as the following questions are asked:

2. **What feelings surround the problem or need as felt by**
   a. **Me, my agency, my profession?**

TABLE 10-1.   The General Method

I.   Engagement
    a. Problems
    b. Feelings
    c. Goals

II. Data Collection
    a. Problems
    b. Persons
    c. Environment

III. Assessment
    a. Assessment statements
    b. Problem prioritization
    c. Contracting (plan)

IV. Intervention
    a. Direct
    b. Indirect
    c. Teamwork
    d. Referral

V.   Evaluation
    a. Goal analysis
    b. Contract review
    c. Contract reformulation

VI. Termination
    a. Decision: transfer, refer, terminate
    b. Plan: timing, follow-up
    c. Termination: feelings, life-cycle approach

    b. The power systems?
    c. Others: those with the problem or need, society at large?
3. **What goals related to the problem or need can be identified by**
    a. Me, my agency, my profession?
    b. The power systems?
    c. Others: those with the problem or need, society at large?

Moving into data collection (stage II), the worker gathers information about problems, persons, and environment. Questions to be answered in this stage are as follows:

4. **What is the scope (number of people), the duration (length of time), and the severity (degree to which it is a life-or-death issue) of the problem or need?**

5. Who are the persons suffering from the problem or unmet need? What is their motivation and capacity to work on the problem or need?
6. Who are the people in the power systems (titles, roles, personal characteristics)? What is their motivation and capacity to work on the problem or need?
7. What are the power systems—structure, channels, lines of authority, processes, rules of procedure? How are decisions made?

Question 7 is extremely important if a worker is to intervene effectively in a power system. If, for example, a worker enters the legislative arena with the intent to have a bill introduced or passed, it is imperative that the worker have knowledge of the legislative process, as well as of the legislators themselves. A diagram of a state's legislative process, such as that provided in Figure 10–5, may help a worker to visualize the complexity of the procedure.[17]

Supplementing information about the identified power systems, the worker needs to know the following:

8. Are there any other systems with the potential for meeting the identified need or for resolving the problem?
9. Are there other systems that could influence or put pressure on the power systems?
10. Are there other resources to support, or to collaborate with, the worker in his or her efforts?

On the basis of the data collected, the worker is then in a position to make a clearer assessment of the problem or need and to plan interventions. The questions raised in the assessment (stage III) include these:

11. *Who* has *what* (problem or need) and *why?*
12. If more than one problem or need has been identified, how should they be prioritized?
13. What is the most effective plan to work on the problems or needs as prioritized?

As a plan is developed, the worker would recall and may plan to use the political skills, program analysis, tactics, and testimony guide suggested earlier. As tasks are listed sequentially on a contracted-plan sheet, a worker might include efforts to mobilize other individuals, groups, or organizations to work with him or her on mutual goals stated on the contract. If others become involved in the action, the tasks may be distributed and contracted among the participants. As pointed out, however, it is possible that all of the tasks will have to be carried out by the worker alone.

FIGURE 10–5. How a Bill Becomes a Law

348

In intervention (stage IV) during indirect work, a worker may have face-to-face contact with the power systems and use various political skills and tactics. (Because a power system is not a client system, such intervention is not considered direct intervention, as defined in Chapter 5.) The worker may act as a team member in a coalition or may refer the issue to another resource for action. Throughout the intervention stage, the worker (team) asks these questions:

14. Am I (are we) completing the tasks as planned?
15. Am I (are we) ready to move on to the next planned task?

As the worker moves into evaluation, the questions asked are the following:

16. To what extent has (have) the goal(s) been accomplished?
17. If there has been goal accomplishment, was this the result of my (our) efforts? If there has not been goal accomplishment, why not?

Here too, the contracted plan developed during assessment is carefully reviewed if goals have not been accomplished. Timing anticipated, resources contracted, and tasks sequenced along with stated goals and problems on the plan are reconsidered.

The worker (team) then asks the following question:

18. Is there a need to reformulate goals or any other dimension of the plan? Are more overt political behaviors needed?

In the final stage, the worker (team) makes the decision regarding termination of his or her involvement in the issue with the identified power systems. Questions raised in this stage include these:

19. Is it time for me (us) to refer, transfer, or terminate my (our) efforts to bring about change in the extended environment in relation to the identified problem or needs?
20. How do I (we) plan to terminate?
  a. When?
  b. Will there be a follow-up?
  c. In terminating, are there feelings that need to be expressed? by me? the power systems? others?
21. Using the life-cycle approach, what is the past, present, and future of my (our) involvement in working on these problems or needs in the extended environment?

If the worker is a beginning generalist, the time may come in the process when a referral or transfer needs to be made to a worker with advanced expertise in political strategies or policy formation. Systems with greater legal access and authority may need to step in and take over the role of advocate. Social problems in society at large are seldom resolved fully. Even when legislation is passed and programs are initiated, ongoing monitoring of change is usually needed. Workers may, therefore, build in a role of monitoring as part of their follow-up plan for the future.

Although beginning generalists may not possess advanced, sophisticated political skills to work in complex political structures, they are the ones most likely to be aware of the pulse and the pain of the disadvantaged in society. Their first-hand experience and documentation, with a strong sense of commitment and perseverance, may be the most valuable forces to bring about change in the extended environment. Ecological generalists, therefore, are prepared primarily for direct practice with client systems, but they do not forget that efforts for social change in society at large are also essential to their holistic identity.

A Place for Radical Social Work

Social workers who have worked primarily on social justice issues to bring about institutional change have been called "radical." In recent years, radical social workers have begun to express the need for a holistic conception of their practice. Rather than limiting the focus of their attention to issues of social justice, they are recognizing the need to understand and to work with psychological problems. Instead of identifying themselves as working only with groups, communities, and institutions, they are finding appropriate roles within their practice for developing relationships with individuals. For example, Peter Leonard writes:

> A radical perspective which ignores or argues away the psychological effects of experience and the need at times to respond to these effects individually, as well as through group, community or organizational action, is in danger of failing to consider others as whole person, of perpetuating in another form, a fragmented, dehumanized view of men and women. Radical social work must therefore encompass direct work with individuals and families as well as with the wider group and collectivities to which they belong, and must seek to relate organizational and individual action.[18]

Although the primary method of radical social workers involves education through group dialogue, there is a growing awareness that radical workers need a range of skills for working with a variety of systems. Leonard supports the notion of shifting the focus of social work from pathology to interactions and from problems related to personal attributes to problems related to social situations. He considers pioneer works on a generalist concept of practice to be groundbreakers for expanded holistic models of social work practice.[19]

The General Method of social work practice as developed in this book provides an organized procedure that may be used by radical social workers.

Throughout the General Method, an ecological perspective is used that sensitizes the worker to the impact of the environment on the individual as well as the individual on the environment. The worker using the General Method is aware of the strong possibility that efforts may need to be directed toward bringing about changes in environmental structures and systems. As radical social workers grow in their search for holism and a balanced perspective in their practice, they may find that the General Method is a relevant guiding framework for their entry-level practice.

A Holistic Vision—Our Future Challenge

As radical social workers move more into direct work with individuals and families and as direct-practice workers become more involved (by choice or necessity) with political or power systems, the quest for holism is becoming an apparent reality in our profession. Social workers are extending their activities to include a broader range of skills and systems. Generalist practice for beginning and advanced workers is becoming more clearly understood and appreciated. The content of this book demonstrates another attempt within the profession to bring together various components of practice into a unified whole.

In addition to breadth, there is an ongoing search for greater depth and height in the profession. We are striving for an understanding and mastery of concentrations and specializations in practice. As pointed out in Chapter 1, further work is needed to develop and articulate the knowledge and skills for advanced practice in areas of concentration. The holistic foundation (Chapter 1) and the generalist perspective and the General Method (Chapters 2–9) described in this book serve as a base on which to build, refine, and extend our efforts to arrive at a holistic conception of all of social work practice. The beginning worker depicted in this text represents the entry level in our profession. To complete the picture, extensive work is needed to identify and integrate the advanced and beginning levels of practice into a holistic conceptualization. As we grow in sensitivity to the interdependence of persons and environments, we are also becoming increasingly aware of the interdependence and complementarity that can be envisioned among practice levels in the profession.

The "advanced generalist practice" concentration, for example, builds on and integrates the theoretical perspective and methodology of generalist practice. In the *Encyclopedia of Social Work*, the advanced generalist concentration is described as a "form of specialization" that "reflects a broader and more in-depth form of generalist practice."[20] As depicted in Figure 10–6 at the advanced generalist level the General Method is extended to apply to indirect practice roles such as supervisor and administrator. The ecological-systems perspective is expanded to the global environment as advanced practitioners grow in sensitivity and skill for practice involving international social work and welfare. Advanced generalist practice is a growing concentration that is beginning to be recognized as having the breadth and depth needed for effective responsiveness to emerging populations and complex problems facing social workers now and in the future.[21] Rather than duplication or competition, to have both an entry-level generalist and an advanced generalist practitioner available in an agency offers complementarity and opportunity for appropriate use of resources.

A skeletal framework for initiating a holistic perspective of social work practice at all educational and practice levels is proposed in Figure 10–7. The inner circle depicts the center of practice, which is foundation knowledge, values, and skills (outlined in Table 1–6 Chapter 1). The circle surrounding the foundation indicates beginning generalist practice (explicated throughout this text). The next circle is divided into sections to highlight the various types of areas of concentration found within the profession. This circle also reflects a place for advanced generalist practice. Practitioners at this level would have M.S.W. degrees. The final outer circle represents the doctoral level, where social workers are engaged in education, research, administration, or advanced specializations. More specific contents for the advanced level, as well as the interrelatedness among various levels and concentrations, continue to be explored and articulated.

Conclusion

I have found it difficult to write a social work textbook that conveys the warmth and depth that I know exists in the profession. Unfortunately, professionals sometimes seem to lose the heart of what they are about as they become engrossed in objectifying their work through scientific or technical language and documentation. The qualities that are not measurable are often described in professional terms that may confuse the student. Sometimes one loses the essential meaning of what is being said. For example, instead of talking about love and compassion, we talk about acceptance and empathy. The desirable qualities of a social worker are often described in terms, for example, of knowledge, skills, dependability, adaptability, and responsibility. Little has been written about that "special" quality that draws a person into social work and that keeps him or her going even when, after repeated efforts, there is no obvious success. The drive behind the profession may be a religious, spiritual, or humanitarian call or commitment. It may be an inner "goodness of person" that has not been defined and is seldom recognized.

To me, social workers are like the person in the Bible who kept on knocking at a neighbor's door until bread was given to another in need.[22] The person knocking did not break the door down, but neither did he or she go away. Social workers are often unnoticed, but they are there—listening to needs, calling on resources, visiting homes, and waiting at capitol buildings or legislative hearings to speak about realities that have to be addressed.

Today, there are doors of complex and powerful systems that need to be opened. There is great need for "whole" social workers—those with a vision of what could be as well as what is and has been; workers with sensitivity, warmth, and hope—as well as purpose and skills.

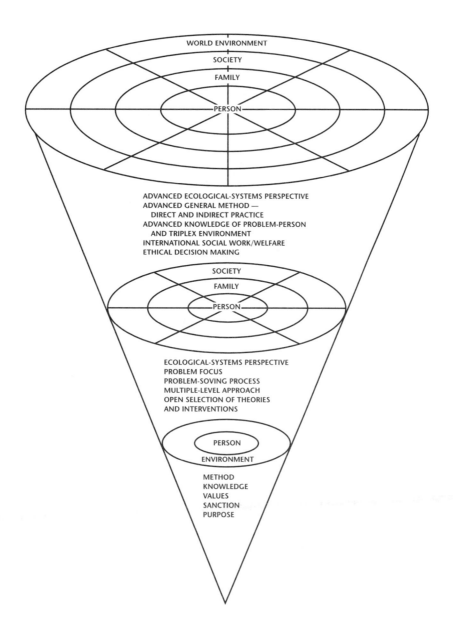

FIGURE 10-6. Advanced Generalist Perspective

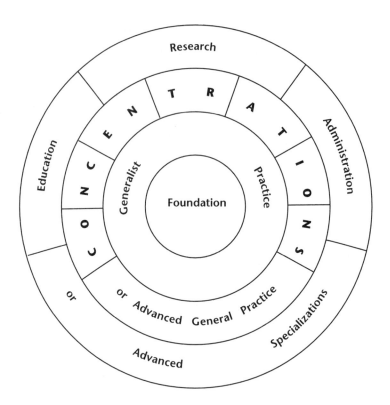

FIGURE 10-7. A Holistic View of Social Work Practice and Education

In ending this book it is time to recall the passage, "To everything there is a season" (Eccles. 3:1). The season has come for social workers to move tradition into contemporary action as we develop holistic conceptualizations and relevant methodologies. But I would not be faithful to the concept of season if I maintained that what has been presented in this text is above change. Beginning professionals are encouraged to take what is here as a proposed guide and not as definitive. Newly developed frameworks will continue to be in process as long as we have a dynamic, responsive profession. We in this profession need you, ecological generalists, with your vitality, creativity, and unifying perspective. We welcome you and encourage your full participation in our vital and growing profession.

NOTES

1. Helen Harris Perlman, *Social Casework: A Problem Solving Process* (Chicago: University of Chicago Press, 1967), p. vii.

2. Allen Pincus and Anne Minahan, *Social Work Practice: Model and Method* (Itasca, Ill.: Peacock, 1973), p. 63.

3. Council on Social Work Education, *Curriculum Policy Statement for the Master's Degree and Baccalaureate Degree Programs in Social Work Education,* approved by the Board of Directors July 19, 1992 and revised October 1993. (New York: Council on Social Work Education), B5.2, p. 3.

4. See Thomas Walz, "The Mission of Social Work Revisited: An Agenda for the 1990's," William R. Hodson Lecture, quoted in "The Public Social Services: The Social Work Role," *School of Social Work Alumni Report* (Minneapolis: University of Minnesota, 1989, p. 1. Also, Alan Keith-Lucas, "A Socially Sanctioned Profession?" in P. Nelson Reid and Philip R. Popple, eds. *The Moral Purposes of Social Work* (Chicago: Nelson-Hall Publishers, 1992), p. 51.

5. Maria O'Neil McMahon, "Responding to the Call," in P. Nelson Reid and Philip R. Popple, *The Moral Purposes of Social Work* (Chicago: Nelson-Hall Publishers, 1992), p. 173.

6. Ibid., pp. 175–177.

7. Robert P. Stewart, "Watershed Days: How Will Social Work Respond to the Conservative Revolution?" *Social Work* 26, no. 4 (July 1981): 273.

8. Bertram H. Beck, "Social Work's Future: Triumph or Disaster?" *Social Work* 26, no. 5 (September 1981): 371.

9. Ronald C. Federico, *The Social Welfare Institution*, 3rd ed. (Lexington, Mass.: Heath 1980), p. 327.

10. Bonnie Brown Morell, "Comments on Currents, ABC's of Block Grants," *Social Work* 27, no. 2 (March 1982): 126–27.

11. Anne Minahan, "Editorial Page, Social Workers and Politics," *Social Work* 26, no. 4 (July 1981): 371.

12. James S. Wolk, "Are Social Workers Politically Active?" *Social Work* 26, no. 4 (July 1981): 268.

13. Harry Specht, *New Directions for Social Work Practice* (Englewood Cliffs, N.J.: Prentice-Hall, 1988), p. 251.

14. Cecilia Kleinkauf, "A Guide to Giving Legislative Testimony," copyright 1981, National Association of Social Workers, Inc. Reprinted with permission, from *Social Work* 26, no. 4 (July 1981), 297–303 (adaptation).

15. Winifred Bell, "Obstacles to Shifting from the Descriptive to the Analytical Approach in Teaching Social Services," *Journal of Education for Social Work* 5, no. 2 (Spring 1969): 5–11.

16. Ronald B. Dear and Rino J. Patti, "Legislative Advocacy: Seven Effective Tactics." Copyright 1981, National Association of Social Workers, Inc. Reprinted with permission, from *Social Work* 26, no. 4 (July 1981): 289–96 (adapted).

17. "How a Bill Becomes a Law." (Diagram prepared and published by the League of Women Voters of Connecticut, Education Fund, and the Joint Committee on Legislative Management of the Connecticut General Assembly, August 1975).

18. Peter Leonard, "Toward a Paradigm for Radical Practice," Roy Bailey and Mike Broke, eds., *Radical Social Work* (New York: Pantheon Books, 1975), p. 51.

19. Ibid.

20. Bradford W. Sheafor and Pamela S. Landon, "Generalist Perspective" in *Encyclopedia of Social Work,* Eighteenth Edition. (Silver Springs, Md.: NASW, 1987): 665.

21. Maria O'Neil McMahon, *Advanced Generalist Practice With an International Perspective* (Englewood Cliffs, N.J.: Prentice-Hall, 1994), pp. 236–237.

22. Luke 11:5–8.

The NASW Code of Ethics

I. The Social Worker's Conduct and Comportment as a Social Worker

A. Propriety—The social worker should maintain high standards of personal conduct in the capacity or identity as social worker.

1. The private conduct of the social worker is a personal matter to the same degree as is any other person's, except when such conduct compromises the fulfillment of professional responsibilities.
2. The social worker should not participate in, condone, or be associated with dishonesty, fraud, deceit, or misrepresentation.
3. The social worker should distinguish clearly between statements and actions made as a private individual and as a representative of the social work profession or an organization or group.

B. Competence and Professional Development—The social worker should strive to become and remain proficient in professional practice and the performance of professional functions.

1. The social worker should accept responsibility or employment only on the basis of existing competence or the intention to acquire the necessary competence.
2. The social worker should not misrepresent professional qualifications, education, experience, or affiliations.
3. The social worker should not allow his or her own personal problems, psychosocial distress, substance abuse, or mental health difficulties to interfere with professional judgment and performance or jeopardize the best interests of those for whom the social worker has a professional responsibility.

Source: Copyright 1993, National Association of Social Workers, Inc.

4. The social worker whose personal problems, psychosocial distress, substance abuse, or mental health difficulties interfere with professional judgment and performance should immediately seek consultation and take appropriate remedial action by seeking professional help, making adjustments in workload, terminating practice, or taking any other steps necessary to protect clients and others.

C. Service—The social worker should regard as primary the service obligation of the social work profession.

1. The social worker should retain ultimate responsibility for the quality and extent of the service that individual assumes, assigns, or performs.
2. The social worker should act to prevent practices that are inhumane or discriminatory against any person or group of persons.

D. Integrity—The social worker should act in accordance with the highest standards of professional integrity and impartiality.

1. The social worker should be alert to and resist the influences and pressures that interfere with the exercise of professional discretion and impartial judgement required for the performance of professional functions.
2. The social worker should not exploit professional relationships for personal gain.

E. Scholarship and Research—The social worker engaged in study and research should be guided by the conventions of scholarly inquiry.

1. The social worker engaged in research should consider carefully its possible consequences for human beings.
2. The social worker engaged in research should ascertain that the consent of participants in the research is voluntary and informed, without any implied deprivation or penalty for refusal to participate, and with due regard for participants' privacy and dignity.
3. The social worker engaged in research should protect participants from unwarranted physical or mental discomfort, distress, harm, danger, or deprivation.
4. The social worker who engages in the evaluation of services or cases should discuss them only for the professional purposes and only with persons directly and professionally concerned with them.
5. Information obtained about participants in research should be treated as confidential.
6. The social worker should take credit only for work actually done in connection with scholarly and research endeavors and credit contributions made by others.

II. The Social Worker's Ethical Responsibility to Clients

F. Primacy of Clients' Interests—The social worker's primary responsibility is to clients.

1. The social worker should serve clients with devotion, loyalty, determination, and the maximum application of professional skill and competence.

2. The social worker should not exploit relationships with clients for personal advantage.

3. The social worker should not practice, condone, facilitate or collaborate with any form of discrimination on the basis of race, color, sex, sexual orientation, age, religion, national origin, marital status, political belief, mental or physical handicap, or any other preference or personal characteristic, condition or status.

4. The social worker should not condone or engage in any dual or multiple relationships with clients or former clients in which there is a risk of exploitation of or potential harm to the client. The social worker is responsible for setting clear, appropriate, and culturally sensitive boundaries.

5. The social worker should under no circumstances engage in sexual activities with clients.

6. The social worker should provide clients with accurate and complete information regarding the extent and nature of the services available to them.

7. The social worker should apprise clients of their risks, rights, opportunities, and obligations associated with social service to them.

8. The social worker should seek advice and counsel of colleagues and supervisors whenever such consultation is in the best interest of clients.

9. The social worker should terminate service to clients, and professional relationships with them, when such service and relationships are no longer required or no longer serve the clients' needs or interests.

10. The social worker should withdraw services precipitously only under unusual circumstances, giving careful consideration to all factors in the situation and taking care to minimize possible adverse effects.

11. The social worker who anticipates the termination or interruption of service to clients should notify clients promptly and seek the transfer, referral, or continuation of service in relation to the clients' needs and preferences.

G. Rights and Prerogatives of Clients—The social worker should make every effort to foster maximum self-determination on the part of clients.

1. When the social worker must act on behalf of a client who has been adjudged legally incompetent, the social worker should safeguard the interests and rights of that client.

2. When another individual has been legally authorized to act in behalf of a client, the social worker should deal with that person always with the client's best interest in mind.

3. The social worker should not engage in any action that violates or diminishes the civil or legal rights of clients.

H. Confidentiality and Privacy—The social worker should respect the privacy of clients and hold in confidence all information obtained in the course of professional service.

1. The social worker should share with others confidences revealed by clients, without their consent, only for compelling professional reasons.
2. The social worker should inform clients fully about the limits of confidentiality in a given situation, the purposes for which information is obtained, and how it may be used.
3. The social worker should afford clients reasonable access to any official social work records concerning them.
4. When providing clients with access to records, the social worker should take due care to protect the confidences of others contained in those records.
5. The social worker should obtain informed consent of clients before taping, recording, or permitting third party observation of their activities.

I. Fees—When setting fees, the social worker should ensure that they are fair, reasonable, considerate, and commensurate with the service performed and with due regard for the clients' ability to pay.

1. The social worker should not accept anything of value for making a referral.

III. The Social Worker's Ethical Responsibility to Colleagues

J. Respect, Fairness, and Courtesy—The social worker should treat colleagues with respect courtesy, fairness, and good faith.

1. The social worker should cooperate with colleagues to promote professional interests and concerns.
2. The social worker should respect confidences shared by colleagues in the course of their professional relationships and transactions.
3. The social worker should create and maintain conditions of practice that facilitate ethical and competent professional performance by colleagues.
4. The social worker should treat with respect, and represent accurately and fairly, the qualifications, views, and findings of colleagues and use appropriate channels to express judgements on these matters.
5. The social worker who replaces or is replaced by a colleague in professional practice should act with consideration for the interest, character, and reputation of that colleague.
6. The social worker should not exploit a dispute between a colleague and employers to obtain a position or otherwise advance the social worker's interest.
7. The social worker should seek arbitration or mediation when conflicts with colleagues require resolution for compelling professional reasons.
8. The social worker should extend to colleagues of other professions the same respect and cooperation that is extended to social work colleagues.
9. The social worker who serves as an employer, supervisor, or mentor to colleagues should make orderly and explicit arrangements regarding the conditions of their continuing professional relationship.
10. The social worker who has the responsibility for employing and evaluating the performance of other staff members, should fulfill such responsibility in a fair, considerate, and equitable manner, on the basis of clearly enunciated criteria.

11. The social worker who has the responsibility for evaluating the performance of employees, supervisees, or students should share evaluations with them.
12. The social worker should not use a professional position vested with power, such as that of employer, supervisor, teacher, or consultant, to his or her advantage or to exploit others.
13. The social worker who has direct knowledge of a social work colleague's impairment due to personal problems, psychosocial distress, substance abuse, or mental health difficulties should consult with that colleague and assist the colleague in taking remedial action.

K. Dealing with Colleagues' Clients—The social worker has the responsibility to relate to the clients of colleagues with full professional consideration.
1. The social worker should not assume professional responsibility for the clients of another agency or a colleague without appropriate communication with that agency or colleague.
2. The social worker who serves the clients of colleagues, during a temporary absence or emergency, should serve those clients with the same consideration as that afforded any client.

IV. The Social Worker's Ethical Responsibility to Employers and Employing Organizations

L. Commitments to Employing Organization—The social worker should adhere to commitments made to the employing organization.
1. The social worker should work to improve the employing agency's policies and procedures, and the efficiency and effectiveness of its services.
2. The social worker should not accept employment or arrange student field placements in an organization which is currently under public sanction by NASW for violating personnel standards, or imposing limitations on or penalties for professional actions on behalf of clients.
3. The social worker should act to prevent and eliminate discrimination in the employing organization's work assignments and in its employment policies and practices.
4. The social worker should use with scrupulous regard, and only for the purpose for which they are intended, the resources of the employing organization.

V. The Social Worker's Ethical Responsibility to the Social Work Profession

M. Maintaining the Integrity of the Profession—The social worker should uphold and advance the values, ethics, knowledge, and mission of the profession.
1. The social worker should protect and enhance the dignity and integrity of the profession and should be responsible and vigorous in discussion and criticism of the profession.
2. The social worker should take action through appropriate channels against unethical conduct by any other member of the profession.

3. The social worker should act to prevent the unauthorized and unqualified practice of social work.
4. The social worker should make no misrepresentation in advertising as to qualifications, competence, service, or results to be achieved.

N. Community Service—The social worker should assist the profession in making social services available to the general public.

1. The social worker should contribute time and professional expertise to activities that promote respect for the utility, the integrity, and the competence of the social work profession.
2. The social worker should support the formulation, development, enactment and implementation of social policies of concern to the profession.

O. Development of Knowledge—The social worker should take responsibility for identifying, developing, and fully utilizing knowledge for professional practice.

1. The social worker should base practice upon recognized knowledge relevant to social work.
2. The social worker should critically examine, and keep current with emerging knowledge relevant to social work.
3. The social worker should contribute to the knowledge base of social work and share research knowledge and practice wisdom with colleagues.

VI. The Social Worker's Ethical Responsibility to Society

P. Promoting the General Welfare—The social worker should promote the general welfare of society.

1. The social worker should act to prevent and eliminate discrimination against any person or group on the basis of race, color, sex, sexual orientation, age, religion, national origin, marital status, political belief, mental or physical handicap, or any other preference or personal characteristic, condition, or status.
2. The social worker should act to ensure that all persons have access to the resources, services, and opportunities which they require.
3. The social worker should act to expand choice and opportunity for all persons, with special regard for disadvantaged or oppressed groups and persons.
4. The social worker should promote conditions that encourage respect for the diversity of cultures which constitute American society.
5. The social worker should provide appropriate professional services in public emergencies.
6. The social worker should advocate changes in policy and legislation to improve social conditions and to promote social justice.
7. The social worker should encourage informed participation by the public in shaping social policies and institutions.

APPENDIX II

"Curriculum Policy Statement for Baccalaureate Degree Programs in Social Work Education," Council on Social Work Education

Approved by Board of Directors July 19, 1992

B1.0   SCOPE AND INTENT OF THE CURRICULUM POLICY STATEMENT

B1.1   This document sets forth the official curriculum policy for the accreditation of baccalaureate (BSW) programs of social work education by the Council on Social Work Education (CSWE). It supersedes all prior statements of curriculum policy for the baccalaureate program level.

B1.2   The curriculum policy statement establishes mandates for minimum requirements for the curricula of baccalaureate programs to be accredited by CSWE. The policy statement specifies certain content areas and requires that they be logically related to each other, to the purposes and values of social work as set forth in this document, and to the purposes, mission, resources, and educational context of each professional program. The statement does not prescribe any particular curriculum design.

B1.3   Each program is responsible for making every faculty member, student, field instructor, and administrator associated with the program aware of the content of the Curriculum Policy Statement.

B2.0   RELATIONSHIP TO ACCREDITATION STANDARDS

B2.1   The Commission on Accreditation of CSWE develops standards by which social work education programs are evaluated for accreditation. These standards pertain to the organization, administration, and curriculum implementation of programs of social work education. Curriculum standards are derived from and must conform with this Curriculum Policy Statement.

Source: Council on Social Work Education, "Curriculum Policy Statement for Baccalaureate Degree Programs in Social Work Education," approved by the Board of Directors, July 19, 1992 (Alexandria, VA: Council on Social Work Education, 1992), p. 5, B5.10.

B3.0   PREMISES UNDERLYING SOCIAL WORK EDUCATION

B3.1   The purpose of social work education is to prepare competent and effective social work professionals who are committed to practice that includes services to the poor and oppressed, and who work to alleviate poverty, oppression, and discrimination.

B3.2   Social work education is based upon a specific body of knowledge, values, and professional skills. It is grounded in the profession's history and philosophy. Education for the profession promotes the development and advancement of knowledge, practice skills, and services that further the well-being of people and promote social and economic justice. Social work education is responsible for the production and application of research and scholarship aimed at advancing social work practice.

B3.3   Programs of social work education are offered at the baccalaureate, master's, and doctoral levels. Doctoral programs are not accredited by CSWE.

B3.4   Programs of social work education maintain close, reciprocal, and ongoing relationships with social work practitioners and with groups and organizations that promote, provide, or seek to influence social policies and social work services. Responsibility for initiating these relationships rests with social work education programs. Effective programs develop and maintain a systematic process of communication with these individuals and groups.

B3.5   The effectiveness of any profession depends on the active engagement of its members in continuous learning. Programs of social work education strive to promote continuing professional development of students and faculty. Programs seek to teach students how to become lifelong learners who are motivated to continue the development of knowledge and skills throughout their careers.

B3.6   Effective social work education programs recognize the interdependence of nations and the need for worldwide professional cooperation.

B3.7   Social work education programs assume a leadership role within the profession by offering curricula that are at the forefront of the new and changing knowledge base of social work and its supporting disciplines.

B4.0   PURPOSE OF SOCIAL WORK

B4.1   The profession of social work is committed to the enhancement of human well-being and to the alleviation of poverty and oppression. The social work profession receives its sanction from public and private auspices and is the primary profession in the provision of social services. Within its general scope of concern, professional social work is practiced in a wide variety of settings and has four related purposes:

B4.1.1 The promotion, restoration, maintenance, and enhancement of the functioning of individuals, families, groups, organizations, and communities by helping them to accomplish tasks, prevent and alleviate distress, and use resources.

B4.1.2 The planning, formulation, and implementation of social policies, services, resources, and programs needed to meet basic human needs and support the development of human capacities.

B4.1.3   The pursuit of policies, services, resources and programs through organizational or administrative advocacy and social or political action, so as to empower groups at risk and promote social and economic justice.

B4.1.4   The development and testing of professional knowledge and skills related to these purposes.

B5.0   PURPOSE AND STRUCTURE OF BACCALAUREATE SOCIAL WORK EDUCATION

B5.1   The purpose of professional social work education is to enable students to integrate the knowledge, values, and skills of the social work profession into competent practice. The achievement of this purpose requires clarity about learning objectives and expected student outcomes, flexibility in programming and teaching to accommodate a diverse student population, and commitment of sufficient time and resources to the educational process.

B5.2   Two levels of social work education are accredited by the Council on Social Work Education: the baccalaureate and the master's. The baccalaureate level prepares students for generalist social work practice, and the master's level prepares students for advanced social work practice in an area of concentration. These levels of education differ from each other in the depth, breadth, and specificity of knowledge and skill that students are expected to synthesize and apply in practice.

Both levels of social work education must provide a professional foundation curriculum which contains the common body of knowledge, values, and skills of the profession. This common base is transferable among settings, population groups, and problem areas. The baccalaureate level of social work education must include a liberal arts perspective and the professional foundation content, which prepares students for direct services with client systems of various sizes and types.

B5.3   Professional social work education at the baccalaureate level takes place in accredited baccalaureate degree granting colleges and universities.

B5.4   All baccalaureate social work programs must:

B5.4.1   Provide content about social work practice with client systems of various sizes and types.

B5.4.2   Prepare graduates to practice with diverse populations.

B5.4.3   Provide content about the social contexts of social work practice, the changing nature of those contexts, the behavior of organizations, and the dynamics of change.

B5.4.4   Infuse throughout the curriculum the values and ethics that guide professional social workers in their practice.

B5.4.5   Prepare graduates who are aware of their responsibility to continue their professional growth and development.

B5.5   The baccalaureate curriculum must be based upon a liberal arts perspective and must include the professional foundation.

B5.6   The baccalaureate curriculum must be developed and organized as a coherent and integrated whole.

B5.7   Graduates of a baccalaureate social work program will be able to:

B5.7.1   Apply critical thinking skills within the context of professional social work practice.

B5.7.2   Practice within the values and ethics of the social work profession and with an understanding of and respect for the positive value of diversity.

B5.7.3   Demonstrate the professional use of self.

B5.7.4   Understand the forms and mechanisms of oppression and discrimination and the strategies of change that advance social and economic justice.

B5.7.5   Understand the history of the social work profession and its current structures and issues.

B5.7.6   Apply the knowledge and skills of generalist social work to practice with systems of all sizes.

B5.7.7   Apply knowledge of bio-psycho-social variables that affect individual development and behavior, and use theoretical frameworks to understand the interactions among individuals and between individuals and social systems (i.e., families, groups, organizations, and communities).

B5.7.8   Analyze the impact of social policies on client systems, workers, and agencies.

B5.7.9   Evaluate research studies and apply findings to practice, and, under supervision, evaluate their own practice interventions and those of other relevant systems.

5.7.10   Use communication skills differentially with a variety of client populations, colleagues, and members of the community.

5.7.11   Use supervision appropriate to generalist practice.

5.7.12   Function within the structure of organizations and service delivery systems and, under supervision, seek necessary organizational change.

5.8   LIBERAL ARTS PERSPECTIVE

B5.9   A liberal arts perspective enriches understanding of the person-environment context of professional social work practice and is integrally related to the mastery of social work content. The baccalaureate professional program in social work is built upon a liberal arts perspective.

B5.10   A liberal arts perspective provides an understanding of one's cultural heritage in the context of other cultures; the methods and limitations of various systems of inquiry; and the knowledge, attitudes, ways of thinking, and means of communication that are characteristic of a broadly educated person. Students must be capable of thinking critically about society, about people and their problems, and about such expressions of culture as art, literature, science, history, and philosophy. Students must have direct knowledge about social, psychological, and biological determinants of human behavior and of diverse cultures, social conditions, and social problems.

B5.11   Determination of whether students have acquired a liberal arts perspective is left to the judgment of the faculty of each social work program. Each program must clearly explicate the requirements for attaining a liberal arts perspective and the rationale for those requirements.

B6.0   BACCALAUREATE CURRICULUM CONTENT

B6.1   The baccalaureate curriculum must include a liberal arts perspective and the professional foundation. The professional foundation includes content on social work values and ethics, diversity, social and economic justice, populations-at-risk, human behavior and the social environment, social welfare policy and services, social work practice, research, and field practicum. Baccalaureate programs must achieve integration among these professional content areas. Curriculum areas do not need to be taught in discrete courses, but mastery of the professional curriculum must occur through classroom experiences and field practica. The baccalaureate social work curriculum must cover but is not necessarily limited to the professional foundation.

B6.2   The curriculum design of each program must identify a coherent approach for the selection of research and theories offered. Every part of the baccalaureate curriculum must strengthen the student's understanding and appreciation of a scientific, analytic approach to building knowledge for the delivery and evaluation of practice. Content provided in each curricular area must be relevant to the objectives, philosophy, and mission of the individual program and must facilitate the student's understanding of how the knowledge relates to social work practice.

Social Work Values and Ethics

B6.3   Programs of social work education must provide specific knowledge about social work values and their ethical implications and must provide opportunities for students to demonstrate their application in professional practice. Students must be assisted to develop an awareness of their personal values and to clarify conflicting values and ethical dilemmas. Among the values and principles that must be infused throughout every social work curriculum are the following:

B6.3.1 Social workers' professional relationships are built on regard for individual worth and dignity and are furthered by mutual participation, acceptance, confidentiality, honesty, and responsible handling of conflict.

B6.3.2 Social workers respect people's right to make independent decisions and to participate actively in the helping process.

B6.3.3 Social workers are committed to assisting client systems to obtain needed resources.

B6.3.4 Social workers strive to make social institutions more humane and responsive to human needs.

B6.3.5 Social workers demonstrate respect for and acceptance of the unique characteristics of diverse populations.

B6.3.6 Social workers are responsible for their own ethical conduct, the quality of their practice, and seeking continuous growth in the knowledge and skills of their profession.

Diversity

B6.4   Professional social work education is committed to preparing students to understand and appreciate human diversity. Programs must provide curriculum content about differences and similarities in the experiences, needs, and beliefs of people. The curriculum must include content about differential assessment and intervention skills that will enable practitioners to serve diverse populations.

Each program is required to include content about population groups that are particularly relevant to the program's mission. These include, but are not limited to groups distinguished by race, ethnicity, culture, class, gender, sexual orientation, religion, physical or mental ability, age, and national origin.

Promotion of Social and Economic Justice

B6.5   Programs of social work education must provide an understanding of the dynamics and consequences of social and economic injustice, including all forms of human oppression and discrimination. They must provide students with the skills to promote social change and to implement a wide range of interventions that further the achievement of individual and collective social and economic justice. Theoretical and practice content must be provided about strategies of intervention for achieving social and economic justice and for combatting the causes and effects of institutionalized forms of oppression.

Populations-At-Risk

B6.6   Programs of social work education must present theoretical and practice content about patterns, dynamics, and consequences of discrimination, economic deprivation, and oppression. The curriculum must provide content about people of color, women, and gay and lesbian persons. Such content must emphasize the impact of discrimination, economic deprivation, and oppression upon these groups.

Each program must include content about populations-at-risk that are particularly relevant to its mission. In addition to those mandated above, such groups include, but are not limited to, those distinguished by age, ethnicity, culture, class, religion, and physical or mental ability.

Human Behavior and the Social Environment

B6.7   Programs of social work education must provide content about theories and knowledge of human bio-psycho-social development, including theories and knowledge about the range of social systems in which individuals live (families, groups, organizations, institutions, and communities). The human behavior and the social environment curriculum must provide an understanding of the interactions between and among human biological, social, psychological, and cultural systems as they affect and are affected by human behavior. The impact of social and economic forces on individuals and social systems must be presented. Content must be provided about the ways in which systems promote or deter people in the maintenance or attainment of optimal health and well-being. Content about values and ethical issues related to bio-psycho-social theories must be included. Students must be taught to evaluate theory and apply theory to client situations.

Social Welfare Policy and Services

B6.8   Social welfare policy and services content must include the history, mission, and philosophy of the social work profession. Content must be presented about the history and current patterns of provision of social welfare services, the role of social policy in helping or deterring people in the maintenance or attainment of optimal health and well-being, and the effect of policy on social work practice. Students must be taught to analyze current social policy within the context of historical and contemporary factors that shape policy. Content must be presented about the political and organizational processes used to influence policy, the process of policy formulation, and the frameworks for analyzing social policies in light of the principles of social and economic justice.

Social Work Practice

B6.9   At the baccalaureate level, professional social work education prepares students for generalist practice with systems of all sizes. Practice content emphasizes professional relationships that are characterized by mutuality, collaboration, and respect for the client system. Content on practice assessment focuses on the examination of client strengths and problems in the interactions among individuals and between people and their environments.

Social work practice content must include knowledge, values, and skills to enhance the well-being of people and to help ameliorate the environmental conditions that affect people adversely. Practice content must include the following skills: defining issues; collecting and assessing data; planning and contracting; identifying alternative interventions; selecting and implementing appropriate courses of action; using appropriate research to monitor and evaluate outcomes; applying appropriate research-based knowledge and technological advances; and termination. Practice content also includes approaches and skills for practice with clients from differing social, cultural, racial, religious, spiritual, and class backgrounds and with systems of all sizes.

B6.10   Each program must explicate the ways in which students are prepared for generalist practice.

Research

B6.11   The research curriculum must provide an understanding and appreciation of a scientific, analytic approach to building knowledge for practice and for evaluating service delivery in all areas of practice. Ethical standards of scientific inquiry must be included in the research content.

The research content must include quantitative and qualitative research methodologies; analysis of data, including statistical procedures; systematic evaluation of practice; analysis and evaluation of theoretical bases, research questions, methodologies, statistical procedures, and conclusions of research reports; and relevant technological advances.

B6.12   Each program must identify how the research curriculum contributes to the student's use of scientific knowledge for practice.

Field Practicum

B6.13   The field practicum is an integral component of the curriculum in social work education. It engages the student in supervised social work practice and provides opportunities to apply classroom learning in the field setting.

B6.14   Field education at the baccalaureate level requires a minimum of 400 hours in field practicum.

B6.15   Each educational program must establish standards for field practicum settings that define their social work services and practices, field instructor assignments and activities, and student learning expectations and responsibilities. Individual programs may organize their practica in different ways but must insure educationally directed, coordinated, and monitored practicum experiences for all students. All programs must provide:

a.   A placement that is based upon the objectives of the educational program and the learning needs of each student.

b.   Structured learning opportunities that enable students to compare their practice experiences, integrate knowledge acquired in the classroom, and expand knowledge beyond the scope of the practicum setting.

c.   Support for field practicum instructors by:

1.   Sharing pertinent information about practicum students.

2.   Providing information about the organization and content of the educational curriculum, emphasizing the interrelationships among human behavior, social policy, research, and practice content.

3.   Providing information about the sequencing of course content.

4.   Articulating clear practice and evaluation goals for the field practicum and for each student.

5.   Offering orientation and training programs.

B6.16   The baccalaureate practicum must provide the student with opportunities for:

a.   The development of an awareness of self in the process of intervention.

    b. Supervised practice experience in the application of knowledge, values and ethics, and practice skills to enhance the well-being of people and to work toward the amelioration of environmental conditions that affect people adversely.

    c. Use of oral and written professional communications which are consistent with the language of the practicum setting and of the profession.

    d. Use of professional supervision to enhance learning.

    e. Critical assessment, implementation, and evaluation of agency policy within ethical guidelines.

B7.0   AVENUES OF RENEWAL

B7.1   Programs of social work education must remain vital and progressive by actively pursuing ongoing exchanges with the practice community and other essential groups, and by developing and assessing new knowledge and technology.

B7.1.1   Programs must establish and maintain close, reciprocal and ongoing relationships with social work practitioners, and use those relationships to continuously evaluate the total curriculum.

B7.1.2   Programs must establish and maintain relationships with groups that develop, implement, and benefit from social policies and services.

7.1.3   Programs must establish and maintain involvement with the professional associations and with disciplines and departments in the academic community.

7.1.4   Programs must assume responsibility for systematic and high quality scholarship that assesses social work practice and develops new knowledge.

APPENDIX III

A Commitment to Service Today

A Talk Delivered to Workers in Public Social Services

Introduction

I was asked to be the guest speaker at an annual meeting for over 500 employees of a State County Social Services Department where, I was told, there was low staff-morale and high burnout. Workers needed an uplift to increase their motivation. When I finished giving the following talk to the group, I received a long, standing ovation.

Excerpts from Transcript of Tape

Thank you very much. I want to sincerely thank you for inviting me to be with you for your annual meeting. I am not here to talk about money, social events, jobs, or the organization; you heard that earlier. I treasure this time with you to talk about "commitment," "service," "self-concept," and "meaning to life." Because really, isn't that the bottom line of what we are all about? And it is very fitting I think that at least once a year we take a little distance from the pressures, the demands, the policies and procedures, to reflect and to recommit ourselves to what, in fact, we are all about. Yes, we all have jobs, but your job and you are very special because what you are about is truly a type of "calling," a very necessary role if we are to be a caring society.

All of you know that there was a time when our country went through a depression. We were in trouble and people were going under. And, our society, the nation, instituted a means to demonstrate care. It was not going to be a society built on "survival of the fittest." There would be a means to help people in need through the rough times so that, hopefully, they could once again become productive members of society. And to do that, our nation in 1935, with our Social Security Act, established a system which reflects the highest value of our society, that is, the value of the potential and worth of every human being. And to fill the role of demonstrating that value, to service the institution of Public Assistance, the government officials looked at many disciplines and people. They did not choose individuals from psychology or psychiatry, those who deal primarily with the individual. They did not choose people from the fields of sociology or social planning, those who deal primarily with the social environment. They tried to find people who understood both, because they knew that the purpose of the Act was to help individuals to function effectively in society. And so the primary discipline that was looked to was that of social work. Social workers were hired to carry out the job because social workers have always had the person and environment perspective. But it did not take long for social workers to know that they could not do it alone. Public social service is a challenge day in and day out, and no discipline can do it alone. And so other disciplines were added to meet the recognized need for clerks, typists, receptionists, and people who could do investigations as well as counseling. An effort was made to have a team approach to meeting the goal of servicing people in need. Throughout the years, that is what the effort has been, a team effort; and that is what the goal has been, to service people in need. Because the public welfare system is such a large system involving a large amount of money, politics and many politicians have been involved, and continue to be involved, with the system. But the service has survived. And people have been helped mainly because the people in the service at the grass roots level for many, many years have been individuals with a commitment to serve. They are people who see that their job gives them the opportunity to find meaning in their lives. Many noted philosophers and writers and leaders have said that when under stress, whether it is caused by living in a concentration camp or whether it is from experiencing abandonment or desertion, what can keep you alive is that you have a meaning and purpose to your life, that you are not just alive but you live. And so with your pressures, your stresses and your jobs, what keeps you going and what keeps many noble, seasoned, wonderful people in jobs such as yours, has been the fact that there is meaning and purpose to what they are about, the fact that they and you have a commitment, a commitment to human service.

So let me talk with you some more about that. What does "commitment" mean? Most dictionaries will define it as "a declaration of adherence to an ideal or doctrine." Another way to define commitment is in terms of "a decisive moral choice for a definite course of action." It is a decisive choice. What does "service" mean? The definition of service is "to meet the needs of others" or "to repair or provide maintenance for others" (*Webster's Third New International Dictionary*). Within the public social service system, there is the need for commitment to service. There is the need for a decisive choice or declaration of adherence to the ideal and a definite course of action to serve, which means to meet the needs of others and to repair or provide maintenance for others. Oh, that is a noble cause when you think about it. So often in large services, the larger it gets, the less you realize how important you are. And yet so often the larger the service gets the more important every single link is because that chain is getting so large that if one link is weak or broken, the whole thing can break down. And so, no matter what your role is, if you are a member of a public social service department, you are in a noble role and you are needed. And you need each other, especially today, and let's talk about "today."

What's going on today? Have you noticed that in the past when indigent people walked the streets, they were often called "bums." And then we went through a period where some poor people who walked the streets were called "bag ladies." What's going on today? Have you noticed that in the literature, we now hear about "homeless families?" People out on the streets are no longer called "bums." They are no longer ladies that are called "bag ladies." Today in America, we have children and mothers and fathers; we have "families" walking our streets because they are homeless. And do we as a society realize that when we decrease opportunities for people, the more we pull back on our programs and services for those in need, there is a negative correlation with an increase in crime, suicide, drug addiction, and breakdown? Do we see that result in society today where there is obviously a pulling back of opportunities for food and clothing and shelter for people in need? Do we see why there could be such an increase in suicides, in crime, or in drug addiction, which there is today? And who is there to be a voice? Who is there to hold on to those high values that say, yes, we are going to care, yes we are going to provide opportunities? Who is there, as the book says, "When I was hungry, you fed me? When I was homeless, you found a place for me to live? When I was anxious, you calmed my fears? When I was naked, you clothed me?" Who is there today to feed, to clothe, to find homes for? You know who's doing it? You are. What you are doing is so needed today.

You and I have come to see that no one system is the cause of the problem or can give the solution to the problem. Our poor and our needy have a problem. It's called "poverty." And it is a multifaceted problem. It involves the health system, the education system, the social service system, transportation, housing, unemployment, and it involves all of these things together. There is no simple answer. And you are not to blame and your system is not to blame because people are dependent on you. The sad thing is that there are not enough resources to give you not only what the poor basically need, but opportunities for them to go beyond that—not just the fish, but the fishing rod. And so, first, to truly serve today, we have to grow in our skills, to become more sophisticated ourselves in doing justice to what we are all about. Just as one of the key messages we have learned is that poverty is not a simple problem, one of the things we have also learned is that there's a need for collaboration, teamwork, a holistic understanding, and commitment. Everybody has to get on board. Everybody is called to care.

Now, where do we begin? Well, we begin at home in our offices. You begin with the sense of unity, together with the people in the different disciplines in your own services—teamwork—we're in it together. Shared commitment is what brings us together. And then, as you work together toward your goal, you grow in seeing that it is not enough. Others are needed. Well, come to us, a School of Social Work, committed to the same goals because that's what can bring us together. We need each other. Today, more than ever, we realize how much we need each other. If we are preparing students to get out there, and many times without supervision or to be very much on their own, to take responsible leadership roles in human services, then they better be taught what it is really all about out there. And how are we going to teach them that if we practiced twenty years ago, and since then, we have been in academia? We need you to keep us informed of what is going on. We need your field placements, we need your data, we need your information, we need your communication. And, what do you need from us? You need someone to be able to have the time to take distance, to research it, to document it, to publicize it, to share with you in spreading the news of the needs of people today.

You probably heard the story of two people who were walking down a river bank. And as they walked along, they saw people drowning in the river. One of them took off his coat and went and jumped into the water, and started to pull the people out, one at a time. And every time he came to the shore, he looked for his friend to get his friend to help him but his friend had disappeared. You know the story? So finally, he got all the people out and they were all on the shore panting and puffing when his friend came back down toward him. He said, "Where were you, we needed you?" And the friend said, "I went up to the top of the river to see who or what was pushing them in, and I stopped it." Now, who did the right thing? Both of them did. They needed someone to pull the people out from drowning and they needed someone to get at the cause of it and try to stop it. And that is the way I think schools and services need each other. You have people coming to you who are without housing, who are hungry, who are drowning. You're meeting those immediate needs. Yes, and some of us in this audience have the time and the responsibility to gather information to do research on causes, effects, and intervening modes, and to publicize our findings. We are needed to teach and prepare people to work with you or take over when you are ready to retire, or for when you need more people to be able to come into your agencies and know what it is about and to assume the same kind of jobs that you're doing.

Yes, we need each other. Yes, it is a team effort, and not just for workers and agencies or teachers and schools such as ours. We need more than that; we need political support. We need power system support. How do we get it? I'll tell you how. We don't rant and rave and go into violence; we know that doesn't help. We don't give up and burn out; that doesn't help. That same book that I told you about that says, "When I was hungry you fed me," has a story in it that I think describes what we are all about. And it is a story about a man who was awakened in the night by someone who was hungry. And the man said, "I have a neighbor who has bread, let us go and get some for you." And so he went and knocked at the door, but the neighbor didn't answer. And he kept knocking, and the neighbor came to the top window and said, "Who is it? Go away, I'm sleeping." You know that story? The man didn't swear and curse; he just said, "We have someone here who is hungry." The neighbor said, "I'm sleeping, don't bother me," and went back to bed. And what did the man do? He kept knocking. So the neighbor came again to the window and said, "I told you to leave me alone." The man said, "We have someone here who is hungry." You know that story? The neighbor went back to bed. The man kept knocking. Finally, what happened? The neighbor said, "I can't get any sleep, for God's sake here's the bread." That is a story in our Bible and that is what we are. We are the people that keep knocking who don't go away because if we do, what's going to happen? Who will be there? What's going to happen to an uncaring, survival-of-the-fittest society? But what keeps us going so that we don't give up, so that we don't burn out, so that we don't get tired of knocking? What keeps us going is what was brought out by Viktor Frankl in his book, *Man's Search for Meaning,* or what was brought out by John Steinbeck in his book, *The Grapes of Wrath,* or what Abraham Maslow talked about when he described how people can really be "self-actualized." What keeps us going is the recognition that we have meaning and purpose in our lives and that's what keeps us going. And yes, we have our goals and we have our dreams and we have our past experiences. But most of all what keeps us going is the belief in human life, and our commitment to human service. We know we can't do it all. But we sure can do something, and that's what keeps us going. We are doing what we can to make a difference, and that gives us purpose and meaning. That makes us more than just alive; it truly helps us to live.

Now let me just briefly talk about "self-concept." You know, I know some people who are very wealthy who seem to have it all and have the worst self-concept. They seem to hate everyone including themselves. And you know clients who have very low, negative self-concepts. And many researchers have tried to study what's this about. How do we get a self-concept that helps us to truly live a happy productive life? It is not a simple answer. Self-concept has been described as a concept with four dimensions to it. To have a healthy, fully mature self-concept, you have four dimensions to you. The four dimensions are (1) within yourself you have a sense of competence, (2) within yourself you have a sense of self-determination, (3) you have a sense of unity—someone who has it together, and (4) within yourself you have a sense of moral worth (C. Gordon, "Self Conceptions", *The Self in Social Interaction,* 1968, pp. 126–130). This breakdown helps us to understand how we can build a self-concept in our children, our clients, and ourselves. To check it out, we need to ask are we, or they, confident? Do we, or they, feel confident? If not, then what can we and they do to grow? Kierkegaard, noted philosopher, points out that we are all in the process of becoming. We can grow into the sense of competence by developing greater skills. Do we have a sense of self-determination? Do we have some opportunity to choose, to plan, to suggest, to think? We try to give that to our clients, and we try to give that to our children. Can we give that to ourselves? Do we have a sense of unity or are we feeling we're at loose ends—scattered? Do we have that sense of having it together? Can we create that? Can we give that security to ourselves? To those we work with? And finally, do we have a sense of moral worth? And what I'm here to talk to you about is the need to recognize how moral and worthy you are and the worth of what you are about. And with that self-concept, yes, you can hold on to your dreams and your ideals and your purpose. Yes, you can stand the pressures and the hurts and the frustrations and the ingratitude or lack of appreciation from so many in terms of what you're about. But most of all, you can find meaning here and now in the present moment. And that's what it is all about—to live fully the present. No matter what you're doing, when you're within the human service system, you have meaning and purpose within the present moment for those people who are presently in need. Whether they know it or not, whether they appreciate it or not, they are human beings and you and I value and believe in the potential of human life. And we are called to tell others to believe in their potential and that things possibly can change. I could go on and on but let me ask you to take a little time to think about this. And yes, now is a good time; you are a little removed from your offices today. Think about your call to recommit yourself to service today. Think about your call to really live the gift of the present moment. Let me give you this quote from Buechner: "Listen to your life. See it for the fathomless mystery that it is. In the boredom and pain of it, no less than in the excitement and gladness: touch, taste, smell your way into the holy and hidden of it because in the last analysis, all moments are key moments, and life itself is a grace" (Frederick Buechner, *Godric*, 1983, p. 86). My parting words are, know that you are a grace to many in your own way. You might be the only grace to many. And my hope is that through your recommitment, you will continue to do the marvelous job that those of you in public social services, and those of you that stay in public social services, are really doing today. Thank you.

Maria O. McMahon, DSW

Index